CAREER OPPORTUNITIES FOR BILINGUALS AND MULTILINGUALS

a directory of resources in
education, employment,
and business
Second Edition

by
VLADIMIR F. WERTSMAN

The Scarecrow Press, Inc.
Metuchen, N.J., & London
1994

British Library Cataloguing-in-Publication data available

Library of Congress Cataloging-in-Publication Data

Wertsman, Vladimir F., 1929–
    Career opportunities for bilinguals and multilinguals : a
directory of resources in education, employment, and
business, second edition. / by Vladimir F. Wertsman.
        p.   cm.
    Includes bibliographical references and indexes.
    ISBN 0-8108-2764-6 (printed on acid-free paper)
    1. Vocational guidance—United States—Directo-
ries. 2. Language and languages—Study and
teaching—Vocational guidance—United States—
Directories. 3. Businessmen—Foreign language
competency—Vocational guidance—United States
—Directories. 4. United States—Officials and
employees—Foreign countries—Foreign language
competency—Directories. 5. Linguistics—Vocational guidance—United States—Directories.
    I. Title.
  HF5382.5.U5W44   1994
  331.7'02'02573—dc20   93-34130

I am always sorry when any language is lost, because languages are the pedigree of nations.

—Samuel Johnson (1709–84)

Every language is a temple in which the soul of those who speak it is enshrined.

—Oliver Wendell Holmes
(1809–94)

The sum of human wisdom is not contained in any one language, and not a single language is capable of expressing all forms and degrees of human comprehension.

—Ezra Pound (1885–1972)

CONTENTS

ACKNOWLEDGMENTS
TO FIRST EDITION

My thanks are due, first of all, to the following staff members of the New York Public Library: Mario Gonzalez (Office of Special Services, Branch Libraries), Edward Kasinec (Slavonic Division, Research Libraries), Wol Sue Lee (General Reference, Mid-Manhattan Library), Valerie Sandoval Mwalilino (Schomburg Center for Research in Black Culture), George Mycak (Office of Reference and Information, Branch Libraries), Barbara Shapiro (General Reference, Mid-Manhattan Library), Bosiljka Stevanovic (Foreign Language Library, Donnell Library Center) and Ellen Viggiano (formerly of General Reference, Mid-Manhattan Library), for useful suggestions, fine cooperation, and encouragement to write this book.

Special thanks are expressed to Esfira Annenberg (formerly of Karbra, Inc., New York), Lester Annenberg (Time Inc., New York), Patricia Beilke (Ball State University, Indiana), Natalia Bezugloff (Cleveland Public Library), David Cohen (Queens College, New York), Palmina Grella (Nassau Community College), Sylva Manoogian (Los Angeles Public Library), Enikö Molnar Bosza (Library of Congress), Nelly Obando Molina (Ministry of Culture and Education, Ecuador), Adriana A. Tandler (Queens Borough Public Library), Tamiye Treho-Meehan (Chicago Public Library), and Marie Zielinska (National Library of Canada), for inspirational conversations, correspondence, and research materials brought to my attention.

I would also like to acknowledge Saadin Abulhab (General Reference, Mid-Manhattan Library), Rita Bott (General Reference, Mid-Manhattan Library), Edmond Fursa (Education Department, Mid-Manhattan Library), Georgia

Donati (Job Information Center, Mid-Manhattan Library), Bobbie Jones (Project Access, Mid-Manhattan Library), Joe Keenan (Job Information Center, Mid-Manhattan Library), Renée Kotler (Bronx Borough Office), Patricia Moore (General Reference, Research Libraries), Gerald O'Sullivan (Cataloging Department, Branch Libraries), Sam Register (General Reference, Research Libraries), and Steve Unger (General Reference, Mid-Manhattan Library), for various forms of assistance during the research process and other phases of preparing the present volume.

Vladimir F. Wertsman
Senior Librarian
Job Information Center
Mid-Manhattan Library
New York City

ACKNOWLEDGMENTS TO SECOND EDITION

For assistance extended to me during the preparation of the second edition, I am grateful to Bosiljka Stevanovic (Head Donnell Foreign Language Library, New York Public Library), Marie Zielinska (Head Biblio-service, National Library of Canada), Irina Kuharets (Russian Specialist, Donnell Foreign Language Library, New York Public Library) as well as to Deborah Abraham (Head Reference Department, Brookline Public Library—Washington Branch), Jerry Cirillo (Brookline Public Library—Coolidge Corner Branch) and Robert Sullivan (Reference Department, Brookline Public Library—Washington Branch).

I am also indebted—for fine cooperation—to Harriet Alter (Salmagundi Club, New York), Joseph Brill (formerly with ICRA Bacau, Romania), Jon Butnaru (formerly with Boston University Library), Liviu Floda (Radio "Free Europe" New York Office), Justin Liuba (Radio "Free Europe" New York Office), Suzana Obuvalina (P.S. 231 Brooklyn, New York), Joseph Palladino (Reference Department, Mid-Manhattan Library, New York), Alexandra Sax (Job Information Center, Mid-Manhattan Library, New York), Irene Shields ("Creative Concepts" Company, New Jersey), and Paul Zaplitny (Brooklyn Public Library-Arlington Branch).

May 1993, New York
Vladimir F. Wertsman, Chair
Publishers & Multicultural
Materials Committee, EMIE
(Ethnic Materials Information
Exchange) Round Table,
American Library Association

V.W.

ix

PREFACE TO THE FIRST EDITION

America is by its very nature a multilingual and multiethnic society. Census data have recorded over 140 U.S. ethnic groups, and tens of millions of Americans have preserved—in various degrees—the native language spoken by their immigrant parents or grandparents. Dozens and dozens of foreign languages are taught in our colleges, universities, and private schools, not to mention high schools. In the last decade, over 300,000 college students have annually registered for foreign language courses, representing about 8 percent of the total number of college registrants. Presently, over 40,000 government jobs and over 60,000 private business and industry jobs require competence in at least one language other than English. In 1986 alone, about 20,000 applicants with foreign language competence applied for foreign service positions. In addition, there are 17,000 U.S. firms operating in over 120 countries around the world, and over 2,500 foreign firms operating in the United States. Hundreds of nonprofit organizations send thousands of employees and volunteers to over a hundred countries on all continents.

The importance of knowing languages other than English in various fields—diplomatic, military, academic, computer, engineering, medicine, marketing, export/import, to name just a few—will grow even more in the future. Intensification of trade, cultural, art, technical, scientific, tourism, and other relations between the United States and virtually all countries around the globe requires a constantly increasing pool in all fields of people who, in addition to their specialty, also know one or more foreign languages. According to David Win, author of *International Careers: An Insider's Guide* (annotated in the Selected Bibliography), "many U.S. employers now realize this fact, which means that they will tend to hire people with language skills over those who lack them." And even more recently, a panel of the National Governors' Association warned that "the economic well-being of the United States was in jeopardy because many Americans are ignorant of languages and cultures of other nations." In its report, the panel—chaired by Governor Thomas H. Kean of New Jersey—called for "all college and university graduates to be conversant in another language" (*New York Times*, February 26, 1989).

Given this demand for foreign languages—both inside and outside the United States—over 30 states have instituted, in the last few years, a language requirement in public schools, and over 30 colleges and universities have added foreign languages as a graduation requirement. Moreover, in 1986 several private foundations—the Pew Memorial Trust, the Ford Foundation, and the Exxon Educational Foundation—provided grants of over $3 million for the establishment of a National Foundation for Foreign Languages. The proposed foundation is to be modeled after the National Science Foundation, the National Endowments for the Arts and Humanities, and the Smithsonian Institution. It will receive funding from the federal government, and will be authorized to receive private funds, too. It seems obvious that the era of bilinguals and multilinguals, which has already begun, will certainly make further progress in the forthcoming decades.

The present directory is a compact, selective, yet comprehensive reference book, culled from about 100 books, periodicals, and other sources. Its purpose is to offer in one volume the most direct and the quickest way of (*a*) locating educational resources (colleges, universities, libraries, and booksellers) for learning languages other than English; (*b*) identifying important prospective U.S. employers (government, nonprofit, private, and networking organizations), as well as foreign employers (United Nations units, foreign countries) interested in hiring American bilingual or multilingual professionals and paraprofessionals. The book consists of three chapters, with over 2,500 annotated entries, listing over 3,500 national and international institutions, firms, and organizations, and covering over 300 languages. Each chapter is accompanied by explanatory notes. At the end there is an extensive annotated bibliography, an appendix, and three indexes: languages, educational and occupational backgrounds, and geographic names. All entries are numbered and arranged alphabetically within their respective sections. The nature of information found in this directory, and its organization and retrieval structure, make it a very handy reference tool for education, job and career information, and foreign language and general reference units of public libraries. It is equally useful to academic, special, private, or school libraries. It also could benefit counselors, teachers, linguists, and other categories of interested researchers in the United States and abroad, especially immigrants who want to come to or who have recently arrived in this country. Finally, the directory gives a good opportunity for high school and college students to review the field of bilinguals and multilinguals before making a decision to learn foreign languages or to embrace a specific major combined with foreign languages.

Although every attempt has been made to provide current addresses, as with any directory, some of the information herein may have undergone changes since this work was completed.

PREFACE TO THE SECOND EDITION

The publication of this second-revised, updated and en-larged-edition has been generated, in the first place, by the positive feedback from the users of the first edition, and the constructive suggestions made by American and foreign readers in their letters addressed to the author. In addition, many entries in all sections were affected by changes of names of institutions or organizations, addresses and zip codes, as well as other modifications (e.g. adjustment of indexes) needed to keep the text up-to-date. We also have witnessed very rapid geopolitical changes in the former Soviet Union and Eastern Europe, and the appearance of new independent states, which were not included in the previous edition. New economic realities (e.g. regional trade pacts and bilateral agreements between various countries), plus inflations and recessions in several countries on all continents, have demonstrated that national economies be-came more and more interdependent. A similar interdependence occurred on the national job markets, and in this context job hunters with language skills were better equipped than those who lacked them.

Despite a constantly increasing global economy and a growing consciousness about this aspect, language study in America is still far from satisfying the actual needs in the national and international job markets. According to the *Statistical Abstract of the United States 1992* the total college/university population grew from *8,581,000* in 1970 to *13,710,000* in 1990, which means a jump of over 50%, while the number of enrollments in foreign language studies only increased by less than 1%, from *1,100,000* in 1970 to *1,183,000* in 1990. Students have expressed more interest in Spanish, Chinese, Japanese, Hebrew and Arabic, Russian, and Italian, while the number of enrollees in German and French has substantially declined.

In order to remedy this situation, some universities have increased the number of foreign language courses offered. Brigham Young University, for instance, presently teaches 54 languages (*The New York Times,* February 18, 1993, p. A-16). They range from Akkadian and Afrikaans to Navajo, Syriac, and Welsh. Similar efforts were recorded at the University of Wisconsin, Madison and Yale University. We can expect much larger enrollments in foreign language courses during the forthcoming years going beyond the 20th century, and, of course, the expansion of the job market for bilinguals and multilinguals. Competition between job seekers with language skills is going to be tough because employers want higher language proficiency or fluency.

With all these factors in mind, the present edition offers several hundred more annotated entries than the previous one. Each section has been carefully reviewed, updated, and augmented with an addendum of new entries. The Appendix "Reminders and Recommendations for Successful Job Hunting" was substantially enlarged with details regarding the presentation of résumés and cover letters, the conduct of the job hunter during the interview, plus a list of job titles for which knowledge of one or more foreign languages proved helpful in finding a job. Readers are reminded *not to overlook* the preface to the first edition since the structure, methodology, and objectives of the book remain the same as during the publication of the first edition. Researchers should also peruse the short introductions to each section, all abbreviations, and the bibliographic suggestions geared to each chapter. Together, all these aspects will speed-up the process of research and retrieval of the information needed during the stage of job hunting, and, hopefully, be useful in locating potential employers and finding a suitable job. Finally, as in the previous edition, any constructive comments and suggestions are always welcome, and eventually— if warranted—could inspire a third edition in a few years.

                                                      V.W.

SYMBOLS, ABBREVIATIONS, AND ACRONYMS

SYMBOLS

★ = Internship
◤ = Translation/Interpretation Courses and/or Services
Ⓧ = Two-Year College Courses
Ⓥ = Volunteers Accepted

INDIVIDUAL LANGUAGES

AA	Aramaic	BG	Bengali
AB	Arabic	BI	Bubi
AC	Aztec	BK	Bashkir
AF	Afrikaans	BL	Bulgarian
AG	Algonquin	BM	Bambara
AH	Ahtena	BN	Bantu
AI	Aino (Ainu)	BR	Breton
AK	Akkadian	B/R	Brahui
AL	Albanian	BS	Basque
AM	Amharic	BT	Buriat
AR	Armenian	B/T	Buthanese
AS	Assyrian	BU	Burmese
AT	Athabaskan	BY	Byelorussian
AV	Avestan	CA	Cambodian (Khmer)
AY	Aymara	CC	Chichewa
AZ	Azerbaijani (Azeri)	CE	Cebuano
BA	Balinese	CG	Chagatay
BB	Berber	CH	Chinese
BC	Baluchi	CI	Chippewa
BE	Bemba	CL	Celtic
BF	Blackfoot	CN	Cornish

C/N	Chimwi-Ni	GJ	Gujarati
CO	Colville	GL	Gulah
CP	Coptic	GM	Guamanian
CR	Cree	GN	Ganda
C/R	Creole	GO	Gothic
CS	Cheremyssian (Mari)	GR	Greek
CT	Catalan	GS	Gourounsi
CV	Chuvashian	GU	Guarani
CW	Cowichan	GY	Gilyak
CZ	Czech	HA	Haida
DA	Danish	HC	Huichol
D/C	Dutch-Creole	H/C	Haitian-Creole
DE	Dende	HE	Hebrew
DJ	Djema	HI	Hindi
DK	Dakota	HL	Hualapi
DR	Dravidian	HM	Hmong
DU	Dutch (Flemish)	HO	Hopi
DY	Dyola	HR	Hiri Moto
EB	Eblaic	HS	Hausa
ED	Edo	HT	Hittite
EG	Egyptian	HU	Hungarian
EK	Eskimo (Inuit)	H/U	Hindi-Urdu
EN	English	HV	Hova
EP	Esperanto	HW	Hawaiian
ES	Estonian	IC	Icelandic
ET	Ethiopic	IG	Igbo (Ibo)
EW	Ewe	IK	Inuktitut
FA	Fanti	IL	Ilocano
FC	Franconian	I/L	Interlingua
F/C	French-Creole	IN	Indonesian
FF	Fufulde	IP	Iplili
FJ	Fijian	IQ	Iroquois
FI	Finnish	IR	Irish (Gaelic-Irish)
FL	Filipino (Tagalog)	IT	Italian
FN	Fang	J/A	Judeo-Arabic
FO	Faroese	JC	Jacaltec
F/O	Fon	JP	Japanese
FR	French	J/P	Judeo-Persian
FS	Frisian	JV	Javanese
FU	Fulani (Peul)	KA	Kanada
GA	Ga	KC	Kutchin
GC	Galician	KD	Kurdish
GE	German	KG	Kongo
GG	Georgian	KH	Khakhas

KI	Kihunde	MN	Manchu
KK	Kikungo	M/N	Mainke (Malinke)
K/K	Koyukon	MO	Mongolian (Khalkha)
KM	Kamayura	M/O	Maori
KN	Kansa	M/Q	Maya-Quiche
KO	Korean	MR	Marathi
KR	Koryak	MS	Malaysian
K/R	Kinairuanda	M/S	Mossi
KS	Kashmiri	MT	Maltese
K/S	Kiswahili	M/T	Montagnaise
KT	Kituba	MU	Moudang
KU	Kirundi (Rundi)	MW	Miwok-Lake
K/U	Kimeru	MY	Mayan
KW	Kingwan	M/Y	Maya-Yucatec
KY	Kikuyo	MX	Manx
KZ	Kazakh	NA	Nahuatl
K/Z	Kirghiz	ND	Ndebele
LA	Latin	NE	Nepali
LB	Luba (Lubi)	NI	Nitihani
LD	Ladino	NJ	Nyanja
LG	Lingala	NR	Norse
LI	Lithuanian	NS	Naskapi
LK	Lakota	NV	Navajo
LM	Lamut	NW	Norwegian
LN	Luganda	NY	Nyangumarda
LO	Lao	OJ	Ojibwa
LP	Lapp	ON	Oneida
LT	Latvian	OS	Ossetic
LU	Luala	O/U	Oscan-Umbrian
LZ	Lozi	PA	Pali
MA	Macedonian	P/C	Portuguese-Creole
M/A	Masa	PE	Persian (Farsi)
MC	Malecite	PI	Pidgin
MD	Mandinka	PJ	Punjabi
ME	Mande (Mende)	PK	Prakrit
MG	Malagasy	PL	Palaic (Palawi)
M/G	Mandingo	PO	Polish
MH	Mohawk	PP	Papago
M/H	Mahri	P/P	Papiamento
MI	Micmac	PR	Prussian
M/I	Mina	PS	Pushto (Afghan)
MK	Makua	PT	Portuguese
ML	Malay	PV	Provençal
MM	Malaylam	QC	Quechua

RM	Rhaeto-Romance (Rumansh)	TI	Tibetan
		TJ	Tajik
RO	Romanian (Rumanian)	TK	Tukolor
		T/K	Tamashek
RU	Russian	TL	Tlingit
RW	Rwanda	TM	Tamil
SA	Salishan-Coast	T/M	Turkoman
S/A	Sara	TN	Tangale
SC	Scottish (Gaelic-Scottish)	T/N	Tenne
		TO	Tocharian
S/C	Serbo-Croatian	TR	Turkic
SD	Sindhi	TS	Tsimshian
SE	Setswana	T/S	Tshiluba
SG	Sogdian	TT	Tatar
S/G	Songhai	T/T	Taki Taki
SH	Swahili	TU	Turkish
S/H	Sangho	T/U	Turko-Tataric
SI	Sinhalese	TV	Tiv
SK	Skokleng	T/V	Tuva (Soyot)
SL	Slovak	TW	Twi
SM	Samoan	T/W	Tswana
S/M	Samo	TY	Tegrinya
SN	Shona	UA	Urartian
SO	Somali	UD	Udi
SP	Spanish	UG	Ugaritic
S/P	Salish-Puget	UI	Uigur
SR	Shuar	UK	Ukrainian
SS	Sanskrit	UM	Umbundu
S/S	Slavic/Slavonic (Old Church)	UR	Urdu
		UT	Ute
ST	Sotho	UY	Uygur-Turki
S/T	Sesotho	UZ	Uzbek
SU	Sumerian	VA	Vai
SV	Slovenian	VD	Vedic
SW	Swedish	VI	Vietnamese
S/W	Si-Swati	VL	Valencian
SY	Syriac	VN	Venda
S/Y	Syryenian	VO	Votiak (Udmuri)
SX	Saxon	VT	Votish
TA	Tahitian	WE	Welsh
TE	Telugu	WN	Wendic (Sorbian)
TG	Tonga	WO	Wolof
T/G	Tsonga	XH	Xhosa
TH	Thai	YA	Yakut

YD	Yiddish	YU	Yupik
YM	Yuman	ZA	Zapotek
YO	Yoruba	ZU	Zulu

LANGUAGE SUBDIVISIONS AND DIALECTS

They are always in parentheses, lowercase, and follow a main
language; e.g. "CH(cl)" means Chinese, classical.

(af)	Afghani	(lu)	Louisiana
(am)	Amoy	(mc)	Moroccan
(an)	Ancient	(md)	Medieval
(az)	Azeri	(mh)	Middle High
(bi)	Biblical	(mi)	Middle
(bl)	Baltic	(ml)	Moldavian
(br)	Brazilian	(mn)	Mandarin
(ca)	Cairo	(mo)	Modern
(ch)	Chicano	(n/g)	New Guinea
(cl)	Classical	(ni)	Nigerian
(cm)	Comoran	(nt)	New Testament
(cn)	Cantonese	(od)	Old
(cr)	Carpatho-Russian	(oh)	Old High
(dr)	Dari	(ot)	Ottoman
(es)	Eastern	(pe)	Pennsylvania
(hi)	Hispanic	(po)	Portuguese
(hk)	Hokyen	(pt)	Patois
(hl)	Hellenistic	(si)	Siberian
(in)	Inupiak	(sw)	Swiss
(ir)	Iraqi	(ta)	Taiwanese
(ko)	Koine	(w/a)	West African

OTHER ABBREVIATIONS AND ACRONYMS

AFL	African Languages	FJI	Federal Job Information
ASL	Asian Languages		
BIL	Biblical Languages	GEL	Germanic Languages
CTR	Commerce/Trade Representative	GRD	Graduate Degree
		IBO	Information on Business Overseas (setting up)
EMB	Embassy		
ESL	English as a Second Language		

INL	Indic Languages	SCL	Scandinavian Languages
KFL	Knowledge of a Foreign Language	SES	State Employment Service
MOL	Modern Languages (usually FR, GE, IT, RU, SP, but not specified)	SLL	Slavic Languages
		UGD	Undergraduate Degree
MUL	Multiple Language Emphasis (various languages and cultures)	UND	United Nations Development Programs
NAL	Native American Languages (American Indian and Eskimo)	UNI	United Nations Information Centers
		USA	United States of America

1. EDUCATION RESOURCES IN THE UNITED STATES AND CANADA

This chapter has three sections: A) Colleges and Universities Teaching Foreign Languages, with 1,376 entries; B) Public Libraries, Museum Libraries, and Others with Foreign-Language Collections, with 391 entries; and C) Suppliers Specializing in Foreign-Language Books and/or Audiovisual Materials, with 284 entries. Entries are arranged in alphabetical order by state (and province for Canada) within each section. Each entry shows the name of the institution, address, and appropriate languages (in symbols).

Section A lists only those colleges or universities which offer majors, graduate studies, or specialization in a specific language or languages, as reflected in standard catalogs for the last three years. Two-year colleges are marked "⊗," and colleges and universities offering special courses in translation and interpretation are marked "◪." Where the language symbols are italicized, the respective college or university does not presently teach these languages, but has only library collections in these languages. Noncredit courses—offered either by colleges and universities, or by commercial institutions, various organizations, or private schools—were not included. They are reflected in a multitude of brochures and catalogs, and could be the object of another book. ESL courses were also excluded, since they are already amply covered in *English Language and Orientation Programs in the United States* (New York: Institute of International Education, 1988).

Section B lists libraries with at least a hundred books in a specific language collection. It should be understood that all colleges and universities mentioned in Section A also have adequate library collections to support their language

1

courses, and several universities (as well as many public or private libraries) have extensive library collections. For details regarding the composition, size, and characteristics of such libraries, one should consult Lee Ash's *Subject Collections,* listed in the Selected Bibliography.

Section C refers to book dealers who sell foreign-language books as well as various audiovisual materials (cassettes, records, videos, etc.) facilitating the learning of languages.

Note that all three sections can be utilized, not only for language-learning purposes, but also for job-finding aims.

A. COLLEGES AND UNIVERSITIES TEACHING FOREIGN LANGUAGES

United States

ALABAMA (AL)

A-1.   ALABAMA AGRICULTURAL AND MECHANICAL UNIVERSITY, Normal 35762/ FR.

A-2.   ALABAMA STATE UNIVERSITY, Montgomery 36101/ FR, SP.

A-3.   AUBURN UNIVERSITY, Auburn 36849/ FR, GE, RU, SP.

A-4.   BIRMINGHAM-SOUTHERN COLLEGE, Birmingham 35254/ FR, GE, SP.

⊗A-5.   GADSDEN STATE COMMUNITY COLLEGE, Gadsden 35902/ FR, SP.

⊗A-6.   GEORGE C. WALLACE STATE COMMUNITY COLLEGE AT DOTHAN, Dothan 36303/ FR, SP.

A-7.   JUDSON COLLEGE, Marion 36756/ SP.

A-8.   MOBILE COLLEGE, Mobile 36663/ FR, SP.

A-9.   SAMFORD UNIVERSITY, Birmingham 35229/ FR, GE, SP.

A-10.   STILLMAN COLLEGE, Tuscaloosa 35403/ FR, SP.

A-11.   UNIVERSITY OF ALABAMA, Tuscaloosa 35487/ FR, FR(od), GE, GO, GR, HE(bi), NR, PT, RU, SP.

A-12.   UNIVERSITY OF ALABAMA IN BIRMINGHAM, Birmingham 35294/ FR, GE, SP.

A-13.   UNIVERSITY OF ALABAMA IN HUNTSVILLE, Huntsville 35899/ FR, GE, RU.

A-14.   UNIVERSITY OF MONTEVALLO, Montevallo 35115/ FR, SP.

A-15.   UNIVERSITY OF NORTH ALABAMA, Florence 35632/ FR, GE, SP.

A-16.   UNIVERSITY OF SOUTH ALABAMA, Mobile 36688/ CH(cn), FR, GE, RU, SP.

ALASKA (AK)

A-17. ALASKA PACIFIC UNIVERSITY, Anchorage 99508-4672/ MUL.

⊗A-18. KUSKOKWIM COMMUNITY COLLEGE, Bethel 99559/ NAL.

A-19. UNIVERSITY OF ALASKA–FAIRBANKS, Fairbanks 99775/ AH, AT, EK, EK(in), EK(si), FR, GE, HA, KC, K/K, RU, SP, TL, TS, YU.

ARIZONA (AZ)

A-20. AMERICAN GRADUATE SCHOOL OF INTERNATIONAL MANAGEMENT, Glendale 85306/ AB, CH, FR, GE, JP, PT, SP.

A-21. ARIZONA STATE UNIVERSITY, Tempe 85287/ CH, FR, GE, GE(m/h), HO, IC, IC(od), IT, JP, NV, PP, PT, RU, SP, TH, *UR*.

⊗A-22. ARIZONA WESTERN COLLEGE, Yuma 85366/ SP.

A-23. COCHISE COLLEGE, Douglas 85607/ SP.

A-24. EASTERN ARIZONA COLLEGE, Thatcher 85552/ FR, GE, SP.

⊗A-25. GLENDALE COMMUNITY COLLEGE, Glendale 85302/ FR, GE, IT, JP, RU, SP.

A-26. GRAND CANYON COLLEGE, Phoenix 85061-1097/ SP.

⊗A-27. MESA COMMUNITY COLLEGE, Mesa 85202/ FR, GE, SP.

A-28. NORTHERN ARIZONA UNIVERSITY, Flagstaff 86011/ FR, HO, NV, SP.

A-29. PRESCOTT COLLEGE, Prescott 86301/ SP.

◢A-30. UNIVERSITY OF ARIZONA, Tucson 85721/ AB, CH, FR, GE, GR, GR(mo), HE, HE(bi), H/U, IT, JP, LA, NV, PE, PT(br), RU, SD, SP, TU.

⊗A-31. YAVAPAI COLLEGE, Prescott 86301/ FR, GE, SP.

ARKANSAS (AR)

A-32. ARKANSAS STATE UNIVERSITY, Arkansas 72467/ FR, GE, SP.

A-33. ARKANSAS TECH UNIVERSITY, Russellville 72801/ FR, GE, SP.

⊗A-34. CROWLEY'S RIDGE COLLEGE, Paragould 72450/ GR.

A-35. HARDING UNIVERSITY, Searcy 72143/ FR, SP.

A-36. HENDERSON STATE UNIVERSITY, Arkadelphia 71923/ SP.

A-37. HENDRIX COLLEGE, Conway 72032/ FR, GE, SP.

A-38. OUACHITA BAPTIST UNIVERSITY, Arkadelphia 71923/ FR, GE, GR, SP.

A-39. PHILANDER SMITH COLLEGE, Little Rock 72202/ MOL.

A-40.   SOUTHERN ARKANSAS UNIVERSITY, Magnolia 71753/ FR, SP.

⊗ A-41.   SOUTHERN BAPTIST COLLEGE, Walnut Ridge 72476/ GR.

A-42.   UNIVERSITY OF ARKANSAS, Fayetteville 72701/ FR, GE, SP.

◪ A-43.   UNIVERSITY OF ARKANSAS AT LITTLE ROCK, Little Rock 72204/ CH, FR, GR, GR(cl), HE, JP, LA, SP.

A-44.   UNIVERSITY OF CENTRAL ARKANSAS, Conway 72032/ FR, SP.

⊗ A-45.   WESTARK COMMUNITY COLLEGE, Fort Smith 72913/ FR, SP.

CALIFORNIA (CA)

⊗ A-46.   ANTELOPE VALLEY COLLEGE, Lancaster 93536/ MOL.

A-47.   AZUSA PACIFIC UNIVERSITY, Azusa 91702/ *KO,* SP.

⊗ A-48.   BAKERSFIELD COLLEGE, Bakersfield 93305/ GE, SP.

⊗ A-49.   BARSTOW COLLEGE, Barstow 92311/ SP.

A-50.   BIOLA UNIVERSITY, La Mirada 90639/ FR, GE, GR.

⊗ A-51.   CABRILLO COLLEGE, Aptos 95003/ CH, FR, GE, IT, JP, RU, SP.

A-52.   CALIFORNIA BAPTIST COLLEGE, Riverside 92504/ SP.

A-53.   CALIFORNIA LUTHERAN UNIVERSITY, Thousand Oaks 91360/ FR, GE, SP.

A-54.   CALIFORNIA STATE UNIVERSITY–BAKERSFIELD, Bakersfield 93311-1099/ SP, SY.

A-55.   CALIFORNIA STATE UNIVERSITY–CHICO, Chico 95929/ FR, GE, SP.

A-56.   CALIFORNIA STATE UNIVERSITY–DOMINGUEZ HILLS, Carson 90747/ CH, CT, FR, GR, JP, LA, NR, PT, SP.

A-57.   CALIFORNIA STATE UNIVERSITY–FRESNO, Fresno 93740/ AB, AR, CH, FR, GE, GR, HE, JP, RU, SP, SS.

A-58.   CALIFORNIA STATE UNIVERSITY–FULLERTON, Fullerton 92634/ AB, CH, FR, GE, HE, JP, RU, SH, SP, SS.

A-59.   CALIFORNIA STATE UNIVERSITY–HAYWARD, Hayward 94542/ FR, GE, SP.

A-60.   CALIFORNIA STATE UNIVERSITY–LONG BEACH, Long Beach 90840/ CH, FL, FR, GE, GR, JP, LA, SH, SS.

A-61.   CALIFORNIA STATE UNIVERSITY–LOS ANGELES, Los Angeles 90032/ FR, JP, SP.

A-62.   CALIFORNIA STATE UNIVERSITY–NORTHRIDGE, Northridge 91330/ AR, CH, FR, GE, HE, JP, *RU, SLL,* SP.

A-63.   CALIFORNIA STATE UNIVERSITY–SACRAMENTO, Sacramento 95819/ FR, GE, SP.

A-64.   CALIFORNIA STATE UNIVERSITY–SAN BERNARDINO, San Bernardino 92407/ FR, MUL, SP.

A-65. CALIFORNIA STATE UNIVERSITY–STANISLAUS, Turlock 95380/ FR, SP, *SY.*

⊗A-66. CERRITOS COLLEGE, Norwalk 90650/ FR, GE, IT.

⊗A-67. CHABOT COLLEGE, Hayward 94545/ FR, GE, IT, PT, SP.

⊗A-68. CHAFFEY COMMUNITY COLLEGE, Alta Loma 91701/ FR, GE, SP.

A-69. CHAPMAN COLLEGE, Orange 92666/ FR, SP.

⊗A-70. CITRUS COLLEGE, Glendora 91740/ FR, GE, SP.

A-71. CLAREMONT McKENNA COLLEGE, Claremont 91711/ AB, CH, FR, GE, GR, HE, HI, H/U, IC, IC(od), IN, JP, KO, ML, NE, SP, SS, TO, UR.

⊗A-72. COLLEGE OF ALAMEDA, Alameda 94501/ SP.

⊗A-73. COLLEGE OF THE CANYONS, Valencia 91355/ FR, GE, SP.

⊗A-74. COLLEGE OF THE DESERT, Palm Desert 92260/ FR, IT, SP.

A-75. COLLEGE OF NOTRE DAME, Belmont 94002/ FR, SP.

⊗A-76. COLLEGE OF THE REDWOODS, Eureka 95501/ FR, GE, SP.

⊗A-76/a. COLLEGE OF SAN MATEO, San Mateo 94420/ FR, GE, SP.

⊗A-77. COLLEGE OF THE SEQUOIAS, Visalia 93277/ FR, SP.

⊗A-78. COLLEGE OF THE SISKIYOUS, Weed 96094/ FR, SP.

⊗A-79. COMPTON COMMUNITY COLLEGE, Compton 90221/ FR, GE, SP.

⊗A-80. CONTRA COSTA COLLEGE, San Pablo 94806/ FR, GE, IT, SP.

⊗A-81. CRAFTON HILLS COLLEGE, Yucaipa 92339/ FR, SP.

⊗A-82. CYPRESS COLLEGE, Cypress 90630/ FR, GE, SP.

⊗A-83. EAST LOS ANGELES COLLEGE, Monterey Park 91754/ FR, GE, JP, SP.

⊗A-84. EL CAMINO COLLEGE, Torrance 90506/ FR, GE, IT, JP, RU, SP.

A-85. FOOTHILL COLLEGE, Los Altos Hills 94022/ FR, GE, IT, JP, SP.

A-86. FULLERTON COLLEGE, Fullerton 92632/ FR, GE, RU, SP.

⊗A-87. GLENDALE COMMUNITY COLLEGE, Glendale 91208/ FR, SP.

A-88. HEBREW UNION COLLEGE, Los Angeles 90007/ *HE, YD.*

A-89. HOLY NAMES COLLEGE, Oakland 94619/ SP.

A-90. HUMBOLDT STATE UNIVERSITY, Arcata 95521/ FR, GE, SP.

⊗A-91. IMPERIAL VALLEY COLLEGE, Imperial 92251/ FR, SP.

⊗A-92. KING'S RIVER COMMUNITY COLLEGE, Reedley 93654/ SP.

⊗A-93. LANEY COLLEGE, Oakland 94607/ MOL.

A-94. LOMA LINDA UNIVERSITY, Riverside 92515/ FR, GE, SP.

⊗A-95. LOS ANGELES CITY COLLEGE, Los Angeles 90029/ FR, GE, SP.

ⓧA-96.   LOS ANGELES MISSION COLLEGE, San Fernando 91342/
         FR, IT, SP.
ⓧA-97.   LOS ANGELES SOUTHWEST COLLEGE, Los Angeles 90047/
         FR, SP.
ⓧA-98.   LOS ANGELES VALLEY COLLEGE, Van Nuys 91401-4096/
         FR, GE, HE, IT, SP.
 A-99.   LOYOLA MARYMOUNT UNIVERSITY, Los Angeles 90045/
         FR, GE, GR, LA, SP.
ⓧA-100. MENDOCINO COLLEGE, Ukiah 95482/ FR, SP.
 A-101. MENLO COLLEGE, Atherton 94025/ FR, GE, SP.
ⓧA-102. MERCED COLLEGE, Merced 95348/ FR, GE, IT, SP.
ⓧA-103. MERRITT COLLEGE, Oakland 94619/ AFL.
 A-104. MILLS COLLEGE, Oakland 94613/ FR, GE, SP.
ⓧA-105. MIRA COSTA COLLEGE, Oceanside 92056/ FR, GE, PT,
         SP.
ⓧA-106. MODESTO JUNIOR COLLEGE, Modesto 95350/ FR, GE,
         IT, SP.
◪A-107. MONTEREY INSTITUTE OF INTERNATIONAL STUDIES,
         Monterey 93940/ CH, FR, GE, JP, RU, SP.
 A-108. MOUNT ST. MARY'S COLLEGE, Los Angeles 90049/ FR,
         SP.
ⓧA-109. NAPA VALLEY COLLEGE, Napa 94558/ FR, GE, SP.
 A-110. OCCIDENTAL COLLEGE, Los Angeles 90041/ FR, GE,
         LA, SP.
ⓧA-111. OHLONE COLLEGE, Fremont 94539/ FR, GE, SP.
ⓧA-112. ORANGE COAST COLLEGE, Costa Mesa 92628/ FR, GE,
         JP, SP.
ⓧA-113. OXNARD COLLEGE, Oxnard 93033/ SP.
 A-114. PACIFIC UNION COLLEGE, Angwin 94508/ FR, GE, PT,
         SP.
ⓧA-115. PASADENA CITY COLLEGE, Pasadena 91106/ FR, GE, IT,
         JP.
 A-116. PEPPERDINE UNIVERSITY, Malibu 90263/ FR, GE, SP.
 A-117. PITZER COLLEGE, Claremont 91711/ FR, GE, SP.
 A-118. POINT LOMA NAZARENE COLLEGE, San Diego 92106/
         HE, JP, LA, RU, SP.
 A-119. POMONA COLLEGE, Claremont 91711/ CH, FR, GE, GR,
         HE, JP, RU.
ⓧA-120. RANCHO SANTIAGO COLLEGE, Santa Ana 92706/ MUL.
 A-121. ST. MARY'S COLLEGE OF CALIFORNIA, Moraga 94575/ FR,
         GR, LA, SP.
ⓧA-122. SAN BERNARDINO VALLEY COLLEGE, San Bernardino
         92410/ FR, GE, SP.
ⓧA-123. SAN DIEGO CITY COLLEGE, San Diego 92101/ AB, FR,
         GE, HE, IT, RU, SP.

◼A-124. SAN DIEGO STATE UNIVERSITY, San Diego 92182/ CH(mn), FR, GE, GR, HE, JP, RU, SP.

A-125. SAN FRANCISCO STATE UNIVERSITY, San Francisco 94132/ CH, FR, GE, IT, JP, RU, SP.

⊗A-126. SAN JOAQUIN DELTA COLLEGE, Stockton 95207/ FR, GE, SP.

⊗A-127. SAN JOSE CITY COLLEGE, San Jose 95128/ FR, GE, SP.

A-128. SAN JOSE STATE UNIVERSITY, San Jose 95192/ AB, CH(mn), FR, GE, GR, HE, JP, LA, PT, SP.

⊗A-129. SANTA BARBARA CITY COLLEGE, Santa Barbara 93109/ FR, GE, SP.

A-130. SANTA CLARA UNIVERSITY, Santa Clara 95053/ FR, GE, IT, SP.

⊗A-131. SANTA MONICA COLLEGE, Santa Monica 90405/ FR, GE, SP.

⊗A-132. SANTA ROSA JUNIOR COLLEGE, Santa Rosa 95401/ FR, GE, SP.

A-133. SCRIPPS COLLEGE, Claremont 91711/ CH, FR, GE, GR, IT, JP, LA, SP.

⊗A-134. SIERRA COLLEGE, Rocklin 95677/ FR, GE, SP.

⊗A-134/a. SKYLINE COLLEGE, San Bruno 94066/ FR, SP.

⊗A-135. SOLANO COMMUNITY COLLEGE, Suisun City 94585/ FR, GE, SP.

A-136. SONOMA STATE UNIVERSITY, Rohnert Park 94928/ FR, GE, HI, *SC,* SP, SS.

⊗A-137. SOUTHWESTERN COLLEGE, Chula Vista 92010/ FR, IT, SP.

◼A-138. STANFORD UNIVERSITY, Stanford 94305/ AB, AR, CH, CZ, FL, FR, GE, *GE(sw),* GR, HE, HI, HS, HU, IN, IR, IT, JP, KO, NW, PE, *PO,* RU, S/C, SH, SP, SW, TH, TI, *TU,* UK, *WN,* YO.

◼A-139. UNIVERSITY OF CALIFORNIA–BERKELEY, Berkeley 94720/ AA, AB(ca), AB(hi), AK, BR, BT, CA, CH(cl), CH(mn), CT, CZ, DA, DU, DU(md), EG, FR, FR(od), *FS,* GE, GE(mh), GE(oh), GO, GR, HE, HI, *HM,* HT, HU, IN, IR, IC(od), IT, JP, JP(cl), KO, LA, ML, MN, MO, *NE,* NW, PA, PE, PE(md), PK, PO, PT, PV(od), RO, RU, RU(od), S/C, SH, SP, SP(ch), SP(od), SS, S/S, SU, SW, SY, TH, TI, UG, UI, UR, WE, YD.

A-140. UNIVERSITY OF CALIFORNIA–DAVIS, Davis 95616/ FR, GE, GR, IT, JP, LA, RU, SP, SW.

◼A-141. UNIVERSITY OF CALIFORNIA–IRVINE, Irvine 92717/ CH, FR, GE, RU, SP.

◼A-142. UNIVERSITY OF CALIFORNIA–LOS ANGELES, Los Angeles 90024/ AB, AF, A/I, AR, BB, BM, CH, CH(cn),

CH(mn), CL, CZ, DA, DU, FI, *FL,* FR, *FS,* GE, GR,
HE, HU, IC, IR, IT, JP, *KO,* LA, MO, NW, *PA,* PE,
PO, PT, QC, RO, RU, S/C, SH, *SL,* SP, SW, *TH,* TU,
UK, *UZ, VI,* WE, YD, YO, ZU.

A-143.   UNIVERSITY OF CALIFORNIA–RIVERSIDE, Riverside
92521/ AB(ea), AB(ir), AB(mc), FR, GE, GE(mh), PT,
PT(br), RU, SP.

A-144.   UNIVERSITY OF CALIFORNIA–SAN DIEGO, La Jolla 92093/
AB(ca), AF, AL, BG, BL, BU, CH(am), CH(mn), CZ,
DA, DU, EP, *FI,* FL, FR, GE, H/C, HE, HI, HS, HU,
HW, IG, IR, IT, JP, KA, KO, ML, NV, NW, PE, PO,
PT, RU, S/C, SH, SP, SW, TH, TI, TU, TW, VI, YO.

◪A-145.   UNIVERSITY OF CALIFORNIA–SANTA BARBARA, Santa
Barbara 93106/ AB, CH(cn), CH(mn), CP, FR, FR(od),
GE, GE(mh), GR, HE, IT, JP, LA, PT, RU, SP, SP(od),
SS, SW.

A-146.   UNIVERSITY OF CALIFORNIA–SANTA CRUZ, Santa Cruz
95064/ AB, CH(mn), FR, GE, GR, HE, IT, JP, LA, NR,
PT, RU, SP, SS, TU.

A-147.   UNIVERSITY OF JUDAISM, Los Angeles 90077/ BIL, *HE,
YD.*

A-148.   UNIVERSITY OF LA VERNE, La Verne 91750/ FR, GE, SP.

A-149.   UNIVERSITY OF THE PACIFIC, Stockton 95211/ FR, GE,
GR, JP, LA, SP.

A-150.   UNIVERSITY OF REDLANDS, Redlands 92374/ FR, GE,
SP.

A-151.   UNIVERSITY OF SAN DIEGO, San Diego 92110/ FR, SP.

A-152.   UNIVERSITY OF SAN FRANCISCO, San Francisco 94117-
1080/ FR, SP.

A-153.   UNIVERSITY OF SOUTHERN CALIFORNIA, Los Angeles
90089/ AB, *AC,* CH, FR, GE, GE(mh), GE(oh),
GR(cl), HE, IT, JP, KO, LA, PO, PT, RU, S/C, SP.

⊗A-154.   VENTURA COLLEGE, Ventura 93003/ FR, GE, SP.

⊗A-155.   WEST HILLS COLLEGE, Coalinga 93210/ MUL.

⊗A-156.   WEST LOS ANGELES COLLEGE, Culver City 90230/ FR, SP.

⊗A-157.   WEST VALLEY COLLEGE, Saratoga 95070/ FR, GE, IT,
SP.

A-158.   WESTMONT COLLEGE, Santa Barbara 93108/ FR, SP.

A-159.   WHITTIER COLLEGE, Whittier 90608/ CH, FR, SP.

A-160.   WORLD COLLEGE WEST, Petaluma 94952/ MUL, SP.

COLORADO (CO)

A-161.   ADAMS STATE COLLEGE, Alamosa 81102/ SP.

A-162.   COLORADO COLLEGE, Colorado Springs 80903/ FR, GE,
SP.

A-163. COLORADO STATE UNIVERSITY, Fort Collins 80523/ FR, GE, SP.
A-164. FORT LEWIS COLLEGE, Durango 81301/ SP.
⊗A-165. FRONT RANGE COMMUNITY COLLEGE, Westminster 80030/ SP.
A-166. METROPOLITAN STATE COLLEGE, Denver 80217/ MUL, SP.
⊗A-167. OTERO JUNIOR COLLEGE, La Junta 81050/ MOL.
A-168. REGIS UNIVERSITY, Denver 80221/ FR, SP.
A-169. UNIVERSITY OF COLORADO AT BOULDER, Boulder 80309/ CH(mn), EG(an), FR, GE, GR, HE, IC(od), IT, JP, LA, LK, NR, NW, PT, PV, RU, *SLL,* SP, S/S, SW.
A-170. UNIVERSITY OF COLORADO AT COLORADO SPRINGS, Colorado Springs 80933-7150/ SP.
A-171. UNIVERSITY OF COLORADO AT DENVER, Denver 80202/ FR, GE, SP.
A-172. UNIVERSITY OF DENVER, Denver 80208/ FR, GE, RU, SP.
A-173. UNIVERSITY OF NORTHERN COLORADO, Greeley 80639/ FR, GE, RU, SP.
A-174. UNIVERSITY OF SOUTHERN COLORADO, Pueblo 81001/ MUL.
A-175. WESTERN STATE COLLEGE OF COLORADO, Gunnison 81231/ FR, SP.

CONNECTICUT (CT)

A-176. ALBERTUS MAGNUS COLLEGE, New Haven 06511/ FR, IT, SP.
A-177. CENTRAL CONNECTICUT STATE UNIVERSITY, New Britain 06050/ CH(mn), FR, GE, HE, IT, JP, LA, PO, SP.
A-178. CONNECTICUT COLLEGE, New London 06320/ CH, FR, GE, GR, IT, JP, LA, RU, SP.
A-179. EASTERN CONNECTICUT STATE UNIVERSITY, Willimantic 06226/ SP.
A-180. FAIRFIELD UNIVERSITY, Fairfield 06430/ FR, GE, SP.
A-181. SACRED HEART UNIVERSITY, Fairfield 06432/ FR, IT, JP, LA, SP.
A-182. ST. JOSEPH COLLEGE, West Hartford 06117/ FR, SP.
A-183. SOUTHERN CONNECTICUT STATE UNIVERSITY, New Haven 06515/ FR, GE, IT, SP.
A-184. TRINITY COLLEGE, Hartford 06106/ FR, GE, IT, *NAL,* RU, SP.
A-185. UNIVERSITY OF CONNECTICUT, Storrs 06269/ FR, FR(od), GE, GR, HE, IC(od), IT, LA, PO, PT, PV, RU, S/C, SP, SP(od), *TU,* WE.

A-186.   UNIVERSITY OF HARTFORD, West Hartford 06117/ AB, CH, DU, FR, GE, GE(mh), GE(oh), GR, IT, JP, SP.
A-187.   WESLEYAN UNIVERSITY, Middletown 96459/ CH, FR, GE, GR, HE, IT, JP, LA, RU, SP.
A-188.   WESTERN CONNECTICUT STATE UNIVERSITY, Danbury 06810/ SP.
A-189.   YALE UNIVERSITY, New Haven 06520/ AA, AB, AF, AK, AV, BM, BU, CH(cl), CH(mn), CL, CP, CZ, EG(an), FL, FR, FR(od), GE, GE(mh), GE(oh), GR, HE, HS, HT, IG, IR(od), IT, JP, JP(cl), JV, KO, KT, LA, LI, NR, PA, PE(md), PE(od), PI(wa), PK, PO, PT, RU, S/C, SH, SP, S/S, S/S(bi), SU, SY, *TH,* TI, *TU,* UG, VD, YO.

DELAWARE (DE)
A-190.   DELAWARE STATE COLLEGE, Dover 19901/ FR, SP.
A-191.   UNIVERSITY OF DELAWARE, Newark 19716/ AB, CH, FR, GE, HE, IT, JP, LA, RU, *SC,* SP.
A-192.   WESLEY COLLEGE, Dover 19901/ FR, SP.

DISTRICT OF COLUMBIA (DC)
◪A-193.   AMERICAN UNIVERSITY, Washington 20016/ FR, GE, GR, HE, JP, LA, RU, SP.
A-194.   CATHOLIC UNIVERSITY OF AMERICA, Washington 20064/ AB, FR, GE, GR, HE, IT, LA, SP.
A-195.   GALLAUDET UNIVERSITY, Washington 20002/ FR, GE, GR, IT, LA, RU, SP.
A-196.   GEORGE WASHINGTON UNIVERSITY, Washington 20052/ CH, FR, GE, RU, SP.
◪A-197.   GEORGETOWN UNIVERSITY, Washington 20057/ AB(cl), CH, CH(mn), FR, GE, GR, HE, IT, JP, PO, PT, RU, SS, S/S.
A-198.   HOWARD UNIVERSITY, Washington 20059/ AFL, FR, GE, *H/C, LA,* RU, SP.
A-199.   TRINITY COLLEGE, Washington 20017/ FR, SP.
A-200.   UNIVERSITY OF THE DISTRICT OF COLUMBIA, Washington 20008/ FR, GE, SP.

FLORIDA (FL)
A-201.   BARRY UNIVERSITY, Miami Shores 33161/ FR, SP.
⊗A-202.   BREVARD COMMUNITY COLLEGE, Cocoa 32922/ FR, GE, SP.
⊗A-203.   DAYTONA BEACH COMMUNITY COLLEGE, Daytona Beach 32120/ FR, SP.

A-204. ECKERD COLLEGE, St. Petersburg 33711/ FR, GE, RU, SP.

A-205. FLAGLER COLLEGE, St. Augustine 32085/ SP.

A-206. FLORIDA ATLANTIC UNIVERSITY, Boca Raton 33431/ FR, GE, SP.

◢A-207. FLORIDA INTERNATIONAL UNIVERSITY, Miami 33199/ AB, CH, FR, GE, H/C, HE, IT, JP, PT.

A-208. FLORIDA SOUTHERN COLLEGE, Lakeland 33801/ CH, FR, GE, SP.

A-209. FLORIDA STATE UNIVERSITY, Tallahassee 32306/ CH, FR, GE, GR, IT, JP, LA, RU, SP, S/S.

⊗A-209/a. GULF COAST COMMUNITY COLLEGE, Panama City 32401/ MUL.

⊗A-210. INDIAN RIVER COMMUNITY COLLEGE, Fort Pierce 33450/ SP.

A-211. JACKSONVILLE UNIVERSITY, Jacksonville 32211/ FR, GE, SP.

A-212. MIAMI CHRISTIAN COLLEGE, Miami 33101/ CH, GR, HE.

A-213. NEW COLLEGE OF THE UNIVERSITY OF SOUTH FLORIDA, Sarasota 34243/ FR, GE, GR, LA, RU, SP.

⊗A-214. POLK COMMUNITY COLLEGE, Winter Haven 33881/ FR, GE, SP.

A-215. ROLLINS COLLEGE, Winter Park 32789/ FR, GE, RU, SP.

A-216. ST. THOMAS UNIVERSITY, Miami 33054/ SP.

⊗A-217. SOUTH FLORIDA COMMUNITY COLLEGE, Avon Park 33825/ SP.

A-218. No entry.

A-219. STETSON UNIVERSITY, De Land 32720/ FR, GE, RU, SP.

A-220. UNIVERSITY OF CENTRAL FLORIDA, Orlando 32816/ FR, GE, SP.

A-221. UNIVERSITY OF FLORIDA, Gainesville 32611/ CH(mn), DU, FR, GE, GR, HE, JP, LΛ, NW, PO, RU, PT, SH, SN, SW, *YD,* YO.

A-222. UNIVERSITY OF MIAMI, Coral Gables 33124/ CH, FR, GE(mh), GR, HE, HE(bi), JP, RU, SP, SW.

A-223. UNIVERSITY OF SOUTH FLORIDA, Tampa 33620/ AB, AY, CH, FR(od), GE, GE(oh), GR, HE, HE(bi), IT, LA, PO, PT, RU, SP.

A-224. UNIVERSITY OF TAMPA, Tampa 33606/ FR, SP.

A-225. UNIVERSITY OF WEST FLORIDA, Pensacola 32514/ FR, SP.

GEORGIA (GA)

A-226. AGNES SCOTT COLLEGE, Decatur 30030/ FR, GE, GR, LA, SP.

ⓍA-227.   ALBANY JUNIOR COLLEGE, Albany 31707/ FR, SP.
A-228.   ALBANY STATE COLLEGE, Albany 31705/ FR, SP.
ⓍA-229.   ATLANTA JUNIOR COLLEGE, Atlanta 30310/ MUL.
A-230.   ATLANTA UNIVERSITY, Atlanta 30314/ FR, SP. Merged with A-233.
ⓍA-231.   BAINBRIDGE JUNIOR COLLEGE, Bainbridge 31717/ FR, SP.
A-232.   BERRY COLLEGE, Mount Berry 30145/ FR, GE, SP.
A-233.   CLARK ATLANTA UNIVERSITY, Atlanta 30314/ FR, GE, SP.
A-234.   CLAYTON STATE COLLEGE, Morrow 30260/ FR, SP.
A-235.   EMANUEL COUNTY JUNIOR COLLEGE, Swainsboro 30401/ FR, SP.
A-236.   EMORY UNIVERSITY, Atlanta 30322/ FR, GE, GR, LA, RU, SP.
A-237.   FORT VALLEY STATE COLLEGE, Fort Valley 31030/ FR.
A-238.   GEORGIA COLLEGE, Milledgeville 31061/ FR, SP.
A-239.   GEORGIA SOUTHERN UNIVERSITY, Statesboro 30460/ FR, GE, SP.
A-240.   GEORGIA STATE UNIVERSITY, Atlanta 30303/ FR, GE.
ⓍA-241.   GORDON COLLEGE, Barnsville 30204/ SP, MUL.
A-242.   LaGRANGE COLLEGE, LaGrange 30240/ SP.
A-243.   MACON COLLEGE, Macon 31297/ FR, SP.
A-244.   MERCER UNIVERSITY, Macon 31207/ FR, GE, GR, LA, SP.
ⓍA-245.   MIDDLE GEORGIA COLLEGE, Cochran 31014/ MUL, SP.
ⓍA-246.   SOUTH GEORGIA COLLEGE, Douglas 31533/ FR, SP.
A-247.   SPELMAN COLLEGE, Atlanta 30314/ FR, GE, SP.
ⓍA-248.   TRUETT McCONNELL COLLEGE, Cleveland 30582/ FR, SP.
A-249.   UNIVERSITY OF GEORGIA, Athens 30602/ AA, CT, DA, DU, FR, FR(od), GE, GE(mh), GE(oh), GO, GR, HE(bi), IC(od), IR(od), IT, LA, NW, PT, PV, RO, SLL, SP(od), SS, SW, SY.
A-250.   VALDOSTA STATE COLLEGE, Valdosta 31698/ FR, SP.
A-251.   WEST GEORGIA COLLEGE, Carrollton 30118/ FR, SP.
ⓍA-252.   YOUNG HARRIS COLLEGE, Young Harris 30582/ FR, SP.

HAWAII (HI)
A-253.   HAWAII LOA COLLEGE, Kaneohe 96744/ CH, FR, JP.
A-254.   UNIVERSITY OF HAWAII AT HILO, Hilo 96720-4091/ HW, JP.
A-255.   UNIVERSITY OF HAWAII AT MANOA, Manoa 96822/ AB(cl), BA, BU, CA, CH(cl), CH(cn), CH(mn), DU, FL, FR, GE, GE(mh), GR, HI, HW, IL, IN, JP, JV,

KO, LA, LO, *MR,* PA, PI(n/g), PK, PT, RU, SM, SP, SS, TA, TH, TI, TI(cl), VI.

IDAHO (ID)
A-256. IDAHO STATE UNIVERSITY, Pocatello 83209/ FR, GE, SP.
ⓍA-257. NORTH IDAHO COLLEGE, Coeur d'Alene 83814/ FR, GE, SP.
A-258. NORTHWEST NAZARENE COLLEGE, Nampa 83651/ MUL.
A-259. RICKS COLLEGE, Rexburg 83460/ FR, GE, RU, SP.
A-260. UNIVERSITY OF IDAHO, Moscow 83843/ *BS,* FR, GE, LA, SP.

ILLINOIS (IL)
A-261. AUGUSTANA COLLEGE, Rock Island 61201/ CH, FR, GE, GR, LA, SP, SW.
ⓍA-262. BLACK HAWK COLLEGE, Moline 61265/ FR, GE, SP.
A-263. BLACKBURN COLLEGE, Carlinville 62626/ SP.
A-264. BRADLEY UNIVERSITY, Peoria 61625/ FR, GE, SP.
A-265. BRISK RABBINICAL COLLEGE, Chicago 60659/ HE.
A-266. CHICAGO STATE UNIVERSITY, Chicago 60628/ SP.
ⓍA-267. CITY COLLEGES OF CHICAGO: HARRY S TRUMAN COLLEGE, Chicago 60640/ FR, SP.
ⓍA-268. CITY COLLEGES OF CHICAGO: KENNEDY-KING COLLEGE, Chicago 60621/ FR, SP.
ⓍA-269. CITY COLLEGES OF CHICAGO: LOOP COLLEGE, Chicago 60601/ FR, SP.
ⓍA-270. CITY COLLEGES OF CHICAGO: MALCOLM X COLLEGE, Chicago 60612/ FR, SP.
ⓍA-271. CITY COLLEGES OF CHICAGO: OLIVE-HARVEY COLLEGE, Chicago 60628/ FR, SP.
ⓍA-272. CITY COLLEGES OF CHICAGO: RICHARD F. DALEY COLLEGE, Chicago 60552/ FR, SP.
A-273. CONCORDIA UNIVERSITY, River Forest 60305/ BIL, GE, MUL.
A-274. DE PAUL UNIVERSITY, Chicago 60604/ FR, GE, SP.
A-275. EASTERN ILLINOIS UNIVERSITY, Charleston 61920/ FR, GE, SP.
A-276. ELMHURST COLLEGE, Elmhurst 60126/ FR, GE, SP.
A-277. GREENVILLE COLLEGE, Greenville 62246/ FR, SP.
A-278. HEBREW THEOLOGICAL COLLEGE, Skokie 60077/ BIL, HE, YD.
A-279. ILLINOIS COLLEGE, Jacksonville 62650/ FR, GE, SP.
A-280. ILLINOIS STATE UNIVERSITY, Normal 61761/ FR, GE, SP.
A-281. ILLINOIS WESLEYAN UNIVERSITY, Bloomington 61702/ FR, GE, SP.

⊗A-282.   JOHN WOOD COMMUNITY COLLEGE, Quincy 62301/ FR, GE, GR, JP, SP.

A-283.   KNOX COLLEGE, Galesburg 61401/ FR, GE, JP, RU, SP.

A-284.   LAKE FOREST COLLEGE, Lake Forest 60045/ FR, GE, SP.

⊗A-285.   LINCOLN LAND COMMUNITY COLLEGE, Springfield 62794/ MUL.

A-286.   LOYOLA UNIVERSITY OF CHICAGO, Chicago 60611/ FR, GE, GR, IT, LA, SP.

A-287.   MacMURRAY COLLEGE, Jacksonville 62650/ FR, SP.

A-288.   MILLIKIN UNIVERSITY, Decatur 62522/ FR, GE, SP.

A-289.   MONMOUTH COLLEGE, Monmouth 61462/ FR, GR, LA, SP.

A-290.   MUNDELEIN COLLEGE, Chicago 60660/ FR, HE, SP.

A-291.   NORTH CENTRAL COLLEGE, Naperville 60566/ FR, GE, GR, JP, LA, RU, SP.

A-292.   NORTH PARK COLLEGE AND THEOLOGICAL SEMINARY, Chicago 60625/ *DA, FI,* FR, GE, *NW,* SP, *SW.*

A-293.   NORTHEASTERN ILLINOIS UNIVERSITY, Chicago 60625/ AB, *AFL,* CH(mn), FR, GE, GR, HE, IN, JP, *LO,* NV, PO, RU, SH, SP, SW, TH, TU.

A-294.   NORTHERN ILLINOIS UNIVERSITY, DeKalb 60115/ FR, HE, *IT,* PT, SP.

A-295.   NORTHWESTERN UNIVERSITY, Evanston 60204/ AB, AM, CH(mn), CZ, FR, GE, GE(mh), GR(mo), H/C, HE, HS, IT, JP, LA, MD, ME, MS, PO, PT, RU, S/C, SH, SP, S/S.

A-296.   PRINCIPIA COLLEGE, Elsah 62028/ FR, GE, RU, SP.

⊗A-297.   REND LAKE COLLEGE, INA 62846/ FR, GE, SP.

A-298.   ROCKFORD COLLEGE, Rockford 61108/ FR, GE, GR, LA, SP.

A-299.   ROOSEVELT UNIVERSITY, Chicago 60605/ FR, SP.

A-300.   ROSARY COLLEGE, River Forest 60305/ FR, GE, IT, SP.

A-301.   ST. XAVIER COLLEGE, Chicago 60655/ FR, SP.

⊗A-302.   SAUK VALLEY COMMUNITY COLLEGE, Dixon 61021/ FR, SP.

A-303.   SOUTHERN ILLINOIS UNIVERSITY AT CARBONDALE, Carbondale 62901/ CH, FR, FR(od), GE, GR, GR(an), LA, *PT,* RU, SP, SP(od), VI.

A-304.   SOUTHERN ILLINOIS UNIVERSITY AT EDWARDSVILLE, Edwardsville 62026/ EP, FR, GE, GR, LA, PT, SP.

A-305.   UNIVERSITY OF CHICAGO, Chicago 60637/ AB, AB(cl), AK, AL, AS, BL, BN, CA, CH, CL, CZ, EG, EK, ET, ET(cl), FR, FR(od), GE, GG, GR, HE, HE(bi), HI, HT, H/U, IN, IR, IT, JP, JP(cl), LA, M/Y, NR, NW, PE,

PO, PT, RO, RU, RU(od), S/C, SP, SS, S/S, SU, SW, TM, TM(cl), TU, UG, UK, UR, UR(cl), WE, YD.

A-306. UNIVERSITY OF ILLINOIS AT CHICAGO, Chicago 60680/ AB, AB(ca), AB(cl), CH, CH(mn), CZ, FR, GE, GE(oh), HE, HE(bi), IT, JP, LI, PO, PT, RU, S/C, SP, S/S, YD.

A-307. UNIVERSITY OF ILLINOIS AT URBANA-CHAMPAIGN, Urbana 61801/ AB(ca), AB(cl), AB(es), AF, AL, AM, BU, CH, CH(cl), CH(cn), CH(mn), C/N, CP, CT, FR, FR(od), GE, GE(mh), GE(oh), GR, GR(cl), HE, HE(bi), HI, HS, HT, H/U, IN, IT, JP, KO, KS, K/U, LG, MD, MK, NR, NW, PA, PE, PO, PT, QC, *RO,* RU, S/C, SH, SN, SO, SP, SP(od), SS, S/S, *SV,* SW, TH, TN, TY, UK, WO, YO.

A-308. WESTERN ILLINOIS UNIVERSITY, Macomb 61455/ FR, GE, SP.

A-309. WHEATON COLLEGE, Wheaton 60187/ FR, GE, GR, *KO,* SP.

INDIANA (IN)

A-310. ANDERSON UNIVERSITY, Anderson 46012/ FR, GE, SP.

A-311. BALL STATE UNIVERSITY, Muncie 47306/ AB, CH, FR, GE, GR(cl), HE, JR, LA, PT, SP.

A-312. BUTLER UNIVERSITY, Indianapolis 46208/ FR, GE, GR, LA, SP.

A-313. DePAUW UNIVERSITY, Greencastle 46135/ FR, GE, GR, LA, RU, SP.

A-314. EARLHAM COLLEGE, Richmond 47374/ FR, GE, *JP,* SP.

A-315. FRANKLIN COLLEGE, Franklin 46131/ FR, SP.

A-316. GOSHEN COLLEGE, Goshen 46526/ GE, SP.

A-317. GRACE COLLEGE, Winona Lake 46590/ FR, GE, GR, HE, RU, SP.

A-318. HANOVER COLLEGE, Hanover 47243/ FR, GE, SP.

A-319. INDIANA STATE UNIVERSITY, Terre Haute 47809/ FR, GE, LA, *PT,* RU, SP.

A-320. INDIANA UNIVERSITY–BLOOMINGTON, Bloomington 47405/ AB, AZ, BL, BM, CC, CH, CV, CZ, DA, DU, ES, EW, FI, FL, FR, GE, GE(oh), GG, GR, GR(cl), H/C, HE, HS, HU, IC(od), IT, JP, KI, KO, KU, LA, LG, LI, LT, MO, NA, *NAL,* ND, PO, PT, QC, RO, RU, S/C, SN, SO, SP, S/S, SV, SW, TI, TT, TU, TV, UK, UZ, WO, YO, ZA, ZU.

A-321. INDIANA UNIVERSITY NORTHWEST, Gary 46408/ FR, SP.

A-322. INDIANA UNIVERSITY AT SOUTH BEND, South Bend 46615/ FR, GE, SP.

A-323.   INDIANA UNIVERSITY–PURDUE UNIVERSITY AT FORT WAYNE, Fort Wayne 46805/ FR, GE, SP.
A-324.   INDIANA UNIVERSITY–PURDUE UNIVERSITY AT INDIANAPOLIS, Indianapolis 46202/ FR, GE, SP.
A-325.   MANCHESTER COLLEGE, North Manchester 46962/ FR, GE, SP.
A-326.   MARIAN COLLEGE, Indianapolis 46260/ FR, GE, SP.
A-327.   MARION COLLEGE, Marion 46953/ SP.
A-328.   OAKLAND CITY COLLEGE, Oakland City 47660/ HI.
A-329.   PURDUE UNIVERSITY, West Lafayette 47907/ CH, FR, GE, RU, SP.
A-330.   PURDUE UNIVERSITY–CALUMET, Hammond 46323/ FR, GE, HE, SP.
A-331.   ST. MARY-OF-THE-WOODS COLLEGE, St. Mary-of-the-Woods 47876/ *FR,* SP.
A-332.   ST. MARY'S COLLEGE, Notre Dame 46556/ FR, SP.
A-333.   ST. MEINRAD COLLEGE, St. Meinrad 47577/ SP.
A-334.   TAYLOR UNIVERSITY, Upland 46989/ FR, GE, SP.
A-335.   UNIVERSITY OF EVANSVILLE, Evansville 47722/ FR, GE, SP.
A-336.   UNIVERSITY OF INDIANAPOLIS, Indianapolis 46227/ FR, GE, SP.
A-337.   UNIVERSITY OF NOTRE DAME, Notre Dame 46556/AB, FR, GE, GR, HE, IT, JP, LA, RU, SP.
A-338.   UNIVERSITY OF SOUTHERN INDIANA, Evansville 47712/ GE, SP.
A-339.   VALPARAISO UNIVERSITY, Valparaiso 46383/ FR, GE, GR, LA, SP.
⊗ A-340.   VINCENNES UNIVERSITY, Vincennes 47591/ FR, GE, SP.
A-341.   WABASH COLLEGE, Crawfordsville 47933/ FR, GE, GR, LA, RU, SP.

IOWA (IA)
A-342.   BRIAR CLIFF COLLEGE, Sioux City 51104/ SP.
A-343.   BUENA VISTA COLLEGE, Storm Lake 50588/ MUL, SP.
A-344.   CENTRAL UNIVERSITY OF IOWA, Pella 50219/ DU, FR, GE, GR, HE, HE(bi), M/Y, PT, SP, WE.
A-345.   CLARKE COLLEGE, Dubuque 52001/ FR, GE, SP.
A-346.   COE COLLEGE, Cedar Rapids 52402/ FR, GE, SP.
A-347.   CORNELL COLLEGE, Mount Vernon 52314/ FR, GE, LA, RU, SP.
A-348.   DORDT COLLEGE, Sioux Center 51250/ GE, SP.
A-349.   DRAKE UNIVERSITY, Des Moines 50311/ FR, GE, SP.
A-350.   GRACELAND COLLEGE, Lamoni 50140/ FR, GE, SP.
A-351.   GRAND VIEW COLLEGE, Des Moines 50316/ *DA.*

A-352. GRINNELL COLLEGE, Grinnell 50112/ CH, FR, GE, GR, RU, SP.

A-353. IOWA STATE UNIVERSITY OF SCIENCE & TECHNOLOGY, Ames 50011/ FR, GE, GR, GR(cl), PT, RU, SP.

⊗A-354. KIRKWOOD COMMUNITY COLLEGE, Cedar Rapids 52406/ FR, GE, SP.

A-355. LORAS COLLEGE, Dubuque 52004/ FR, GE, GR, LA, SP.

A-356. LUTHER COLLEGE, Decorah 52101/ FR, GE, GR, HE, LA, SP, SW.

⊗A-357. MARSHALLTOWN COMMUNITY COLLEGE, Marshalltown 50158/ SP.

A-358. MORNINGSIDE COLLEGE, Sioux City 51106/ FR, SP.

A-359. MOUNT ST. CLAIRE COLLEGE, Clinton 52732/ FR, SP.

A-360. NORTHWESTERN COLLEGE, Orange City 51041/ *DU,* FR, SP.

A-361. ST. AMBROSE UNIVERSITY, Davenport 52803/ FR, GE, GR, LA, RU, SP.

A-362. SIMPSON COLLEGE, Indianola 50125/ FR, GE, RU, SP.

⊗A-363. SOUTHERN COMMUNITY COLLEGE, NORTH CAMPUS, West Burlington 52655/ GE.

A-364. UNIVERSITY OF DUBUQUE, Dubuque 52001/ FR, SP.

A-365. UNIVERSITY OF IOWA, Iowa City 52242/ CH, FR, GE, GR, IT, JP, LA, PT, RU, SP, SS.

A-366. UNIVERSITY OF NORTHERN IOWA, Cedar Falls 50614/ CH, FR, GE, SP.

A-367. VENNARD COLLEGE, University Park 52595/ HE, SP.

⊗A-368. WALDORF COLLEGE, Forest City 50436/ GE, SP.

A-369. WARTBURG COLLEGE, Waverly 50677/ FR, GE, GR, SP.

A-370. WESTMAR COLLEGE, Le Mars 51031/ GE.

KANSAS (KS)

A-371. BAKER UNIVERSITY, Baldwin City 66006/ FR, GE, SP.

A-372. BENEDICTINE COLLEGE, Atchinson 66002/ FR, GR, LA, SP.

A-373. BETHEL COLLÉGE, North Newton 67117/ GE.

A-374. EMPORIA STATE UNIVERSITY, Emporia 66801/ MUL.

A-375. FORT HAYS STATE UNIVERSITY, Hays 67601/ FR, GE, SP.

⊗A-376. FORT SCOTT COMMUNITY COLLEGE, Fort Scott 66701/ SP.

A-377. FRIENDS UNIVERSITY, Wichita 67213/ SP.

⊗A-378. HUTCHINSON COMMUNITY COLLEGE, Hutchinson 67501/ SP.

⊗A-379. INDEPENDENCE COMMUNITY COLLEGE, Independence 67301/ FR, SP.

⊗A-380. KANSAS CITY KANSAS COMMUNITY COLLEGE, Kansas City 66112/ FR, GE, SP.

A-381.   KANSAS WESLEYAN UNIVERSITY, Salina 67401/ SP.
⊗A-382.   LABETTE COMMUNITY COLLEGE, Parsons 67357/ MUL.
A-383.   McPHERSON COLLEGE, McPherson 67460/ GE, SP.
A-384.   MID-AMERICA NAZARENE COLLEGE, Olathe 66061/ MOL, SP.
⊗A-384/a. NEOSHO COUNTY COMMUNITY COLLEGE, Chanute 66720/ MOL.
A-385.   OTTAWA UNIVERSITY, Ottawa 66067/ FR.
A-386.   PITTSBURG STATE UNIVERSITY, Pittsburg 66762/ FR, SP.
⊗A-387.   PRATT COMMUNITY COLLEGE, Pratt 67124/ FR, SP.
A-388.   ST. MARY COLLEGE, Leavenworth 66048/ NAL, SP.
A-389.   ST. MARY OF THE PLAIN COLLEGE, Dodge City 67801/ SP.
A-390.   SOUTHWESTERN COLLEGE, Winfield 67156/ FR, GE, SP.
A-391.   UNIVERSITY OF KANSAS, Lawrence 66045/ AB, BL, CH, CZ, DA, FR, FR(od), GE, GE(mh), GE(oh), GR, GU, H/C, HE, HL, IP, IT, JP, KN, KO, LA, NR, NW, PO, PT, RU, SLL, SP, SP(od), SS, S/S, SV, SW.
A-392.   WASHBURN UNIVERSITY OF TOPEKA, Topeka 66621/ FR, GE, SP.
A-393.   WICHITA STATE UNIVERSITY, Wichita 67208-1595/ FR, GE, LA, SP.

KENTUCKY (KY)
A-394.   ASBURY COLLEGE, Wilmore 40390/ FR, GR, SP.
A-395.   BELLARMINE COLLEGE, Louisville 40205/ FR, GE.
A-396.   BEREA COLLEGE, Berea 40404/ FR, GE, LA, SP.
A-397.   CENTRE COLLEGE, Danville 40422/ FR, GE, SP.
A-398.   EASTERN KENTUCKY UNIVERSITY, Richmond 40475/ FR, GE, RU, SP.
A-399.   GEORGETOWN COLLEGE, Georgetown 40324/ FR, GE, SP.
A-400.   KENTUCKY WESLEYAN COLLEGE, Owensboro 42302/ FR, GE, SP.
A-401.   MOREHEAD STATE UNIVERSITY, Morehead 40351/ FR.
A-402.   MURRAY STATE UNIVERSITY, Murray 42071/ FR, GE, SP.
A-403.   TRANSYLVANIA UNIVERSITY, Lexington 40508/ FR, GE, SP.
A-404.   UNIVERSITY OF KENTUCKY, Lexington 40506/ DA, FI, FR, FR(od), GE, GE(mh), GE(oh), GO, HE, HU, IC(od), IT, NW, PV(od), RU, SP, SP(od), SW.
A-405.   UNIVERSITY OF LOUISVILLE, Louisville 40292/ FR, GE, GR, RU, SP.

A-406. WESTERN KENTUCKY UNIVERSITY, Bowling Green 42101/ FR, GE, SP.

LOUISIANA (LA)
A-407. CENTENARY COLLEGE OF LOUISIANA, Shreveport 71104/ FR, SP.
A-408. DILLARD UNIVERSITY, New Orleans 70122/ FR, GE, JP, SP.
A-409. GRAMBLING STATE UNIVERSITY, Grambling 71245/ FR, GE, SP.
A-410. LOUISIANA STATE UNIVERSITY AND AGRICULTURAL AND MECHANICAL COLLEGE, Baton Rouge 70803/ FR, GE, IT, LA, PT, RU, SP.
A-411. LOUISIANA STATE UNIVERSITY IN SHREVEPORT, Shreveport 71115/ FR, FR(lu), FR(od), GE, GE(mh), GE(oh), GO, GR, HE(bi), JP, NR, SP, SP(od).
A-412. LOUISIANA TECH UNIVERSITY, Ruston 71272/ FR, SP.
A-413. LOYOLA UNIVERSITY, New Orleans 70118/ FR, GE, RU, SP.
A-414. McNEESE STATE UNIVERSITY, Lake Charles 70609/ AB, FR, SP.
A-415. NICHOLLS STATE UNIVERSITY, Thibodaux 70310/ FR.
A-416. NORTHEAST LOUISIANA UNIVERSITY, Monroe 71202/ FR, SP.
A-417. SOUTHERN LOUISIANA UNIVERSITY, Hammond 70402/ FR, SP.
A-418. TULANE UNIVERSITY, New Orleans 70118/ CH, FR, GE, GR, HE, IR, IT, JP, LA, LI, M/Y, NA, NV, NW, PT, RU, SP, SS.
A-419. UNIVERSITY OF SOUTHWESTERN LOUISIANA, Lafayette 70504/ FR, GE, SP.
A-420. XAVIER UNIVERSITY OF LOUISIANA, New Orleans 70125/ EG, FR, GE, SP.

MAINE (ME)
A-421. BATES COLLEGE, Lewiston 04240/ FR, GE, RU, SP.
A-422. BOWDOIN COLLEGE, Brunswick 04011/ FR, GE, RU, SP.
A-423. COLBY COLLEGE, Waterville 04901/ FR, GE, SP.
A-424. COLLEGE OF THE ATLANTIC, Bar Harbor 04609/ LA.
A-425. UNIVERSITY OF MAINE, Orono 04469/ FR, GE, LA, SP.
A-426. UNIVERSITY OF MAINE AT FORT KENT, Fort Kent 04743/ FR.
A-427. UNIVERSITY OF MAINE AT PRESQUE ISLE, Presque Isle 04769/ FR.
A-428. UNIVERSITY OF SOUTHERN MAINE, Portland 04103/ FR.

MARYLAND (MD)

A-429. BALTIMORE HEBREW UNIVERSITY, Baltimore 21215/ AB, HE, YD.

A-430. COLLEGE OF NOTRE DAME OF MARYLAND, Baltimore 21210/ FR, SP.

A-431. FROSTBURG STATE UNIVERSITY, Frostburg 21532/ FR, GE, RU, SP.

A-432. GOUCHER COLLEGE, Baltimore 21204/ FR, GE, RU, SP.

A-433. HOOD COLLEGE, Frederick 21701/ FR, GE, SP.

A-434. JOHNS HOPKINS UNIVERSITY: SCHOOL OF ARTS & SCIENCES & ENGINEERING, Baltimore 21218/ *DA, ET,* FR, GE, GR, IT, LA, *MN, MO,* SP, *SS.*

A-435. LOYOLA COLLEGE IN MARYLAND, Baltimore 21210/ FR, GE, GR, LA, SP.

A-436. MORGAN STATE UNIVERSITY, Baltimore 21239/ FR, GE, SP.

A-437. MOUNT ST. MARY'S COLLEGE, Emmitsburg 21727/ FR, GE, SP.

A-438. NER ISRAEL RABBINICAL COLLEGE, Baltimore 21208/ HE, YD.

A-439. SALISBURY STATE UNIVERSITY, Salisbury 21801/ FR, SP.

A-440. TOWSON STATE UNIVERSITY, Towson 21204/ FR, GE, SP.

A-441. UNIVERSITY OF MARYLAND–BALTIMORE COUNTY, Catonsville 21228/ FR, GE, RU, SP.

A-442. UNIVERSITY OF MARYLAND–COLLEGE PARK, College Park 20742/ FR, GE, IT, LA, RU, SLL, SP.

A-443. UNIVERSITY OF MARYLAND–UNIVERSITY COLLEGE, College Park 20742/ CH, FR, GE, GR, *JP, KO,* SP.

A-444. WASHINGTON COLLEGE, Chestertown 21620/ FR, GE, SP.

A-445. WESTERN MARYLAND COLLEGE, Westminster 21157/ FR, GE, SP.

MASSACHUSETTS (MA)

A-446. AMERICAN INTERNATIONAL COLLEGE, Springfield 01109/ FR, SP.

A-447. AMHERST COLLEGE, Amherst 01002/ FR, GE, GR, LA, RU, SP.

A-448. ANNA MARIA COLLEGE, Paxton 01612/ FR, SP.

A-449. ASSUMPTION COLLEGE, Worcester 01615/ FR, SP.

A-450. ATLANTIC UNION COLLEGE, South Lancaster 01561/ FR, SP.

A-451. BOSTON COLLEGE, Chestnut Hill 02167/ AR(cl), AV, BL, CH(mn), CZ, FR, FR(od), GE, GR, HE, IR(od), IT, LA, PE(od), PO, PV, RO, RU, RU(od), S/C, SP, SP(od), SS, S/S.

A-452. BOSTON UNIVERSITY, Boston 02215/ CH, CT, FR, GE, GR, GR(mo), HE, H/U, IT, JP, LA, MD, PT, RU, S/C, SE, SP, SS, TM, YD, YO, ZU.

A-453. BRANDEIS UNIVERSITY, Waltham 02254/ AA, AB, AK, CP, EG(an), FR, GE, GR, HE, HE(bi), HT, IT, LA, RU, SP, S/S, SU, UG, YD.

A-454. BRIDGEWATER STATE COLLEGE, Bridgewater 02324/ FR, SP.

A-455. CLARK UNIVERSITY, Worcester 01610/ FR, GE, *LA,* SP.

A-456. COLLEGE OF THE HOLY CROSS, Worcester 01610/ FR, GE, GR, LA, RU, SP.

A-457. EASTERN NAZARENE COLLEGE, Quincy 02170/ FR, GE, SP.

A-458. ELMS COLLEGE, Chicopee 01013/ FR, GE, SP.

A-459. EMMANUEL COLLEGE, Boston 02115/ FR, GE, IT, SP.

⊗A-460. ENDICOTT COLLEGE, Beverly 01915/ MUL.

A-461. FITCHBURG STATE COLLEGE, Fitchburg 01420/ *FI.*

A-462. FRAMINGHAM STATE COLLEGE, Framingham 01701/ FR, SP.

A-463. GORDON COLLEGE, Wenham 01984/ FR, GE, HE, SP.

A-464. HARVARD AND RADCLIFFE COLLEGES, Cambridge 02138/ AB, CH, FR, GE, GR, GR(mo), HE, IT, JP, LA, PT, RU, SCL, SLL, SP.

A-465. HARVARD UNIVERSITY, Cambridge 02138/ AA, AB, AB(cl), *AFL,* AK, AR, AR(cl), AV, BL, BR, CH, CH(cl), CH(mn), CP, CZ, DU, EB, ET, *FI,* FR, *FS,* GE, GE(mh), GE(oh), GG(cl), GJ, GO, GR, HE, HE(bi), HI, HT, IR, IR(md), IR(od), IT, *JP, KD,* KO, LA, *LD, MA,* MN, MO, MO(cl), MO(md), PA, *PE,* PE(md), *PO,* PS, *PT, PV, RM,* RO, RU, SC, S/C, SD, SG, *SL,* SP, SS, S/S, SU, SV, SW, SY, SX, TI, TR(od), TU, UG, UI, UK, UR, VD, VI, WE, WE(es), *WN,* YD.

A-466. HEBREW COLLEGE, Brookline 02146/ HE.

⊗A-467. HOLYOKE COMMUNITY COLLEGE, Holyoke 01040/ GE, SP.

A-468. MASSACHUSETTS INSTITUTE OF TECHNOLOGY, Cambridge 02139/ FR, GE, JP, RU, SP.

A-469. MOUNT HOLYOKE COLLEGE, South Hadley 01075/ FR, GE, GR, IT, LA, RU, SP.

A-470. NORTHEASTERN UNIVERSITY, Boston 02115/ FR, GE, IT, RU, SP.

A-471. PINE MANOR COLLEGE, Chestnut Hill 02167/ FR.

A-472. REGIS COLLEGE, Weston 02193/ FR, GE, SP.

A-473. ST. HYACINTH COLLEGE AND SEMINARY, Granby 01033/ *PO.*

A-474. SIMMONS COLLEGE, Boston 02115/ FR, SP.
A-475. SIMON'S ROCK COLLEGE OF BARD, Great Barrington 01230/ AB, IR, GE, RU, SP.
A-476. SMITH COLLEGE, Northampton 01063/ FR, GE, GR, IT, LA, PT, RU, SP.
A-477. SOUTHEASTERN MASSACHUSETTS UNIVERSITY (New name: UNIVERSITY OF MASSACHUSETTS-DARTMOUTH), North Dartmouth 02747/ FR, GE, IT, PT, RU, SP.
A-478. STONEHILL COLLEGE, North Easton 02357/ FR, SP.
A-479. SUFFOLK UNIVERSITY, Boston 02108/ FR, SP.
A-480. TUFTS UNIVERSITY, Medford 02155/ CH, FR, GE, GR, IT, LA, RU, SP.
A-481. UNIVERSITY OF LOWELL, Lowell 01854/ FR, GR(mo), SP.
A-482. UNIVERSITY OF MASSACHUSETTS, AMHERST, Amherst 01003/ CH, CH(cl), FR, FR(od), GE, GE(mh), GE(oh), GO, HE, IC(od), IT, JP, LA, PT, RU, RU(od), SP, SS, S/S, S/S(md).
A-483. UNIVERSITY OF MASSACHUSETTS, BOSTON, Boston 02125/ AB, DA, FR, GE, GR, IT, LA, RU, SP.
A-484. WELLESLEY COLLEGE, Wellesley 02181/ CH, FR, GE, HE, GR, IT, JP, LA, RU, SP.
A-485. WESTFIELD STATE COLLEGE, Westfield 01086/ FR, SP.
A-486. WHEATON COLLEGE, Norton 02766/ FR, GE, GR, IT, LA, RU, SP.
A-487. WILLIAMS COLLEGE, Williamstown 02167/ FR, GE, GR, LA, NR, RU, SP.
A-488. WORCESTER STATE COLLEGE, Worcester 01602/ FR, SP.

MICHIGAN (MI)

A-489. ADRIAN COLLEGE, Adrian 49221/ FR, GE, SP.
A-490. ALBION COLLEGE, Albion 49224/ FR, GE, SP.
A-491. No entry.
A-492. ALMA COLLEGE, Alma 48801/ FR, GE, SP.
A-493. ANDREWS UNIVERSITY, Berrien Springs 49104/ FR, GE, SP.
A-494. AQUINAS COLLEGE, Grand Rapids 49506/ FR, GE, SP.
A-495. CALVIN COLLEGE, Grand Rapids 49506/ CH, DU, FR, GE, GR, LA, SP.
A-496. CENTRAL MICHIGAN UNIVERSITY, Mount Pleasant 48859/ FR, GE, LA, SP.
A-497. CONCORDIA COLLEGE, Ann Arbor 48105/ GR, HE.
A-498. EASTERN MICHIGAN UNIVERSITY, Ypsilanti 48197/ FR, GE, JP, PO, RU, SP.

A-499. GRAND VALLEY STATE UNIVERSITY, Allendale 49401/ FR, GE, RU, SP.

A-500. HILLSDALE COLLEGE, Hillsdale 49242/ FR, GE, SP.

A-501. HOPE COLLEGE, Holland 49422/ FR, GE, GR, LA, SP.

A-502. KALAMAZOO COLLEGE, Kalamazoo 49006/ FR, GE, LA, SP.

⊗A-503. LAKE MICHIGAN COLLEGE, Benton Harbor 49002/ FR, GE, SP.

⊗A-504. LANSING COMMUNITY COLLEGE, Lansing 48901/ FR, GE, SP.

◪A-505. MADONNA UNIVERSITY, Livonia 48150/ FR, SP.

◪A-506. MARYGROVE COLLEGE, Detroit 48221/ FR, GE, SP.

A-507. MICHIGAN STATE UNIVERSITY, East Lansing 48824/ AB, AM, CH, CH(mn), FF, FR, GE, HE, HI, HS, JP, KO, LA, *MR,* NR, PI(ni), PT, RU, SH, SN, SP, *SS,* SW, *UR, VI,* YD.

A-508. NORTHERN MICHIGAN UNIVERSITY, Marquette 49855/ *FI,* FR, GE, SP.

A-509. OAKLAND UNIVERSITY, Rochester 48309/ CH, FR, GE, JP, RU, SP.

A-510. OLIVET COLLEGE, Olivet 49076/ FR, SP.

A-511. SAGINAW VALLEY STATE UNIVERSITY, University Center 48710/ FR, SP.

⊗A-512. SCHOOLCRAFT COLLEGE, Livonia 48152/ FR, GE, SP.

A-513. SIENA HEIGHTS COLLEGE, Adrian 49221/ SP.

A-514. SPRING ARBOR COLLEGE, Spring Arbor 49283/ FR, SP.

A-515. UNIVERSITY OF DETROIT, Detroit 48221/ FR, GE, GR, SP.

A-516. UNIVERSITY OF MICHIGAN, Ann Arbor 48109-1316/ AB, AK, AR, AV, BU, CG, CH, CZ, DA, DU, FC(od), FL, FR, GE, GR, HE, HE(bi), IC(od), IN, IT, JP, KD, LA, LT, *MR,* OJ, PA, PE(od), PO, PT, RU, S/C, SCL, SP, SS, TH, TI, TU(az), TU(ot), UK, *UR,* VI.

A-517. WAYNE STATE UNIVERSITY, Detroit 48202/ AA, AB, AR, FR, FR(od), GE, GE(mh), GE(oh), GR, HE, IT, LA, PO, PT, RU, RU(od), SH, SP, SP(od).

A-518. WESTERN MICHIGAN UNIVERSITY, Kalamazoo 49008/ FR, GE, LA, SP.

A-519. WESTERN THEOLOGICAL SEMINARY, Holland 49423/ *DU.*

MINNESOTA (MN)

A-520. AUGSBURG COLLEGE, Minneapolis 55454/ CH, FR, GE, NW, RU, SP, SW.

A-521. BEMIDJI STATE UNIVERSITY, Bemidji 56601/ FR, GE, SP.

Ⓧ A-522.   BETHANY LUTHERAN COLLEGE, Mankato 56001/ GE, GR, HE.

A-523.   CARLETON COLLEGE, Northfield 55057/ AB, CZ, FR, GE, GR, HE, LA, RU, SP, SS.

A-524.   COLLEGE OF ST. BENEDICT, St. Joseph 56374/ FR, GE, LA, SP.

A-525.   COLLEGE OF ST. CATHERINE, St. Paul 55105/ *CI,* FR, GE, RU, SP.

A-526.   COLLEGE OF ST. TERESA, Winona 55987/ FR, SP.

A-527.   COLLEGE OF ST. THOMAS, St. Paul 55105/ FR, GE, *IR,* LA, RU, *SC,* SP, *WE.*

A-528.   CONCORDIA COLLEGE–MOREHEAD, Morehead 56562/ FR, GE, LA, SCL, SP.

A-529.   GUSTAVUS ADOLPHUS COLLEGE, St. Peter 56082/ FR, GE, GR, IT, JP, LA, RU, SP, SW.

A-530.   HAMLINE UNIVERSITY, St. Paul 55104/ FR, GE, RU, SP.

Ⓧ A-531.   ITASKA COMMUNITY COLLEGE, Grand Rapids 55744/ NAL.

A-532.   MACALESTER COLLEGE, St. Paul 55105/ AB, FR, GE, GR, HE, JP, KO, LA, PE, RU, SP, S/C, SS, SW.

A-533.   MANKATO STATE UNIVERSITY, Mankato 56001/ FR, GE, RU, SP.

A-534.   MOORHEAD STATE UNIVERSITY, Moorhead 56563/ FR, GE, SP.

A-535.   NORTH CENTRAL BIBLE COLLEGE, Minneapolis 55404/ GR, HE.

Ⓧ A-536.   NORTH HENNEPIN COMMUNITY COLLEGE, Minneapolis 55445/ GE, SP.

Ⓧ A-537.   RAINY RIVER COMMUNITY COLLEGE, International Falls 56649/ NAL.

A-538.   ST. CLOUD STATE UNIVERSITY, St. Cloud 56301/ AB, AB(cl), CH, DA, FR, GE, GR, JP, SP, SW.

A-539.   ST. JOHN'S UNIVERSITY, Collegeville 56321/ FR, GE, LA, SP.

A-540.   ST. MARY'S COLLEGE OF MINNESOTA, Winona 55987/ FR, SP.

A-541.   ST. OLAF COLLEGE, Northfield 55057/ CH, FR, GE, GR, LA, *NW,* RU, SP.

A-542.   UNIVERSITY OF MINNESOTA–DULUTH, Duluth 55812/ CH, CI, FR, GE, GE(mh), NR, SP, SW.

A-543.   UNIVERSITY OF MINNESOTA–MORRIS, Morris 56267/ FR, GE, SP.

A-544.   UNIVERSITY OF MINNESOTA–TWIN CITIES, Minneapolis–St. Paul 55455/ AA, AB, AK, AV, CH, DA, DK, DU, FI,

FR, FR(od), GE, GE(mh), GE(oh), GO, GR, HE, HE(bi), HI, IC(od), IR, IT, JP, LA, MR, NR, NW, OJ, PE, PO, PT, PV(od), RU, SP, SP(od), SS, S/S, SU, SW, SX, UG, UR.

⊗A-545. WILLMAR COMMUNITY COLLEGE, Willmar 56201/ GE, SP.

A-546. WINONA STATE UNIVERSITY, Winona 55987/ GE, JP, SP.

MISSISSIPPI (MS)

A-547. BELHAVEN COLLEGE, Jackson 39201/ FR, GR, LA, SP.

⊗A-548. COPIAH-LINCOLN COMMUNITY COLLEGE–NATCHEZ CAMPUS, Natchez 39120/ FR, MOL.

A-549. DELTA STATE UNIVERSITY, Cleveland 38733/ FR, GE, SP.

A-550. JACKSON STATE UNIVERSITY, Jackson 39217/ SP.

A-551. MILLSAPS COLLEGE, Jackson 39210/ FR, GE, GR, SP.

A-552. MISSISSIPPI COLLEGE, Clinton 39058/ FR, GE, GR, LA, SP.

A-553. MISSISSIPPI STATE UNIVERSITY, Mississippi State 39762/ MOL.

A-554. RUST COLLEGE, Holly Springs 38635/ FR, GE, SP.

A-555. UNIVERSITY OF MISSISSIPPI, University 38677/ AB, FR, GE, GR, SP.

A-556. UNIVERSITY OF SOUTHERN MISSISSIPPI, Hattiesburg 39406/ CH, MUL.

A-557. WILLIAM CAREY COLLEGE, Hattiesburg 39401/ SP.

MISSOURI (MO)

A-558. ASSEMBLIES OF GOD THEOLOGICAL SEMINARY, Springfield 65802/ HE.

A-559. AVILA COLLEGE, Kansas City 64145/ FR.

A-560. CENTRAL METHODIST COLLEGE, Fayette 65248/ FR, GE, SP.

A-561. CENTRAL MISSOURI STATE UNIVERSITY, Warrensburg 64093/ FR, GE, SP.

A-562. COLUMBIA COLLEGE, Columbia 65216/ SP.

⊗A-563. COTTEY COLLEGE, Nevada 64772/ FR, GE, SP.

A-564. COVENANT THEOLOGICAL SEMINARY, St. Louis 63141/ GR, HE.

A-565. DRURY COLLEGE, Springfield 65803/ FR, GE, SP.

A-566. EVANGEL COLLEGE, Springfield 65802/ FR, SP.

⊗A-567. JEFFERSON COLLEGE, Hillsboro 63050/ FR, SP.

⊗A-568. KEMPER MILITARY JUNIOR COLLEGE, Boonville 65233/ GE, SP.

A-569. LINCOLN UNIVERSITY, Jefferson City 65102/ FR.

A-570. LINDENWOOD COLLEGE, St. Charles 63301/ FR, SP.
A-571. MISSOURI SOUTHERN STATE COLLEGE, Joplin 64801/ SP.
A-572. NORTHEAST MISSOURI STATE UNIVERSITY, Kirksville 63501/ FR, GE, SP.
A-573. NORTHWEST MISSOURI STATE UNIVERSITY, Maryville 64468/ FR, SP.
A-574. ROCKHURST COLLEGE, Kansas City 64110/ FR, SP.
◢A-575. ST. LOUIS UNIVERSITY, St. Louis 63103/ *AB, ET,* FR, GE, GR, *HE,* LA, RU, SP.
A-576. SCHOOL OF THE OZARKS, Point Lookout 65726/ FR, GE, SP.
A-577. SOUTHEAST MISSOURI STATE UNIVERSITY, Cape Girardeau 63701/ FR, GE, LA, SP.
A-578. SOUTHWEST MISSOURI STATE UNIVERSITY, Springfield 65804/ FR, GE, LA, SP.
A-579. STEPHENS COLLEGE, Columbia 65215/ FR, SP.
A-580. UNIVERSITY OF MISSOURI–COLUMBIA, Columbia 65211/ CH, FR, GE, GR, HE, LA, *NAL,* RU, SP, *SS, YM.*
A-581. UNIVERSITY OF MISSOURI–KANSAS CITY, Kansas City 64110/ FR, GE, SP.
A-582. UNIVERSITY OF MISSOURI–ST. LOUIS, St. Louis 63121/ FR, GE(mh), GE(oh), JP, SP.
A-583. WASHINGTON UNIVERSITY, St. Louis 63130/ AB, CH, FR, FR(od), GE, GE(mh), GE(oh), GR, HE, HE(bi), IN, IT, JP, LA, NW, RU, SP, SP(od), SW, YD.
A-584. WESTMINSTER COLLEGE, Fulton 65251/ FR, SP.
A-585. WILLIAM JEWELL COLLEGE, Liberty 64068/ FR, GE, SP.
A-586. WILLIAM WOODS COLLEGE, Fulton 65251/ FR, GE, SP.

MONTANA (MT)
A-587. CARROLL COLLEGE, Helena 59625/ FR, GR, LA, SP.
A-588. EASTERN MONTANA COLLEGE, Billings 59101/ GE, SP.
⊗A-589. LITTLE BIG HORN COLLEGE, Crow Agency 59022/ NAL.
A-590. MONTANA STATE UNIVERSITY, Bozeman 59717/ FR, GE, SP.
A-591. UNIVERSITY OF MONTANA, Missoula 59812/ CH, FR, FR(od), GE, GR, HI, LA, M/Y, PT, RU, SP, SP(od), SS.

NEBRASKA (NE)
A-592. BELLEVUE COLLEGE, Bellevue 68005/ SP.
A-593. CONCORDIA COLLEGE, Seward 68434/ SP.
A-594. CREIGHTON UNIVERSITY, Omaha 68178/ FR, GE, GR, LA, SP.
A-595. DANA COLLEGE, Blair 68008/ *DA,* GE, SP, *SW.*

A-596. DOANE COLLEGE, Crete 68333/ GE, SP.
A-597. HASTINGS COLLEGE, Hastings 68901/ GE, SP.
☒A-598. KEARNEY STATE COLLEGE (New name: UNIVERSITY OF NEBRASKA-KEARNEY), Kearney 68847/ FR, GE, SP.
A-599. MIDLAND LUTHERAN COLLEGE, Fremont 68025/ GE, SP.
A-600. NEBRASKA WESLEYAN UNIVERSITY, Lincoln 68504/ FR, GE, SP.
⊗A-601. NEBRASKA WESTERN COLLEGE, Scotts Bluff 69361/ FR, GE, SP.
⊗A-602. NORTHEAST TECHNICAL COMMUNITY COLLEGE, Norfolk 68701/ FR.
A-603. UNIVERSITY OF NEBRASKA AT OMAHA, Omaha 68182/ FR, GE, SP.
A-604. UNIVERSITY OF NEBRASKA–LINCOLN, Lincoln 68588/ FR, GE, GR, GR(mo), LA, RU, SP.
A-605. WAYNE STATE COLLEGE, Wayne 68787/ FR, GE, SP.

NEVADA (NV)
⊗A-606. NEVADA UNIVERSITY SYSTEM–ELKO COMMUNITY COLLEGE, Elko 89801/ *BS.*
A-607. UNIVERSITY OF NEVADA–LAS VEGAS, Las Vegas 89154/ FR, GE, PT, SP.
☒A-608. UNIVERSITY OF NEVADA–RENO, Reno 89557-0002/ BS, FR, GE, GR, JP, NR, NW, SP.

NEW HAMPSHIRE (NH)
A-609. DARTMOUTH COLLEGE, Hanover 03755/ CH, FR, GE, GR, IT, LA, RU, SP.
A-610. FRANKLIN PIERCE COLLEGE, Rindge 03461/ FR, SP.
A-611. KEENE STATE COLLEGE, Keene 03431/ FR, SP.
A-612. PLYMOUTH STATE COLLEGE, Plymouth 03264/ FR, SP.
A-613. RIVIER COLLEGE, Nashua 03060/ FR, SP.
A-614. ST. ANSELM COLLEGE, Manchester 03102/ FR, LA, RU, SP.
A-615. UNIVERSITY OF NEW HAMPSHIRE, Durham 03824/ CH, FR, FR(od), GE, GR(an), JP, LA, PT, RU, SP, SP(od), S/S.

NEW JERSEY (NJ)
⊗A-616. BERGEN COMMUNITY COLLEGE, Paramus 07652/ MUL.
A-617. BLOOMFIELD COLLEGE, Bloomfield 07003/ FR, SP.
⊗A-618. BROOKDALE COMMUNITY COLLEGE, Lincroft 07738/ FR, GE, SP.
A-619. CALDWELL COLLEGE, Caldwell 07006/ FR, SP.

A-620. COLLEGE OF ST. ELIZABETH, Morristown 07960/ FR, SP.

A-621. DREW UNIVERSITY, Madison 07940/ AK, FR, GE, GE(oh), GO, GR, LA, RU, SP, UG.

A-622. FAIRLEIGH DICKINSON UNIVERSITY: FLORHAM-MADISON CAMPUS, Madison 07940/ FR, SP.

A-623. FAIRLEIGH DICKINSON UNIVERSITY: RUTHERFORD CAMPUS, Rutherford 07070/ FR, SP.

A-624. FAIRLEIGH DICKINSON UNIVERSITY: TEANECK-HACKENSACK CAMPUS, Teaneck 07601/ FR, GE, SP.

A-625. GEORGIAN COURT COLLEGE, Lakewood 08701/ FR, GE, SP.

A-626. GLASSBORO STATE COLLEGE, Glassboro 08028/ FR, SP.

A-627. JERSEY CITY STATE COLLEGE, Jersey City 07305/ MUL, SP.

A-628. KEAN COLLEGE OF NEW JERSEY, Union 07083/ FR, SP.

⊗A-629. MIDDLESEX COUNTY COLLEGE, Edison 08818/ FR, GE, SP.

A-630. MONMOUTH COLLEGE, West Long Branch 07764/ FR, SP.

◪A-631. MONTCLAIR STATE COLLEGE, Upper Montclair 07043/ CH, FR, GE, IT, LA, SP.

⊗A-632. OCEAN COUNTY COLLEGE, Toms River 08753/ MOL.

A-633. PRINCETON UNIVERSITY, Princeton 08544/ AA, AB, CH(cl), CH(mn), FR, FR(od), GE, GE(mh), GE(oh), GO, GR, HE, HE(bi), J/A, JP, KO, *MN, MO,* NR, PE, PT, RU, *SLL,* SP, SP(od), SX, SY, *TI,* TU.

A-634. RABBINICAL COLLEGE OF AMERICA, Morristown 07960/ HE, YD.

A-635. RIDER COLLEGE, Lawrenceville 08648/ FR, GE, RU, SP.

A-636. RUTGERS–THE STATE UNIVERSITY OF NEW JERSEY: CAMDEN COLLEGE OF ARTS AND SCIENCES, Camden 08102/ FR, GE, SP.

A-637. RUTGERS–THE STATE UNIVERSITY OF NEW JERSEY: DOUGLASS COLLEGE, New Brunswick 08903/ CH, FR, FR(od), GE, GR, IT, LA, PT, RU, SP.

A-638. RUTGERS–THE STATE UNIVERSITY OF NEW JERSEY: LIVINGSTON COLLEGE, New Brunswick 08903/ CH, FR, GE, GR, IT, LA, PT, RU, SP.

A-639. RUTGERS–THE STATE UNIVERSITY OF NEW JERSEY: NEWARK COLLEGE OF ARTS AND SCIENCES, Newark 07102/ FR, GE, IT, RU, SP.

A-640. RUTGERS–THE STATE UNIVERSITY OF NEW JERSEY: RUTGERS COLLEGE, New Brunswick 08903/ CH, FR, GE, GR, IT, LA, PT, RU, SP.

A-641. RUTGERS–THE STATE UNIVERSITY OF NEW JERSEY: UNIVERSITY COLLEGE, CAMDEN, Camden 08102/ FR, GE, SP.

A-642. RUTGERS–THE STATE UNIVERSITY OF NEW JERSEY: UNIVERSITY COLLEGE, NEW BRUNSWICK, New Brunswick 08903/ CH, FR, GE, GR, IT, LA, PT, RU, SP.

A-643. RUTGERS–THE STATE UNIVERSITY OF NEW JERSEY: UNIVERSITY COLLEGE, NEWARK, Newark 07102/ SP.

A-644. ST. PETER'S COLLEGE, Jersey City 07306/ FR, SP.

A-645. SETON HALL UNIVERSITY, South Orange 07079/ CH, FR, JP, RU, SP.

A-646. STOCKTON STATE COLLEGE, Pomona 08240/ FR, LA, SP.

A-647. THOMAS A. EDISON STATE COLLEGE, Trenton 08608/ FR, GE, HE, IT, JP, SP.

A-648. UPSALA COLLEGE, East Orange 07019/ FR, GE, SP.

A-649. WILLIAM PATERSON COLLEGE OF NEW JERSEY, Wayne 07470/ FR, SP.

NEW MEXICO (NM)

A-650. EASTERN NEW MEXICO UNIVERSITY, Portales 88130/ FR, SP.

A-651. NEW MEXICO HIGHLANDS UNIVERSITY, Las Vegas 87701/ SP.

A-652. NEW MEXICO MILITARY INSTITUTE, Roswell 88201/ FR, GE, PT, SP.

A-653. NEW MEXICO STATE UNIVERSITY, Las Cruces 88003/ FR, GE, RU, SP.

A-654. UNIVERSITY OF NEW MEXICO, Albuquerque 87131/ FR, GE, GR, JP, PT, PV(od), QC, RU, SP, SP(od).

NEW YORK (NY)

A-655. ADELPHI UNIVERSITY, Garden City 11530/ FR, SP.

A-656. ALFRED UNIVERSITY, Alfred 14802/ FR, GE, HE, SP.

A-657. BARD COLLEGE, Annandale-on-Hudson 12504/ CH, FR, GE, GR, LA, RU, SP.

A-658. BARNARD COLLEGE, New York 10027/ FR, GE, GR, IT, LA, RU, SP.

A-659. CANISIUS COLLEGE, Buffalo 14208/ FR, GE, SP.

⊗A-660. CAYUGA COUNTY COMMUNITY COLLEGE, Auburn 13021/ FR, GE, SP.

A-661. CITY UNIVERSITY OF NEW YORK–BARUCH COLLEGE, New York 10010/ FR, HE, SP.

◼A-662. CITY UNIVERSITY OF NEW YORK–BROOKLYN COLLEGE, Brooklyn 11210/ AB, CH(cn), FR, GE, GR, HE, IT, LA, RU, SP, YD.

A-663.   CITY UNIVERSITY OF NEW YORK–CITY COLLEGE, New York 10031/ FR, GE, GR, HE, IT, LA, RU, SP.

A-664.   CITY UNIVERSITY OF NEW YORK GRADUATE SCHOOL AND UNIVERSITY CENTER, New York 10036/ FR, GE, GL, IN, JP, KO, NR, NW, SP, SS.

A-665.   CITY UNIVERSITY OF NEW YORK–HUNTER COLLEGE, New York 10021/ CH, FR, GE, GR, HE, IT, LA, RU, SP.

A-666.   CITY UNIVERSITY OF NEW YORK–LEHMAN COLLEGE, Bronx 10468/ FR, GE, GR, HE, IT, LA, PT, RU, SP.

A-667.   CITY UNIVERSITY OF NEW YORK–QUEENS COLLEGE, Flushing 11367/ AB, CH, FR, GE, GR, HE, HE(bi), IT, PT, RU, SH, SP, YD.

A-668.   CITY UNIVERSITY OF NEW YORK–YORK COLLEGE, Jamaica 11451/ FR, IT, SP.

A-669.   COLGATE UNIVERSITY, Hamilton 13346/ CH, FR, GE, GR, JP, LA, SP.

A-670.   COLLEGE OF MOUNT ST. VINCENT, Riverdale 10471/ FR, LA, RU, SP.

A-671.   COLLEGE OF NEW ROCHELLE, New Rochelle 10805/ FR, LA.

A-672.   COLLEGE OF ST. ROSE, Albany 12203/ SP.

A-673.   COLUMBIA UNIVERSITY–COLUMBIA COLLEGE, New York 10027/ AB, AM, AR, AR(cl), BG, CA, CH, FI, FR, GE, GR, HE, HI, HU, H/U, IC(od), IT, JP, JP(cl), *KO*, LA, *MN, MO,* NE, PE, PE(od), PO, PT, RU, S/C, SH, SI, SP, SW, TI, TU, UR, UZ, YD.

A-674.   COLUMBIA UNIVERSITY–SCHOOL OF GENERAL STUDIES, New York 10027/ FR, GE, GR, IT, LA, RU, SP.

A-675.   CORNELL UNIVERSITY, Ithaca 14853/ AB, AF, AK, AR(cl), BL, BU, CE, CH, CH(am), CH(hk), CH(mn), CZ, FA(od), FC(od), FR(md), FR, FS, GE, GE(mh), GE(oh), GO, GR(mo), HC, HE, HI, H/U, IC(od), IN, IR(od), IT, JP, JV, LI, MA, NW, PA, PO, PT, PV(od), QC, RO, RU, RU(od), *SC,* S/C, SH, SP(od), SS, S/S, SU, SW, SX, TE, TH, TM, TO, TU, UK, WE.

A-676.   DAEMEN COLLEGE, Amherst 14226/ FR, SP.

A-677.   DOMINICAN COLLEGE OF BLAUVELT, Orangeburg 10962/ MUL, SP.

A-678.   ELMIRA COLLEGE, Elmira 14901/ FR, GE, GR, LA, SP.

A-679.   EUGENE LANG COLLEGE/NEW SCHOOL FOR SOCIAL RESEARCH, New York 10011/ MUL.

A-680.   FORDHAM UNIVERSITY, Bronx 10458/ FR, GE, GR, IT, LA, RU, SP.

A-681. FRIENDS WORLD COLLEGE, Huntington 11743/ AB, CH, FR, GE, GR, HE, HI, IT, JP, KO, PT, SLL, SP, SW, YO.
A-682. HAMILTON COLLEGE, Clinton 13323/ FR, GE, GR, JP, LA, *PV,* RU, SP.
A-683. HARTWICK COLLEGE, Oneonta 13820/ FR, GE, SP.
A-684. HEBREW UNION COLLEGE, New York 10012/ HE, YD.
A-685. HOBART & WILLIAM SMITH COLLEGES, Geneva 14456/ CH, FR, GE, GR, JP, LA, RU, SP.
A-686. HOFSTRA UNIVERSITY, Hempstead 11550/ FR, GE, GR, HE, IT, LA, RU, SP.
A-687. HOUGHTON COLLEGE, Houghton 14744/ FR, GE, SP.
A-688. IONA COLLEGE, New Rochelle 10801/ FR, IT, SP.
A-689. ITHACA COLLEGE, Ithaca 14850/ FR, GE, SP.
⊗A-690. JAMESTOWN COMMUNITY COLLEGE, Jamestown 14701/ FR, SP.
A-691. JEWISH THEOLOGICAL SEMINARY OF AMERICA, New York 10027/ HE, YD.
A-692. LE MOYNE COLLEGE, Syracuse 13214/ FR, SP.
A-693. LONG ISLAND UNIVERSITY–BROOKLYN CAMPUS, Brooklyn 11201/ MUL.
A-694. LONG ISLAND UNIVERSITY–C. W. POST CAMPUS, Brookville 11548/ FR, GE, HE, IT, SP.
A-695. MANHATTAN COLLEGE, Riverdale 10471/ FR, GE, GR, IT, LA, RU, SP.
A-696. MANHATTANVILLE COLLEGE, Purchase 10577/ FR, GE, RU, *SLL,* SP.
A-697. MARIST COLLEGE, Poughkeepsie 12601/ FR, RU, SP.
A-698. MARYMOUNT COLLEGE, Tarrytown 10591/ FR, RU, SP.
A-699. MARYMOUNT MANHATTAN COLLEGE, New York 10021/ FR, IT, SP.
A-700. MERCY COLLEGE, Dobbs Ferry 10522/ FR, IT, SP.
⊗A-701. MOHAWK VALLEY COLLEGE, Utica 13501/ MUL.
A-702. MOLLOY COLLEGE, Rockville Centre 11570/ FR, SP.
A-703. NAZARETH COLLEGE OF ROCHESTER, Rochester 14618/ FR, GE, IT, RU, SP.
A-704. NEW YORK UNIVERSITY, New York 10003/ AA, AB, AB(ca), AB(cl), AK, CH, CH(mn), EG(an), FR, FR(od), GE, GE(mh), GO, GR, HE, HE(bi), HT, IR(od), IT, JP, LA, PE, PT, PV, RU, SP, SS, TU, UG, WE.
A-705. NIAGARA UNIVERSITY, Niagara University 14109/ FR, SP.
⊗A-706. ORANGE COUNTY COMMUNITY COLLEGE, Middletown 10940/ FR, GE, SP.

A-707.   PACE UNIVERSITY–NEW YORK CITY, New York 10038/ FR, SP.

A-708.   PACE UNIVERSITY–PLEASANTVILLE/BRIARCLIFF, Pleasantville 10570/ FR, SP.

A-709.   PACE UNIVERSITY–WHITE PLAINS, White Plains 10603/ FR, SP.

A-710.   RENSSELAER POLYTECHNIC INSTITUTE, Troy 12180/ GE.

A-711.   RUSSELL SAGE COLLEGE, Troy 12180/ FR, SP.

A-712.   ST. BONAVENTURE UNIVERSITY, St. Bonaventure 14778/ FR, GE, GR, LA, SP.

A-713.   ST. JOHN FISHER COLLEGE, Rochester 14618/ FR, GE, IT, SP.

A-714.   ST. JOHN'S UNIVERSITY, Jamaica 11439/ FR, GE, IT, SP.

A-715.   ST. JOSEPH'S COLLEGE, Brooklyn 11205/ FR, SP.

A-716.   ST. LAWRENCE UNIVERSITY, Canton 13617/ FR, GE, SP.

A-717.   ST. THOMAS AQUINAS COLLEGE, Sparkill 10976/ FR, SP.

A-718.   SARAH LAWRENCE COLLEGE, Bronxville 10708/ FR, GE, GR, IT, LA, RU, SP.

A-719.   SIENA COLLEGE, Loudonville 12211/ FR, GR, LA, SP.

A-720.   SKIDMORE COLLEGE, Saratoga Springs 12866/ FR, GE, SP.

A-721.   STATE UNIVERSITY OF NEW YORK AT ALBANY, Albany 12222/ BL, CH, CH(cl), CH(mn), FR, FR(od), GE, GE(mh), GE(oh), GO, GR, HE, HE(bi), IT, LA, MH, M/Q, M/Y, NA, PO, PT, RU, S/C, SP, SP(od), SX.

A-722.   STATE UNIVERSITY OF NEW YORK AT BINGHAMTON, Binghamton 13902/ AB, CH, FR, GE, GE(mh), GE(oh), GO, GR, HE, IC(od), IT, JP, LA, NR, PE, RU, SP, SS, TU.

A-723.   STATE UNIVERSITY OF NEW YORK AT BUFFALO, Buffalo 14260/ AB, AM, FR, GE, HE, HI, IN, IT, KO, LA, PT, QC, RU, S/C, SS, S/S, SW, TH, TI, TU, UR, YO.

A-724.   STATE UNIVERSITY OF NEW YORK COLLEGE AT BROCKPORT, Brockport 14420/ FR, SP.

A-725.   STATE UNIVERSITY OF NEW YORK COLLEGE AT BUFFALO, Buffalo 14222/ BG, FL, FR, GE(mh), GE(oh), GR, HS, HU, IT, JP, *PO,* RU, SP.

A-726.   STATE UNIVERSITY OF NEW YORK COLLEGE AT CORTLAND, Cortland 13045/ FR, GE, SP.

A-727.   STATE UNIVERSITY OF NEW YORK COLLEGE AT FREDONIA, Fredonia 14063/ FR, GE, SP.

A-728. STATE UNIVERSITY OF NEW YORK COLLEGE AT GENESEO, Geneseo 14454/ AB(ca), AB(cl), AB, AB(ir), AZ, CH, CV, FR, KZ, LA, MO(cl), PT, SP, SX, TU, TU(az), UY, UZ, YA.

A-729. STATE UNIVERSITY OF NEW YORK COLLEGE AT NEW PALTZ, New Paltz 12561/ FR, GE, SP.

A-730. STATE UNIVERSITY OF NEW YORK COLLEGE AT OLD WESTBURY, Old Westbury 11568/ FR, SP.

A-731. STATE UNIVERSITY OF NEW YORK COLLEGE AT ONE-ONTA, Oneonta 13820/ FR, GE, SP.

A-732. STATE UNIVERSITY OF NEW YORK COLLEGE AT OSWEGO, Oswego 13126/ FR, GE, RU, SP.

A-733. STATE UNIVERSITY OF NEW YORK COLLEGE AT PLATTS-BURGH, Plattsburgh 12901/ FR, SP.

A-734. STATE UNIVERSITY OF NEW YORK COLLEGE AT POTSDAM, Potsdam 13676/ FR, SP.

A-735. STATE UNIVERSITY OF NEW YORK COLLEGE AT PUR-CHASE, Purchase 10577/ FR, IT, SP.

A-736. STATE UNIVERSITY OF NEW YORK AT STONY BROOK, Stony Brook 11794/ AB, *CA, CH,* FR, GE, GR, HE, IR, IT, KO, PT, RU, SLL, SP, *SS, TI,* VI.

ⓍA-737. SUFFOLK COUNTY COMMUNITY COLLEGE, Riverhead 11901/ MUL.

A-738. SYRACUSE UNIVERSITY, Syracuse 13244/ CH, FR, GE, GE(mh), GE(oh), GO, GR, HE, HI, IT, LA, PO, RU, SP, UK, UR.

A-739. TOURO COLLEGE, New York 10001/ FR, HE, MUL.

A-740. UNION COLLEGE, Schenectady 12308/ FR, GE, GR, LA, SP.

A-741. UNITED STATES MILITARY ACADEMY, West Point 10996/ AB, CH, FR, GE, *JP,* PT, RU, SP.

A-742. UNIVERSITY OF ROCHESTER, Rochester 14627/ CH, CZ, FR, GE, JP, MR, RO, RU, SP, *SS.*

A-743. UNIVERSITY OF THE STATE OF NEW YORK REGENTS COL-LEGE DEGREES, Albany 12203/ FR, GE, SP.

A-744. VASSAR COLLEGE, Poughkeepsie 12601/ FR, GE, GR, IT, LA, RU, SP.

A-745. WAGNER COLLEGE, Staten Island 10301/ FR, GE, SP.

A-746. WELLS COLLEGE, Aurora 13026/ FR, GE, IT, RU, SP.

A-747. WILLIAM SMITH COLLEGE, Geneva 14456/ FR, GE, GR, LA, RU, SP. Merged with A-685.

A-748. YESHIVA UNIVERSITY, New York 10033/ FR, GE, GR, HE, LA.

NORTH CAROLINA (NC)

A-749. APPALACHIAN STATE UNIVERSITY, Boone 28608/ FR, SP.

A-750. ATLANTIC CHRISTIAN COLLEGE, Wilson 27893/ FR, SP.

A-751. BENNETT COLLEGE, Greensboro 27401/ FR, SP.

⊗ A-752. BREVARD COLLEGE, Brevard 28712/ FR, GE, SP.

A-753. CAMPBELL UNIVERSITY, Buies Creek 27506/ FR, SP.

A-754. CATAWBA COLLEGE, Salisbury 28144/ FR, SP.

⊗ A-755. CHOWAN COLLEGE, Murfreesboro 27855/ FR, SP.

A-756. DAVIDSON COLLEGE, Davidson 28036/ FR, GE, GR, LA, RU, SP.

A-757. DUKE UNIVERSITY, Durham 22706/ AB, CH, *DA,* FR, GE, GR, HI, H/U, *IT,* JP, LA, *NW,* PE, PO, RU, SH, SP, SP(od), *SW,* UR.

A-758. EAST CAROLINA UNIVERSITY, Greenville 27858/ FR, GE, SP.

A-759. ELON COLLEGE, Elon College 27244/ MUL, SP.

A-760. FAYETTEVILLE STATE UNIVERSITY, Fayetteville 28301/ GE.

A-761. GARDNER-WEBB COLLEGE, Boiling Springs 28017/ FR, SP.

A-762. GREENSBORO COLLEGE, Greensboro 27401/ FR, SP.

A-763. GUILFORD COLLEGE, Greensboro 27410/ FR, GE, SP.

A-764. HIGH POINT UNIVERSITY, High Point 27262/ FR, SP.

⊗ A-765. LEES-McRAE COLLEGE, Banner Elk 28604/ FR, SP.

A-766. LENOIR-RHYNE COLLEGE, Hickory 28601/ FR, GE, SP.

A-767. LIVINGSTONE COLLEGE, Salisbury 28144/ FR.

⊗ A-768. LOUISBURG COLLEGE, Louisburg 27549/ FR, SP.

A-769. MARS HILL COLLEGE, Mars Hill 28754/ FR, SP.

A-770. MEREDITH COLLEGE, Raleigh 27607/ FR, SP.

A-771. METHODIST COLLEGE, Fayetteville 28311/ FR, GE, SP.

A-772. NORTH CAROLINA AGRICULTURAL AND TECHNICAL STATE UNIVERSITY, Greensboro 27411/ FR, SP.

A-773. NORTH CAROLINA CENTRAL UNIVERSITY, Durham 27707/ FR, SP.

A-774. NORTH CAROLINA STATE UNIVERSITY, Raleigh 27695/ FR, SP.

⊗ A-775. PEACE COLLEGE, Raleigh 27604/ MUL.

A-776. QUEENS COLLEGE, Charlotte 28274/ FR, SP.

A-777. ST. ANDREWS PRESBYTERIAN COLLEGE, Laurinburg 28352/ FR, MUL.

A-778. ST. AUGUSTINE'S COLLEGE, Raleigh 27610/ FR, GE, SP.

A-779. SALEM COLLEGE, Winston-Salem 27108/ FR, GE, LA, SP.

A-780. UNIVERSITY OF NORTH CAROLINA AT ASHEVILLE, Asheville 28804/ FR, GE, SP.

A-781. UNIVERSITY OF NORTH CAROLINA AT CHAPEL HILL, Chapel Hill 27599/ AB, AK, AL, BL, CH(mn), CL, CT, CZ, DU, FR, FR(od), GE, GE(mh), GE(oh), GG, GO, GR, HE, HE(bi), IC(od), IR, IT, JP, LA, MA, NW, PO, PT, PV(od), RO, RU, S/C, SP, SP(od), SS, S/S, TU, WE.

A-782. UNIVERSITY OF NORTH CAROLINA AT CHARLOTTE, Charlotte 28223/ FR, GE, SP.

A-783. UNIVERSITY OF NORTH CAROLINA AT GREENSBORO, Greensboro 27412/ FR, GE, GR, LA, RU, SP.

A-784. UNIVERSITY OF NORTH CAROLINA AT WILMINGTON, Wilmington 28403/ FR, SP.

A-785. WAKE FOREST UNIVERSITY, Winston-Salem 27109/ FR, GE, GR, LA, RU, SP.

A-786. WESTERN CAROLINA UNIVERSITY, Cullowhee 28723/ FR, GE, SP.

A-787. WINSTON-SALEM STATE UNIVERSITY, Winston-Salem 27110/ SP.

NORTH DAKOTA (ND)

Ⓧ A-788. BISMARCK STATE COLLEGE, Bismarck 58501/ GE, SP.

A-789. DICKINSON STATE UNIVERSITY, Dickinson 58601/ SP.

A-790. MINOT STATE UNIVERSITY, Minot 58702/ GE, FR, SP.

A-791. NORTH DAKOTA STATE UNIVERSITY, Fargo 58105/ FR, GE, SP.

A-792. UNIVERSITY OF NORTH DAKOTA, Grand Forks 58202/ FR, GE, LA, NW, RU, SP, SW.

A-793. STATE UNIVERSITY OF AGRICULTURE & APPLIED SCIENCE, VALLEY CITY, Valley City 58072/ SP.

OHIO (OH)

A-794. ASHLAND UNIVERSITY, Ashland 44805/ FR, SP.

A-795. BALDWIN-WALLACE COLLEGE, Berea 44017/ FR, GE, SP.

A-796. BLUFFTON COLLEGE, Bluffton 45817/ SP.

A-797. BORROMEO COLLEGE OF OHIO, Wickliffe 44092/ GR, LA.

A-798. BOWLING GREEN STATE UNIVERSITY, Bowling Green 43403/ FR, GE, LA, RU, SP.

A-798/a. CAPITAL UNIVERSITY, Columbus 43209/ FR, GE, SP.

A-799. CASE WESTERN RESERVE UNIVERSITY, Cleveland 44106/ FR, GE, GR, LA.

A-800.   CEDARVILLE COLLEGE, Cedarville 45314/ SP.

A-801.   CENTRAL STATE UNIVERSITY, Wilberforce 45384/ FR, LA, RU, SP.

A-802.   CLEVELAND COLLEGE OF JEWISH STUDIES, Cleveland 44122/ HE, YD.

A-803.   CLEVELAND STATE UNIVERSITY, Cleveland 44115/ AL, AR, FR, GE, GR, MY, SP, SS.

A-804.   COLLEGE OF WOOSTER, Wooster 44691/ FR, GE, GR, IT, LA, RU, SP.

A-805.   DEFIANCE COLLEGE, Defiance 43512/ MUL.

A-806.   DENISON UNIVERSITY, Granville 43023/ FR, GE, SP.

A-807.   FINDLAY COLLEGE, Findlay 45840/ SP.

A-808.   FRANCISCAN UNIVERSITY OF STEUBENVILLE, Steubenville 43952/ FR, SP.

A-809.   HEBREW UNION COLLEGE JEWISH INSTITUTE OF RELIGION, Cincinnati 45520/ BIL, HE, *LD*, YD.

A-810.   HEIDELBERG COLLEGE, Tiffin 44883/ GE, SP.

A-811.   HIRAM COLLEGE, Hiram 44234/ FR, GE, SP.

A-812.   JOHN CARROLL UNIVERSITY, University Heights 44118/ FR, GE, GR, LA, SP.

A-813.   KENT STATE UNIVERSITY, Kent 44242/ *ES, FI,* FR, GE, GR, LA, *LI, LT, PO,* RU, *S/C, SL,* SP, *SV, SW, UK.*

A-814.   KENYON COLLEGE, Gambier 43022/ CH, FR, GE, GR, IT, JP, LA, RU, SP.

A-815.   LAKE ERIE COLLEGE, Painesville 44077/ MUL.

ⓧA-816.   LORAIN COUNTY COMMUNITY COLLEGE, Elyria 44035/ MUL.

A-817.   LOURDES COLLEGE, Sylvania 43560/ FR, SP.

A-818.   MARIETTA COLLEGE, Marietta 45750/ FR, SP.

A-819.   MIAMI UNIVERSITY–OXFORD CAMPUS, Oxford 45056/ FR, GE, GR, LA, RU, SP.

A-820.   MOUNT UNION COLLEGE, Alliance 44601/ FR, GE, SP.

A-821.   MOUNT VERNON NAZARENE COLLEGE, Mount Vernon 43050/ SP.

A-822.   MUSKINGUM COLLEGE, New Concord 43762/ FR, GE, SP.

A-823.   OBERLIN COLLEGE, Oberlin 44074/ CH, FR, GE, GR, LA, RU, SP.

A-824.   OHIO NORTHERN UNIVERSITY, Ada 45810/ FR, SP.

A-825.   OHIO STATE UNIVERSITY–COLUMBUS CAMPUS, Columbus 43210/ AA, AB, AB(cl), BL, BN, CH, CH(cl), CR, CZ, ES, FR, FR(od), GE, GE(mh), GE(oh), GO, GR, GR(mo), GR(nt), HE, HE(bi), HM, HU, IT, JP, JP(cl), KO, LA, LI, MA, MW, NR, PE, PT, RO, RU, S/C, SH, SP, S/S, SV, SW, TU, UK, VD, YD.

A-826.   OHIO UNIVERSITY, Athens 45701/ AB, AF, CH, FR, GE, IN, JP, LA, RU, SP.

A-827.   OHIO WESLEYAN UNIVERSITY, Delaware 43015/ FR, GE, SP.

A-828.   OTTERBEIN COLLEGE, Westerville 43081/ FR, SP.

A-829.   UNIVERSITY OF AKRON, Akron 44325/ CH, FR, GE, GR, HE, IT, LA, RU, SP.

A-830.   UNIVERSITY OF CINCINNATI, Cincinnati 45221/ CH, CH(mn), CL, FR, GE, GE(mh), GE(oh), GR, HE, IC(od), IR, JP, LA, NR, PT, RU, SC, SH, SP, SP(od), SW, WE.

A-831.   UNIVERSITY OF DAYTON, Dayton 45469/ CH, FR, GE, GR, IT, RU, SP.

A-832.   UNIVERSITY OF TOLEDO, Toledo 43606/ FR, GE, GR, LA, SP.

A-833.   URSULINE COLLEGE, Pepper Pike 44124/ FR, SP.

A-834.   WALSH COLLEGE, North Canton 44720/ FR, SP.

A-835.   WILMINGTON COLLEGE, Wilmington 45177/ FR, GE, SP.

A-836.   WITTENBERG UNIVERSITY, Springfield 45501/ CH, FR, GE, JP, RU, SP.

A-837.   WRIGHT STATE UNIVERSITY, Dayton 45435/ FR, GE, GR, LA, SP.

A-838.   XAVIER UNIVERSITY, Cincinnati 45207/ FR, GE, GR, LA, SP.

A-839.   YOUNGSTOWN STATE UNIVERSITY, Youngstown 44555/ FR, GE, IT, LA, RU, SP.

OKLAHOMA (OK)

A-840.   CAMERON UNIVERSITY, Lawton 73505/ MUL.

A-841.   CENTRAL STATE UNIVERSITY (New name: UNIVERSITY OF CENTRAL OKLAHOMA), Edmond 73034/ FR, GE, SP.

A-842.   NORTHEASTERN STATE UNIVERSITY, Tahlequah 74464/ FR, GE, SP.

A-843.   OKLAHOMA BAPTIST UNIVERSITY, Shawnee 74801/ FR, GE, SP.

⊗ A-844.   OKLAHOMA CITY COMMUNITY COLLEGE, Oklahoma City 73159/ MUL.

A-845.   OKLAHOMA CITY UNIVERSITY, Oklahoma City 73106/ FR, GE, SP.

A-846.   OKLAHOMA STATE UNIVERSITY, Stillwater 74078/ CH, FR, GE, JP, LA, RU, SP.

A-847.   ORAL ROBERTS UNIVERSITY, Tulsa 74171/ FR, GE, SP.

A-848.   PHILLIPS UNIVERSITY, Enid 73702/ GE, SP.

✘A-849. ROSE STATE COLLEGE, Midwest City 73110/ FR, GE, SP.

A-850. SOUTHEASTERN OKLAHOMA STATE UNIVERSITY, Durant 74701/ FR, SP.

A-851. SOUTHERN NAZARENE UNIVERSITY, Bethany 73008/ FR, GE, SP.

A-852. SOUTHWESTERN OKLAHOMA STATE UNIVERSITY, Weatherford 73008/ FR.

A-853. UNIVERSITY OF OKLAHOMA, Norman 73109/ CH, GE, GR, HE, JP, LA, RU, SP.

A-854. UNIVERSITY OF SCIENCE AND ARTS OF OKLAHOMA, Chickasha 73018/ SP.

A-855. UNIVERSITY OF TULSA, Tulsa 74104/ FR, SP.

✘A-856. WESTERN OKLAHOMA STATE COLLEGE, Altus 73524/ SP.

OREGON (OR)

✘A-857. CENTRAL OREGON COMMUNITY COLLEGE, Bend 97701/ FR, GE, SP.

✘A-858. LANE COMMUNITY COLLEGE, Eugene 97405/ FR, GE, SP.

A-859. LEWIS AND CLARK COLLEGE, Portland 97219/ FR, GE, SP.

A-860. LINFIELD COLLEGE, McMinnville 97128/ FR, GE, JP, SP.

✘A-861. MOUNT HOOD COMMUNITY COLLEGE, Gresham 97030/ MUL.

A-862. OREGON STATE UNIVERSITY, Corvallis 97331/ FR, GE, SP.

A-863. PACIFIC UNIVERSITY, Forest Grove 97116/ CH, FR, GE, HE(bi), JP, SP.

✘A-864. PORTLAND COMMUNITY COLLEGE, Portland 97219/ FR, GE, JP, RU, SP.

A-865. PORTLAND STATE UNIVERSITY, Portland 97201/ FR, GE, JP, RU, SP.

A-866. REED COLLEGE, Portland 97202/ CH, FR, GE, GR, LA, RU, SP.

A-867. SOUTHERN OREGON STATE COLLEGE, Ashland 97520/ MUL, SP.

✘A-868. TREASURE VALLEY COMMUNITY COLLEGE, Ontario 97914/ SP.

A-869. UNIVERSITY OF OREGON–EUGENE, Eugene 97403/ CH, CH(mn), *EP,* FR, GE, GE(mh), GO, GR, HE, IN, IT, JC, JP, LA, NW, PV, RO, RU, S/C, SP, TH, TI, UT.

A-870. UNIVERSITY OF PORTLAND, Portland 97203/ MUL.

A-871. WESTERN CONSERVATIVE BAPTIST SEMINARY, Portland 97215/ GR, HE.

A-872. WESTERN EVANGELICAL SEMINARY, Portland 97267/ GR, HE.

A-873. WESTERN OREGON STATE COLLEGE, Monmouth 97361/ FR, GE, SP.

PENNSYLVANIA (PA)

A-874. ALBRIGHT COLLEGE, Reading 19612/ FR, GE, SP.

A-875. ALLEGHENY COLLEGE, Meadville 16335/ FR, GE, GR, LA, RU, SP.

A-876. ALLENTOWN COLLEGE OF ST. FRANCIS DE SALES, Center Valley 18034/ FR, SP.

A-877. ALLIANCE COLLEGE, Cambridge Springs 16403/ *PO, SLL.*

A-878. ALVERNIA COLLEGE, Reading 19607/ FR, *PO,* SP.

A-879. BLOOMSBURG UNIVERSITY OF PENNSYLVANIA, Bloomsburg 17815/ FR, GE, SP.

A-880. BRYN MAWR COLLEGE, Bryn Mawr 19010/ AB, FR, FR(od), GE, GR, GR(an), HE, IT, LA, LA(md), RU, SP, S/S.

A-881. BUCKNELL UNIVERSITY, Lewisburg 17837/ FR, GE, GR, JP, LA, RU, SP.

A-882. BYZANTINE CATHOLIC SEMINARY, Pittsburgh 15214/ UK(cr).

A-883. CABRINI COLLEGE, Radnor 19087/ FR, IT, SP.

A-884. CALIFORNIA UNIVERSITY OF PENNSYLVANIA, California 15419/ FR, GE, RU, SLL, SP.

◢A-885. CARNEGIE-MELLON UNIVERSITY, Pittsburgh 15213/ FR, GE, SP.

A-886. CEDAR CREST COLLEGE, Allentown 18104/ FR, GE, SP.

A-887. CHATHAM COLLEGE, Pittsburgh 15232/ FR, GE, SP.

A-888. CHESTNUT HILL COLLEGE, Philadelphia 19118/ FR, GE, LA, SP.

A-889. CHEYNEY UNIVERSITY OF PENNSYLVANIA, Cheyney 19319/ FR, SP.

A-890. CHRIST THE SAVIOUR SEMINARY, Johnstown 15906/ *S/S,* UK(cr).

A-891. CLARION UNIVERSITY OF PENNSYLVANIA, Clarion 16214/ FR, GE, RU, SP.

⊗A-892. COMMUNITY COLLEGE OF ALLEGHENY COUNTY, Pittsburgh 15237/ FR, GE, IT, RU, SP.

A-893. DICKINSON COLLEGE, Carlisle 17013/ FR, GE, GR, LA, RU, SP.

A-894. DUQUESNE UNIVERSITY, Pittsburgh 15282/ *AFL,* FR, GE, GR, *HS,* LA, SP.

A-895. EAST STROUDSBURG UNIVERSITY OF PENNSYLVANIA, East Stroudsburg 18301/ FR, GE, SP.

A-896. EASTERN COLLEGE, St. Davids 19087/ FR, SP.

A-897. EDINBORO UNIVERSITY OF PENNSYLVANIA, Edinboro 16444/ FR, GE, RU, SP.

A-898. ELIZABETHTOWN COLLEGE, Elizabethtown 17022/ FR, GE, SP.

A-899. FRANKLIN AND MARSHALL COLLEGE, Lancaster 17604/ FR, GE, GR(mo), LA, RU, SP.

A-900. GANNON UNIVERSITY, Erie 16541/ FR, GE, JP, LA, RU, SP.

A-901. GENEVA COLLEGE, Beaver Falls 15010/ SP.

A-902. GETTYSBURG COLLEGE, Gettysburg 17325/ FR, GE, GR, LA, SP.

A-903. GRATZ COLLEGE, Melrose Park 19126/ HE, YD.

A-904. GROVE CITY COLLEGE, Grove City 16127/ FR, GE, SP.

A-905. HAVERFORD COLLEGE, Haverford 19041/ FR, GE, GR, IT, LA, RU, SP.

A-906. HOLY FAMILY COLLEGE, Philadelphia 19114/ FR, *PO,* SP.

A-907. IMMACULATA COLLEGE, Immaculata 19345/ FR, GE, IT, LA, RU, SP.

A-908. INDIANA UNIVERSITY OF PENNSYLVANIA, Indiana 15705/ FR, GE, RU, SP.

A-909. JUNIATA COLLEGE, Huntingdon 16652/ FR, GE, RU, SP.

A-910. KING'S COLLEGE, Wilkes-Barre 18711/ FR, SP.

A-911. KUTZTOWN UNIVERSITY OF PENNSYLVANIA, Kutztown 19530/ FR, GE, RU, SP.

A-912. LA SALLE UNIVERSITY, Philadelphia 19141/ FR, GE, GR, IT, LA, RU, SP.

A-913. LAFAYETTE COLLEGE, Easton 18042/ FR, GE, RU, SP.

A-914. LANCASTER THEOLOGICAL SEMINARY, Lancaster 17603/ *GR, HE.*

A-915. LEBANON VALLEY COLLEGE OF PENNSYLVANIA, Annville 17003/ FR, GE, SP.

A-916. LEHIGH UNIVERSITY, Bethlehem 18015/ FR, GE, GR, LA, RU, SP.

A-917. LINCOLN UNIVERSITY, Lincoln University 19352/ CH, FR, RU, SP.

A-918. LOCK HAVEN UNIVERSITY OF PENNSYLVANIA, Lock Haven 17745/ FR, GE, SP.

A-919. LYCOMING COLLEGE, Williamsport 17701/ FR, GE, SP.

A-920. MANSFIELD UNIVERSITY OF PENNSYLVANIA, Mansfield 16933/ FR, GE, SP.

A-921. MARYWOOD COLLEGE, Scranton 18509/ FR, SP.

A-922. MESSIAH COLLEGE, Grantham 17027/ FR, GE, SP.

A-923. MILLERSVILLE UNIVERSITY OF PENNSYLVANIA, Millersville 17551/ FR, GE, GR, LA, RU, SP.

A-924. MORAVIAN COLLEGE, Bethlehem 18018/ FR, GE, GR, LA, SP.

A-925. MUHLENBERG COLLEGE, Allentown 18104/ FR, GE, GR, LA, RU, SP.

⊗ A-926. NORTHEASTERN CHRISTIAN JUNIOR COLLEGE, Villanova 19085/ FR, HE.

A-927. PENN STATE UNIVERSITY, UNIVERSITY PARK CAMPUS, University Park 16802/ CH, FR, GE, GE(mh), GE(oh), GO, GR, HE, IT, JP, LI, *PO, SLL,* SP, SS, S/S, *UK.*

A-928. POINT PARK COLLEGE, Pittsburgh 15222/ FR, SP.

A-929. ROSEMONT COLLEGE, Rosemont 19010/ FR, GE, IT, SP.

A-930. ST. CLEMENT UKRAINIAN CATHOLIC UNIVERSITY, Philadelphia 19117/ UK.

A-931. ST. FRANCIS COLLEGE, Loretto 15940/ FR, SP.

A-932. ST. JOSEPH'S UNIVERSITY, Philadelphia 19131/ FR, GE, SP.

A-933. ST. VINCENT COLLEGE, Latrobe 15650/ FR, SP.

A-934. SETON HILL COLLEGE, Greensburg 15601/ FR, SP.

A-935. SHIPPENSBURG UNIVERSITY OF PENNSYLVANIA, Shippensburg 17257/ FR, GE, SP.

A-936. SLIPPERY ROCK UNIVERSITY OF PENNSYLVANIA, Slippery Rock 16057/ FR, GE, SP.

A-937. SUSQUEHANNA UNIVERSITY, Selinsgrove 17870/ FR, GE, GR, LA, SP.

A-938. SWARTHMORE COLLEGE, Swarthmore 19081/ CH, FR, GE, GR, HE, LA, RU, SP.

A-939. TALMUDICAL YESHIVA OF PHILADELPHIA, Philadelphia 19131/ HE, YD.

A-940. TEMPLE UNIVERSITY, Philadelphia 19122/ CH, DU, FR, GE, GR, HE, HE(bi), HU, IN, IT, JP, KO, PO, RU, SP, WE.

A-941. THIEL COLLEGE, Greensville 16125/ FR, SP.

A-942. UNIVERSITY OF PENNSYLVANIA, Philadelphia 19104/ AB, AB(cl), AK, AR(cl), AR(md), AS, AV, BG, CH, CH(cl), CH(mn), DA, DU, FR, FR(od), GE, GE(mh), GE(oh), GJ, GO, GR, HE, HE(bi), HI, HT, H/U, IC, IC(od), IT, JP, JP(cl), LA, *LI,* MR, MY, NR, O/U, PA, PE, PE(md), PE(od), PK, PR, PT, PV, PV(od), RU, SG, SLL, SP, SP(od), SS, SU, SW, SX, TE, TM, TM(cl), TR, TU, UR, UR(cl), VD, VI.

◪A-943. UNIVERSITY OF PITTSBURGH, Pittsburgh 15260/ AB, AB(ca), CH, DU, FI, FR, FS, GE, GR, HI, HU, IN, IR, IT, JP, KO, LA, PE, RU, QC, SH, SP, SV, TH, TU.

A-944. UNIVERSITY OF PITTSBURGH AT BRADFORD, Bradford 16701/ FR, IT.

A-945. UNIVERSITY OF SCRANTON, Scranton 18510/ FR, GE, GR, LA, SP.

A-946. URSINUS COLLEGE, Collegeville 19426/ FR, GE, GR, LA, SP.

A-947. VILLANOVA UNIVERSITY, Villanova 19085/ FR, GE, GR, IT, LA, RU, SP.

A-948. WASHINGTON AND JEFFERSON COLLEGE, Washington 15301/ FR, GE, SP.

A-949. WEST CHESTER UNIVERSITY OF PENNSYLVANIA, West Chester 19383/ FR, GE, LA, RU, SP.

A-950. WESTMINSTER COLLEGE, New Wilmington 16172/ FR, GE, LA, SP.

A-951. WIDENER UNIVERSITY, Chester 19061/ FR, GE, SP.

A-952. WILKES UNIVERSITY, Wilkes-Barre 18766/ FR, GE, SP.

A-953. WILSON COLLEGE, Chambersburg 17201/ FR, GE, LA, SP.

A-954. YORK COLLEGE OF PENNSYLVANIA, York 17405/ FR, GE, SP.

PUERTO RICO (PR) See A-1180+

RHODE ISLAND (RI)

A-955. BROWN UNIVERSITY, Providence 02912/ AB, BL, CH, CH(cn), CH(mn), EG(an), FR, FR(od), GE, GE(mh), GR, HE, HE(bi), HI, IR, IT, JP, KO, LA, NR, PO, PT, RU, RU(od), SP, SS, S/S, SV, SW, TU, *YD.*

A-956. PROVIDENCE COLLEGE, Providence 02918/ FR, IT, SP.

A-957. RHODE ISLAND COLLEGE, Providence 02908/ FR, SP.

A-958. SALVE REGINA COLLEGE, Newport 02840/ FR, SP.

A-959. UNIVERSITY OF RHODE ISLAND, Kingston 02881/ FR, GE, IT, RU, SP.

SOUTH CAROLINA (SC)

A-960. BAPTIST COLLEGE AT CHARLESTON, Charleston 29411/ SP.

A-961. BOB JONES UNIVERSITY, Greenville 29614/ AA, FR, GE, GR, HE(bi), SP.

A-962. THE CITADEL, Charleston 29409/ FR, GE, SP.

A-963. CLEMSON UNIVERSITY, Clemson 29634/ FR, GE, SP.

A-964. COKER COLLEGE, Hartsville 29550/ FR, SP.

A-965. COLLEGE OF CHARLESTON, Charleston 29424/ FR, GE, SP.
A-966. COLUMBIA COLLEGE, Columbia 29203/ FR, GE, SP.
A-967. CONVERSE COLLEGE, Spartanburg 29302/ FR, SP.
A-968. ERSKINE COLLEGE, Due West 29639/ FR, SP.
A-969. FRANCIS MARION COLLEGE, Florence 29501/ FR, SP.
A-970. FURMAN UNIVERSITY, Greenville 29613/ FR, GE, GR, LA, SP.
A-971. LANDER COLLEGE, Greenwood 29646/ FR.
A-972. NEWBERRY COLLEGE, Newberry 29108/ FR, SP.
A-973. PRESBYTERIAN COLLEGE, Clinton 29325/ FR, GE, SP.
A-974. SOUTH CAROLINA STATE COLLEGE, Orangeburg 29117/ FR, SP.
A-975. UNIVERSITY OF SOUTH CAROLINA, Columbia 29208/ CH, FR, FR(od), GE, GR, HE, IT, JP, LA, PT, SH, SP.
ⓧA-976. UNIVERSITY OF SOUTH CAROLINA AT LANCASTER, Lancaster 29720/ FR, GE.
A-977. WINTHROP COLLEGE, Rock Hill 29733/ FR, SP.
A-978. WOFFORD COLLEGE, Spartanburg 29303/ FR, GE, SP.

SOUTH DAKOTA (SD)
A-979. AUGUSTANA COLLEGE, Sioux Falls 57197/ FR, GE, GR, SP, *SW*.
A-980. BLACK HILLS STATE UNIVERSITY, Spearfish 57799/ SP.
A-981. DAKOTA WESLEYAN UNIVERSITY, Mitchell 57301/ GE, SP.
A-982. NORTHERN STATE UNIVERSITY, Aberdeen 57401/ FR, GE, SP.
A-983. SOUTH DAKOTA STATE UNIVERSITY, Brookings 57007/ FR, GE, SP.
A-984. UNIVERSITY OF SOUTH DAKOTA, Vermillion 57069/ FR, GE, GR, LA, SP.

TENNESSEE (TN)
A-985. AUSTIN PEAY STATE UNIVERSITY, Clarksville 37044/ FR, SP.
A-986. CARSON-NEWMAN COLLEGE, Jefferson City 37760/ FR, GE, SP.
A-987. DAVID LIPSCOMB UNIVERSITY, Nashville 37204/ BIL, FR, GE, SP.
ⓧA-988. DYERSBURG STATE COMMUNITY COLLEGE, Dyersburg 38025/ SP.
A-989. EAST TENNESSEE STATE UNIVERSITY, Johnson City 37614/ FR, GE, SP.
A-990. FISK UNIVERSITY, Nashville 37208/ FR, SP.

⊗A-991.   HIWASEE COLLEGE, Madisonville 37354/ FR, GE, HE, LA.

A-992.   KING COLLEGE, Bristol 37620/ FR, LA.

A-993.   LAMBUTH COLLEGE, Jackson 38301/ FR, SP.

A-994.   LEE COLLEGE, Cleveland 37320/ FR, SP.

A-995.   MEMPHIS STATE UNIVERSITY, Memphis 38152/ MUL.

A-996.   MIDDLE TENNESSEE STATE UNIVERSITY, Murfreesboro 37132/ FR, GE, SP.

A-997.   RHODES COLLEGE, Memphis 38112/ FR, GE, GR, LA, SP.

A-998.   SOUTHERN COLLEGE OF SEVEN-DAY ADVENTISTS, Collegedale 37315/ FR, GE, SP.

A-999.   TENNESSEE STATE UNIVERSITY, Nashville 37209/ FR, SP.

A-1000.   TENNESSEE TECHNOLOGICAL UNIVERSITY, Cookeville 38505/ FR, GE, SP.

A-1001.   TENNESSEE WESLEYAN COLLEGE, Athens 37371/ SP.

A-1002.   UNION UNIVERSITY, Jackson 38305/ FR, GR, SP.

A-1003.   UNIVERSITY OF THE SOUTH, Sewanee 37375/ FR, GE, GR, LA, RU, SP.

A-1004.   UNIVERSITY OF TENNESSEE AT CHATTANOOGA, Chattanooga 37403/ FR, GE, GR, LA, SP.

A-1005.   UNIVERSITY OF TENNESSEE AT KNOXVILLE, Knoxville 37996/ FR, GE, GR, IT, LA, RU, SLL, SP.

A-1006.   UNIVERSITY OF TENNESSEE AT MARTIN, Martin 38238/ FR, GE, SP.

A-1007.   VANDERBILT UNIVERSITY, Nashville 37212/ AB, CH, CP, FR, FR(od), GE, GE(mh), GR, GR(hk), HE, HE(bi), JP, LA, NA, PT, RU, SP, SY.

⊗A-1008.   VOLUNTEER STATE COMMUNITY COLLEGE, Gallatin 37066/ MOL.

TEXAS (TX)

A-1009.   ABILENE CHRISTIAN UNIVERSITY, Abilene 79699/ FR, GE, GR, LA, SP.

A-1010.   AMARILLO COMMUNITY COLLEGE, Amarillo 79178/ MUL.

A-1011.   ANGELO STATE UNIVERSITY, San Angelo 76909/ FR, SP.

A-1012.   AUSTIN COLLEGE, Sherman 75091/ FR, GE, SP.

⊗A-1013.   AUSTIN COMMUNITY COLLEGE, Austin 78714/ FR, GE, SP.

A-1014.   BAYLOR UNIVERSITY, Waco 76798/ FR, GE, GR, LA, RU, SP.

⊗A-1015.   BEE COUNTY COLLEGE, Beeville 78102/ FR, GE, SP.

A-1016.   BISHOP COLLEGE, Dallas 75241/ SP.

⊗A-1017.   CENTRAL TEXAS COLLEGE, Killeen 76542/ FR, GE, SP.

A-1018.   CORPUS CHRISTI STATE UNIVERSITY, Corpus Christi 78412/ SP.

A-1019.   EAST TEXAS BAPTIST UNIVERSITY, Marshall 75670/ SP.

A-1020.   EAST TEXAS STATE UNIVERSITY, Commerce 75428/ FR, GE, SP.

⊗A-1021.   EL PASO COMMUNITY COLLEGE, El Paso 79998/ FR, GE.

⊗A-1022.   GALVESTON COLLEGE, Galveston 77550/ MOL.

A-1023.   HARDIN-SIMMONS UNIVERSITY, Abilene 79698/ FR, GE, SP.

A-1024.   HOUSTON BAPTIST UNIVERSITY, Houston 77074/ FR, SH, SP.

⊗A-1025.   HOUSTON COMMUNITY COLLEGE SYSTEM, Houston 77270/ MUL.

A-1026.   HOWARD PAYNE UNIVERSITY, Brownwood 76801/ FR, SP.

A-1027.   INCARNATE WORD COLLEGE, San Antonio 78209/ SP.

⊗A-1028.   JACKSONVILLE COLLEGE, Jacksonville 75766/ FR, GE, SP.

⊗A-1029.   KILGORE COLLEGE, Kilgore 75662/ FR, GE, SP.

A-1030.   LAMAR UNIVERSITY, Beaumont 77710/ FR, SP.

⊗A-1031.   LON MORRIS COLLEGE, Jacksonville 75766/ FR, SP.

A-1032.   LUBBOCK CHRISTIAN UNIVERSITY, Lubbock 79407/ BIL, SP.

A-1033.   McLENNAN COMMUNITY COLLEGE, Waco 76708/ SP.

A-1034.   McMURRY UNIVERSITY, Abilene 79697/ FR, GE, SP.

A-1035.   MIDLAND COLLEGE, Midland 79705/ FR, GE, SP.

A-1036.   MIDWESTERN STATE UNIVERSITY, Wichita Falls 76308/ SP.

A-1037.   NORTH TEXAS STATE UNIVERSITY, Denton 76203/ FR, GE, LA, SP.

A-1038.   OUR LADY OF THE LAKE UNIVERSITY OF SAN ANTONIO, San Antonio 78207/ SP.

⊗A-1039.   PARIS JUNIOR COLLEGE, Paris 75460/ FR, GE, SP.

A-1040.   PRAIRIE VIEW A&M UNIVERSITY, Prairie View 77446/ SP.

◢A-1041.   RICE UNIVERSITY, Houston 77251/ CH, FR, FR(od), GE, GE(mh), GE(oh), GO, GR, IC(od), LA, PO, PT, RU, SP, SP(od), SW, SX.

A-1042.   ST. MARY'S UNIVERSITY OF SAN ANTONIO, San Antonio 78228/ FR, GE, SP.

⊗A-1043.   ST. PHILLIP'S COLLEGE, San Antonio 78203/ SP.

⊗A-1044.   SAN JACINTO COLLEGE-NORTH CAMPUS, Houston 77049/ GE, PT, SP.

A-1045. SCHREINER COLLEGE, Kerrville 78028/ FR, GE, SP.
A-1046. SOUTHERN METHODIST UNIVERSITY, Dallas 75275/ FR, GE, IT, RU, SP.
A-1047. SOUTHWEST TEXAS STATE UNIVERSITY, San Marcos 78666/ FR, GE, SP.
A-1048. SOUTHWESTERN ADVENTIST COLLEGE, Keene 76059/ SP.
A-1049. SOUTHWESTERN UNIVERSITY, Georgetown 78626/ FR, GE, LA, SP.
A-1050. STEPHEN A. AUSTIN STATE UNIVERSITY, Nacogdoches 75962/ FR, SP.
A-1051. SUL ROSS STATE UNIVERSITY, Alpine 79832/ SP.
A-1052. TARLETON STATE UNIVERSITY, Stephenville 76402/ SP.
⊗A-1053. TEMPLE JUNIOR COLLEGE, Temple 76504/ FR, GE, SP.
A-1054. TEXAS A&I UNIVERSITY, Kingsville 78363/ SP.
A-1055. TEXAS A&M UNIVERSITY AT GALVESTON, Galveston 77533-1675/ SP.
A-1056. TEXAS CHRISTIAN UNIVERSITY, Fort Worth 76129/ FR, GE, SP.
A-1057. TEXAS LUTHERAN COLLEGE, Seguin 78155/ GE, SP.
A-1058. TEXAS SOUTHERN UNIVERSITY, Houston 77004/ FR, SP.
⊗A-1059. TEXAS SOUTHMOST COLLEGE, Brownsville 78520/ FR, SP.
A-1060. TEXAS TECH UNIVERSITY, Lubbock 79430/ CH, CZ, FR, GE, GR, LA, PT, SP, *YD.*
A-1061. TEXAS WESLEYAN UNIVERSITY, Fort Worth 76105/ FR, SP.
A-1062. TEXAS WOMAN'S UNIVERSITY, Denton 76204/ SP.
A-1063. TRINITY UNIVERSITY, San Antonio 78284/ FR, GE, GR, RU, SP.
⊗A-1064. TYLER JUNIOR COLLEGE, Tyler 75711/ MUL.
A-1065. UNIVERSITY OF DALLAS, Irving 75062/ FR, GE, GR, LA, SP.
A-1066. UNIVERSITY OF HOUSTON, Houston 77002/ FR, GE, RU, SP.
A-1067. UNIVERSITY OF ST. THOMAS, Houston 77006/ FR, GE, GR, LA, SP.
A-1068. UNIVERSITY OF TEXAS AT ARLINGTON, Arlington 76019/ FR, FR(od), GE, HE(bi), LA, RU, SP, SP(od).
A-1069. UNIVERSITY OF TEXAS AT AUSTIN, Austin 78712/ AA, AB, AB(ca), CH, CT, CZ, DA, DR, FR, FR(od), GE, GR, GR(mo), HE, HE(bi), HI, IT, JP, KA, KM, LA, MM, M/Y, NW, *PA,* PE, PO, PT, QC, RU, S/C, SK, SP, SR, SW, TE, TM, TU, *UR,* YD.

A-1070. UNIVERSITY OF TEXAS AT EL PASO, El Paso 79968/ CH(mn), FR, GE, JP, SP.
A-1071. UNIVERSITY OF TEXAS AT SAN ANTONIO, San Antonio 78249/ FR, GE, SP.
Ⓧ A-1072. UNIVERSITY OF TEXAS OF THE PERMIAN BASIN, Odessa 79762/ SP.
Ⓧ A-1073. VICTORIA COLLEGE, Victoria 77901/ MUL.
A-1074. WEST TEXAS STATE UNIVERSITY, Canyon 79016/ SP.
Ⓧ A-1075. WESTERN TEXAS COLLEGE, Snyder 79549/ GE, SP.
Ⓧ A-1076. WHARTON COUNTY JUNIOR COLLEGE, Wharton 77488/ SP.

UTAH (UT)
A-1077. BRIGHAM YOUNG UNIVERSITY, Provo 84602/ AA, AB, AF, AK, AY, CH, CH(cn), CH(mn), CP, CT, DA, DU, FI, FJ, FL, FR, GE, GE(mh), GE(oh), GO, GR, HE, HE(bi), HI, HU, IC, IT, JP, JP(cl), KO, LA, M/O, M/Y, NV, NW, PE, PO, PT, QC, RU, S/C, SM, SP, SW, TA, TG, TU, UG, WE.
Ⓧ A-1078. DIXIE COLLEGE, St. George 84770/ FR, GE, RU, SP.
Ⓧ A-1079. SNOW COLLEGE, Ephraim 84627/ FR, GE, SP.
A-1080. SOUTHERN UTAH UNIVERSITY, Cedar City 84720/ FR, GE, SP.
A-1081. UNIVERSITY OF UTAH, Salt Lake City 84112/ AB(ca), CH(mn), FR, GE, GE(mh), GE(oh), GO, GR, HE, HT, JP, LA, NR, NV, PE, RU, SP, SS, S/S, TR, TU, YD.
A-1082. UTAH STATE UNIVERSITY, Logan 84322/ FR, GE, SP.
A-1083. WEBER STATE UNIVERSITY, Ogden 84408/ FR, GE, SP.

VERMONT (VT)
A-1084. BENNINGTON COLLEGE, Bennington 05201/ CH, FR, GE, GR, IT, LA, SP.
A-1085. CASTLETON STATE COLLEGE, Castleton 05735/ FR, SP.
A-1086. MARLBORO COLLEGE, Marlboro 05344/ FR, GE, GR, IT, JP, LA, PT, RU, SP.
A-1087. MIDDLEBURY COLLEGE, Middlebury 05753/ AB, CH, FR, GE, GR, IT, JP, LA, RU, SP.
A-1088. NORWICH UNIVERSITY, Northfield 05663/ FR, GE, RU, SP.
A-1089. ST. MICHAEL'S COLLEGE, Colchester 05404/ FR, SP.
A-1090. SCHOOL FOR INTERNATIONAL TRAINING, Brattleboro 05301/ AB, CH, FR, GE(sw), HI, JP, PE(af), SP.
A-1091. TRINITY COLLEGE OF VERMONT, Burlington 05401/ FR, SP.

A-1092. UNIVERSITY OF VERMONT, Burlington 05405/ FR, GE, GE(mh), GE(oh), GO, GR, HE, IR, JP, LA, PO, RU, SP, SS, TH, TI.

VIRGIN ISLANDS (VI) See A-1189

VIRGINIA (VA)

A-1093. BRIDGEWATER COLLEGE, Bridgewater 22812/ FR, GE, SP.

A-1094. CHRISTENDOM COLLEGE, Front Royal 22630/ FR.

A-1095. CHRISTOPHER NEWPORT COLLEGE, Newport News 23606/ FR, GE, SP.

A-1096. COLLEGE OF WILLIAM AND MARY, Williamsburg 23187/ FR, GE, SP.

A-1097. EASTERN MENNONITE COLLEGE AND SEMINARY, Harrisonburg 22801/ FR, GE, SP.

A-1098. EMORY AND HENRY COLLEGE, Emory 24327/ FR, GE, LA, SP.

A-1099. FERRUM COLLEGE, Ferrum 24088/ FR, RU, SP.

A-1100. GEORGE MASON UNIVERSITY, Fairfax 22030/ FR, GE, JP, RU, SP.

A-1101. HAMPDEN-SYDNEY COLLEGE, Hampden-Sydney 23901/ FR, GE, GR, LA, RU, SP.

A-1102. HOLLINS COLLEGE, Roanoke 24020/ FR, GE, GR, LA, SP.

A-1103. JAMES MADISON UNIVERSITY, Harrisonburg 22807/ FR, GE, RU, SP.

A-1104. LONGWOOD COLLEGE, Farmville 23901/ MUL.

A-1105. LYNCHBURG COLLEGE, Lynchburg 24501/ FR, GE, SP.

A-1106. MARY BALDWIN COLLEGE, Staunton 24401/ FR, SP.

A-1107. MARY WASHINGTON COLLEGE, Fredericksburg 22401/ FR, GE, GR, IT, LA, RU, SP.

A-1108. OLD DOMINION UNIVERSITY, Norfolk 23529/ FR, GE, RU, SP.

A-1109. RADFORD UNIVERSITY, Radford 24142/ FR, GE, LA, SP.

A-1110. RANDOLPH-MACON COLLEGE, Ashland 23005/ FR, GE, GR, LA, RU, SP.

A-1111. RANDOLPH-MACON WOMAN'S COLLEGE, Lynchburg 24503/ GE, GR, LA, SP.

A-1112. ROANOKE COLLEGE, Salem 24153/ FR, GE, SP.

A-1113. SWEET BRIAR COLLEGE, Sweet Briar 24595/ FR, GE, GR, IT, LA, SP.

A-1114. UNIVERSITY OF RICHMOND, Richmond 23173/ FR, GE, GR, LA, RU, SP.

A-1115. UNIVERSITY OF VIRGINIA, Charlottesville 22906/ AB, CH, FR, GE, GR, HE, HE(bi), HI, IC(od), IR(od), IT, JP, LA, PO, PT, RU, RU(od), S/C, SH, SP, SP(od), SS, S/S, WE.

A-1116. VIRGINIA MILITARY INSTITUTE, Lexington 24450/ MOL.

A-1117. VIRGINIA POLYTECHNIC INSTITUTE AND STATE UNIVERSITY, Blacksburg 24061/ FR, GE, SP.

A-1118. VIRGINIA STATE UNIVERSITY, Petersburg 23803/ MUL.

A-1119. VIRGINIA UNION UNIVERSITY, Richmond 23220/ FR.

A-1120. VIRGINIA WESLEYAN COLLEGE, Norfolk 23502/ FR, SP.

A-1121. WASHINGTON AND LEE UNIVERSITY, Lexington 24450/ FR, GE, SP.

WASHINGTON (WA)

A-1122. CENTRAL WASHINGTON UNIVERSITY, Ellensburg 98926/ FR, GE, SP.

⊗A-1123. CLARK COLLEGE, Vancouver 98663/ FR, GE, JP, SP.

A-1124. EASTERN WASHINGTON UNIVERSITY, Cheney 99004/ CH, FR, GE, KO, RU, SP.

⊗A-1125. EVERETT COMMUNITY COLLEGE, Everett 98201/ FR, GE, JP, SP.

A-1126. EVERGREEN STATE COLLEGE, Olympia 98505/ FR, GE, RU, SP.

A-1127. GONZAGA UNIVERSITY, Spokane 99258/ FR, GE, GR, IT, LA, NAL, SP.

⊗A-1128. OLYMPIC COLLEGE, Bremerton 98310/ FR, GE, SP.

A-1129. PACIFIC LUTHERAN UNIVERSITY, Tacoma 98447/ FR, GE, SP, SW.

⊗A-1130. SEATTLE CENTRAL COMMUNITY COLLEGE, Seattle 98122/ FR, GE, JP, LA, SP.

A-1131. SEATTLE PACIFIC UNIVERSITY, Seattle 98119/ FR, GE, GR, RU, SP.

A-1132. SEATTLE UNIVERSITY, Seattle 98122/ FR, GE, JP, SP.

⊗A-1133. SPOKANE COMMUNITY COLLEGE, Spokane 99207/ FR, GE, SP.

⊗A-1134. SPOKANE FALLS COMMUNITY COLLEGE, Spokane 99204/ CH, FR, GE, JP, RU, SP.

⊗A-1135. TACOMA COMMUNITY COLLEGE, Tacoma 98465/ SP.

A-1136. UNIVERSITY OF PUGET SOUND, Tacoma 98416/ FR, GE, SP.

A-1137. UNIVERSITY OF WASHINGTON, Seattle 98195/ AB, AK, BL, CH(cl), CZ, DA, FI, *FO,* FR, GE, GR, *GY,* HE, HI, IC, IT, JP, KO, *KR,* LA, *LM,* NW, PE, PO, PT,

PV, RO, RU, S/C, *SLL,* SP, S/P, SS, S/S, SW, TH, TR,
TU, *UD,* UG, UI(od), VD.

A-1138. WALLA WALLA COLLEGE, Washington 99324/ BIL, FR,
GE, SP.

A-1139. WASHINGTON STATE UNIVERSITY, Pullman 99163/AB,
AB(ca), AB, CII, CH(mn), FR, GE, GR, IC(od), JP,
KO, NR, RU, SP, SW.

⊗A-1140. WENATCHEE VALLEY COLLEGE, Wenatchee 98801/ SP.

A-1141. WESTERN WASHINGTON UNIVERSITY, Bellingham 98225/
FR, GE, RU, SP.

A-1142. WHITMAN COLLEGE, Walla Walla 99362/ CH, FR, GE,
JP, SP.

A-1143. WHITWORTH COLLEGE, Spokane 99251/ FR, GE, SP.

WEST VIRGINIA (WV)

A-1144. BETHANY COLLEGE, Bethany 26032/ FR, GE, SP.

A-1145. DAVIS AND ELKINS COLLEGE, Elkins 26241/ FR, SP.

A-1146. FAIRMONT STATE COLLEGE, Fairmont 26554/ FR.

A-1147. MARSHALL UNIVERSITY, Huntington 25755/ FR, GE,
LA, SP.

⊗A-1148. POTOMAC STATE COLLEGE OF WEST VIRGINIA UNIVER-
SITY, Keyser 26726/ FR, GE, SP.

A-1149. SHEPHERD COLLEGE, Shepherdstown 25443/ FR.

A-1150. WEST VIRGINIA UNIVERSITY, Morgantown 26506/AB,
CH, CT, FR, GE, GR, JP, LA, PO, PT, RU, SP.

A-1151. WHEELING JESUIT COLLEGE, Wheeling 26003/ FR, SP.

WISCONSIN (WI)

A-1152. BELOIT COLLEGE, Beloit 53511/ FR, GE, GR, LA, *RU,*
SP.

A-1153. CARDINAL STRICH COLLEGE, Milwaukee 53217/ FR,
SP.

A-1154. CARROLL COLLEGE, Waukesha 53186/ FR, GE, SP.

A-1155. CARTHAGE COLLEGE, Kenosha 53140/ FR, GE, SP.

A-1156. CONCORDIA UNIVERSITY WISCONSIN, Mequon 53092/
GE, GR, HE.

A-1157. EDGEWOOD COLLEGE, Madison 53711/ FR, SP.

A-1158. LAKELAND COLLEGE, Sheboygan 53082/ GE.

A-1159. LAWRENCE UNIVERSITY, Appleton 54912/ CH, FR, GE,
GR, LA, RU, SP.

A-1160. MARQUETTE UNIVERSITY, Milwaukee 53233/ FR, GE,
LA, SP.

A-1161. MOUNT MARY COLLEGE, Milwaukee 53222/ FR, GE, SP.

A-1162. NORTHLAND COLLEGE, Ashland 54806/ FR, SP.

A-1163.   RIPON COLLEGE, Ripon 54971/ FR, GE, SP.
A-1164.   ST. NORBERT COLLEGE, De Pere 54115/ FR, GE, SP.
A-1165.   UNIVERSITY OF WISCONSIN–EAU CLAIRE, Eau Clair 54702/ FR, GE, SP.
A-1166.   UNIVERSITY OF WISCONSIN–GREEN BAY, Green Bay 54311/ FR, GE, ON, SP.
A-1167.   UNIVERSITY OF WISCONSIN–LA CROSSE, La Crosse 54601/ FR, SP.
A-1168.   UNIVERSITY OF WISCONSIN–MADISON, Madison 53706/ AA, AB(ca), BL, CH, CH(cl), CH(mn), CZ, EG(an), FI, FR, FR(od), GE, GE(mh), GE(oh), GO, GR, HE, HE(bi), HI, IC(od), IT, JP, LA, PK, PO, PT, RU, S/C, SH, SP, SP(od), S/S, ST, TE, TH, TI, TI(cl), TM, VD, XH.
A-1169.   UNIVERSITY OF WISCONSIN–MILWAUKEE, Milwaukee 53201/ CH(mn), DA, FR, GE, *GE*(sw), GR, HE, HT, IN, IT, JP, LA, *LT,* MM, MO(cl), NE, NR, NW, PA, PT, PV, QC, *RO,* RU, S/C, SP, SW, SX, TU, UR.
A-1170.   UNIVERSITY OF WISCONSIN–OSHKOSH, Oshkosh 54901/ FR, GE, SP.
A-1171.   UNIVERSITY OF WISCONSIN–PARKSIDE, Kenosha 53141/ FR, GE, SP.
A-1172.   UNIVERSITY OF WISCONSIN–PLATTEVILLE, Platteville 53818/ FR, GE, SP.
A-1173.   UNIVERSITY OF WISCONSIN–RIVER FALLS, River Falls 54022/ FR, GE.
A-1174.   UNIVERSITY OF WISCONSIN–STEVENS POINT, Stevens Point 54481/ FR, GE, RU, SP.
A-1174/a.   UNIVERSITY OF WISCONSIN–WHITEWATER, Whitewater 53190/ FR, GE, SP.

WYOMING (WY)
⊗A-1175.   CASPER COLLEGE, Casper 82601/ FR, GE, IT, SP.
⊗A-1176.   EASTERN WYOMING COLLEGE, Torrington 82240/ FR, SP.
⊗A-1177.   NORTHWEST COLLEGE, Powell 82435/ GE, SP.
A-1178.   UNIVERSITY OF WYOMING, Laramie 82071/ FR, GE, GR, LA, RU, SP.
⊗A-1179.   WESTERN WYOMING COMMUNITY COLLEGE, Rock Springs 82901/ FR, GE, SP.

PUERTO RICO (PR)
A-1180.   ANTILLIAN COLLEGE, Mayagüez 00709/ SP.
A-1181.   BAYAMON CENTRAL UNIVERSITY, Bayamon 00960/ SP.

A-1182.   CATHOLIC UNIVERSITY OF PUERTO RICO, Ponce 00732/ FR, GE, SP.

A-1183.   INTERAMERICAN UNIVERSITY OF PUERTO RICO– METROPOLITAN CAMPUS, Hato Rey 00919/ SP, UK.

A-1184.   UNIVERSITY OF PUERTO RICO–CAYEY UNIVERSITY COLLEGE, Cayey 00736/ SP.

A-1185.   UNIVERSITY OF PUERTO RICO–MAYAGÜEZ CAMPUS, Mayagüez 00680/ FR, SP.

A-1186.   UNIVERSITY OF PUERTO RICO–MEDICAL SCIENCES CAMPUS, Rio Piedras 00936/ SP.

☑A-1187.   UNIVERSITY OF PUERTO RICO–RIO PIEDRAS CAMPUS, Rio Piedras 00931/ FR, SP.

A-1188.   UNIVERSITY OF THE SACRED HEART, Santurce 00914/ FR, SP.

VIRGIN ISLANDS (VI)

A-1189.   UNIVERSITY OF THE VIRGIN ISLANDS, Charlotte Amalie 00802/ SP.

Canada

ALBERTA (A)

A-1190.   UNIVERSITY OF ALBERTA, Edmonton T6G 2M7/AB(cl), BF, CR, CT, GE, GE(mh), GO, GR, HE, HE(bi), JP, NW, PO, PT, RO, SP, SP(od), S/S, UK.

A-1191.   UNIVERSITY OF CALGARY, Calgary T2N 1N4/ CR, FR, GE, GR, LA, RU, SP, SS, TI.

BRITISH COLUMBIA (BC)

A-1192.   SIMON FRASER UNIVERSITY, Burnaby V5A 1S6/ CH, CH(mn), FR, GR, HE, SP.

A-1193.   UNIVERSITY OF BRITISH COLUMBIA, Vancouver V6T 1Z1/ CH, CH(mn), FR, GE, GE(oh), GO, GR, HE, HI, H/U, IC(od), IT, JP, JP(cl), LT, NY, PO, PT, RU, SA, S/C, SP, SS, S/S, SW, UK.

MANITOBA (M)

A-1194.   BRANDON UNIVERSITY, Brandon R7A 6A9/ FR, GE, LA.

A-1195.   UNIVERSITY OF MANITOBA, Winnipeg R3T 2N2/ AB, CO, CR, DK, DU, FR, FR(od), GE, GE(mh), GE(oh), GO, GR, HE, HI, HU, IC, LA, NR, OJ, PO, RU, SP, SS, S/S, SY, UK, YD.

A-1196. UNIVERSITY OF WINNIPEG, Winnipeg R3B 2E9/ FR, GE, GR, LA.

NEW BRUNSWICK (NB)
A-1197. UNIVERSITY OF NEW BRUNSWICK, Fredericton E2L 4L5/ FR, GE, GR, LA, MC, RU, SP.

NEWFOUNDLAND (NF)
A-1198. MEMORIAL UNIVERSITY OF NEWFOUNDLAND, St. John's A1C 5S7/ CR, FR, GE, GR, HE, JP, LA, MI, M/T, PT, RU, SP, SS.

NOVA SCOTIA (NS)
A-1199. ACADIA UNIVERSITY, Wolfville B0P 1X0/ FR.
A-1200. DALHOUSIE UNIVERSITY, Halifax B3H 4H6/ FR, GE, GR, LA, RU, SP.
A-1201. MOUNT ST. VINCENT UNIVERSITY, Halifax B3M 2J6/ FR, GE, SP.
A-1202. ST. FRANCIS XAVIER UNIVERSITY, Antigonish B2G 1C0/ FR, SP.
A-1203. UNIVERSITÉ SAINT-ANNE, Pointe-de-L'Église B0W 1M0/ FR.
A-1204. UNIVERSITY OF KING'S COLLEGE, Halifax B3H 2A1/ FR, GE, RU, SP.

ONTARIO (O)
A-1205. BRESCIA COLLEGE, London N6G 1H2/ FR, GE, SP.
A-1206. KING'S COLLEGE, London N6A 2M3/ FR, GE, GR, LA, RU, SP.
A-1207. McMASTER UNIVERSITY, Hamilton L8S 4L8/ FR, GE, GR, IT, JP, LA, PT, RU, SP.
A-1208. QUEEN'S UNIVERSITY, Kingston K7L 3N6/ FR, GE, GR, IT, HE(bi), LA, NR(od), SP.
◢A-1209. UNIVERSITY OF OTTAWA, Ottawa K1N 6N5/ GE, GR, IT, LA, RU, SLL, SP.
A-1210. UNIVERSITY OF TORONTO, Toronto M5S 1A1/ AA, AB, AB(cl), AK, AV, CH, CH(cl), CH(cn), CH(mn), CL, CP, CT, CZ, DU, EG, ET, FR, FR(od), GE, GE(mn), GR, HE, HE(bi), HT, HU, H/U, IT, JP, JP(cl), KO, LA, MO, MO(md), NR(od), PA, PE, PO, PT, PV, RU, SC, S/C, SL, SP, SP(od), SS, S/S, SU, TI, TU, UK, UR, WE, YD.

A-1211.   UNIVERSITY OF WESTERN ONTARIO, London N6A 3K7/ FR, GE, GR, LA, OJ, ON, RU, SP, TS.

A-1212.   UNIVERSITY OF WINDSOR, Windsor N9B 3P4/ FR, GE, GR, IT, JP, LA, RU, SLL, SP.

A-1213.   VICTORIA UNIVERSITY, Toronto M5S 1K7/ CH, CH(cl), CH(mn), CW, EP, FR, GE, IC, JP, NI, NY, SA, SC, S/C, SS, SW.

◨A-1214.   YORK UNIVERSITY, North York M3J 1P3/ CH, FR, GE, GE(mh), GR, HE, IT, JP, LA, PO, PT, RU, SP, UK.

PRINCE EDWARD ISLAND (PE)

A-1215.   UNIVERSITY OF PRINCE EDWARD ISLAND, Charlotte-town C1A 4P3/ FR, GE, SP.

QUEBEC (Q)

A-1216.   BISHOP'S UNIVERSITY, Lenoxville J1M 1Z7/ FR, GE, IT, SP.

A-1217.   CONCORDIA UNIVERSITY, Montreal H3G 1M8/ FR, GE, IT, LA, RU, SP.

A-1218.   LAVAL UNIVERSITÉ, Cité Universitaire G1K 7P4/ FR, GE, GR, SP.

A-1219.   McGILL UNIVERSITY, Montreal H3A 2T5/ AA, AB, AB(cl), BL, CH, CH(mn), CR, FR, FR(od), GE, GE(mh), GE(oh), GR, HE, HE(bi), HU, IK, IT, JP, MH, M/T, NR(od), NS, OJ, PA, PE, PO, PT, RU, SH, SP, SP(od), SS, S/S, TU, UR, YD.

A-1220.   UNIVERSITÉ DE MONTRÉAL, Montréal H3C 3T5/ AB, BL, CH, FR, FR(od), GE, GR, HE, HI, JP, IT, LA, NR(od), PO, PT, PV, RU, SP.

A-1221.   UNIVERSITÉ DE QUÉBEC, Montreal H3C 3P8/ FR.

SASKATCHEWAN (S)

A-1222.   ST. THOMAS MORE COLLEGE, Saskatoon S7N 0W6/ FR, GE, GR, RU, SP, UK.

A-1223.   UNIVERSITY OF SASKATCHEWAN, Saskatoon S7N 0W0/ AA, AB, CR, FR, GE, GR, HE, LA, RU, SP, SY, UK.

Addendum Section A

CALIFORNIA

⊗A-1224.   CANADA COLLEGE, Redwood City 94061/ GE, FR, SP.

A-1225.   CHRIST COLLEGE IRVINE, Irvine 92175/ BIL.

⊗A-1226.   DE ANZA COLLEGE, Cupertino 95014/ FR, GE, SP.

⊗A-1227.   FEATHER RIVER COLLEGE, Quincy 95971/ SP.

Ⓧ A-1228. FRESNO CITY COLLEGE, Fresno 93741/ CH, PT, SP.
Ⓧ A-1229. GAVILAN COMMUNITY COLLEGE, Gilroy 95020/ SP.
Ⓧ A-1230. GROSSMONT COMMUNITY COLLEGE, El Cajon 92020/ FR, GE, SP.
Ⓧ A-1231. IRVINE VALLEY COLLEGE, Irvine 92720/ FR, SP.
   A-1232. LA SIERRA UNIVERSITY, Riverside 92515/ FR, SP.
Ⓧ A-1233. LONG BEACH CITY COLLEGE, Long Beach 90808/ MUL.
   A-1234. NAVAL POSTGRADUATE STUDIES, Monterey 94943/ RU.
Ⓧ A-1235. PALOMAR COMMUNITY COLLEGE, San Marcos 92069/ SP.
Ⓧ A-1236. SADDLEBACK COLLEGE, Mission Viejo 92962/ MUL.
Ⓧ A-1237. SAN DIEGO MESA COLLEGE, San Diego 92111/ MUL.

COLORADO
Ⓧ A-1238. PIKES PEAK COMMUNITY COLLEGE, Colorado Springs 80906/ MUL.
Ⓧ A-1239. RED ROCKS COMMUNITY COLLEGE, Lakewood 80401/ GE.
   A-1240. No entry.

FLORIDA
   A-1241. BETHUNE-COOKMAN COLLEGE, Daytona Beach 32115/ MUL.
Ⓧ A-1242. BROWARD COMMUNITY COLLEGE, Fort Lauderdale 33301/ MUL.
Ⓧ A-1243. EDISON COMMUNITY COLLEGE, Fort Meyers 33906/ MUL.
Ⓧ A-1244. MIAMI DADE COMMUNITY COLLEGE, Miami 33132/ FR, GE, IT, PT, RU, SP.
Ⓧ A-1245. OKALOOSA-WALTON COMMUNITY COLLEGE, Niceville 32578/ FR, GE, SP.

GEORGIA
Ⓧ A-1246. ANDREW COLLEGE, Cuthbert 31740/ FR.
Ⓧ A-1247. ATLANTA METROPOLITAN COLLEGE, Atlanta 30310/ MUL.
   A-1248. AUGUSTA COLLEGE, Augusta 30910/ FR, SP.
   A-1249. BRENAU COLLEGE, Gainsville 30501/ FR.
Ⓧ A-1250. DARTON COLLEGE, Albany 31707/ FR, SP.
Ⓧ A-1251. DE KALB COLLEGE, Decatur 30034/ MUL.
Ⓧ A-1252. EAST GEORGIA COLLEGE, Swainsboro 30401/ FR, SP.
   A-1253. KENNESAW STATE UNIVERSITY, Marietta 30061/ FR, SP.
   A-1254. MOREHOUSE COLLEGE, Atlanta 30314/ FR, GE, JP, SP.

A-1255. MORRIS BROWN COLLEGE, Atlanta 30314/ FR, SP.
A-1256. NORTH GEORGIA COLLEGE, Dahlonega 30597/ FR.
ⓧA-1257. OXFORD COLLEGE-EMORY UNIVERSITY, Oxford 30267/
         FR, GE, HE, IT, RU, SP.
Λ 1258. PIEDMONT COLLEGE, Demorest 30535/ SP.
A-1259. WESLEYAN COLLEGE, Macon 31297/ SP.

IDAHO
ⓧA-1260. COLLEGE OF SOUTHERN IDAHO, Twin Falls 83303/ FR.

ILLINOIS
ⓧA-1261. CHICAGO CITY COLLEGES: HAROLD WASHINGTON COL-
         LEGE, Chicago 60601/ FR, GE, JP, RU, SP.
ⓧA-1262. CHICAGO CITY-WIDE COLLEGE, Chicago 60606/ FR,
         GE, HE, IT, JP, RU, SP.
A-1263. EAST–WEST UNIVERSITY, Chicago 60605/ AB.
A-1264. EUREKA COLLEGE, Eureka 61530/ SP.
A-1265. ILLINOIS BENEDICTINE COLLEGE, Lisle 60532/ SP.
A-1266. ILLINOIS CENTRAL COLLEGE, East Peoria 61635/ MUL.
ⓧA-1267. JOLIET JUNIOR COLLEGE, Joliet 60436/ FR, GE, SP.
ⓧA-1268. OAKTON COMMUNITY COLLEGE, De Plaines 60016/ SP.
A-1269. OLIVET NAZARENE UNIVERSITY, Kankakee 60901/
         MUL.
ⓧA-1270. PRAIRIE STATE COLLEGE, Chicago Heights 60411/
         MUL.
ⓧA-1271. RICHLAND COMMUNITY COLLEGE, Decatur 62521/ FR,
         GE, SP.

INDIANA
A-1271/a. INDIANA UNIVERSITY-SOUTH BEND, South Bend 46634/
         FR.
A-1272. INDIANA WESLEYAN UNIVERSITY, Marion 46953/ BIL.
A-1273. PURDUE UNIVERSITY, West Lafayette 47907/ FR.
ⓧA-1274. SUMMIT CHRISTIAN COLLEGE, Fort Wayne 46807/ HE.

IOWA
A-1275. TEIKYO WESTERN UNIVERSITY, Le Mars 51031/ GE.
A-1276. No entry.

KANSAS
ⓧA-1277. ALLEN COUNTY COMMUNITY COLLEGE, Iola 66749/ SP.
ⓧA-1278. BARTON COUNTY COMMUNITY COLLEGE, Great Bend
         67530/ MUL.

A-1279. CENTRAL BAPTIST THEOLOGICAL SEMINARY, Kansas 66102/ GR(cl), HE.
ⓧ A-1280. COLBY COMMUNITY COLLEGE, Colby 67701/ MUL.
ⓧ A-1281. GARDEN CITY COMMUNITY COLLEGE, Garden City 67846/ CH, GE, SP.
A-1282. KANSAS STATE UNIVERSITY, Manhattan 66506/ FR, GE, JP, RU, SP.

KENTUCKY
ⓧ A-1283. JEFFERSON COMMUNITY COLLEGE, Louisville 40202/ FR, SP.

LOUISIANA
A-1284. LOUISIANA COLLEGE, Pineville 71360/ FR, MUL.
A-1285. NEW ORLEANS BAPTIST THEOLOGICAL SEMINARY, New Orleans 70126/ BIL.
A-1286. SOUTHERN LOUISIANA UNIVERSITY, Hammond 70361/ SP.
A-1287. SOUTHERN UNIVERSITY AT NEW ORLEANS, New Orleans 70126/ FR.
A-1288. UNIVERSITY OF NEW ORLEANS, New Orleans 70148/ FR, SP.
A-1289. UNIVERSITY OF SOUTHWESTERN LOUISIANA, Lafayette 70504/ FR, GE, SP.

MAINE
A-1290. UNIVERSITY OF MAINE-FARMINGTON, Farmington 04938/ MUL.

MARYLAND
A-1291. LOYOLA COLLEGE IN MARYLAND, Baltimore 21210/ FR.
A-1292. WASHINGTON BIBLE COLLEGE, Lanham 20706/ BIL.

MASSACHUSETTS
A-1293. BRADFORD COLLEGE, Bradford 01835/ FR, SP.

MICHIGAN
A-1294. GRAND RAPIDS BAPTIST COLLEGE & SEMINARY, Grand Rapids 49505/ BIL.
A-1295. MADONNA UNIVERSITY, Livonia 48150/ FR.
A-1296. SAINT MARY'S COLLEGE, Orchard Lake 48324/ MUL.
ⓧ A-1297. SUOMI COLLEGE, Hancock 49930/ SCL.
A-1298. UNIVERSITY OF DETROIT-MERCY, Detroit 48221/ FR, GE.
A-1299. UNIVERSITY OF MICHIGAN-FLINT, Flint 48502/ FR, SP.

MINNESOTA
ⓧ A-1300. AUSTIN COMMUNITY COLLEGE, Austin 55912/ FR, GE, SP.
A-1301. BETHEL THEOLOGICAL SEMINARY, St. Paul 55712/ BIL.
A-1302. COLLEGE OF ST. CATHERINE, St. Paul 55105/ FR, LA, SP.
A-1303. CONCORDIA COLLEGE: ST. PAUL, St. Paul 55104/ MUL.
ⓧ A-1304. MINNEAPOLIS COMMUNITY COLLEGE, Minneapolis 55403/ MUL.
ⓧ A-1305. NORTHLAND COMMUNITY COLLEGE, Thief River Falls 56701/ SP.
A-1306. UNIVERSITY OF ST. THOMAS, St. Paul 55105/ CH, FR, GE, LA, RU, SP.

MISSISSIPPI
A-1307. BLUE MOUNTAIN COLLEGE, Blue Mountain 38610/ MUL.

MISSOURI
A-1308. CALVARY BIBLE COLLEGE, Kansas City 38610/ BIL.
ⓧ A-1309. EAST CENTRAL COLLEGE, Union 63084/ FR, SP.
ⓧ A-1310. MINERAL AREA COLLEGE, Flat River 63601/ MUL.
A-1311. MISSOURI WESTERN STATE UNIVERSITY, St. Joseph 64507/ FR.
A-1312. NAZARENE THEOLOGICAL SEMINARY, Kansas City 64131/ BIL.
A-1313. SOUTHWEST BAPTIST UNIVERSITY, Bolivar 65613/ SP.
A-1314. WEBSTER UNIVERSITY, St. Louis 63119/ FR, SP.

MONTANA
ⓧ A-1315. MILES COMMUNITY COLLEGE, Miles City 59301/ SP.
A-1316. ROCKY MOUNTAIN COLLEGE, Billings 59102/ SP.

NEBRASKA
A-1317. UNION COLLEGE, Lincoln 68506/ SP.
ⓧ A-1318. WESTERN NEBRASKA COMMUNITY COLLEGE: SCOTT BLUFF, Scott Bluff 69361/ FR, GE, SP.

NEW MEXICO
ⓧ A-1319. NEW MEXICO JUNIOR COLLEGE, Hobbs 88240/ SP.
A-1320. WESTERN NEW MEXICO UNIVERSITY, Silver City 88062/ SP.

NEW YORK
A-1321. CITY UNIVERSITY OF NEW YORK: COLLEGE OF STATEN ISLAND, New York 10301/ MUL, SP.
A-1322. DOWLING COLLEGE, Oakdale 11769/ MUL.
A-1323. PACE UNIVERSITY, New York 10038/ FR.

NORTH CAROLINA
A-1324. BARTON COLLEGE, Wilson 27893/ SP, SR.

OHIO
A-1325. NOTRE DAME COLLEGE OF OHIO, Cleveland 44121/ FR, SP, MUL.
A-1326. UNITED THEOLOGICAL SEMINARY, Dayton 45406/ GR, HE.
A-1327. UNIVERSITY OF FINDLAY, Findlay 45840/ SP.
A-1328. UNIVERSITY OF RIO GRANDE, Rio Grande 45674/ SP.

OKLAHOMA
⊗A-1329. TULSA JUNIOR COLLEGE, Tulsa 74135/ FR, GE, IT, LA, JP, RU, SP.
A-1330. UNIVERSITY OF CENTRAL OKLAHOMA, Edmond 73034/ FR.

OREGON
⊗A-1331. CHEMEKETA COMMUNITY COLLEGE, Chemeketa 97309/ MUL.
A-1332. NORTH WEST CHRISTIAN COLLEGE, Eugene 97401/ FR, GE, RU, SP.
⊗A-1333. PORTLAND COMMUNITY COLLEGE, Portland 97219/ GE.
A-1334. UNIVERSITY OF OREGON–ROBERT DONALD CLARK HONORS COLLEGE, Eugene 97403/ CH, FR, GE, GR, IT, JP, LA, RU, SP.
A-1335. WILLIAMETTE UNIVERSITY, Salem 97301/ FR, GE, SP.

PENNSYLVANIA
A-1335/a. EVANGELICAL SCHOOL OF THEOLOGY, Myerstown 17067/ BIL.
A-1336. LA ROCHE COLLEGE, Pittsburgh 15237/ FR, GE, SP.
⊗A-1337. PINEBROOK JUNIOR COLLEGE, Coopersburg 18036/ GE.
⊗A-1338. VALLEY FORGE MILITARY JUNIOR COLLEGE, Wayne 19087/ SP.

SOUTH CAROLINA
A-1339.   CENTRAL WESTERN COLLEGE, Central 29630/ BIL.
A-1340.   CHARLESTON SOUTHERN UNIVERSITY, Charleston 29411/ SP.
A-1341.   COLUMBIA BIBLE COLLEGE AND SEMINARY, Columbia 29230/ BIL.

TENNESSEE
A-1342.   BELMONT UNIVERSITY, Nashville 37212/ FR.
A-1343.   MID-AMERICA BAPTIST THEOLOGICAL SEMINARY, Memphis 38104/ BIL.
⊗ A-1344.   SHELBY STATE COMMUNITY COLLEGE, Memphis 38174/ FR, SP.

TEXAS
⊗ A-1345.   BLINN COLLEGE, Brenham 77833/ SP.
⊗ A-1346.   BRAZOSPORT COLLEGE, Lake Jackson 77566/ SP.
⊗ A-1347.   COLLIN COUNTY COMMUNITY COLLEGE, McKinney 75070/ FR, GE, LA, SP.
A-1348.   CONCORDIA LUTHERAN COLLEGE, Austin 78705/ SP.
A-1349.   DALLAS CHRISTIAN COLLEGE, Dallas 75234/ BIL.
A-1350.   DALLAS THEOLOGICAL SEMINARY, Dallas 75204/ BIL.
⊗ A-1351.   DEL MAR COLLEGE, Corpus Christi 78404/ MUL.
⊗ A-1352.   FRANK PHILIPPS COLLEGE, Borger 79008/ FR, SP.
A-1353.   ODESSA COLLEGE, Odessa 79764/ SP, MUL.
A-1354.   SAM HOUSTON STATE UNIVERSITY, Huntsville 77341/ FR, GE, SP.
A-1355.   SOUTHWESTERN ASSEMBLIES OF GOD SEMINARY, Waxahachie 75165/ BIL, SP.
⊗ A-1356.   TRINITY VALLEY COMMUNITY COLLEGE, Athens 75751/ SP.
A-1357.   UNIVERSITY OF MARY HARDIN-BAYLOR, Belton 76513/ FR, SP.
A-1358.   UNIVERSITY OF NORTH TEXAS, Denton 76203/ FR, GE, SP.
A-1359.   UNIVERSITY OF TEXAS: TYLER, Tyler 75701/ SP.

VIRGINIA
A-1360.   BLUEFIELD COLLEGE, Bluefield 24605/ BIL.
A-1361.   HAMPTON UNIVERSITY, Hampton 23668/ FR.
A-1362.   LIBERTY UNIVERSITY, Lynchburg 24506/ FR, SP.
A-1363.   VIRGINIA COMMONWEALTH UNIVERSITY, Richmond 23284/ FR, GE, SP.

WASHINGTON
⊗A-1364.　GRAYS HARBOR COLLEGE, Aberdeen 98520/ CH, JP.
　A-1365.　HERITAGE COLLEGE, Toppenish 98948/ SP.
⊗A-1366.　HIGHLINE COMMUNITY COLLEGE, Highland Park 98198/
　　　　　　CH, LA.
⊗A-1367.　SKAGIT VALLEY COLLEGE, Mount Vernon 98273/ SP.

WEST VIRGINIA
⊗A-1368.　OHIO VALLEY COLLEGE, Parkersburg 26101/ HE, SP.

WISCONSIN
　A-1369.　NASHOTAH HOUSE, Nashotah 53058/ BIL.
　A-1370.　NORTHWESTERN COLLEGE, Watertown 53094/ BIL.

WYOMING
⊗A-1371.　CENTRAL WYOMING COLLEGE, Riverton 82501/ MUL.
　A-1372.　SHERIDAN COLLEGE, Sheridan 82801/ MUL.

PUERTO RICO
　A-1373.　INTER-AMERICAN UNIVERSITY OF PUERTO RICO: AREC-
　　　　　　IBO UNIVERSITY COLLEGE, Arecibo 00613/ SP.
　A-1374.　INTER-AMERICAN UNIVERSITY OF PUERTO RICO: SAN
　　　　　　GERMAN CAMPUS, San German 00683/ SP.

CANADA

ONTARIO
　A-1375.　CARLETON UNIVERSITY, Carleton K1S 5B6/ FR, GE,
　　　　　　GR, LA, RU.
　A-1376.　UNIVERSITY OF WATERLOO, Waterloo N2L 3G1/ FR,
　　　　　　GE, GR, LA, RU, SLL.

B. PUBLIC LIBRARIES, MUSEUM LIBRARIES, AND OTHERS WITH FOREIGN-LANGUAGE COLLECTIONS

United States Libraries

ALASKA (AK)
B-1.　　ALASKA STATE LIBRARY/DEPARTMENT OF EDUCATION,
　　　　State Office Building, Pouch G, Juneau 99811/ RU.
B-2.　　ANCHORAGE MUNICIPAL LIBRARIES, 3600 Denali
　　　　Street, Anchorage 99503/ FR, GE, RU, SP.

B-3. ANCHORAGE MUSEUM OF HISTORY & ARTS LIBRARY, 121 West Seventh Street, Anchorage 99501/ NAL.

B-4. PETERSBURG PUBLIC LIBRARY, Box 549, Petersburg 99833/ NW.

B-5. SHELDON MUSEUM AND CULTURAL CENTER LIBRARY, P.O. Box 269, Haines 99827/ NAL.

ARIZONA (AZ)

B-6. AGUILA PUBLIC LIBRARY, 51310 First Street, P.O. Box 188, Aguila 85320/ SP.

B-7. CHANDLER PUBLIC LIBRARY, 75 East Commonwealth Avenue, Chandler 85225/ SP.

B-8. DOUGLAS PUBLIC LIBRARY, 625 Tenth Street, Douglas 85607/ SP.

B-9. HAYDEN PUBLIC LIBRARY, Velasco Avenue, Box 99, Hayden 85235/ SP.

B-10. MUSEUM OF NORTHERN ARIZONA LIBRARY, Route 4, Box 729, Flagstaff 86001/ NAL.

B-11. NOGALES CITY–SANTA CRUZ COUNTY LIBRARY, 518 Grand Avenue, Nogales 85621/ SP.

B-12. PHOENIX PUBLIC LIBRARY, 12 East McDowell Road, Phoenix 85004/ CH, DA, DU, FR, GE, GR(mo), HE, HU, IT, JP, NW, PO, PT, RU, SP, SW, VI, YD.

B-13. TOLLESON PUBLIC LIBRARY, 9555 West Van Buren Street, Tolleson 85353/ SP.

B-14. TUCSON MUSEUM OF ARTS LIBRARY, 140 North Main Street, Tucson 85701/ SP(ch).

B-15. TUCSON-PIMA LIBRARY, 101 North Stone Avenue, P.O. Box 27470, City Hall Annex, Tucson 85726/ FR, GE, IT, SP, VI.

ARKANSAS (AR)

B-16. CENTRAL ARKANSAS LIBRARY SYSTEM, 700 Louisiana Street, Little Rock 72201/ FR, GE, SP.

CALIFORNIA (CA)

B-17. ALAMEDA COUNTY LIBRARY, 3121 Diabolo Street, Hayward 94545/ SP.

B-18. ALAMEDA FREE LIBRARY, 1433 Oak Street, Alameda 94501/ CH, FR, GE, IT, JP, SP.

B-19. ASSYRIAN FOUNDATION OF AMERICA LIBRARY, 1920 San Pablo Avenue, Berkeley 94702/ AS.

B-20. AZUSA CITY LIBRARY, 729 North Dalton Avenue, Azusa 91702/ SP.

B-21. BEVERLY HILLS PUBLIC LIBRARY, 444 North Rexford Drive, Beverly Hills 90210/ FR, GE, IT, PE, SP, VI.

B-22. BRUGGEMEYER MEMORIAL LIBRARY, 318 South Ramona Street, Monterey 91754/ CH, JP, KO, SP, VI.

B-23. CALIFORNIA HUNGARIAN-AMERICAN CULTURAL FOUNDATION LIBRARY, Northright 91324/ HU.

B-24. CALIFORNIA STATE LIBRARY, 914 Capitol Mall, P.O. Box 942837, Sacramento 94237/ AB, CH, CZ, DA, FI, GJ, GR(mo), HE, HU.

B-25. CHICANO RESOURCE CENTER, 4801 East Third Street, Los Angeles 90022/ SP(ch).

B-26. CITY OF COMMERCE PUBLIC LIBRARY, 5655 Jillson Street, Commerce 90040/ SP.

B-27. COUNTY OF LOS ANGELES PUBLIC LIBRARY, P.O. Box 7011, 7400 East Imperial Highway, 90241/AR, CH, DU, FR, GE, HU, IT, JP, KO, RU, SP, VI, YD.

B-28. EL SEGUNDO PUBLIC LIBRARY, 111 West Mariposa Avenue, El Segundo 90245/ SP.

B-29. FRESNO COUNTY FREE LIBRARY, 2420 Mariposa Street, Fresno 93721/ CH, JP, KO, SP.

B-30. GLENDALE PUBLIC LIBRARY, 222 East Harvard Street, Glendale 91205/ AR, CH, FR, GE, IT, JP, KO, SP, VI.

B-31. GOETHE INSTITUTE, 432 Clay Street, San Francisco 94111/ GE.

B-32. INGLEWOOD CITY PUBLIC LIBRARY, 101 West Manchester Boulevard, Inglewood 90301/ FR, GE, IT, SP, VI.

B-33. THE INSTITUTE OF BUDDHIST STUDIES LIBRARY, 2717 Haste Street, Berkeley 94704/ JP.

B-34. IRISH FOUNDATION LIBRARY, 2123 Market Street, San Francisco 94114/ IR.

B-35. JUDAH MAGNES MEMORIAL MUSEUM LIBRARY, 2911 Russell Street, Berkeley 94705/ HE, YD.

B-36. LOS ANGELES PUBLIC LIBRARY/FOREIGN LANGUAGES DEPARTMENT, 630 West Fifth Street, Los Angeles 90071/ AB, AR, CH, CZ, DA, DU, FI, FL, FR, GE, GR(mo), HE, IT, JP, KO, LI, LT, NW, PE, PO, PT, RU, S/C, SP, SW, VI, YD.

B-37. MONROVIA PUBLIC LIBRARY, 321 South Myrtle Avenue, Monrovia 91016/ SP.

B-38. MUSEUM OF RUSSIAN CULTURE LIBRARY, 2450 Sutter Street, San Francisco 94115/ RU.

B-39. NATIONAL CITY PUBLIC LIBRARY, 200 East 12th Street, National City 91950/ SP.

B-40. OAKLAND PUBLIC LIBRARY, 125 14th Street, Oakland 94612/ CA, CH, FL, JP, KO, LO, SP, TH, VI.

B-41. OCEANSIDE PUBLIC LIBRARY, 330 Nee Hill Street, Oceanside 92054/ FR, SP.

B-42. ORANGE COUNTY PUBLIC LIBRARY, 101 North Center Street, Orange 92666/ CH, IC, IT, JP, KO, SP, VI.

B-43. PALOS VERDES LIBRARY DISTRICT, 650 Deep Valley Drive, Rolling Hills Estates 90274/ CH, FR, GE, IT, JP, PE, PT, RU, SP.

B-44. PLACENTIA LIBRARY DISTRICT, 411 East Chapman Street, Placentia 92670/ AB.

B-45. POLAND'S MILLENNIUM LIBRARY, 3424 West Adams Boulevard, Los Angeles 90018/ PO.

B-46. POLISH ARTS AND CULTURE FOUNDATION LIBRARY, 166 Geary Street, Suite 1202–1203, San Francisco 94108/ PO.

B-47. POMONA PUBLIC LIBRARY, 625 South Garey Avenue, Pomona 91766/ CH, FR, GE, IT, JP, KO, SP, VI.

B-48. REDWOOD CITY PUBLIC LIBRARY/FAIR OAKS BRANCH, 2600 Middlefield Road, Redwood City 94065/ SP.

B-49. SAN DIEGO PUBLIC LIBRARY/LANGUAGES AND LITERATURES SECTION, 820 East Street, San Diego 92101/ FR, GE, IT, JP, PT, RU, SP, VI.

B-50. SAN FRANCISCO PUBLIC LIBRARY, Civic Center, San Francisco 94102/ CH, CZ, DA, DU, FI, FR, GE, GR(mo), HU, IT, JP, NW, PO, PT, RU, S/C, SP, SW, YD.

B-51. SAN JOSE PUBLIC LIBRARY/BIBLIOTECA LATINA AMERICANA, 690 Locust Street, San Jose 95110/ SP.

B-52. SANTA ANA PUBLIC LIBRARY, 26 Civic Center Plaza, Santa Ana 92702/ FR, GE, IT, JP, RU, SP, VI.

B-53. SANTA FE SPRINGS CITY LIBRARY, 11700 East Telegraph Road, Santa Fe Springs 90670/ SP.

B-54. SANTA MONICA PUBLIC LIBRARY, 1343 Sixth Street, Santa Monica 90406/ CH, FR, GE, HU, IT, JP, RU, SP, SW, YD.

B-55. STANISLAUS COUNTY FREE LIBRARY, 1500 I Street, Modesto 95354/ CA, LO, SP, VI.

B-56. TORRANCE PUBLIC LIBRARY, 3301 Torrance Boulevard, Torrance 90503/ CH, DA, FR, GE, GR(mo), HU, IT, JP, KO, PO, RU, SP, SW, TH.

B-57. UNITED IRISH CULTURAL CENTER LIBRARY, 2700 45th Avenue, San Francisco 94116/ IR.

B-58. U.P.E.C. CULTURAL CENTER LIBRARY, 1120 East 14th Street, San Leandro 94577/ PT.

COLORADO (CO)

B-59. COSTILLA COUNTY LIBRARY, 402 Main Street, P.O. Box 351, San Luis 81152/ SP.

B-60. DENVER PUBLIC LIBRARY, 1357 Broadway, Denver 80203/ AB, CH, CZ, DA, DU, FR, GE, GR(mo), HU, IT, JP, KO, NW, PO, PT, RU, S/C, SV, SW, UK, YD.

B-61. LIBRARY OF THE UKRAINIAN RESEARCH FOUNDATION, 6931 South Yosemite Street, Englewood 80110/ UK.

B-62. MUSLIM BIBLIOGRAPHIC CENTER LIBRARY, P.O. Box 10191, Denver 80210/ AB.

CONNECTICUT (CT)

B-63. AMERICAN LITHUANIAN CULTURAL ARCHIVES LIBRARY, Thurber Road, Putnam 06260/ LI.

B-64. BRIDGEPORT PUBLIC LIBRARY, 925 Broad Street, Bridgeport 06604/ FR, GE, HU, IT, PO, PT, RU, SL, SP, SW, YD.

B-65. NORWALK PUBLIC LIBRARY, 1 Belden Avenue, Norwalk 06850/ FR, GE, GR(mo), HU, IT, PO, SP.

B-66. STAMFORD PUBLIC LIBRARY/THE FERGUSON LIBRARY, 1 Public Library Plaza, Stamford 06904/ FR, GE, IT, PO, RU, SP.

DELAWARE (DE)

B-67. NEWARK FREE LIBRARY, 750 Library Avenue, Newark 19711/ SP.

B-68. WILMINGTON INSTITUTE LIBRARY, Tenth and Market Streets, Wilmington 19801/ SP.

DISTRICT OF COLUMBIA (DC)

B-69. BRAZILIAN-AMERICAN CULTURAL INSTITUTE, 4103 Connecticut Avenue NW, Washington 20008/ PT(br).

B-70. FREDERICK DOUGLASS INSTITUTE MUSEUM OF AFRICAN ART LIBRARY, 318 A Street NW, Washington 20002/AFL.

B-71. LIBRARY OF CONGRESS, 101 Independence Avenue SE, Washington 20540/ AB, AC, AF, AL, AR, AY, AZ, BG, BL, BR, BS, B/T, BU, BY, CA, CH, CT, CZ, DA, DU, ES, ET, FI, FL, FO, FR, GC, GE, GG, GR, GR(mo), H/C, HE, HI, HS, HU, IC, IN, IR, IT, JP, J/P, KO, LA, LD, LI, LO, LT, MA, ML, MM, MR, MT, MX, NA, NE, NW, PA, PE, PO, PS, PT, PV, QC, RM, RO, RO(ml), RU, SC, S/C, SD, SH, SL, SN, SP, SV, SW, SY, TH, TI, TM, TR, TT, TU, UK, UR, UZ, VI, WE, XH, and several hundred others.

B-72.   ORGANIZATION OF AMERICAN STATES/COLUMBUS MEMO-
RIAL LIBRARY, 19th Street and Constitution Avenue NW,
Washington 20006/ SP.

B-73.   PUBLIC LIBRARY OF THE DISTRICT OF COLUMBIA/MARTIN
LUTHER KING MEMORIAL LIBRARY, 901 G Street NW,
Washington 20001/ CH, DA, DU, FR, GE, GR(mo), HE,
HU, IT, JP, NW, PO, PT, RU, SP, SW, YD.

FLORIDA (FL)

B-74.   AMERICAN INSTITUTE OF POLISH CULTURE LIBRARY, 1000
Brickell Avenue, Suite 600, Miami 33131/ PO.

B-75.   BELLE GLADE MUNICIPAL LIBRARY, 530 South Main
Street, Belle Glade 33430/ SP.

B-76.   BLACK RESOURCES INFORMATION COORDINATING SERV-
ICES, 614 Howard Avenue and 222 West Pensacola Street,
Suite 125-9, Tallahassee/ AFL.

B-77.   BROWARD COUNTY DIVISION OF LIBRARIES, 100 South
Andrews Avenue, Fort Lauderdale 33301/ FR, GE, IT,
RU, SP, YD.

B-78.   DUNEDIN PUBLIC LIBRARY, 223 Douglas Avenue, Dunedin
34698/ FR, GE.

B-79.   GULFPORT PUBLIC LIBRARY, 5501 28th Avenue South,
Gulfport 33707/ RU.

B-80.   HIALEAH JOHN F. KENNEDY LIBRARY, 190 West 49th
Street, Hialeah 33012/ SP.

B-81.   JACKSONVILLE PUBLIC LIBRARIES, 122 North Ocean
Street, Jacksonville 32202/ FR, GE, IT, SP.

B-82.   MIAMI-DADE PUBLIC LIBRARY, 101 West Flagler
Street, Miami 33130/ FR, GE, HU, IT, PO, PT, RU, SP,
YD.

B-83.   ORLANDO COUNTY LIBRARY HEADQUARTERS, 101 East
Central Boulevard, Orlando 32801/ FR, GE, KO, SP,
VI.

B-84.   STATE LIBRARY OF FLORIDA/DIVISION OF LIBRARY SERV-
ICES, R. A. Gray Building, Tallahassee 32399/ SP.

B-85.   TARPON SPRINGS PUBLIC LIBRARY, Craig Park, Spring
Boulevard, Springs 34689/ GR(mo).

GEORGIA (GA)

B-86.   ATLANTA FULTON PUBLIC LIBRARY, 1 Margaret Mitchell
Square NW, Atlanta 30303/ FR, GE, IT, RU, SP.

B-87.   HUNGARIAN CULTURAL FOUNDATION LIBRARY, 755 Columbia Drive, Suite 612, Decatur 30030/ HU.

HAWAII (HI)

B-88.　HAWAII STATE PUBLIC LIBRARY SYSTEM, 465 South King Street, Honolulu 96813/ CH, FL, FR, GE, IT, JP, KO, SP, VI.

IDAHO (ID)

B-89.　BOISE PUBLIC LIBRARY AND INFORMATION CENTER, 715 Capitol Boulevard, Boise 83702/ FR, SP.

B-90.　IDAHO STATE LIBRARY, 325 West State Street, Boise 83702/ SP.

B-91.　TWIN FALLS PUBLIC LIBRARY, 434 Second Street East, Twin Falls 83301/ FR, GE, SP.

ILLINOIS (IL)

B-92.　AMERICAN LITHUANIAN MUSICIANS ALLIANCE LIBRARY, 7310 South California Avenue, Chicago 60629/ LI.

B-93.　BALZEKAS MUSEUM OF LITHUANIAN CULTURE LIBRARY, 6500 South Pulaski Road, Chicago 60629/ LI.

B-94.　BUDDHIST EDUCATIONAL CENTER LIBRARY, 4645 North Racine Avenue, Chicago 60640/ JP.

B-95.　CENTER FOR BELGIAN CULTURE OF WESTERN ILLINOIS LIBRARY, 712 18th Avenue, Moline 61265/ FR.

B-96.　CHICAGO PUBLIC LIBRARY/FOREIGN LANGUAGE SECTION, 400 South State Street, Chicago 60605/ AB, AL, AR, BG, BL, CH, CZ, DA, DU, FI, FR, GE, GJ, HE, HI, HU, IR, IT, JP, KO, LI, LT, NW, PE, PO, PT, RO, RU, S/C, SV, SW, UK, UR, VI, YD.

B-97.　CROATIAN ETHNIC INSTITUTE LIBRARY, 4851 South Drexel Boulevard, Chicago 60616/ S/C.

B-98.　CZECHOSLOVAK HERITAGE AND MUSEUM LIBRARY, 2701 South Harlem Avenue, Berwyn 60402/ CZ, SL.

B-99.　ELMWOOD PARK PUBLIC LIBRARY, 4 Conti Parkway, Elmwood Park 60635/ IT.

B-100.　FIELD MUSEUM OF NATURAL HISTORY LIBRARY, Roosevelt Road and Lake Shore Drive, Chicago 60605/ TI.

B-101.　HIGHWOOD PUBLIC LIBRARY, 102 Highwood Avenue, Highwood 60040/ IT.

B-102.　LIBRARY OF LITHUANIAN MUSICOLOGY, 2345 West 56th Street, Chicago 60636/ LI.

B-103.　NEWBERRY LIBRARY, 60 West Walton Street, Chicago 60610/ BS, CN, FL, FR, GE, HW, IR, IT, MX, NAL, PT, RU, SP, WE, and others.

B-104.　POLISH MUSEUM OF AMERICA LIBRARY, 984 North Milwaukee Street, Chicago 60622/ PO.

B-105. POLISH WOMEN'S ALLIANCE OF AMERICA LIBRARY, 984 North Milwaukee Street, Chicago 60622/ PO.
B-106. SISTERS OF ST. CASIMIR LITHUANIAN CULTURAL MUSEUM LIBRARY, 2601 West Marquette Road, Chicago 60629/ LI.
B-107. SWEDISH AMERICAN HISTORICAL SOCIETY LIBRARY, 5125 North Spaulding Street, Rockford 60625/ SW.
B-108. SZATHMARY ARCHIVES LIBRARY, 2218 North Lincoln Avenue, Chicago 60614/ HU.
B-109. TINLEY PARK PUBLIC LIBRARY, 17101 South 71st Avenue, Tinley Park 60477/ GE.
B-110. UKRAINIAN NATIONAL MUSEUM LIBRARY, 2453 West Chicago Avenue, Chicago 60622/ UK.
B-111. VIVEKANANDA VEDANTA SOCIETY LIBRARY, 5423 South Hyde Park Boulevard, Chicago 60615/ HI.
B-112. WESTMONT PUBLIC LIBRARY, 37 East Richmond Street, Westmont 60559/ CZ.
B-113. WORLD LITHUANIAN ARCHIVES LIBRARY, 5620 South Claremont Avenue, Chicago 60636/ LI.

INDIANA (IN)
B-114. ASSOCIATION OF ROMANIAN CATHOLICS OF AMERICA LIBRARY, 4309 Olcott Avenue, East Chicago 46312/ RO.
B-115. INDIANAPOLIS–MARION COUNTY PUBLIC LIBRARY, 40 East Saint Clair Street, Indianapolis 46206/ FR, GE, IT, JP, RU, SP.

IOWA (IA)
B-116. CZECH HERITAGE FOUNDATION LIBRARY, P.O. Box 761, Cedar Rapids 52406/ CZ, SL.
B-117. DAVENPORT PUBLIC LIBRARY, 321 Main Street, Davenport 52801/ SP.
B-118. KIMBALTON PUBLIC LIBRARY, Box 67, Kimbalton 51543/ DA.
B-119. PUBLIC LIBRARY OF DES MOINES, 100 Locust Avenue, Des Moines 50309/ FR.

KANSAS (KS)
B-120. DODGE CITY PUBLIC LIBRARY, 1001 Second Avenue, Dodge City 67801/ SP.
B-121. GRANT COUNTY LIBRARY, 215 East Grant Street, Ulysses 67780/ SP.
B-122. JOHNSON COUNTY LIBRARY, Shawney Mission Parkway, P.O. Box 2901, Shawnee Mission 66201/ FR, SP.

B-123. KANSAS CITY PUBLIC LIBRARY, 625 Minnesota Avenue, Kansas City 66101/ SP.

B-124. NEWTON PUBLIC LIBRARY, 720 North Oak Street, Newton 67114/ SP.

B-125. WICHITA PUBLIC LIBRARY, 223 South Main Street, Wichita 67202/ FR, SP.

KENTUCKY (KY)

B-126. LOUISVILLE FREE PUBLIC LIBRARY, 301 York Street, Louisville 40203/ FR.

LOUISIANA (LA)

B-127. JEFFERSON PARISH LIBRARY, 3420 North Causeway Boulevard, P.O. Box 7490, Metairie 70010/ FR, GE, SP.

B-128. LOUISIANA STATE LIBRARY, 760 Riverside North, Baton Rouge 70802/ FR, GE, IT, SP.

B-129. NEW ORLEANS PUBLIC LIBRARY, 219 Loyola Avenue, New Orleans 70140/ CH, FR, GE, IT, SP, VI.

MAINE (ME)

B-130. LE CENTRE D'HÉRITAGE FRANCO-AMÉRICAIN, 81 Ash Street, Lewiston 04240/ FR.

B-131. MAINE STATE LIBRARY, LMA Building, State House Station 64, Augusta 04333/ FR.

MARYLAND (MD)

B-132. ENOCH PRATT FREE LIBRARY, 400 Cathedral Street, Baltimore 21201/ CZ, DA, DU, FI, FR, GE, GR(mo), HE, HU, IT, JP, LI, NW, PO, PT, RU, S/C, SL, SP, SW, UK, VI.

B-133. VIETNAMESE CULTURAL ASSOCIATION OF NORTH AMERICA LIBRARY, P.O. Box 1884, Rockville 20850/ VI.

MASSACHUSETTS (MA)

B-134. ALBANIAN ORTHODOX DIOCESE OF AMERICA LIBRARY, 54 Burroughs Street, Jamaica Plain 02130/ AL.

B-135. AMERICAN JEWISH HISTORICAL SOCIETY LIBRARY, Waltham 02154/ YD.

B-136. ARMENIAN LIBRARY AND MUSEUM OF AMERICA, 65 Main Street, Watertown 02172/ AR.

B-137. BOSTON PUBLIC LIBRARY, 666 Boylston Street, Box 286, Boston 02117/ AB, AF, AL, AR, BG, BL, CH, CZ, DA,

ES, FI, FR, GE, GJ, GR(mo), HE, HI, HU, IC, IT, JP, KO, LI, LT, NW, PO, PT, RO, RU, S/C, SH, SL, SP, SV, SW, TU, VI, YD.

B-138.   BROOKLINE PUBLIC LIBRARY, 361 Washington Street, Brookline 02146/ FR, GE, IT, RU, SP, YD.

B-139.   CAMBRIDGE PUBLIC LIBRARY/CENTRAL SQUARE BRANCH, 45 Pearl Street, Cambridge 02139/ FR, GR(mo), SP.

B-140.   CHELSEA PUBLIC LIBRARY, 569 Broadway, Chelsea 02150/ SP, YD.

B-141.   CHICOPEE PUBLIC LIBRARY SYSTEM, Market Square, Chicopee 01013/ PO.

B-142.   FALL RIVER PUBLIC LIBRARY, 104 North Main Street, Fall River 02720/ GE, GR(mo), PO, PT.

B-143.   FITCHBURG PUBLIC LIBRARY, 610 Main Street, Fitchburg 01420/ FI, FR, GE, SP.

B-144.   FORBES LIBRARY, 20 West Street, Northampton 01060/ AB, DA, FR, GE, GR(mo), HE, IR, IT, JP, NW, PO, PT, RU, SP.

B-145.   FRAMINGHAM PUBLIC LIBRARY, 49 Lexington Street, Framingham 01701/ SP.

B-145/a.   FRENCH LIBRARY/BOSTON, 53 Marlborough Street, Boston 02116/ FR.

B-146.   NATIONAL ASSOCIATION FOR ARMENIAN STUDIES AND RESEARCH LIBRARY, 175 Mount Auburn Street, Cambridge 02138/ AR.

B-147.   NATIONAL YIDDISH BOOK CENTER LIBRARY, Old East Street School, P.O. Box 969, Amherst 01002/ YD.

B-148.   NEW BEDFORD FREE PUBLIC LIBRARY/CASA DE SAUDADE BRANCH, 58 Crapo Street, New Bedford 02740/ PT.

B-149.   PORTUGUESE CONTINENTAL UNION OF THE U.S. LIBRARY, 899 Boylston Street, Boston 02115/ PT.

B-150.   SHATTUCK LIBRARY, 75-A Newbury Street, Boston 02116/ SP.

B-151.   SPRINGFIELD CITY LIBRARY, 220 State Street, Springfield 01103/ FR, GE, GR(mo), IT, PO, RU, SP.

B-152.   TURKISH-AMERICAN CULTURAL SOCIETY LIBRARY, 678 Massachusetts Avenue, Cambridge 02139/ TU.

B-153.   WATERTOWN FREE PUBLIC LIBRARY, 123 Main Street, Watertown 02172/ AR.

MICHIGAN (MI)

B-154.   A.G.B.U. ALEX MANOOGIAN SCHOOL LIBRARY, 22001 Northwestern Highway, Southfield 48075/ AR.

B-155. ALBION PUBLIC LIBRARY, 501 South Superior Street, Albion 49224/ SP.

B-156. ANN ARBOR PUBLIC LIBRARY, 343 South Fifth Avenue, Ann Arbor 48104/ FR, GE, SP.

B-157. CALVIN LIBRARY, Burton Street, Grand Rapids 49506/ DU.

B-158. CENTER FOR AFRO-AMERICAN AND AFRICAN STUDIES, 1100 South University, Ann Arbor 48109/ AFL.

B-159. DETROIT PUBLIC LIBRARY, 5201 Woodward Avenue, Detroit 48202/ AB, AR, BL, CH, CZ, DA, DU, FI, FR, GE, GR(mo), HE, HI, HU, IT, JP, LI, LT, NW, PO, RO, RU, S/C, SL, SP, SV, SW, UK, UR, YD.

B-160. ESTONIAN EDUCATIONAL SOCIETY OF DETROIT LIBRARY, P.O. Box 344, Trenton 48183/ ES.

B-161. HAMTRAMCK PUBLIC LIBRARY/ALBERT J. ZAK MEMORIAL, 2360 Caniff Street, Hamtramck 48212/ PO, RU, UK.

B-162. HERRICK PUBLIC LIBRARY, 300 South River Avenue, Holland 49423/ DU, GE, SP, VI.

B-163. LATVIAN CENTER GAREZERS LIBRARY, Route 3, Box 363, Three Rivers 49093/ LT.

B-164. LIBRARY AND MUSEUM OF SLOVAK LANGUAGE, HISTORY, LITERATURE, AND CULTURE, 775 West Drahner Road, Oxford 48051/ SL.

B-165. MACEDONIAN ETHNIC LIBRARY, 920 Shoreham Road, Grosse Pointe Woods 48236/ MA.

B-166. MACOMB COUNTY LIBRARY, 16480 Hall Road, Mount Clemens 48044/ FR, GE, IT, PO.

B-167. MALTESE-AMERICAN BENEVOLENT SOCIETY LIBRARY, 1832 Michigan Avenue, Detroit 48216/ MT.

B-168. NETHERLANDS MUSEUM LIBRARY, 8 East 12th Street, Holland 49423/ DU.

B-169. OAK PARK LIBRARY, 14200 Oak Park Boulevard, Oak Park 48237/ RU.

B-170. PETER WHITE PUBLIC LIBRARY, 217 North Front Street, Marquette 49855/ FI.

B-171. PRENTIS MEMORIAL LIBRARY OF THE TEMPLE BETH EL, 7400 Telegraph Street, Birmingham 48010/ HE, YD.

B-172. ROMANIAN-AMERICAN HERITAGE CENTER, 2522 Grey Tower Road, Jackson 49201/ RO.

B-173. SOKOL DETROIT, 23600 West Warren Avenue, Dearborn Heights 48127/ CZ, SL.

B-174. WAKEFIELD PUBLIC LIBRARY, 401 Hancock Street, Wakefield 49968/ FI, PO.

B-175.   WARREN PUBLIC LIBRARY/ARTHUR J. MILLER BRANCH, 4700 East 13 Mile Road, Warren 48092/ FR, GE, IT, PO, RU, SP, UK.

MINNESOTA (MN)

B-176.   AMERICAN SWEDISH INSTITUTE LIBRARY, 2600 Park Avenue, Minneapolis 55407/ SW.

B-177.   BUHL PUBLIC LIBRARY, 400 Jones Avenue, Box 664, Buhl 55713/ FI, IT, SV.

B-178.   MINNEAPOLIS PUBLIC LIBRARY AND INFORMATION CENTER/LANGUAGE AND LITERATURE DEPARTMENT, 300 Nicollet Mall, Minneapolis 55401/ AB, CH, CZ, DA, DU, FI, FR, GE, GR, HU, IT, JP, LI, LT, NW, PO, RU, SP, SW, UK, VI, WE.

B-179.   SAINT PAUL PUBLIC LIBRARY, 90 West Fourth Street, Saint Paul 55102/ CZ, FR, GE, IT, NW, PO, RU, SP, SW, UK, YD.

B-180.   SONS OF NORWAY INTERNATIONAL LIBRARY, 1455 West Lake Street, Minneapolis 55408/ NW.

B-181.   VALDRES SAMBAND LIBRARY, Route No. 3, Box 86, Granite Falls 56241/ NW.

MISSOURI (MO)

B-182.   KANSAS CITY PUBLIC LIBRARY, 311 East 12th Street, Kansas City 64106/ FR, GE, PT, RU, SP, VI, YD.

B-183.   SAINT LOUIS PUBLIC LIBRARY, 1301 Olive Street, Saint Louis 63103/ CH, FR, GE, GR(mo), IT, PT, RU, SP, YD.

MONTANA (MT)

B-184.   GREAT FALLS PUBLIC LIBRARY/PATHFINDER FEDERATION OF LIBRARIES HEADQUARTERS, 301 Second Avenue North and Third Streets, Great Falls 59401/ DA, NW, SW.

NEBRASKA (NE)

B-185.   DVORACEK MEMORIAL LIBRARY, 419 West Third Street, Wilber 68465/ CZ.

B-186.   LINCOLN CITY LIBRARIES, 136 South 14th Street, Lincoln 68508/ FR, GE, SP.

B-187.   OMAHA PUBLIC LIBRARY/W. DALE CLARK LIBRARY, 215 South 15th Street, Omaha 68102/ AB, CH, CZ, DA, DU, FI, FR, GE, GR(mo), HE, HU, IT, JP, KO, LI, NW, PO, PT, RU, SP, SW, TH, UK, VI, YD.

NEVADA (NV)

B-188. LAS VEGAS-CLARK COUNTY LIBRARY DISTRICT, 1401 East Flamingo Road, Las Vegas 89109/ SP.

NEW HAMPSHIRE (NH)

B-189. ASSOCIATION CANADO-AMÉRICAINE LIBRARY AND MUSEUM, 52 Concord Street, Manchester 03101/ FR.

B-190. BERLIN PUBLIC LIBRARY, 270 Main Street, Berlin 03570/ FR.

B-191. ROCHESTER PUBLIC LIBRARY, 65 South Main Street, Rochester 03867/ FR.

NEW JERSEY (NJ)

B-192. BYELORUSSIAN INSTITUTE OF ARTS AND SCIENCES, 230 Springfield Avenue, Rutherford 07070/ BY.

B-193. DR. ANDREW T. UDVARY REFERENCE LIBRARY, 66 Plum Street, New Brunswick 08901/ HU.

B-194. ELIZABETH PUBLIC LIBRARY, 11 South Broad Street, Elizabeth 07202/ FR, GE, PO, SP, YD.

B-195. ENGLEWOOD PUBLIC LIBRARY, 31 Engle Street, Englewood 07631/ FR, GE, IT, SP.

B-196. LINDEN FREE PUBLIC LIBRARY, 31 East Henry Street, Linden 07036/ CZ, FR, GE, GR(mo), HU, IT, LI, LT, PO, RU, SL, SP, UK.

B-197. LODI MEMORIAL LIBRARY, 1 Memorial Drive, Lodi 07644/ IT, PT, SP.

B-198. NEW BRUNSWICK FREE PUBLIC LIBRARY, 60 Livingston Avenue, New Brunswick 08901/ GE, HU, RU, SP.

B-199. NEWARK PUBLIC LIBRARY, P.O. Box 630, Newark 07101/ CZ, DU, FR, GE, GR(mo), HE, HU, IT, LI, PO, PT, RU, SP, SW, UK, VI, YD.

B-200. SOUTH RIVER PUBLIC LIBRARY, 55 Appleby Avenue, South River 08882/ FR, GE, HU, PO, PT, RU.

B-201. WEST NEW YORK PUBLIC LIBRARY, 425 60th Street, West New York 07093/ SP.

NEW MEXICO (NM)

B-202. ALBUQUERQUE BERNALILLO COUNTY PUBLIC LIBRARY, 501 Cooper Avenue NW, Albuquerque 87102/ SP.

B-203. SOCORRO PUBLIC LIBRARY, 401 Park Street, Socorro 87801/ SP.

B-204. WHEELWRIGHT MUSEUM LIBRARY, 704 Camino Lejo, Sante Fe 87502/ NAL.

NEW YORK (NY)

B-205.   AMERICAN IRISH HISTORICAL SOCIETY LIBRARY, 991 Fifth Avenue, New York 10028/ IR.

B-206.   AMERICAN MUSEUM OF NATURAL HISTORY, 79th Street and Central Park West, New York 10024/ NAL.

B-207.   ASIAN AMERICAN RESOURCE CENTER, 199 Lafayette Street, New York 10012/ ASL.

B-208.   ASSOCIATION FOR PUERTO-RICAN HISPANIC CULTURE LIBRARY, 381 West Broadway, New York 10012/ SP.

B-209.   BANGLADESH CULTURAL ASSOCIATION LIBRARY, 60 Second Avenue, New York 10003/ BG.

B-210.   BRAZILIAN-AMERICAN SOCIETY LIBRARY, 57 West 46th Street, 2nd Floor, New York 10036/ PT(br).

B-211.   BROOKLYN MUSEUM LIBRARY, Eastern Parkway, Brooklyn 11238/ EG.

B-212.   BROOKLYN PUBLIC LIBRARY, Grand Army Plaza, Brooklyn 11238/ AB, BG, CH, CZ, DA, DU, FR, GE, GR(mo), HE, HI, HU, IN, IT, LI, LT, NW, PE, PO, PT, RO, RU, SP, SW, UK, UR, YD.

B-213.   BUFFALO AND ERIE COUNTY PUBLIC LIBRARY, Lafayette Square, Buffalo 14203/ FR, GE, HU, IT, PO, SP, SW, UK.

B-214.   BULGARIAN EASTERN ORTHODOX CHURCH/DIOCESE OF NEW YORK, 312 West 101st Street, New York 10025/ BL.

B-215.   BUND ARCHIVES OF THE JEWISH LABOR MOVEMENT/ LIBRARY, 25 East 21st Street, New York 10010/ FR, GE, PO, RU, YD.

B-216.   CHIAN FEDERATION OF AMERICA LIBRARY, 44-01 Broadway, New York 11103/ GR(mo).

B-217.   CHINESE INFORMATION SERVICE LIBRARY, 159 Lexington Avenue, New York 10016/ CH.

B-218.   CENTRAL YIDDISH CULTURAL ORGANIZATION LIBRARY, 25 East 78th Street, New York 10021/ YD.

B-219.   DIOCESE OF THE ARMENIAN CHURCH OF AMERICA/LIBRARY, 630 Second Avenue, New York 10016/AR.

B-220.   EL MUSEO DEL BARRIO LIBRARY, 1945 Third Avenue, New York 10020/ SP.

B-221.   ESTONIAN HOUSE LIBRARY, 243 East 34th Street, New York 10016/ ES.

B-222.   FILIPINAS AMERICAS SCIENCE AND ARTS FOUNDATION LIBRARY, 1209 Park Avenue, New York 10028/ FL.

B-223.   FRENCH INSTITUTE/ALLIANCE FRANÇAISE LIBRARY, 22 East 60th Street, New York 10022/ FR.

B-224. GATES PUBLIC LIBRARY, 1605 Buffalo Road, Rochester 14624/ IT.

B-225. GOETHE HOUSE LIBRARY, 1014 Fifth Avenue, New York 10028/ GE.

B-226. HARRISON PUBLIC LIBRARY, Bruce Avenue, Harrison 10528/ IT, JP.

B-227. HEMPSTEAD PUBLIC LIBRARY, 115 Nichols Court, Hempstead 11550/ CH, DU, FR, GE, GR(mo), HE, HU, JP, PO, PT, RU, SP, YD.

B-228. HOLY TRINITY MONASTERY AND ORTHODOX SEMINARY LIBRARY, Jordanville 13361/ RU.

B-229. HOWLAND PUBLIC LIBRARY COMPANY, 313 Main Street, Beacon 12508/ SP.

B-230. ISLAMIC CENTER OF NEW YORK LIBRARY, 1 Riverside Drive, New York 10023/ AB.

B-231. ITALIAN CULTURAL INSTITUTE LIBRARY, 686 Park Avenue, New York 10021/ IT.

B-232. JACQUES MANCHAIS CENTER OF TIBETAN ART LIBRARY, 338 Lighthouse Avenue, New York 10306/ TI.

B-233. JAMES PRENDERGAST LIBRARY ASSOCIATION, 509 Cherry Street, Jamestown 14701/ DA, NW, SW.

B-234. JAPAN SOCIETY/LIBRARY, 333 East 47th Street, New York 10017/ JP.

B-235. KOSCIUSZKO FOUNDATION LIBRARY, 15 East 65th Street, New York 10021/ PO.

B-236. LITHUANIAN CULTURAL CENTER LIBRARY, 361 Highland Boulevard, New York 11207/ LI.

B-237. LONG BEACH PUBLIC LIBRARY, 111 West Park Avenue, Long Beach 11561/ HE, SP.

B-238. MASTICS-MORICHES-SHIRLEY COMMUNITY LIBRARY, William Floyd Parkway, Shirley 11967/ IT.

B-239. NEW YORK HISPANIC SOCIETY OF AMERICA, 613 West 155th Street, New York 10032/ CT, PT, SP.

B-240. NEW YORK PUBLIC LIBRARY/BELMONT REGIONAL BRANCH, 610 East 186th Street, New York 10458/ IT.

B-241. NEW YORK PUBLIC LIBRARY/BRONX REFERENCE CENTER, 2556 Bainbridge Avenue, New York 10458-4698/ SP.

B-242. NEW YORK PUBLIC LIBRARY/CHATHAM SQUARE REGIONAL BRANCH, 33 East Broadway, New York 10002/ CH.

B-243. NEW YORK PUBLIC LIBRARY/DONNELL LIBRARY CENTER/ FOREIGN LANGUAGE LIBRARY, 20 West 53rd Street, New York 10019/ AB, AL, AR, BG, BL, CH, CZ, DA, DU, ES, FI, FR, GE, GJ, GR(mo), H/C, HE, HI, HU, IT, JP,

KO, LI, LT, MR, NW, PE, PO, PT, RO, RU, S/C, SL, SP, SW, TE, TH, TM, TU, UK, UR, VI, YD, and several others in smaller collections.

B-244. NEW YORK PUBLIC LIBRARY/HUNT'S POINT REGIONAL BRANCH, 877 Southern Boulevard, New York 10459/ SP.

B-245. NEW YORK PUBLIC LIBRARY/RESEARCH LIBRARIES, Fifth Avenue and 42nd Street, New York 10018/ AA, AB, AI, AR, AS, BL, BY, CA, CH, CS, CV, CZ, EG, ES, ET, FL, FR, GE, HE, HI, HS, HU, IT, JP, KH, KO, LI, LT, MA, MO, MR, NAL, NW, OS, PA, PE, PL, PO, PR, PT, PV, RO, RO(ml), RU, S/C, SD, SI, SL, SP, SS, S/S, S/Y, TH, TI, TJ, T/M, TU, T/U, T/V, UA, UI, UK, UR, VI, VO, VT, WE, YA, YD, and several others in smaller collections.

B-246. NEW YORK PUBLIC LIBRARY/SAINT GEORGE LIBRARY CENTER, 450 Saint Mark's Place, New York 10301/ SP.

B-247. NEW YORK PUBLIC LIBRARY/SCHOMBURG CENTER FOR RESEARCH IN BLACK CULTURE, 515 Lenox Avenue, New York 10037/ AM, BE, BM, EW, FA, FU, GA, GN, HS, IG, KG, KU, KY, LB, LG, LZ, ME, MG, M/G, ND, NJ, RW, S/G, SH, SN, SO, ST, TG, T/G, TW, T/W, VA, VN, XH, YO, ZU, and hundreds of other AFL in smaller collections.

B-248. NEW YORK PUBLIC LIBRARY/SEWARD PARK BRANCH, 192 East Broadway, New York 10002/ CH, HE, SP, YD.

B-249. NEW YORK STATE LIBRARY/DEPARTMENT OF EDUCA-TION, Empire State Plaza, Albany 12230/ AG, DU, IQ.

B-250. PAN-MACEDONIAN ASSOCIATION LIBRARY, 246 Eighth Avenue, New York 10011/ MA.

B-251. PILSUDSKI INSTITUTE OF AMERICA LIBRARY, 381 Park Avenue South, New York 10016/ FR, PO.

B-252. POLISH INSTITUTE OF ARTS AND SCIENCES IN AMERICA/ LIBRARY, 208 East 30th Street, New York 10016/ PO.

B-253. PUERTO RICAN HERITAGE MUSEUM LIBRARY, 150 Fifth Avenue, New York 10011/ SP.

B-254. QUEENS BOROUGH PUBLIC LIBRARY/CENTRAL LIBRARY, 89-11 Merrick Boulevard, New York 11432/ AB, AL, AR, BG, BL, CH, CZ, DA, DU, ES, FI, FR, GE, GJ, GR(mo), HE, HI, HU, IT, JP, KO, LI, LT, NW, PJ, PO, PT, RO, RU, S/C, SL, SV, SW, UK, UR, VI, YD.

B-255. ROCHESTER PUBLIC LIBRARY, 115 South Avenue, Rochester 14604/ FR, GE, HE, HU, IT, PO, RU, SP, UK, YD.

B-256. ROMANIAN LIBRARY, 200 East 38th Street, New York 10016/ RO.

B-257. SHEVCHENKO SCIENTIFIC SOCIETY LIBRARY, 63 Fourth Avenue, New York 10003/ UK.

B-258. SUFFOLK COOPERATIVE LIBRARY SYSTEM, 627 North Sunrise Service Road, Bellport 11713/ AB, CH, CZ, DA, DU, FI, FR, GE, GR(mo), HE, HI, HU, IT, JP, KO, NW, PO, PT, RU, SL, SP, SW, TU, UK, UR, VI, YD.

B-259. TAMIL SANGHAM NEW YORK/LIBRARY, 166 Logan Avenue, New York 10301/ TM.

B-260. TOLSTOY FOUNDATION/ALEXANDRA TOLSTOY MEMORIAL LIBRARY, Rockland Lake Road, Valley Cottage 10989/ RU.

B-261. TURKISH-AMERICAN ASSOCIATION LIBRARY, 1472 Broadway, New York 10036/ TU.

B-262. UKRAINIAN ACADEMY OF ARTS AND SCIENCES IN THE U.S./LIBRARY, 206 West 100th Street, New York 10025/ UK.

B-263. WILLIAM HENRY SCHOFELD MEMORIAL LIBRARY, 127 East 73rd Street, New York 10021/ DA, FI, IC, NW, SW.

B-264. YIVO INSTITUTE FOR JEWISH RESEARCH LIBRARY, 1048 Fifth Avenue, New York 10028/ HE, YD.

NORTH CAROLINA (NC)

B-265. NORTH CAROLINA FOREIGN LANGUAGE CENTER/CUMBERLAND COUNTY PUBLIC LIBRARY, 300 Maiden Lane, Fayetteville 28301/ AB, BG, CH, CZ, DA, DU, FI, FR, GE, GJ, GR(mo), HE, HI, HU, IT, JP, KO, MR, PJ, PO, PT, RU, SP, TH, UR, VI, YD.

B-266. PUBLIC LIBRARY OF CHARLOTTE AND MECKLENBURG COUNTY, 310 North Tryon Street, Charlotte 28202/ FR, GE.

OHIO (OH)

B-267. AKRON–SUMMIT COUNTY PUBLIC LIBRARY, 55 South Main Street, Akron 44236/ DU, FR, GE, HU, IT, RO, RU, SL, SP.

B-268. CINCINNATI HISTORICAL SOCIETY LIBRARY, 1301 Western Avenue, Cincinnati 45202/ GE.

B-269. CLEVELAND PUBLIC LIBRARY/FOREIGN LANGUAGE DEPARTMENT, 325 Superior Avenue, Cleveland 44114/ AB, AR, BL, BY, CH, CZ, DA, DU, EG, ES, FI, FR, GE, GR(mo), HE, HU, IR, IT, JP, KO, LI, LT, NW, PO,

PT, RO, RU, S/C, SH, SL, SP, SV, SW, TI, TU, UK, VI, WE, YD.

B-270. CLEVELAND ROMANIAN CULTURAL AND ART CENTER, 3256 Warren Road, Cleveland 44111/ RO.

B-271. CUYAHOGA COUNTY PUBLIC LIBRARY, 4510 Memphis Avenue, Cleveland 44144/ FR, GE, IT, RU, SP.

B-272. DAYTON AND MONTGOMERY COUNTY PUBLIC LIBRARY, 215 East Third Street, Dayton 45402/ FR, GE, HU, RU, SP.

B-273. FAIRPORT PUBLIC LIBRARY, 335 Vine Street, Fairport Harbor 44077/ FI, HU.

B-274. LATVIAN ASSOCIATION OF CLEVELAND LIBRARY, 1385 Andrews Avenue, Lakewood 44107/ LT.

B-275. METROPOLITAN LIBRARY OF COLUMBUS, 69 South Grant Avenue, Columbus 43215/ FR, GE, IT, SP.

B-276. PUBLIC LIBRARY OF CINCINNATI AND HAMILTON COUNTY, 800 Vine Street, Cincinnati 45202/ DA, DU, FR, GE, GR(mo), HE, HU, IT, PO, PT, RU, SP, SW, YD.

B-277. REUBEN McMILLAND FREE LIBRARY ASSOCIATION, 305 Wick Avenue, Youngstown 44503/ FR, GE, HU, IT, PO, RU, S/C, SL, SP.

B-278. SAINT EPHREM EDUCATIONAL CENTER LIBRARY, 155 South Meridian Road, Youngstown 44511/ AR, SY.

B-279. SLOVAK INSTITUTE LIBRARY, 2900 East Boulevard, Cleveland 44104/ SL.

B-280. TOLEDO–LUCAS COUNTY PUBLIC LIBRARY, 325 Michigan Street, Toledo 43624/ AB, FR, GE, GR(mo), IT, PO, RU, SP, YD.

B-281. UKRAINIAN MUSEUM-ARCHIVES LIBRARY, 1202 Kenilworth Avenue, Cleveland 44113/ UK.

B-282. WAUSEON PUBLIC LIBRARY, 117 East Elm Street, Wauseon 43567/ SP.

B-283. WELSH-AMERICAN HERITAGE MUSEUM LIBRARY, East Main Street, Oak Hill 45656/ WE.

B-283/a. WESTERN RESERVE HISTORICAL SOCIETY LIBRARY, 10825 East Boulevard, Cleveland 44106/ CZ, GE, IT, MX, PO, YD.

OKLAHOMA (OK)

B-284. FIVE CIVILIZED TRIBES MUSEUM LIBRARY, Agency Hill, Honor Heights Drive, Muskogee 74401/ NAL.

B-285. SOUTHERN PRAIRIE LIBRARY SYSTEM, 421 North Hudson Street, Drawer U, Altus 83521/ SP.

B-286. TULSA CITY-COUNTY LIBRARY, 400 Civic Center, Tulsa 74103/ FR, GE.

OREGON (OR)

B-287. ASTORIA PUBLIC LIBRARY, 450 Tenth Street, Astoria 97103/ FI, NW, SW.

B-288. INDEPENDENCE PUBLIC LIBRARY, 311 South Monmouth Street, Independence 97351/ SP.

B-289. LIBRARY ASSOCIATION OF PORTLAND/MULTNOMAH COUNTY LIBRARY, 205 NE Russell Street, Portland 97212/ CH, DU, FR, GE, GR(mo), HE, HU, IT, KO, NW, PO, RU, SP, SW, VI, YD.

B-290. WOODBURN PUBLIC LIBRARY, 280 Garfield Street, Woodburn 97071/ RU, SP.

PENNSYLVANIA (PA)

B-291. AMERICAN PHILOSOPHICAL SOCIETY LIBRARY, 105 South Fifth Street, Philadelphia 19106/ NAL.

B-292. AMERICAN SWEDISH HISTORICAL MUSEUM LIBRARY, 1900 Pattison Avenue, Philadelphia 19145/ SW.

B-293. BALCH INSTITUTE, Seventh and Ramstead Streets, Philadelphia 19106/ CZ, RU, SL, UK, YD, and others.

B-294. BETHLEHEM PUBLIC LIBRARY, 11 West Church Street, Bethlehem 18018/ SP.

B-295. CARNEGIE LIBRARY OF PITTSBURGH, 4400 Forbes Avenue, Pittsburgh 15213/ FR, GE, HE, IT, RU, S/C, SP, UK, YD.

B-296. CROATIAN FRATERNAL UNION LIBRARY, 100 Delaney Drive, Pittsburgh 15235/ S/C.

B-297. FREE LIBRARY OF PHILADELPHIA, Logan Square, Philadelphia 19103/ CH, DU, FR, GE, GR(mo), HE, HU, IT, JP, KO, PO, PT, RU, SP, SW, UK, VI, YD.

B-298. GERMAN SOCIETY OF PENNSYLVANIA LIBRARY, 611 Spring Garden Street, Philadelphia 14123/ GE.

B-299. JANKOTA LIBRARY AND SLAVIC ARCHIVES, Danville 17821/ SL.

B-300. JEDNOTA MUSEUM AND INSTITUTE LIBRARY, 1015 Rosedale Avenue, Middletown 17057/ SL.

B-301. MENNONITE HERITAGE CENTER LIBRARY, 24 South Main Street, Souderton 18640/ DU, GE, GE(sw).

B-302. MOLODA PROSWITA LIBRARY, 23rd and Brown Streets, Philadelphia 19130/ UK.

B-303. NATIONAL SLOVAK SOCIETY OF THE U.S.A. LIBRARY, 2325 East Carson Street, Pittsburgh 15203/ SL.

B-304. OSTERHOUT FREE LIBRARY, 71 South Franklin Street, Wilkes-Barre 18701/ FR, GE, SP.

B-305. PENNSYLVANIA DUTCH FOLK CULTURE SOCIETY LIBRARY, Lenhartsville 19534/ GE(pa).

B-306. PENNSYLVANIA GERMAN SOCIETY LIBRARY, R.D.I. Box 469, Brenigsville 18031/ GE.

B-307. SCOTCH-IRISH SOCIETY OF THE U.S.A. LIBRARY, 250 Booth Lane, Haverford 19041/ IR, SC.

B-308. WELSH GUILD, 1724 Arch Street, Philadelphia 19103/ WE.

B-309. WILLIAM MORRIS McCLAIN MEMORIAL LIBRARY, 2137 MacLarie Lane, Broomall 19008/ SC.

RHODE ISLAND (RI)

B-310. CENTRAL FALLS FREE PUBLIC LIBRARY, 205 Central Street, Central Falls 02863/ FR, PT, SP.

B-311. CUMBERLAND PUBLIC LIBRARY, 1464 Diamond Hill Road, Cumberland 02864/ PT.

B-312. EAST PROVIDENCE PUBLIC LIBRARY, 41 Grove Avenue, East Providence 02914/ PT.

B-313. MARIAN J. MOHR MEMORIAL LIBRARY, 1 Memorial Drive, Johnston 02919/ IT.

B-314. NEWPORT PUBLIC LIBRARY, Acquidneck Park Box 8, Newport 02840/ FR.

B-315. PAWTUCKET PUBLIC LIBRARY, 13 Summer Street, Pawtucket 02860/ FR, PO, PT, SP.

B-316. PROVIDENCE PUBLIC LIBRARY, 225 Washington Street, Providence 02903/ AB, AR, DA, FI, FR, GE, GR(mo), HE, IT, LI, NW, PO, PT, RU, SP, SW, YD.

B-317. ROGERS FREE LIBRARY, 525 Hope Street, Bristol 02809/ PT.

B-318. WESTERLY PUBLIC LIBRARY, 38 Broad Street, Westerly 02891/ IT.

B-319. WOONSOCKET HARRIS PUBLIC LIBRARY, 303 Clinton Street, Woonsocket 02895/ FR.

SOUTH CAROLINA (SC)

B-320. CHARLESTON COUNTY LIBRARY, 404 King Street, Charleston 29414/ FR, GE, SP.

B-321. GREENVILLE COUNTY LIBRARY, 300 College Street, Greenville 29601/ FR, GE, SP.

SOUTH DAKOTA (SD)

B-322. PHOEBE APPERSON HEARST LIBRARY, 315 West Main Street, P.O.B. 248, Mitchell 57356/ CZ, FI, FR, GE, IT, NW, S/C, SV.

TENNESSEE (TN)

B-323. CHATTANOOGA–HAMILTON COUNTY BICENTENNIAL LIBRARY, 1001 Broad Street, Chattanooga 37402/ FR, GE, SP.

B-324. MEMPHIS–SHELBY COUNTY PUBLIC LIBRARY AND INFORMATION CENTER, 1850 Peabody Street, Memphis 38104/ FR, GE, IT, RU, SP.

TEXAS (TX)

B-325. ALICE PUBLIC LIBRARY, 401 East Third Street, Alice 78332/ SP.

B-326. CENTRAL TEXAS LIBRARY SYSTEM/AUSTIN PUBLIC LIBRARY, 810 Guadalupe Street, P.O. Box 2287, Austin 78768/ SP.

B-327. DALLAS PUBLIC LIBRARY, 1515 Young Street, Dallas 75201/ FR, GE, SP.

B-328. DEAF SMITH COUNTY LIBRARY, 211 East Fourth Street, Hereford 79045/ SP.

B-329. DONNA PUBLIC LIBRARY, 301 South Main Street, Donna 78537/ SP.

B-330. EAGLE PASS PUBLIC LIBRARY, 589 Main Street, Eagle Pass 78852/ SP.

B-331. EL PASO COUNTY LIBRARY, Drawer 788, 601 Tenth Street, Fabens 79838/ SP.

B-332. EL PASO PUBLIC LIBRARY, 501 North Oregon Street, El Paso 79901/ FR, GE, RU, SP.

B-333. HILLSBORO CITY LIBRARY, 118 South Waco Street, Hillsboro 76645/ SP.

B-334. HOUSTON PUBLIC LIBRARY, 500 McKinney Avenue, Houston 77002/ FR, GE, SP.

B-335. McALLEN MEMORIAL LIBRARY, 601 North Main Street, McAllen 78501/ SP.

B-336. MERCEDES MEMORIAL LIBRARY, 434 South Ohio Street, Mercedes 78570/ SP.

B-337. MULESHOE AREA PUBLIC LIBRARY, 322 West Second Street, Muleshoe 79347/ SP.

B-338. PHARR MEMORIAL LIBRARY, 200 South Athol Street, Pharr 78577/ SP.

B-339. SAN ANTONIO PUBLIC LIBRARY, 203 South Saint Mary's Street, San Antonio 78205/ SP.

B-340. SLAVONIC BENEVOLENT ORDER OF TEXAS LIBRARY AND MUSEUM, 520 North Main Street, Temple 76501/ SL.

B-341. TEXAS PANHANDLE LIBRARY SYSTEM, 413 East 4th Street, Box 2171, Amarillo 79189/ SP.

B-342. VAL VERDE COUNTY LIBRARY, 300 Spring Street, Del Rio 78840/ SP.

UTAH (UT)

B-343. SALT LAKE CITY PUBLIC LIBRARY, 209 East Fifth Street, South, Salt Lake City 84111/ AB, DA, DU, FR, GE, GR(mo), IT, RU, SP, SW.

B-344. SALT LAKE COUNTY LIBRARY SYSTEM/WHITMORE LIBRARY, 2197 East 7000, South Salt Lake City 94121/ SP.

VERMONT (VT)

B-345. HASKELL FREE LIBRARY, Box 337, Derby Line 05830/ FR.

B-346. VERMONT DEPARTMENT OF LIBRARIES, Pavillion Office Building, 109 State Street, Montpelier 05609/ FR.

VIRGINIA (VA)

B-347. ARLINGTON COUNTY DEPARTMENT OF LIBRARIES, 2100 Clarendon Boulevard, Arlington 22201/ FR, GE, GR(mo), IT, KO, RU, SP, VI.

B-348. NORFOLK PUBLIC LIBRARY, 301 East City Hall Avenue, Norfolk 23510/ FR, GR(mo), SP.

WASHINGTON (WA)

B-349. OREGON PROVINCE ARCHIVES OF THE SOCIETY OF JESUS/ LIBRARY, NAL(manuscripts). [Transferred to A-1127]

B-350. SEATTLE PUBLIC LIBRARY, 1000 Fourth Avenue, Seattle 98104/ CH, CZ, DA, DU, EK, FI, FR, GE, GR(mo), HE, HU, IC, IT, JP, KO, LI, NW, PO, PT, RU, SP, SW, UK, VI, YD.

B-351. TACOMA PUBLIC LIBRARY, 1102 Tacoma Avenue, South Tacoma 98402/ FR, GE, NW, RU, SP, SW.

B-352. TIMBERLAND REGIONAL LIBRARY, 415 Airdustrial Way SW, Olympia 98501/ FI.

WEST VIRGINIA (WV)

B-353. KANAWHA COUNTY PUBLIC LIBRARY, 123 Capitol Street, Charleston 25301/ FR, GE, IT, SP.

WISCONSIN (WI)

B-354. DODGE COUNTY LIBRARY SERVICE, 311 B North Street, Beaver Dam 53916/ SP.

B-355. MADISON PUBLIC LIBRARY, 201 West Mifflin Street, Madison 53703/ FR, GE, IT, NW, RU, SP, SW.

B-356. MILWAUKEE PUBLIC LIBRARY, 814 West Wisconsin Avenue, Milwaukee 53233/ AB, CH, CZ, DA, DU, FR, GE, GR(mo), HE, HU, IT, JP, LI, LT, NW, PO, PT, RU, S/C, SL, SV, SP, SW, TH, UK, VI, YD.

B-357. NEW PUBLIC LIBRARY, 319 Second Street, New Glarus 53574/ GE.

B-358. SAINT SAVA SERBIAN ORTHODOX CATHEDRAL LIBRARY, 3201 South 51st Street, Milwaukee 53219/ S/C, S/S.

B-359. WATERLOO PUBLIC MEMORIAL LIBRARY, 117 East Madison Street, Waterloo 53594/ GE.

WYOMING (WY)

B-360. LARAMIE COUNTY LIBRARY SYSTEM, 2800 Central Avenue, Laramie 82001/ SP.

Canadian Libraries

ALBERTA (A)

B-361. ALBERTA DEPARTMENT OF CULTURE & MULTICULTURALISM, 16214 114th Avenue, Edmonton T5M 2Z5/AB, CH, CR, DU, ES, FI, FR, GE, GJ, GR(mo), HE, HU, IC, IT, LI, NW, OJ, PJ, PO, PT, RU, SC, SL, SP, SW, UK, UR, VI, WE.

BRITISH COLUMBIA (BC)

B-362. GREATER VANCOUVER LIBRARY FEDERATION, 110-6545 Bonsor Street, Vancouver V5H 1H3/ CH, DU, GE, IT, UK.

B-363. VANCOUVER PUBLIC LIBRARY, 750 Burrard Street, Vancouver V6Z 1X5/ AB, CH, CZ, DA, DU, GE, GR(mo), HI, HU, IT, JP, NW, PJ, PO, PT, RU, SL, SP, SW, UK, UR, VI.

MANITOBA (M)

B-364. CITY OF WINNIPEG LIBRARIES, 251 Donald Street, Winnipeg R3C 3P5/ AB, CH, CZ, DU, FI, GE, HI, IC, IT, MT, NW, PJ, PO, PT, RU, SC, SL, SP, SW, UK, UR, VI.

NORTHWEST TERRITORIES (NT)

B-365.   NORTHWEST TERRITORIES PUBLIC LIBRARY SERVICE, Box 1100, Hay River X0E 0R0/ EK.

ONTARIO (O)

B-366.   EAST YORK PUBLIC LIBRARY/ S. WALTER STEWART BRANCH, 170 Memorial Park Avenue, Toronto M4J 2K5/ CH, DU, ES, GE, GJ, GR(mo), HI, IT, MA, PJ, PO, PT, RU, SP, UK, UR, VI.

B-367.   ETOBICOKE PUBLIC LIBRARY/RICHVIEW LIBRARY, Box 501, Etobicoke M9C 5G1/ CH, GE, GJ, GR(mo), HI, HU, IT, JP, KO, PJ, PO, PT, S/C, SP, UK, UR, VI.

B-368.   HAMILTON PUBLIC LIBRARY, 55 York Boulevard, Hamilton L8N 4G4/ AB, BG, CH, CZ, DU, GE, GJ, GR(mo), HI, HU, IT, LI, LT, PJ, PO, PT, RU, S/C, SP, UK, UR, VI.

B-369.   KITCHENER PUBLIC LIBRARY, 85 Queen Street, Kitchener N2H 2H1/ AB, BG, CH, CZ, DU, GE, GJ, HU, IT, PO, PT, RU, S/C, SP, UK, UR, VI.

B-370.   LONDON PUBLIC LIBRARIES, 305 Queens Avenue, London N6B 3L7/ AB, BG, CH, CZ, DA, DU, GE, GJ, GR(mo), HI, HU, IT, KO, LI, MR, MT, PJ, PO, PT, RU, SL, SP, SW, UK, UR.

B-371.   METROPOLITAN TORONTO LIBRARY BOARD/LANGUAGES DEPARTMENT, 789 Yonge Street, Toronto M4W 2G8/ AB, BG, BL, BY, CH, CZ, DA, DU, EK, ES, FI, GE, GJ, GR(mo), HE, HI, HU, IT, JP, KO, LI, LT, MA, MR, NW, PE, PJ, PO, PT, RO, RU, S/C, SL, SP, SV, SW, TM, TU, UK, UR, VI, YD.

B-372.   MISSISSAUGA PUBLIC LIBRARY, 301 Burnham Thorpe Road, West Mississauga L5B 3Y3/ AB, BG, CH, CZ, DU, GE, GJ, GR(mo), HI, HU, IT, MR, PJ, PO, PT, RU, S/C, SL, SP, SV, TM, UK, UR, VI.

B-373.   NATIONAL LIBRARY OF CANADA/MULTILINGUAL BIBLIO-SERVICE, Ottawa K1A 0N4/ AB, CH, CZ, DA, DU, ES, FI, FL, GE, GJ, GR(mo), HI, HU, IC, IT, LA, LI, MT, NAL, NW, PJ, PO, PT, RU, SC, SL, SP, SW, UK, UR, VI, WE.

B-374.   NORTH YORK PUBLIC LIBRARY, 5120 Young Street, N. York M2N 5N9/ BG, CH, DU, FI, GE, GJ, GR(mo), HE, HI, HU, IT, JP, KO, LT, PJ, PO, PT, RU, S/C, SP, UK, UR, VI.

B-375.   OTTAWA PUBLIC LIBRARY, 120 Metcalfe Street, Ottawa K1P 5M2/ AB, CH, CZ, DU, FI, GE, GR(mo), HE, HI,

HU, IT, JP, NW, PO, PT, RO, RU, S/C, SP, SW, UK, VI.

B-376. SCARBOROUGH PUBLIC LIBRARY, 155 Bonis Avenue, Scarborough M1T 3S4/ AB, BG, CH, DU, ES, FI, GE, GJ, GR(mo), HI, HU, IT, JP, KO, MR, PJ, PO, PT, RU, S/C, SP, UK, UR, VI.

B-377. SUDBURY PUBLIC LIBRARY, 74 Mackenzie Street, Sudbury P3C 4X8/ ES, FI, GE, GR(mo), IT, PO, S/C, UK.

B-378. TORONTO PUBLIC LIBRARY, 281 Orchard Street, East, Toronto M5A 4L2/ BG, CH, CZ, DU, ES, FI, GE, GJ, GR(mo), HE, HI, HU, IT, JP, KO, LI, LT, MT, PJ, PO, PT, RU, S/C, SL, SP, UK, UR, VI, YD.

B-379. WINDSOR PUBLIC LIBRARY, 850 Quellette Avenue, Windsor N9A 4M9/ AB, CH, CZ, DU, FI, GE, GR(mo), HE, HI, HU, IT, JP, LT, MA, PJ, PO, PT, RO, RU, S/C, SL, SP, SW, UK, UR, VI, YD.

B-380. YORK PUBLIC LIBRARY, 1745 Eglinton Avenue, West Toronto M6E 2H4/ BG, CH, CZ, GE, GJ, GR(mo), HI, HU, IT, PO, PT, RU, S/C, SL, SP, UK, UR, VI.

PRINCE EDWARD ISLAND (PE)

B-381. CONFEDERATION CENTER PUBLIC LIBRARY, P.O. Box 7000, Charlottetown C1A 8P3/ CH, DU, GE, VI.

QUEBEC (Q)

B-382. BIBLIOTHÈQUE MUNICIPALE DE MONTRÉAL/PUBLIC LIBRARY OF MONTREAL, 5650 Rue D'iberville, Montreal H2G 3E4/ AB, CH, CZ, DU, FI, FR, GE, GR(mo), HI, HU, IC, IT, NW, PJ, PO, PT, RU, SC, SL, SP, SW, UK, UR, VI.

B-383. BIBLIOTHÈQUE MUNICIPALE ST. LÉONARD, 8420 Boulevard le Cordairo, St. Léonard H1R 3G5/ FR, IT.

SASKATCHEWAN (S)

B-384. SASKATCHEWAN PROVINCIAL LIBRARY, 1352 Winnipeg Street, Regina S4P 3V7/ AB, CH, CZ, DU, FI, GE, GJ, GR(mo), HI, HU, IC, IT, JP, NW, PJ, PO, PT, RO, RU, SP, SW, UK, UR, VI.

Addendum Section B

MARYLAND

B-385. POLISH NOBILITY ASSOCIATION LIBRARY, Villa Anneslie, 529 Dunkirk Road, Baltimore 21212/ PO.

NEW YORK

B-386. AMERICAN BIBLE SOCIETY, 1865 Broadway, New York 10023/ MUL Bibles translated in dozens of languages around the world.

B-387. AUSTRIAN CULTURAL INSTITUTE LIBRARY, 11 East 52nd Street, New York 10022/ GE.

CANADA

MANITOBA

B-388. GERMAN SOCIETY OF WINNIPEG LIBRARY, 121 Charles Street, Winnipeg R2W 4A6/ GE.

B-389. MANITOBA CULTURE, HERITAGE AND RECREATION PUBLIC LIBRARY SERVICES, 1525 First Street, Unit 20, Brandon R7A 7A1/ FR.

NORTHWEST TERRITORIES

B-390. AMITTURMIUT LIBRARY, P.O. Box 158, Igloolik X0A 0L0/ IK.

QUEBEC

B-391. ITALIAN CULTURAL INSTITUTE, 1200 Drive Penfield Avenue, Montreal H3A 1A9/ IT.

C. SUPPLIERS SPECIALIZING IN FOREIGN-LANGUAGE BOOKS AND/OR AUDIOVISUAL MATERIALS

United States Suppliers

ARIZONA (AZ)

C-1. HISPANIC BOOK DISTRIBUTORS, 1870 West Prince Road, Suite 8, Tuscon 85705/ SP.

CALIFORNIA (CA)

C-2. ABRIL ARMENIAN BOOKSTORE, 5450 Santa Monica Boulevard, Los Angeles 90029/ AR.

C-3. ARMENIAN YOUTH FEDERATION SARDARABAD BOOK SERVICE, 108 North Brand Boulevard, Glendale 91203/ AR.

C-4. ASIAN BOOK CENTER, 4810 Melrose Avenue, Los Angeles 90029/ TH.

C-5. BAYON MARKET, 1181 East Tenth Street, Long Beach 90813/ CA.

C-6.   BILINGUAL EDUCATION SERVICES, P.O.B. 669, South Pasadena 91030/ SP.

C-7.   BOOKS NIPPON, 532 West Sixth Street, Los Angeles 90014/ JP.

C-8.   CHINA BOOKS AND PERIODICALS, 2929 24th Street, San Francisco 94110/ CH.

C-9.   CHINA CULTURAL CENTER, 970 North Broadway, Los Angeles 90012/ CH.

C-10. DAINAM CO., P.O.B. 4279, 1334 North Pacific Avenue, Glendale 91202/ VI.

C-11. DE LA ROSA'S LATIN AMERICAN IMPORTS, 80 South First Street, San Jose 95113/ SP.

C-12. DISCOLANDIA, 2964 24th Street, San Francisco 96110/ SP.

C-13. DISCORAMA, 428 South King Road, San Jose 95116/ SP.

C-14. DONG-A-BOOK PLAZA, 3460 West Eighth Street, Los Angeles 90005/ KO.

C-15. EAST WIND BOOKS AND ARTS, 1435-A Stockton Street, San Francisco 94133/ CH.

C-16. EDITORIAL EXCELSIOR CO., 15 North Market Street, San Jose 95113/ SP.

C-17. EUROPEAN BOOK COMPANY, 925 Larkin Street, San Francisco 91409/ FR, GE, SP.

C-18. EVERGREEN PUBLISHING AND STATIONERY, 136 South Atlantic Boulevard, Monterey Park 91754/ CH.

C-19. EVERYBODY'S BOOKSTORE, 17 Brenham Place, San Francisco 94108/ CH, FL.

C-20. FOLLETT LIBRARY BOOK CO., China Basin Building, San Francisco 94107/ SP.

C-21. FONDO CULTURAL LATINOAMERICANO, 6621 Atlantic Avenue, Bell 90201/ SP.

C-22. HAMEL SPANISH BOOKS, 10977 Santa Monica Boulevard, Los Angeles 90029/ SP.

C-23. HOWARD KARNO BOOKS, P.O.B. 431, Santa Monica 90406/ SP.

C-24. IACONI BOOK IMPORTS, 300-A Pennsylvania Avenue, San Francisco 94107/ AR, CA, CH, FR, GE, IT, JP, KO, PT, SP, VI.

C-25. JANSIS, 2350 Barrett Court, Pinole 94564/ GJ, HI, MR, TM.

C-26. JAPANESE-AMERICAN CURRICULUM PROJECT, P.O.B. 367, San Mateo 94401/ JP.

C-27. JEONG-EUM-SA IMPORTS, 3030 West Olympic Boulevard, Los Angeles 90006/ KO.

C-28. J.K. ENTERPRISE, c/o Hankook Ilbo and Korea Times, 141 North Vermont Avenue, Los Angeles 90004/KO.

C-29. KETAB BOOK CORPORATION, 16661 Ventura Boulevard, Encino 91436/ PE.

C-30. KINOKUNIYA BOOK STORES OF AMERICA, Astronaut Ellison Onizouka Street, Suite 106, Los Angeles 90012/ Japan Center West Building, 1581 Webster Street, San Francisco 94115/ JP.

C-31. KOREAN PUBLICATION CENTER, 3343 West Eighth Street, Los Angeles 90005/ KO.

C-32. KOREAONE, 1454 El Camino Real, Santa Clara 95151/540 Balboa Street, Santa Clara 95151/ CH, JP, KO.

C-33. LA LATINA, 2417 Mission Street, San Francisco 94100/ SP.

C-34. LIBRERIA MEXICO, 311 South Broadway, Los Angeles 90013/ 2631 Mission Street, San Francisco 94110/ SP.

C-35. LIBROS LATINOS, P.O.B. 1103, Redlands 97237/ PT, SP.

C-36. MAI HIEN PUBLICATIONS, P.O.B. 1061, Campbell 95009/ VI.

C-37. NATIONAL HISPANIC UNIVERSITY BOOKSTORE, 255 East 14th Street, Oakland 94612/ CA, CH, PJ, SP, VI.

C-38. NG HING KEE, 776 Jackson Street, San Francisco 94133/ CH.

C-39. ORIENTAL BOOK STORE, 630 East Colorado Boulevard, Pasadena 91101/ CA.

C-40. PHILIPPINE BOOK CENTER, 725 Silver Avenue, San Francisco 94135/ FL.

C-41. PHILIPPINE EXPRESSIONS, 1033 Hilgard Avenue, Los Angeles 90024/ FL.

C-42. SPANISH AND EUROPEAN BOOKSTORE, 3117 Wilshire Boulevard, Los Angeles 90010/ SP.

C-43. SZWEDE SLAVIC BOOKS, 2233 El Camino Real, P.O.B. 1214, Palo Alto 94302-1214/ CZ, PO, RU, S/C, SL, UK.

C-44. TRAM-VIETNAM PUBLISHING COMPANY, P.O.B. 11092, Portland 97211/ VI.

C-45. TULUC BOOK STORE, 8377 Westminster Avenue, Garden Grove 92644/ VI.

C-46. UNIVERSAL COMPANY BOOK STORE, 970 Broadway, 214-A, Los Angeles 90012/ SP.

C-47. VAN KHOA DISTRIBUTORS, 9393 Bolsa Ve., Westminster 92683/ VI.

C-48. VIENTIANE MARKET, 233 Jones Street, San Francisco 94102/ VI.

C-49. VIETNAMESE BOOKSTORE, 5480 Katella Avenue, Los Alamitos 90720/ VI.

CONNECTICUT (CT)

C-50.   CORTINA INSTITUTE OF LANGUAGES, Department SRC, 17 Riverside Avenue, Westport 06880/ MUL.

C-51.   No entry.

FLORIDA (FL)

C-52.   DOWNTOWN BOOK CENTRE, 247 SE First Street, Miami 33131/ SP.

C-53.   EDICIONES UNIVERSAL, P.O.B. 450353, Shenandoah Station, Miami 33145/ SP.

C-54.   FIESTA PUBLISHING CORPORATION, 6360 NE Fourth Street, Miami 33138/ SP.

ILLINOIS (IL)

C-55.   ADLER'S FOREIGN BOOKS, 915 Foster Street, Evanston 60201/ FR, GE, SP.

C-56.   DRAUGUS, 4545 West 63rd Street, Chicago 60629/ LI.

C-57.   LIBRERÍA GIRÓN, 3547 West 26th Street, Chicago 60623/ SP.

C-58.   MIDWEST EUROPEAN PUBLICATIONS, 915 Foster Street, Evanston 60201/ GE, SP.

C-59.   POLONIA BOOKSTORE & PUBLISHING COMPANY, 2886 Milwaukee Avenue, Chicago 60618/ PO.

C-60.   TIGERA LUIS, CUBAN BOYS, 1225 West 18th Street, Chicago 60608/ SP.

C-61.   W.J. BOOK STORE, 2235 South Wentworth Avenue, Chicago 60616/ ASL.

C-62.   YUQUIYU PUBLICATIONS, 2546 West Division Street, Chicago 60622/ SP.

MARYLAND (MD)

C-63.   CULTURAL HISPANA, P.O.B. 7729, Silver Spring 20910/ PT, SP.

C-64.   SMOLOSKYP, P.O.B. 561, Ellicott City 21043/ UK.

C-65.   VICTOR KAMKIN, 12224 Parklawn Drive, Rockville 20852/ RU, UK.

MASSACHUSETTS (MA)

C-66.   BIBLIOPHILOS, P.O.B. 268, Harvard Square, Cambridge 02238/ GR(mo), PT, SP.

C-67.   CHENG AND TSUI COMPANY, 25 West Street, Boston 02111/ CH, JP.

C-68.   NATIONAL DISSEMINATION CENTRE, 417 Rocks Street, Fall River 02723/ CH, GR(mo), IT, KO, SP, VI.

C-69.   SCHOENHOF'S FOREIGN BOOKS, 76-A Mount Auburn Street, Cambridge 02138/ GE, IT, RU, SP.

MICHIGAN (MI)

C-70.   ARDIS, 2901 Heatherway, Ann Arbor 48104/ RU.

C-71.   INTERNATIONAL BOOK CENTRE, 2007 Laurel Drive, P.O.B. 295, Troy 48099/ AB, CH, GE, JP, KO, SP, VI.

C-72.   UKRAINS'KA KNYHARNIA, 4340 Bernice Street, Warren 48091/ UK.

MISSOURI (MO)

C-73.   REFUGEE MATERIALS CENTER/INDOCHINESE MATERIALS, 324 East 11th Street, 9th Floor, Kansas City 64106/ CA, HM, LO, SP, VI.

NEVADA (NV)

C-74.   BAKER AND TAYLOR, 380 Edison Way, Reno 89564/ SP.

NEW JERSEY (NJ)

C-75.   TRET'A VOLNA, Alexander Glazer, 286 Barrow Street, Jersey City 07302/ RU.

NEW YORK (NY)

C-76.   AMERICA EAST BOOK COMPANY, 46 Bower Street, Store No. 18, New York 10013/ CH.

C-77.   ARISTIDE D. CARATZAS, P.O.B. 210, 481 Main Street, New Rochelle 10802/ GE, GR(mo), IT.

C-78.   ARKA COMPANY, 26 First Avenue, New York 10003/ UK.

C-79.   ARMENIAN APOSTOLIC CHURCH OF AMERICA, 138 East 39th Street, New York 10016/ AR.

C-80.   ASTRON IMPORTS, 22-81 31st Avenue, Long Island City 11102/ GR.

C-81.   BERLITZ, 257 Park Avenue South, New York 10016/ MUL.

C-82.   BILINGUAL PUBLICATIONS, 270 Lafayette Street, New York 10012/ SP.

C-83.   BOOKS NIPPON, 115 West 57th Street, New York 10019/ JP.

C-84.   CENTRAL YIDDISH CULTURE ORGANIZATION, 25 East 21st Street, New York 10010/ YD.

C-85.   CHINA BOOKS AND PERIODICALS, 136 West 18th Street, New York 10011/ CH.

C-86.   CONVERSA-PHONE, 1 Comac Loop, Ronkonkoma 11779/ MUL.

C-87.   DARBININKAS, 341 Highland Boulevard, Brooklyn 11207/ LI.

C-88.   D.C. DIVRY, 148 West 24th Street, New York 10011/ GR.

C-89.   DIOCESE OF ARMENIAN CHURCH BOOKSTORE, 639 Second Avenue, New York 10016/ AR.

C-90.   EAST INDIA BOOK COMPANY, 635 Second Avenue, Suite 2-R, New York 10016/ BG, GJ, HI, PJ, UR.

C-91.   EICHLER'S RELIGIOUS ARTICLES AND GIFTS, 1429 Coney Island, Brooklyn 11230/ YD.

C-92.   ELISEO TORRES, 1164 Garrison Avenue, Bronx 11207/ SP.

C-93.   FRENCH AND SPANISH BOOK CORPORATION, 115 Fifth Avenue, New York 10003/ FR, SP.

C-94.   GERALD FUCHS, 1841 Broadway, Suite 904, New York 10023/ GE.
INACTIVE(?) NO ADDRESS FOR 2ND EDITION.

C-95.   HAITIAN CORNER, 495 Amsterdam Avenue, New York 10018/ FR, H/C.
INACTIVE(?) NO ADDRESS FOR 2ND EDITION.

C-96.   W. S. HEINMAN, 1780 Broadway, New York 10019/ DU, GE, PO.
INACTIVE(?) NO ADDRESS FOR 2ND EDITION.

C-97.   IDEAL FOREIGN BOOKS, 132-10 Hillside Avenue, Richmond Hills 11418/ GE, IT, SP.

C-98.   ITALIAN PUBLICATIONS, 11-03 46th Avenue, Long Island City 11101/ IT.

C-99.   JUNG-KU BOOKS, 8 Pell Street, New York 10013/ CH.

C-100. KORYO BOOK IMPORTING, 35 West 32nd Street, New York 10001/ KO.

C-101. LAIKS, 73-07 Third Avenue, Brooklyn 11209/ LT.

C-102. LAZAR'S SEFER ISRAEL, 156 Fifth Avenue, New York 10010/ HE.

C-103. LECTORUM PUBLICATIONS, 137 West 14th Street, New York 10011/ SP.

C-104. LUSO-BRAZILIAN BOOKS, 33 Nevins Street, P.O.B. 170286, Brooklyn 11217/ PT(br).

C-105. MACONDO BOOKS, 221 West 14th Street, New York 10011/ SP.

C-106. MARY ROSENBERG, 17 West 60th Street, New York 10023/ FR, GE.
INACTIVE(?)

C-107. ORIENTAL CULTURE ENTERPRISES, 13-17 Elizabeth Street, New York 10013/ CH.

C-108. POLISH AMERICAN BOOK STORE/NOWY DZIENNIK, 21 West 38th Street, New York 10018/ PO.

C-109.   PUSKI-CORVIN HUNGARIAN BOOKS, 251 East 82nd Street, New York 10028/ HU.

C-110.   RASHID SALES, 191 Atlantic Avenue, Brooklyn 11201/ AB.

C-111.   RIZZOLI BOOKSTORE, 31 West 57th Street, New York 10019/ 712 Fifth Avenue, New York 10020/ IT.

C-112.   RUSSICA BOOK AND ART SHOP, 799 Broadway, 3rd Floor, New York 10003/ RU.

C-113.   SFARIM MEHABAIT (BOOKS FROM ISRAEL), 50 West 67th Street, New York 10023/ HE.

C-114.   SHAPOLSKY PUBLISHERS, 56 East 11th Street, New York 10003/ HE.

C-115.   SPEEDIMEX, 45-45 39th Street, Long Island City 11104/ IT.

C-116.   SUCHASNIST', 254 West 31st Street, 15th Floor, New York 10001/ UK. [Moved to New Jersey; see Addendum C-243]

C-117.   SURMA BOOK & MUSIC COMPANY, 11 East Seventh Street, New York 10003/ UK.

C-118.   UKRAINIAN ARTS ARKA COMPANY, 48 East 7th Street, New York 10003/ UK.

C-119.   S. F. VANNI, 30 West 12th Street, New York 10011/ IT.

C-120.   VICTOR KAMKIN, New York 10010/ RU, UK. [See C-65 Main Headquarters]

C-121.   WORKMEN'S CIRCLE, 45 East 33rd Street, New York 10016/ YD.

C-122.   WORLD JOURNAL BOOKSTORE, 377 Broadway, New York 10013/ CH.

C-123.   ZEN ORIENTAL/TOKYO SHOTEN BOOKSTORE, 115 West 57th Street, New York 10019/ JP.

OHIO (OH)

C-124.   AIMS INTERNATIONAL BOOKS, 3216 Montana Avenue, Cleveland 45211/ SP.

C-125.   CROATIAN BOOKS, 6313 Street and Clair Avenue, Cleveland 44103/ S/C.

C-126.   OLGERTS DIKIS, 6571 Clines Chapel Road, Waverly 45690/ LT.

TEXAS (TX)

C-127.   ARTE PUBLICO PRESS, University of Houston, 4800 Calhoun No. 429-AH, Houston 77004/ SP.

C-128.   BOOKS INTERNATIONAL, P.O.B. 27593, Houston 77227/ GE, SP.

C-129.   IMPORTED BOOKS, P.O.B. 4414, 2025 West Clarendon Street, Dallas 75208/ AB, CH, FR, GE, IT, JP, PT, SP, VI.

C-130.   ZIELEKS COMPANY, 11215 Sagerland Drive, Houston 77089/ VI.

VERMONT (VT)

C-131.   CHARLES E. TUTTLE COMPANY, 28 South Main Street, Rutland 05701/ CH, JP, KO, VI.

VIRGINIA (VA)

C-132.   HELLAR GRABBI, 3602 Albee Lane, Alexandria 22309/ ES.

C-133.   VIETNAM BOOKS, 6416 Charnwood Street, Springfield 22152/ VI.

WASHINGTON (WA)

C-134.   SOUTH SKY BOOK COMPANY, 5501 University Way NE, Seattle 98105/ CH.

Canadian Suppliers

ALBERTA (A)

C-135.   KOALA BOOKS OF CANADA, 14327-95A Avenue, Edmonton T5N 0B6/ JP.

C-136.   UKRAINIAN BOOKSTORE, 10215-97th Street, P.O.B. 1640, Edmonton T5J 2N9/ UK.

BRITISH COLUMBIA (BC)

C-137.   J. KOLASKY, 15097 Pheasant Drive, Currey V3R 4X4/ RU, UK.

MANITOBA (M)

C-138.   "KALYNA" UKRAINIAN CO-OPERATIVE, 952 Main Street, Winnipeg R2W 3R4/ UK.

C-139.   UKRAINIAN VOICE BOOKSTORE, 842 Main Street, Winnipeg R2W 3N8/ UK.

ONTARIO (O)

C-139/a.   AJAX BOOKS, c/o F. Verwimp, 106 Bolland Crescent, Ajax L1S 3G9/ DU.

C-140.   ALEXANDER TRADING COMPANY, 310 Tweedsmuir Avenue, No. 610, Toronto M5P 2Y2/ HU.

C-141. APOLLO BOOKS, 1529 Ortona Avenue, Ottawa K2C 1W2/ GR(mo).

C-142. ARKA UKRAINIAN BOOKS AND GIFTS, 575 Queen Street West, Toronto M5V 2B6/ PO, UK.

C-143. ASIAN EDUCATIONAL SUPPLIES, P.O.B. 162, Station E, Toronto M6H 4E2/ BG, GJ, HI, MR, PJ, UR.

C-144. BOHDAN B. FEDCHUCK, 420 Hillsdale Avenue East, Toronto M4S 1T8/ UK.

C-145. BOOK BARREL, 2284 Bloor Street West, Toronto M6S 1N9/ GE.

C-146. BRAMBLE HOUSE, 1087 Dundas Street West, Toronto M6J 1W9/ PT.

C-147. CARAVAN IMPORTS AND TRAVEL, 833 Brown's Line, Alderwood Plaza, Toronto M8W 3V7/ MA, S/C, SV.

C-148. CASA HISPANA, 1836 Weston Road, Weston M9N 1V8/ SP.

C-149. CENTRAL BOOKSTORE, 1414 Dundas Street, Toronto M6J 1Y5/ PT.

C-150. CENTURY PUBLISHING COMPANY, 657 Willard Avenue, Toronto M6S 3S1/ PO.

C-151. CHA HUA BOOKSTORE, 340 Spadian Avenue, Toronto M5T 2G2/ CH.

C-152. CHINA BOOKSTORE, 621 Gerrad Street East, Toronto M4M 1Y2/ CH.

C-153. DAUGHTER'S OF ST. PAUL, 3022 Dufferin Street, Toronto M6B 3T5/ IT.

C-154. DUNHUANG BOOKS AND ARTS, 328 Broadview Avenue, Toronto M4M 3T5/ CH.

C-155. EL CAMINO, 648/A Bloor Street West, Toronto M6G 1K9/ SP.

C-156. ESTONIAN PUBLISHING COMPANY, 958 Broadview Avenue, Toronto M4K 2R6/ ES.

C-157. FAR EASTERN BOOKS, P.O.B. 846, Adelaide Street Station, Toronto M5C 2K1/ BG, GJ, HI, MR, PJ, TM, UR.

C-158. FINNISH BOOK AND MUSIC STORE, 175 Spruce Street, Sudbury P3C 1N2/ FI.

C-159. FINNISH PLACE, 5463 Yonge Street, Willowdale M2N 5S1/ FI.

C-160. GERMAN BOOK AND GIFT SHOP, 457½ Spadina Avenue, Toronto M5S 2G7/ GE.

C-161. GERMAN BOOK BOUTIQUE, 37 Queen Street, Ottawa K1P 5C4/ GE.

C-162. GERMAN BOOK BOUTIQUES, 90 Yorkville Avenue,

Toronto M5R 1B9/ 151 Sparks Street Promenade, Ottawa K1F 5E3/ AB, CH, GE, IT, PO.

C-163. GIROL DISTRIBUTION, 120 Somerset Street West, Ottawa K2P 0H8/ PT, SP.

C-164. GRAND EAST ENTERPRISE, 96 Buddleswood Court, Scarborough M1S 3M9/ CH, JP, KO, VI.

C-165. GREAT WALL BOOKSTORE, 322 Bathurst Street, Toronto M5T 2S3/ CH.

C-166. GREEK PUBLICATIONS, 809 Danforth Avenue, Toronto M4J 1L2/ GR(mo).

C-167. HAMILTON LATVIAN SOCIETY BOOKSTORE, 16 Queen Street North, Hamilton L8R 2T8/ LT.

C-168. HELLAS MUSIC COMPANY, 450 Danforth Avenue, Toronto M4K 1P4/ GR(mo).

C-169. HIMALAYA BOOKS, P.O.B. 2112, Station B, Brampton L6T 3S3/ BG, GJ, HI, MR, PJ, TM, UR.

C-170. H.I.S.A.K.-C.S.A.C., A. H. Lgubo Krasic, 50 Adler Street North, Sudbury P3C 4J8/ S/C.

C-171. HOLLAND BOOKS, 3523 Kingbird Court, Mississauga L5L 2P9/ DU, GE, SW.

C-172. HOMIN UKRAINY PUBLISHING COMPANY, 140 Bathurst Street, Toronto M5V 2R3/ UK.

C-173. HOUSE OF FINLAND, 2027 Long Lake Road, Sudbury P3E 4M8/ FI.

C-174. ISRAEL'S JUDAICA CENTRE, 973 Eglinton Avenue West, Toronto M6C 2C4/ HE, YD.

C-175. ITAL BOOKSTORE, 1337 St. Clair Avenue West, Toronto M6E 1C3/ IT.

C-176. ITALIAN CULTURAL INSTITUTE, 496 Huron Street, Toronto M5R 2R3/ IT.

C-177. KNJIZARA CIRILO I METODIJE, P.O.B. 316, Station A, Toronto M5W 1C2/ S/C, SV.

C-178. LATVIAN BOOKSTORE, 491 College Street, Toronto M6G 1A5/ LT.

C-179. MALTA SERVICE BUREAU, P.O.B. 826, Station B, Ottawa K1P 5P1/ MT.

C-180. MARJULY IMPORTED BOOKS, 596 Bloor Street, Toronto M6G 1K4/ SP.

C-181. MIDEASTERN BOOKS IMPORTS, 2744 St. Joseph Boulevard, Orleans K1C 1G5/ AB, FR.

C-182. MLADOST, 37 Creekwood Drive, Scarborough M1E 4L6/ S/C.

C-183. MOSAIC BOOK IMPORTERS, 805 Dundas Street West, Toronto M9C 4X8/ CH, GR(mo), IT, KO, PT, SP, VI.

C-184.   NEGEV BOOK AND GIFT STORE, 3509 Bathurst Street, Toronto M6A 2C5/ HE, YD.

C-185.   NEW WORLD BOOKSTORE, 496 Dundas Street West, Toronto M5T 1G9/ CH.

C-186.   OVERSEAS COURIER SERVICE CANADA, 83 Galaxy Boulevard, Unit 7 and 8, Rexdale M9W 5X6/ JP.

C-187.   PAN ASIAN PUBLICATIONS, 69 Blue Eagle Trail, Agincourt M1V 1K6/ P.O.B. 31, Agincourt Street, Scarborough M1S 3B4/ CA, CH, JP, KO, LO, VI.

C-188.   PANNONIA BOOKS, P.O.B. 1017, Station B, Toronto M5T 2T8/ HU, UK.

C-189.   PAPELARIA PORTUGAL, 220 Ossington Avenue, Toronto M6T 2Z9/ PT.

C-190.   PLATON CANADIAN-GREEK BOOKSTORE, 781 Danforth Avenue, Toronto M4J 1L2/ GR(mo).

C-191.   POLISH ALLIANCE PRESS, 1638 Bloor Street West, Toronto M6P 4A8/ PO.

C-192.   POLISH-CANADIAN PUBLISHING FUND, P.O.B. 173, Station B, Toronto M5T 2T3/ PO.

C-193.   POLISH VOICE PUBLISHING COMPANY, 390 Roncesvalles Avenue, Toronto M6R 2M9/ PO.

C-194.   PORTUGUESE BOOKSTORE, 86 Nassau Street, Toronto M5T 1M5/ PT.

C-195.   S AND B BOOKS, 4143 Dundas Street West, Toronto M8X 1X2/ DU, GE, IT, SW.

C-196.   SANDOWN MARKET, 221 Kennedy Road, Scarborough M1N 3P4/ JP.

C-197.   SANKO TRADING COMPANY, 221 Spadina Avenue, Toronto M5T 2E2/ JP.

C-198.   SHER ENTERPRISES, P.O.B. 243, Agincourt Post Office, Scarborough M1S 3B6/ AB, GJ, UR.

C-199.   SIANI FLEWOG, 329 Queenston Street, St. Catharines L2P 2X8/ WE.

C-200.   SINO-CANADIAN PUBLICATIONS SERVICES, 25 Glen Watford Drive, Unit 4, Scarborough M1S 2B7/ CH.

C-201.   SIXTY-EIGHT PUBLISHERS, P.O.B. 695, 164 Davenport Road, Toronto M5W 1G2/ CZ.

C-202.   SLOVAK JESUIT FATHERS, P.O.B. 600, Cambridge N1R 5W3/ SL.

C-203.   SPEELMAN'S BOOKHOUSE, 510 Steels Avenue West, Unit 12, Rexdale M5V 5C6/ DU.

C-204.   SUN SHING BOOKSTORE, 463 Dundas Street West, Toronto M5T 1G8/ CH.

C-205.   SUN WA BOOKSTORE, 151 Dundas Street West, Toronto

M5T 1C5/ 421 Dundas Street West, Toronto M5T 2W4/ 482-A Dundas Street West, Toronto M5T 1G9/ CH.

C-206. THIRD WORLD BOOKS AND GIFTS, 942 Bathurst Street, Toronto M5R 3G5/ AF, HI, VI.

C-207. TROYKA, 799 College Street, Toronto M6G 1C7/ RU.

C-208. UKRAINIAN BOOK AND GIFT STORE, 2282 Bloor Street West, Toronto M6S 1N9/ UK.

C-209. UKRAINIAN BOOKSTORE/UKRAINS'KA KNYHA, 962 Bloor Street West, Toronto M6H 1L6/ ES, LI, RU, UK.

C-210. UKRAINIAN ECHO PUBLISHING COMPANY, 140 Bathurst Street, Toronto M5V 2R3/ UK.

C-211. VAPAA SANA PRESS, 400 Queen Street West, Toronto M5V 2A6/ FI.

C-212. WAN KOW, 336 Spadina Avenue, Toronto M5T 2G2/ CH.

C-213. WEST ARKA BOOK AND GIFT STORE, 2282 Bloor Street West, Toronto M6S 1N9/ UK.

C-214. WORLD BOOKSTORE, 119-A Elizabeth Street, Toronto M5G 1P8/ CH.

C-215. YUGOSLAVICA BOOKS, 47 Keegan Crescent, Downsview M3J 1G1/ S/C.

C-216. ZUCKER'S BOOKS AND ART STORE, 3453 Bathurst Street, Toronto M6A 2C5/ HE, YD.

QUEBEC (Q)

C-217. GERMAN BOOK BOUTIQUES/LIVRES ALLEMANDS, Place Bonaventure, P.O.B. 88, Montreal H5A 1A3/ AB, CH, FR, GE, IT, PO.

C-218. LIBRERÍA LAS AMÉRICAS, 2075 Boulevard St. Laurent, Montreal H2X 2T3/ SP.

C-219. LIBRERÍA SELECTA, 6050 Avenue Tisserand, Brossard J4W 3E6/ SP.

C-220. LIVRARIA SILMAR, 4276 Boulevard St. Laurent, Montreal H2W 1Z3/ PT.

Addendum Section C

United States Suppliers

CALIFORNIA (CA)

C-221. CASALINDA BOOKSHOP, 615 South Flower Street, Suite 1920, Los Angeles 90017/ FL.

C-222. HWONG PUBLISHING, 10353 Los Alamitos Boulevard, Los Alamitos 90720/ VI.

C-223.   IRANZAMI, 23361 El Toro Road, No. 112, El Toro 92630/ PE.

C-224.   ITALIAN BOOK STORE, 1875 Century Park East, Suite 2626, Los Angeles 90067/ IT.

C-225.   MAI HIEN XUAT BAN, 889 Peter Pan Avenue, San Jose 95116/ VI.

C-226.   ROMANIAN-AMERICAN ACADEMY OF ARTS & SCIENCES, 3328 Monte Vista Avenue, Davis 95616/ RO.

C-227.   SIAM BOOK CENTER, 5178 Hollywood Boulevard, Hollywood 90027/ TH.

COLORADO (CO)

C-228.   WESTERN CONTINENTAL BOOK, 625 East 70th Avenue, No. 5, Denver 80029/ FR, GE, SP.

CONNECTICUT (CT)

C-229.   AUDIO-FORUM, Suite LA30, Broad Street, Guilford 06437/ FR, GE, IR, IT, RU, SP.

FLORIDA (FL)

C-230.   ASTRAN, 7965 NW 64th Street, Miami 33166/ SP.

C-231.   FRANHIL ENTERPRISES, P.O. Box 650728, Miami 33165/ SP.

ILLINOIS (IL)

C-232.   FACETS VIDEO, 1517 West Fullerton Street, Chicago 60614/ CZ, HU, PO, RU, SLL.

C-233.   QUALITY BOOKS, 400 Anthony Trail, Northbrook 60062/ SP.

C-234.   ROSENBLUM'S WORLD OF JUDAICA, 2906 West Devon Street, Chicago 60611/ HE.

C-235.   SEOUL BOOKS, 3345 North Clark Street, Chicago 60657/ KO.

C-236.   YELLOW BIRD PUBLISHING, 4050 Waveland Street, Chicago 60641/ RO.

MARYLAND (MD)

C-237.   IRANBOOKS, 8014 Old Georgetown Road, Bethesda 20814/ PE.

MASSACHUSETTS (MA)

C-238.   PIMENTEL'S MULTILINGUAL BOOKS & RECORDS, 1659 Acushnet Avenue NW, New Bedford 02740/ FR, PT, SP.

C-239. RUSSIAN BOOK STORE, 1211 Commonwealth Avenue, Brighton 02134/ RU.

MICHIGAN (MI)
C-240. NEW ERA PUBLICATIONS, P.O. Box 130109, Ann Arbor 48113/ AB.
C-241. OLIVIA AND HILL PRESS, P.O. Box 7396, Ann Arbor 48107/ FR, GE, RU, SP.

NEW JERSEY (NJ)
C-242. HERMITAGE, P.O. Box 410, Tenafly 07670/ RU.
C-243. SUCHASNIST', 744 Broad Street, Suite 1115/16, Newark 07102/ UK.

NEW YORK (NY)
C-244. APPLAUSE LEARNING RESOURCES, 85-A Fernwood Lane, Roslyn 11576/ FR, GE, IT, RU, SP.
C-245. BLACK SEA BOOK STORE, 3175 Coney Island Avenue, Brooklyn 11235/ RU.
C-246. "CYCO" PUBLISHING HOUSE & DISTRIBUTION AGENCY, 25 East 21st Street, New York 10010/ YD.
C-247. EFFECT PUBLISHING-POSSEV, 501 Fifth Avenue, Suite 1612, New York 10017/ RU.
C-248. GERARD HAMON, P.O. Box 758, 525 Fenimore Road, Mamaroneck 10543/ FR.
C-249. HAITIANA PUBLICATIONS, 221-09 Linden Boulevard, Cambria Heights 11411/ H/C.
C-250. HOTALING'S NEWS, 142 West 42nd Street & Times Square, New York 10036/ MUL (newspapers from various countries).
C-251. INTERNATIONAL BOOK DISTRIBUTORS, P.O. Box 467, 24 Hudson Street, Kinderhook, NY 12106/ MUL (dictionaries in various languages).
C-252. IRISH ARTS CENTER, 553 West 51st Street, New York 10019/ IR.
C-253. KINOKUNYA BOOK STORE, 10 West 49th Street (Rockefeller Center), New York 10020/ JP.
C-254. KISMET RECORD COMPANY, 227 East 14th Street, New York 10003/ RU.
C-255. LION OF TEPELENA, P.O. Box 340733, Brooklyn 11234/ AL.
C-256. MINERVA BOOKS, 31 Union Square West, New York 10003/ SP (technical).

C-257. N & N BOOKS INTERNATIONAL, 63-73 110th Street, Forest Hills 11375/ RU.

C-258. PENINSULA PUBLISHING COMPANY, 156 Fifth Avenue, New York 10010/ SP (educational).

C-259. RUSSIAN HOUSE, 253 Fifth Avenue, New York 10016/ RU.

C-260. SERBERT, P.O. Box 430 Madison Square Garden, New York 10010/ PT, SP.

C-261. TOKYO SHOTEN, 521 Fifth Avenue, New York 11175/ JP.

C-262. W.J. BOOKSTORE, 141-07 20th Avenue, Whitestone 11427/ CH.

C-263. WORLD JOURNAL BOOKSTORE, 377 Broadway, New York 10013/ CH.

TEXAS (TX)

C-264. VIETNAMESE BOOK STORE, P.O. Box 720065, Houston 77272/ VI.

VIRGINIA (VA)

C-265. MOONFALL PRESS, 7845 Glenister Drive, Springfield 22152/ RO.

PUERTO RICO (PR)

C-266. LIBRERIA INTERNACIONAL, Apartado 23142, Universidad de Puerto Rico, San Juan 00931/ SP.

C-267. UPRED EDITORIAL, Apartado X, Rio Piedras 00931/ SP.

Canadian Suppliers

BRITISH COLOMBIA (BC)

C-268. SOPHIA BOOKSTORE, 725 Nelson Street, Vancouver V6Z 2A8/ JP.

MANITOBA (M)

C-269. DEUTSCHE BUCH GESELLSCHAFT HANS GUENTHER W. FRICKE, 475 Dominion Street, Winnipeg R36 2N1/ GE.

ONTARIO (O)

C-270. ARABIC BOOK OUTLET, P.O. Box 312, Don Mills M3C 2S7/ AB.

C-271. BUI VAN BAO, 15 Rochdale Avenue, Toronto M6E 1W9/ VI.

C-272. ERUDITE, 616 Sheppard Avenue W, Toronto M3H 2S1/ RU.

C-273. HARPER COLLINS, 1995 Markham Road, Scarborough M1B 5M8/ GE, GR, RU, SP.

C-274. LANG VAN, P.O. Box 310, Station W, Toronto M6M 5B9/ VI.

C-275. LAWSON FALLE, 1245 Franklin Boulevard, Cambridge N1R 5X9/ CH, FR, IT, PT.

C-276. LIBRAIRIE TRILLIUM, 321 Dalhousie Street, Ottawa K1N 7G1/ FR.

C-277. MERIDIAN CHEMICAL & TRADING COMPANY, 2077 Mountain Grove Avenue, Burlington L7P 2H8/ GE (technical).

C-278. MONALI BOOKS, P.O. Box 2914, Station D, Ottawa K1P 5W9/ AB.

C-279. MULTICULTURAL AUDIO VIDEO SYSTEMS, 12033 Street, Thomas Crescent, Tecumseh N8N 3V6/ BG, CH, FR, GE, GR, GJ, HI, JP, PO, PJ, RU, SP, UR.

C-280. SPEEDIMEX, Unit 5, 155 Deerhide Crescent, Weston M9M 2Z2/ IT.

C-281. SRBICA, 2192 Dundas Street West, Toronto M6R 1X3/ S/C.

QUEBEC (Q)

C-282. JEWISH PUBLIC LIBRARY, 5151 Chemin de la Cote Sainte Catherine, Montreal H3W 1M6/ YD.

C-283. LIBRAIRIE CHAMPIGNY, 4474 St. Denis, Montreal H2J 2L1/ FR.

C-284. YEVSHAN CORPORATION, P.O. Box 325, Beaconsfield H9W 5T8/ UK.

2. UNITED STATES EMPLOYMENT AND BUSINESS RESOURCES

This chapter consists of four sections—D) Government Sector: Federal and State Departments, Agencies, and Other Related Units, with 151 entries; E) Nonprofit Sector: Cultural, Charity, Social Voluntary, and Other Organizations, with 163 entries; F) Private Sector: Banking, Commercial, Consulting, Research, and Other Firms, with 137 entries; and G) Ethnic and Language Connections: Fraternal, Professional, Trade, and Other Organizations, with 220 entries. Entries are arranged in alphabetical order within each section. In the first three sections, each entry shows the name of agency, firm, or organization; address; nature of activities; job requirements (graduate or undergraduate degree, educational or occupational background); and languages of interest.

Some entries are marked "★" for internships, which means that the respective institution or firm or organization provides a work experience supplementing academic training, or introducing a specific field of work. Internships may be paid or unpaid, and usually last a few weeks or a few months.

Section D has entries for each of the states and territories. Each entry lists addresses of Federal Job Information Centers, State Employment Services, and State Offices for Volunteers (See Addendum). The information will be of interest to bilinguals and multilinguals desiring a job on a state level, or for immigrants from various countries intending to remain and work in the United States.

Section E provides opportunities for both salaried workers and volunteers (marked "Ⓥ"). In some cases, when volunteers are sent to other countries, they may receive a stipend, travel allowance, room and board, or placement with residents of a community. It has been noted that in several cases nonprofit organizations have changed their addresses.

Section G shows—for each entry—the name of the organization, nature of activities and services, and relevant languages. All organizations listed in this section are useful for networking purposes. They organize conventions or other meetings; many have job placement or counseling services; and they put out newsletters, bulletins, or other publications with job listings.

D. GOVERNMENT SECTOR: FEDERAL AND STATE DEPARTMENTS, AGENCIES, AND OTHER RELATED UNITS

★D-1. BOARD OF GOVERNORS OF THE FEDERAL RESERVE SYSTEM, International Finance Division, 20th Street and Constitution Avenue NW, Washington, DC 20557.
—Formulates monetary policy; analyzes international operations and major economic and financial developments; maintains liaison with foreign banks.
—GRD/ accounting, banking, and monetary systems; international economics; international finance, law, statistics/ KFL helpful.

D-2. BUREAU OF THE CENSUS/DEPARTMENT OF COMMERCE, Foreign Trade Division, 14th Street and Pennsylvania Avenue NW, Washington, DC 20230.
—Compiles current statistics on U.S. foreign trade, including imports, exports, shipping, etc.
—GRD/ area studies, demography, economics, statistics/ KFL reading.

★D-3. CENTRAL INTELLIGENCE AGENCY, Personnel Section, P.O.B. 12406, Arlington, VA 22209-8406.
—Collects and evaluates foreign intelligence and furnishes information needed by U.S. government and policy-making officials.
—GRD/ accounting, area studies, cartography, chemistry, computer sciences, economic affairs, economics, engi-

neering, foreign affairs, geography, history, international relations, international trade, journalism, physics, political science, various areas and language studies/ MUL fluency, especially needed are AB, CH, HE, JP, PE, RU, and several others.

D-4.   CIVIL AERONAUTICS BOARD, Bureau of International Aviation, 1825 Connecticut Avenue NW, Washington, DC 20428.
—Promotes and regulates civil air transport in the United States, as well as between the United States and other countries; IBO.
—GRD/ area studies, aviation, economics, trade/ KFL helpful.

D-5.   CONGRESSIONAL BUDGET OFFICE, National Security and International Affairs Division, Second and D Streets SW, Washington, DC 20515.
—Helps Congress to oversee the federal budget and make decisions on taxing, spending, and programs related to defense, international economics, etc.
—GRD/ accounting, economics, finance, national security, taxes, tariffs, trade/ KFL helpful.

D-6.   DEFENSE INTELLIGENCE AGENCY, Civilian Personnel Division, The Pentagon, Washington, DC 20301-0611.
—Provides military intelligence support to unified and specified commands.
—GRD/ area studies, communications, computer science, economics, engineering, international relations, physics, political science, statistics/ MUL.

D-7.   DEFENSE SECURITY ASSISTANCE AGENCY, The Pentagon, Washington, DC 20301-2800.
—Administers and supervises the execution of approved security assistance plans and programs, including military sales.
—GRD/ accounting, administration, business, economics, technology, weapons/ KFL helpful.

★D-8. DEPARTMENT OF AGRICULTURE, Personnel Division, Foreign Agricultural Services, Room 5627, South Building, 14th Street and Independence Avenue SW, Washington, DC 20250.

—Promotes trade of U.S. agricultural products abroad through hundreds of agricultural attachés; IBO.

—GRD/ agricultural economics, economics, international economics, plus a minimum of two years' work or education experience abroad/ FR, JP, SP are significant assets.

★D-9. DEPARTMENT OF COMMERCE, Foreign Service Personnel, Room 3226, 14th Street and Pennsylvania Avenue NW, Washington, DC 20230.

—Administers and promotes U.S. business abroad, and coordinates work in the areas of research, analysis, and formulation of commercial and international programs; IBO.

—GRD/ business, economics, government, history, international trade, marketing, political science, plus a minimum of two years' relevant experience/ KFL fluency according to assigned country/area.

D-10. DEPARTMENT OF DEFENSE, International Security Affairs, Room 3B347, The Pentagon, Washington, DC 20301- 1155.

—Coordinates activities of military forces needed to deter war and maintain security for the U.S.

—GRD/ international affairs, international economics, military technology, national security, studies in the field of Russian, Chinese, East-Central European areas, and their languages/ AB, CH, RU, and East European Languages.

D-11. DEPARTMENT OF DEFENSE DEPENDENT SCHOOLS, Teacher Recruitment Section, Hoffman Building I, 2461 Eisenhower Avenue, Alexandria, VA 22331.

—Recruits teachers for elementary and secondary schools on U.S. military bases located in over 20 countries around the world.

—UGD/GRD/ teaching of foreign languages/ FR, GE, LA, SP.

D-12. DEPARTMENT OF EDUCATION, Office of Personnel, Division of International Education, 400 Maryland Avenue SW, Washington, DC 20202.

—Coordinates foreign and domestic educational programs, including language and area studies, research and service activities, discretionary grants, etc.

—UGD/GRD/ area studies, international exchange/ KFL helpful.

D-13.   DEPARTMENT OF EDUCATION, Office of International Programs, Teacher Exchange Branch, 400 Maryland Avenue SW, Washington, DC 20202.
—Administers exchanges of U.S. teachers with foreign teachers interested in teaching in elementary and secondary schools, colleges, and universities, including teaching foreign languages and ESL.
—UGD/GRD/ education, foreign languages teaching/ MUL (less commonly taught languages are emphasized).

D-14.   DEPARTMENT OF ENERGY, Assistant Secretary for International Affairs, 1000 Independence Avenue SW, Washington, DC 20585.
—Develops and implements U.S. international energy policies; IBO.
—GRD/ economics, energy matters, engineering/ KFL helpful.

D-15.   DEPARTMENT OF HEALTH, Food and Drug Administration, 200 Independence Avenue SW, Washington, DC 20201.
—Protects the health of the U.S. population against impure and unsafe foods, drugs, cosmetics, and other potential hazards; IBO.
—KFL helpful.

D-16.   DEPARTMENT OF HEALTH AND HUMAN SERVICES, Office of International Health, 200 Independence Avenue SW, Washington, DC 20201.
—Shares U.S. experience in the field of health with other countries; coordinates research on cancer, cardiovascular diseases, AIDS, and other diseases, and studies various social security systems around the world.
—GRD/ business administration, chemistry, health, international health, nutrition, physics, statistics/ KFL helpful.

D-17.   DEPARTMENT OF HOUSING AND URBAN DEVELOPMENT, Assistant Secretary of International Affairs, 451 Seventh Street SW, Washington, DC 20410.

—Coordinates programs intended to improve the quality of life in U.S. cities, and has exchanges of experiences with other countries; IBO.

—GRD/ economics, financial analysis, loans, program analysis, realty specialization/ KFL helpful.

D-18.   DEPARTMENT OF JUSTICE, Office of International Affairs, Tenth Street and Constitution Avenue NW, Washington, DC 20530.

—Coordinates policy related to transnational criminal justice, and maintains contacts with several other countries and organizations.

—GRD/ languages, law, statistics/ MUL. *See also* D-31, D-34, D-41.

D-19.   DEPARTMENT OF LABOR, Bureau of International Labor Affairs, 200 Constitution Avenue NW, Washington, DC 20210.

—Formulates international economic and trade policies, establishes guidelines for labor attachés abroad, and sends U.S. representatives to international labor forums; IBO.

—GRD/ area studies, international affairs, labor relations, trade relations/ KFL desirable.

D-20.   DEPARTMENT OF STATE, Employment Information Office, 2201 C Street NW, Room 2815, Washington, DC 20520.

—Overseas employment opportunities for persons specializing in the fields of communications, engineering, medicine (physicians and nurses), and secretarial skills in languages (translation and interpretation)/ KFL.

★D-21.   DEPARTMENT OF STATE, Foreign Service Officer Recruitment Branch, P.O. Box 9317, Rosslyn Station, Washington, DC 22209.

—Assists the U.S. president and the secretary of state to plan, formulate, and implement foreign policy, coordinating a staff of about 4,000 officers; IBO.

—GRD/ business administration, economics, geography, international relations, journalism, law, management, military science, political science, science, translation and interpretation/ MUL competence, especially needed AB, CH, JP, RU.

D-22. DEPARTMENT OF STATE, Language Services Division, 221 C Street NW, Washington, DC 20520.
—GRD/ language training, interpretation, translation skills/ KFL required–fluency and experience.

D-23. DEPARTMENT OF STATE, Office of Overseas Schools, Room 234, SA-6, Washington, DC 20520.
—Recruits teachers for elementary and secondary schools for children of U.S. State Department personnel in dozens of countries around the world.
—UGD/GRD/ education, teaching of foreign languages/ FR, LA, RU, SP.

D-24. DEPARTMENT OF STATE, Office of United Nations System Recruitment, Bureau of International Organizations Affairs, Room 3536, Washington, DC 20520.
—Maintains a computerized list of U.S. citizens with qualifications for United Nations positions when vacancies occur at United Nations units. For specific requirements, *see* H-1 through H-43.
—Interested applicants should send their résumés and cover letters to the above address; suitable candidates are referred via the United States Mission to the United Nations, but the United Nations hiring unit makes the final decision.

D-25. DEPARTMENT OF THE AIR FORCE, Central Overseas Rotation and Recruitment Office, The Pentagon, Washington, DC 20330.
—Maintains U.S. air force capable of preserving peace and security of the country in cooperation with the army and the navy; uses civilian personnel abroad.
—UGD/GRD/ communications, engineering, medicine (physicians), nursing, secretarial, and several other skills/ KFL helpful.

D-26. DEPARTMENT OF THE ARMY, U.S. Army Civilian Personnel Center, Hoffman II Building, 200 Stovail Street, Alexandria, VA 22332.
—Organizes, equips, and trains active duty and reserve armed forces for the defense and security of the nation, using also civilian personnel all around the world.
—UGD/GRD/ communications, engineering, medical sci-

ence, nursing, secretarial, and various other skills and backgrounds/ KFL helpful.

D-27. DEPARTMENT OF THE INTERIOR, Office of Territorial and International Affairs, 1800 C Street NW, Washington, DC 20240.
—Administers nationally owned public land and natural resources.
—IBO/ MUL.

D-28. DEPARTMENT OF THE NAVY, Overseas and Return Placement, 800 North Quincy Street, Room 1219, Arlington, VA 22203.
—Protects the nation at sea, supports forces of all military departments of the United States, and maintains freedom of the seas; uses also civilian personnel abroad.
—UGD/GRD/ communications, engineering, medicine, nursing, secretarial, and various other skills/ KFL helpful.

D-29. DEPARTMENT OF THE TREASURY, 1500 Pennsylvania Avenue NW, Washington, DC 20220.
—Formulates, recommends, and implements economic, financial, and fiscal policies, and serves as financial agent and law enforcer of the U.S. government.
—IBO/ MUL.

D-30. DEPARTMENT OF TRANSPORTATION, Office of International Affairs, 400 Seventh Street SW, Washington, DC 20590.
—Develops and implements international aviation and transportation policies, trade, and foreign assistance programs of U.S. government.
—UGD/GRD/ economics, international relations, law, transportation and related areas/ KFL preferred; IBO/ MUL.

D-31. DRUG ENFORCEMENT ADMINISTRATION/DEPARTMENT OF JUSTICE, 1600-700 Army Navy Drive, Arlington, VA 22202.
—Enforces antidrug laws by immobilizing major trafficking organizations and by removing their leaders and assets; maintains liaison with drug enforcement agencies in over 50 countries.

—UGD/GRD/ intelligence, investigation, law, and foreign affairs/ KFL, especially AB, CH, PE, SP, TH, TU,
and others.

★D-32.   ENVIRONMENTAL PROTECTION AGENCY, Administration
of International Activities, 401 M Street SW, Washington,
DC 20460.
—Coordinates programs aimed at protecting and improving the environment, exchanging experiences with
other countries, and guiding U.S. representatives
abroad.
—UGD/GRD/ environmental protection, health disciplines, international affairs, law, public health/ KFL
desirable; IBO/ MUL.

★D-33.   EXPORT-IMPORT BANK OF THE UNITED STATES, Personnel Office, 811 Vermont Avenue NW, Washington, DC
20571.
—Helps financing and facilitates U.S. exports abroad.
—GRD/ accounting, banking, economics, finance, international affairs, international trade/ FR, SP most useful;
IBO/ MUL.

D-34.   FEDERAL BUREAU OF INVESTIGATION/DEPARTMENT OF
JUSTICE, Ninth Street and Pennsylvania Avenue NW,
Washington, DC 20535.
—Investigates violations of federal laws; provides the
government with information regarding national security; maintains liaison with foreign security and police
agencies.
—UGD/GRD/ accounting, business administration, computers, electronics, engineering, explosives, fin-
gerprinting, firearms, law, public administration, science disciplines, translation and interpretation/ KFL
preferred, especially AB, CH, JP, PE, RU, and others.

D-35.   FEDERAL COMMUNICATIONS COMMISSION, 1919 M Street
NW, Washington, DC 20554.
—Regulates interstate and foreign communications by
radio, television, wire, and cable.
—IBO/ MUL.

D-36.   FEDERAL MARITIME COMMISSION, International Department, 1100 L Street NW, Washington, DC 20573.
—Regulates the waterborne domestic and foreign commerce of the United States.
—GRD/ economics, finance, maritime shipping, trade/ KFL useful; IBO/ MUL.

D-37.   FEDERAL TRADE COMMISSION, Sixth Street and Pennsylvania Avenue NW, Washington, DC 20580.
—Maintains competitive enterprise as the basis of the U.S. economic system and protects it from monopolization, deception, and corrupt practices.
—IBO/ MUL.

D-38.   FOREIGN BROADCAST INFORMATION SERVICE/CENTRAL INTELLIGENCE AGENCY, Personnel Office, P.O. Box 2604, Washington, DC 20013.
—Reviews and scans foreign-language newspapers, journals, and monographs for information needed by analysts and policymakers.
—UGD/GRD/ area studies, international relations, political science, science and technology, social science/ KFL reading plus ability to render in English.

D-39.   FOREIGN CLAIMS SETTLEMENT COMMISSION OF THE UNITED STATES/DEPARTMENT OF JUSTICE, 1111 20th Street NW, Washington, DC 20579.
—Determines claims by U.S. citizens against foreign governments (mostly from Eastern Europe) for loss or injury caused by the respective governments.
—GRD/ finance, law, special knowledge of involved countries/ CZ, HU, PO, RU, and others helpful; IBO/ MUL.

D-39/a.   GENERAL ACCOUNTING OFFICE, International Division, 441 G Street NW, Washington, DC 20548.
—Examines the efficiency of federal government agencies in the executive branch, and maintains offices overseas.
—GRD/ area studies, business administration, international economics, international relations/ KFL helpful.

D-40.   GENERAL SERVICES ADMINISTRATION, General Services Building, 18th and F Streets NW, Washington, DC 20405.

—Manages U.S. property, including property located abroad, and keeps the necessary records of the property.
—GRD/ business administration, economics, finance/ KFL helpful; IBO/ MUL.

D-41.   IMMIGRATION AND NATURALIZATION SERVICE/DEPARTMENT OF JUSTICE, Room 6021, 425 I Street NW, Washington, DC 20536.
—Controls aliens entering the United States and keeps information on alien status; apprehends undocumented aliens; and facilitates naturalization and citizenship for qualified aliens.
—UGD/GRD/ immigration law, investigation, statistics, translation/interpretation/ KFL helpful, especially proficiency in GE, IT, SP.

★D-42.   INTER-AMERICAN FOUNDATION, 1515 Wilson Boulevard, Rosslyn, VA 22209.
—Supports financial, social, economic, and cultural projects in Latin America and the Caribbean region.
—UGD/GRD/ cooperative banking, economics, housing, industrial management, labor, law/ FR, H/C, PT, SP required; IBO/ MUL.

★D-43.   INTERNATIONAL DEVELOPMENT COOPERATION AGENCY, Personnel Division, 320 21st Street NW, Washington, DC 20523.
—Administers U.S. government's economic assistance programs in over 60 countries in Africa, Asia, the Near East, and Latin America.
—GRD/ area studies, developmental assistance, economics, languages, trade/ AB, AFL, FR, SP proficiency.

D-44.   INTERNATIONAL TRADE COMMISSION/DEPARTMENT OF COMMERCE, 50 E Street SW, Washington, DC 20436.
—Formulates and plans policies for coordinating international economic issues affecting dozens of countries around the world.
—GRD/ area studies, international economics, international law, international trade/ FR, GE, JP, SP desirable; IBO/ MUL.

★D-45.　LIBRARY OF CONGRESS, Employment Office, Room LM 107, 101 Independence Avenue SE, Washington, DC 20540.
—Largest public library in U.S., of national and international importance; provides research and reference services to U.S. Congress; serves as copyright depository, and collects books from around the world.
—UGD/GRD/ bibliographic areas, foreign affairs, defense, international affairs, law and government, librarianship, research, social studies, various country and area studies, various languages/ MUL; some positions require only reading and understanding of a language.
—The Library of Congress has a computerized recruitment service for potential applicants according to their employment interest.

D-46.　NATIONAL AERONAUTICS AND SPACE ADMINISTRATION, International Affairs Division, Maryland Avenue SW, Washington, DC 20546.
—Coordinates research for flights inside and outside the earth's atmosphere, and cooperates with other nations involved in similar activities.
—GRD/ administration, aeronautics, engineering, science, technology/ KFL desirable, especially CH, GE, RU.

D-47.　NATIONAL SCIENCE FOUNDATION, Division of International Programs, 1800 G Street NW, Washington, DC 20550.
—Formulates and supports advancement of scientific progress in U.S. and international scientific cooperation.
—GRD/ science, social science, technology/ KFL very helpful, plus international experience.

★D-48.　NATIONAL SECURITY AGENCY, M322 (AA1), Fort Meade, MD 20755-6000.
—Coordinates U.S. communications security, produces information on foreign intelligence, and takes the necessary measures to protect computer security for the federal government.

—UGD/GRD/ business, communications, computers, cryptography, liberal arts, linguistics, physical sciences/ KFL useful, especially AB, ASL, CH, RU.

D-49.   NUCLEAR REGULATORY COMMISSION, Office of International Programs, 1717 H Street NW, Washington, DC 20555/ Personnel Office: Mail Stop W-468, Washington, DC 20555.
—Licenses and regulates uses of nuclear energy, and attempts to protect public health and safety.
—GRD/ economics, law, political science, trade/ KFL helpful, especially FR, GE, JP, RU.

D-50.   OFFICE OF MANAGEMENT AND BUDGET, Job Information Center, 1900 E Street NW, Washington, DC 20541.
—Administers a merit system of federal employment; provides recruitment examinations, training, and promotions of applicants on the basis of skills.
—Has recorded messages and sends information and application forms upon request; for Federal Job Information Centers in each state, *see* D-68 through D-121/ KFL helpful according to requirements.

D-51.   OFFICE OF TECHNOLOGY ASSESSMENT, International Security and Commerce Program Management, 600 Pennsylvania Avenue SE, Washington, DC 20510.
—Assists U.S. Congress to plan for the consequences of technological changes.
—GRD/ international economy, scientific disciplines, world trade/ KFL helpful.

D-52.   OFFICE OF U.S. TRADE REPRESENTATIVE, 600 17th Street NW, Washington, DC 20506.
—Administers trade agreements and represents the United States in discussions and negotiations on bilateral or multilateral matters, or with the United Nations.
—GRD/ economy, international economy, law, trade and negotiations/ KFL helpful.

★D-53.   OVERSEAS PRIVATE INVESTMENT CORPORATION, 1650 M Street NW, Washington, DC 20527.
—Encourages private investment in about 100 countries with developing economies and provides financial assistance, insurance, and counseling.

—GRD/ business, economics, finance, insurance, law, marketing, plus at least two years' relevant experience in developing countries/ CH, FR, SP are preferred; IBO/ MUL.

D-54. PANAMA CANAL COMMISSION, 200 L Street NW, Room 550, Washington, DC 20036.
—Coordinates operations for safe and efficient transit of ships.
—GRD/ business, engineering, maritime disciplines/ SP.

★D-55. PEACE CORPS, Office of Recruitment, 1900 K Street NW, Washington, DC 20526.
—Promotes peace between U.S. and developing countries, and helps these countries in the fields of agriculture, education, health, nutrition, technology, among others.
—UGD/GRD/ accounting, agriculture, economics, education, forestry, health and environmental sciences, physical therapy, teaching, and other backgrounds/AB, FR, SH, SP helpful.

★D-56. RADIO FREE EUROPE/RADIO LIBERTY, 1201 Connecticut Avenue NW, Washington, DC 20036/ Oettingenstrasse 67, 8000 München 22, West Germany.
—Broadcasts programs in several languages to the Soviet Union and other East European countries.
—GRD/ area studies, international affairs, international communications, mass media, social psychology, translation and interpretation skills, plus relevant experience/AR, AZ, BK, BL, BY, CZ, ES, GG, HU, KZ, K/Z, LI, LT, PO, RO, RU, SL, TJ, TT, T/U, UK, UZ.

D-57. SECURITIES AND EXCHANGE COMMISSION, 450 Fifth Street NW, Washington, DC 20549.
—Provides disclosure of security matters to interested public, and protects investors against malpractice and fraud in financial and security markets.
—IBO/ MUL.

D-58. SMALL BUSINESS ADMINISTRATION, Office of International Trade, 1441 L Street NW, Washington, DC 20416.
—Helps, counsels, and protects the interests of small businesses, and provides loans to such firms as needed.
—IBO/ MUL.

D-59.   U.S. ARMS CONTROL AND DISARMAMENT AGENCY, 320
21st Street NW, Washington, DC 20451.
—Formulates and implements arms control and disarmament policy, and promotes U.S. national security interests.
—GRD/ economics, foreign policy, international organizations, military matters, Soviet and East European
studies, weapons technology/ CH, FR, RU helpful.

D-60.   U.S. CUSTOMS SERVICE/DEPARTMENT OF THE TREASURY,
Recruitment Division, 1301 Constitution Avenue NW,
Washington, DC 20229.
—Collects the revenues from imports, and enforces cus-
toms and related laws.
—UGD/GRD/ finance and taxes, investigation, law/ KFL
helpful.

★D-61.   U.S. HOUSE COMMITTEE ON FOREIGN AFFAIRS, Placement
Office, B-26, Cannon House Office Building, Washington,
DC 20515.
—Examines and modifies legislation before submitting it
to the House of Representatives.
—GRD/ area studies, international economics, interna-
tional relations, law, plus previous related experience/
KFL helpful in certain areas.

D-62.   U.S. INFORMATION AGENCY, Office of Personnel, 301
Fourth Street SW, Washington, DC 20547.
—Coordinates the overseas information, broadcasting,
television, publishing, educational, and cultural programs of the U.S. government.
—UGD/GRD/ administration, area studies, communications, engineering, ESL, international relations, liberal
arts, librarianship, journalism, public relations/ KFL
helpful according to country of service.
—U.S. Foreign Service Information Officers are recruited
by the State Department; other positions are filled by
the agency.

◢D-63.   U.S. JOINT PUBLICATIONS RESEARCH SERVICE/CENTRAL
INTELLIGENCE AGENCY, 1000 North Glebe Road, Arlington, VA 22201.
—Translates foreign-language materials in the fields of
science, technology, and social science.

—UGD/GRD/ computers, engineering, science disciplines (theoretical and applied), social science, subject knowledge in all these fields, plus ability to render into proper English the translated materials/ MUL; work can be handled by mail.

D-64.   U.S. MISSION TO THE UNITED NATIONS, 799 United Nations Plaza, New York, NY 10017.
—Maintains computerized lists of U.S. job applicants for United Nations positions, screens résumés and applicants for proper qualifications, and proposes suitable candidates for filling specific vacancies. Final decision on all applications is made by United Nations hiring units. *See also* D-24.

D-65.   U.S. SENATE PLACEMENT OFFICE, Russell Senate Office Building, Basement, Room 26, Washington, DC 20510.
—Examines, modifies, and makes necessary legislative changes before submitting them to the U.S. Senate; also has responsibilities in matters concerning international affairs.
—GRD/ area studies, international economics, international relations, law, political science, plus previous relevant work experience/ KFL helpful.

D-66.   U.S. TRAVEL SERVICES, INTERNATIONAL TRADE ADMINISTRATION/DEPARTMENT OF COMMERCE, 14th Street and Constitution Avenue NW, Washington, DC 20230.
—Develops travel to the United States from abroad; stimulates the U.S. travel industry and its contribution to economic stability and growth.
—UGD/GRD/ advertising, business administration, international economics, marketing, mass media/ KFL helpful according to the country assigned abroad.

★D-67.   VOICE OF AMERICA, Office of Personnel and Recruitment, Room 1192, HHS–North Building, 330 Independence Avenue SW, Washington, DC 20547.
—Produces and broadcasts radio programs in English and over 40 foreign languages for overseas listeners, focusing on U.S. politics, culture, economic and social developments, etc.
—UGD/GRD/ area studies, broadcasting, cultural studies, foreign policy, mass media, political science, social

science, translation/interpretation, various journalism skills/ AB, AL, AM, AR, AZ, BG, BL, BM, CA, CH, CZ, ES, FR, GG, GR(mo), HI, HS, HU, IN, KO, LI, LO, LT, PE, PO, PS, PT, RO, RU, S/C, SH, SL, SP, SV, TH, TU, UK, UR, UZ, VI.

State-by-State Review of Federal Job Information Centers, State Employment Services, and Offices for Volunteers

D-68.   ALABAMA (AL)
FJI: Building 600, Suite 347, 3322 Memorial Parkway South, Huntsville 35801.
SES: 1789 Congress Street and W. L. Dickinson Drive, Montgomery 36130.

D-69.   ALASKA (AK)
FJI: 222 West 7th Avenue No. 22, Anchorage 99513.
SES: P.O. Box 3-7000, Juneau 99802.

D-70.   ARIZONA (AZ)
FJI: Central Plaza Building, Room 1415, 3225 North Central Avenue, Phoenix 85012.
SES: 800 West Washington Street, Phoenix 85005.

D-71.   ARKANSAS (AR)
FJI: *See* Oklahoma Listing.
SES: 10421 West Markham, Little Rock 72205.

D-72.   CALIFORNIA (CA)
FJI: 9650 Flair Drive, Suite 100-A, El Monte, Los Angeles 91731/ 1029 J Street, Room 100, Sacramento 95814/ 880 Front Street, San Diego 92188/ 211 Main Street, 2nd Floor, San Francisco 94105.
SES: 800 Capitol Mall, Room 5000, Sacramento 94280.

D-73.   COLORADO (CO)
FJI: 12345 West Alameda Parkway, Lakewood, Denver 80225.
SES: 600 Grant Street, Denver 80203.

D-74.　CONNECTICUT (CT)
　　　　FJI:　Federal Building, 450 Main Street, Hartford 06103.
　　　　SES:　200 Folly Brook Boulevard, Wethersfield 06109.

D-75.　DELAWARE (DE)
　　　　FJI:　*See* Philadelphia Listing.
　　　　SES:　Carvel State Office Building, 820 N. French Street, Wilmington 19801.

D-76.　DISTRICT OF COLUMBIA (DC)
　　　　FJI:　1900 E Street NW, Washington 20415.
　　　　SES:　500 C Street NW, Room 600, Washington 20001.

D-77.　FLORIDA (FL)
　　　　FJI:　Commodore Building, Suite 125, 3444 McCrory Place, Orlando 32803.
　　　　SES:　303 Hartman Building, 2012 Capital Circle, S.E., Tallahassee 32399.

D-78.　GEORGIA (GA)
　　　　FJI:　Richard R. Russell Federal Building, 75 Spring Street SW, Atlanta 30303.
　　　　SES:　148 International Boulevard NE, Atlanta 30305.

D-79.　HAWAII (HI)
　　　　FJI:　Federal Building, 300 Ala Moana Boulevard, Honolulu 96850. (Lists Also Overseas Jobs.)
　　　　SES:　830 Punchbowl Street, Room 329, Honolulu 96814.

D-80.　IDAHO (ID)
　　　　FJI:　*See* Washington Listing.
　　　　SES:　277 N. 6th Street, Boise 83720.

D-81.　ILLINOIS (IL)
　　　　FJI:　175 West Jackson Boulevard, Room 530, Chicago 60604/ For Some Counties *See* Missouri Listing.
　　　　SES:　310 South Michigan Avenue, Chicago 60604.

D-82.　INDIANA (IN)
　　　　FJI:　Minton-Capehard Federal Building, 575 North Pennsylvania Avenue, Indianapolis 46204/ For Some Counties *See* Ohio Listing.
　　　　SES:　402 West Washington Street, Indianapolis 46204.

D-83.   IOWA (IA)
FJI: *See* Missouri, Kansas, or Illinois Listings.
SES: 1000 East Grand Street, Des Moines 50319.

D-84.   KANSAS (KS)
FJI: 120 Building, Room 101, 120 South Market Street, Wichita 67202.
SES: 401 SW Topeka Boulevard, Topeka 66603.

D-85.   KENTUCKY (KY)
FJI: *See* Ohio or Indiana Listings.
SES: 1049 US 127 South Bay, Frankfort 40601.

D-86.   LOUISIANA (LA)
FJI: 1515 Poydras Street, Suite 608, New Orleans 70112.
SES: P.O.B. 94094, Baton Rouge 70804.

D-87.   MAINE (ME)
FJI: *See* New Hampshire Listing.
SES: 20 Union Street, P.O.B. 309, Augusta 04332.

D-88.   MARYLAND (MD)
FJI: Edward A. Garmatz Federal Building, Room 1200, 101 Lombard Street, Baltimore 21201.
SES: 217 East Redwood Street, Baltimore 21202.

D-89.   MASSACHUSETTS (MA)
FJI: Thomas O'Neal Federal Building, 10 Causeway, Boston 02222.
SES: 100 Cambridge Street, Room 1100, Boston 02220.

D-90.   MICHIGAN (MI)
FJI: 477 Michigan Avenue, Room 585, Detroit 48226.
SES: 1200 Sixth Street, 14th Floor, Detroit 48226.

D-91.   MINNESOTA (MN)
FJI: Federal Building, Fort Snelling, Twin Cities 55111.
SES: 443 Lafayette Road, St. Paul 55155.

D-92.   MISSISSIPPI (MS)
FJI: *See* Alabama Listing.
SES: 1520 West Capitol Building, Jackson 39203.

D-93.   MISSOURI (MO)
FJI: Federal Building, Room 134, 601 East 12th Street, Kansas 64106/ 815 Olive Street, Room 400, St. Louis 63101.
SES: 3315 West Truman Boulevard, P.O.B. 504, Jefferson City 65102.

D-94.   MONTANA (MT)
FJI: *See* Colorado Listing.
SES: P.O. Box 1728, Helena 59624.

D-95.   NEBRASKA (NE)
FJI: *See* Kansas Listing.
SES: P.O. Box 94600, Lincoln 68509.

D-96.   NEVADA (NV)
FJI: *See* California (Sacramento) Listing.
SES: 500 East Third Street, Carson City 89713.

D-97.   NEW HAMPSHIRE (NH)
FJI: Federal Building, Room 104, 80 Daniel Street, Portsmouth 03801.
SES: 32 South Main Street, Concord 03301.

D-98.   NEW JERSEY (NJ)
FJI: Peter Rodino, Jr. Federal Building, 970 Broad Street, Newark 07102.
SES: John Fitch Plaza, Trenton 08625.

D-99.   NEW MEXICO (NM)
FJI: Federal Building, Room 101, 421 Gold Avenue SW, Albuquerque 87102.
SES: P.O.B. 1928, Albuquerque 87103.

D-100.   NEW YORK (NY)
FJI: Jacob J. Javits Federal Building, 26 Federal Plaza, Room 128, New York 10278/ U.S. Courthouse and Federal Building, 100 South Clinton Street, Syracuse 13260.
SES: W.A. Harriman Campus, State Office Building, Albany 12240.

D-101. NORTH CAROLINA (NC)
FJI: 4505 Falls of the Nouse Road, Suite 445, P.O. Box 25069, Raleigh 27611.
SES: Labor Building, 4 West Edenton Street, Raleigh 27601.

D-102. NORTH DAKOTA (ND)
FJI: *See* Minnesota Listing.
SES: P.O. Box 1537, Bismarck 58502.

NORTHERN MARIANA ISLANDS (CM) *See* D-119

D-103. OHIO (OH)
FJI: Federal Building, 200 West Second Street, Dayton 45402/ For Some Counties *See* Michigan Listing.
SES: 145 South Front Street, Columbus 43215.

D-104. OKLAHOMA (OK)
FJI: 200 N.W. Fifth Street, Room 205, Oklahoma City 73102.
SES: 4001 North Lincoln Boulevard, Room G-80, Oklahoma City 73105.

D-105. OREGON (OR)
FJI: Federal Building, Room 376, 1220 SW Third Street, Portland 97204.
SES: 875 Union Street NE, Salem 97311.

D-106. PENNSYLVANIA (PA)
FJI: William J. Green, Jr., Federal Building, 600 Arch Street, Philadelphia 19106/ Federal Building, Room 168, Harrisburg 17108/ Federal Building, 100 Liberty Avenue, Room 119 Pittsburgh 15222.
SES: 7th and Forster Streets, Harrisburg 17120.

PUERTO RICO (PR) *See* D-120

D-107. RHODE ISLAND (RI)
FJI: Pastore Federal Building, Room 310, Kennedy Plaza, Providence 02903.
SES: 101 Friendship Street, Providence 02903.

D-108. SOUTH CAROLINA (SC)
FJI: *See* North Carolina Listing.

SES: 1550 Gadsden Street, P.O. Box 11329, Columbia 29211.

D-109.   SOUTH DAKOTA (SD)
FJI: *See* Minnesota Listing.
SES: 700 Governors Drive, Pierre 57501.

D-110.   TENNESSEE (TN)
FJI: 200 Jefferson Avenue, Suite 1312, Memphis 38103.
SES: 501 Union Building, Suite 200, Nashville 37243.

D-111.   TEXAS (TX)
FJI: 1100 Commerce Street, Dallas 75242/ Corpus Christi: *See San Antonio*/ 8610 Broadway, Room 305, San Antonio 78206/ Houston: *See Dallas*.
SES: 101 East 15th Street, Austin 78778.

D-112.   UTAH (UT)
FJI: *See* Colorado Listing.
SES: 2120 State Office Building, Salt Lake City 84114.

D-113.   VERMONT (VT)
FJI: *See* New Hampshire Listing.
SES: Green Mountain Drive, P.O.B. 488, Montpelier 05602.

VIRGIN ISLANDS (VI) *See* D-121

D-114.   VIRGINIA (VA)
FJI: Federal Building, Room 220, Granby Street, Norfolk 23510.
SES: Powers-Taylor Building, 13th South Street, Richmond 23241.

D-115.   WASHINGTON (WA)
FJI: Federal Building, 915 Second Avenue, Seattle 98174.
SES: P.O.B. 4400, Olympia 98504.

D-116.   WEST VIRGINIA (WV)
FJI: *See* Ohio Listing.
SES: R-151 State Capitol Building, Charleston 25305.

D-117. WISCONSIN (WI)
        FJI: *See* Illinois or Minnesota Listings (Depends On County).
        SES: P.O. Box 7946, Madison 53707.

D-118. WYOMING (WY)
        FJI: *Contact offices in neighboring states.*
        SES: P.O. Box 2760, Casper 82602.

* * *

D-118/a. GUAM (GU)
          SES: ITC Building, 3rd Floor, P.O.B. 9970, Tamuning 96911.

D-119. NORTHERN MARIANA ISLANDS (CM)
        SES: Office of the Governor, Saipan 96950.

D-120. PUERTO RICO (PR)
        FJI: Federico Degetau Federal Office Building, Carlos E. Chardon Street, Hato Rey 00918.
        SES: 505 Muñoz Rivera Avenue, Hato Rey 00918.

D-121. VIRGIN ISLANDS (VI)
        FJI: *See* Puerto Rico Listing.
        SES: 22 Hospital Street, St. Croix 00820.

Addendum Section D

State Offices for Volunteers

D-122. ALABAMA (AL)
        560 South McDonough Street, Montgomery 36130.

D-123. CONNECTICUT (CT)
        80 Washington Street, Hartford 06106.

D-124. DELAWARE (DE)
        P.O. Box 1401, Dover 19930.

D-125. FLORIDA (FL)
        1321 Windwood Boulevard, Building 1, Tallahassee 32301.

D-126.   GEORGIA (GA)
1200 Equitable Building, 100 Peachtree Street NW, Atlanta 30303.

D-127.   HAWAII (HI)
State Capitol, Room 42, Honolulu 96813.

D-128.   ILLINOIS (IL)
100 West Randolph Street, 16th Floor, Chicago 60601.

D-129.   INDIANA (IN)
1 North Capitol, Indianapolis (South) 46204.

D-130.   IOWA (IA)
State Capitol, Des Moines 50319.

D-131.   KENTUCKY (KY)
275 East Main Street NW, Frankfort 40601.

D-132.   MAINE (ME)
State House Station 73, Augusta 04333.

D-133.   MARYLAND (MD)
301 West Preston Street, Room 1501, Baltimore 21201.

D-134.   MINNESOTA (MN)
500 Rile Street, St. Paul 55155.

D-135.   MISSOURI (MO)
615 13th Street, Kansas City 64106.

D-136.   NEW HAMPSHIRE (NH)
State House, Concord 03301.

D-137.   NEW MEXICO (NM)
State Capitol, Santa Fe 87503.

D-138.   NEW YORK (NY)
2 World Trade Center, 57th Floor, New York 10047.

D-139.   NORTH CAROLINA (NC)
116 West Jones Street, Raleigh 27611.

D-140. NORTH DAKOTA (ND)
600 East Boulevard Avenue, Bismarck 58505.

D-141. OHIO (OH)
65 East State Street, Room 1612, Columbus 43226.

D-142. OREGON (OR)
State Capitol Building, Room 160, Salem 97310.

D-143. PENNSYLVANIA (PA)
Penn-Serve, Labor & Industry Building, Room 1304, Harrisburg 17120.

D-144. RHODE ISLAND (RI)
160 Broad Street, Providence 02903.

D-145. SOUTH CAROLINA (SC)
1205 Pendleton Street, Columbia 29201.

D-146. SOUTH DAKOTA (SD)
State Capitol Building, Pierre 57501.

D-147. TENNESSEE (TN)
400 Deedrich Street, Nashville 37248.

D-148. TEXAS (TX)
P.O. Box 12428, Austin 78711.

D-149. VERMONT (VT)
109 State Street, Montpelier 05602.

D-150. VIRGINIA (VA)
223 Governor Street, Richmond 23219.

D-151. WASHINGTON (WA)
9th Street and Columbia Building, Olympia 98504.

E. NONPROFIT SECTOR: CULTURAL, CHARITY, SOCIAL, VOLUNTARY, AND OTHER ORGANIZATIONS

E-1. ACADEMY FOR EDUCATIONAL DEVELOPMENT, Programs Department, 1255 23rd Street NW, Washington, DC 20037.

—Provides consulting services in agriculture, economics, education, health, and other fields to over 80 developing countries.

—GRD/ business, economics, education, health, law, public affairs, plus previous substantial and relevant experience/ AB, FR, SP preferred.

★E-2.   ACCIÓN INTERNACIONAL/AITEC, 130 Prospect Street, Cambridge, MA 02139.

—Conducts research and evaluation programs aimed at generating employment, income opportunities, and small business projects in Latin American and Caribbean countries.

—UGD/GRD/ business, international development, Latin American studies, public adminstration, plus a minimum of four years' relevant experience/ SP.

E-3.   AFRICAN-AMERICAN INSTITUTE, 833 United Nations Plaza, New York, NY 10017/ 1625 Massachusetts Avenue, NW, Washington, DC 20036.

—Assists African countries in the fields of educational development and job training, and disseminates information on Africa in the United States.

—GRD/ African area studies, cultural studies, economic development, economics, educational administration, teaching/ AFL, FR, SP.

E-4.   AFRICAN-AMERICAN LABOR CENTER, 1400 K Street NW, Suite 700, Washington, DC 20005.

—Assists over 25 African countries with the development of democratic, free, and responsible trade unions, and with the education of their cadre.

—UGD/ African area studies, industrial relations, teaching, trade unionism, vocational training/AFL, FR, SP.

E-5.   AFRICAN MEDICAL AND RESEARCH FOUNDATION, 420 Lexington Avenue, New York, NY 10170.

—Provides health care to remote African regions through special medical teams, and immunization, nutrition, research, and other programs.

—GRD/ health management, health planning, maternal and child care, medicine, nutrition, public health/ SH preferred.

E-6.   AGRICULTURAL COOPERATIVE DEVELOPMENT INTERNATIONAL EXECUTIVE ASSISTANCE, 50 F Street NW, Suite 900, Washington, DC 20002.
—Conducts programs in over 15 developing countries and is involved in bank credits, farm exports, and other branches of agriculture.
—GRD/ agriculture, business, economics, financial management, plus at least four years' experience in developing countries/ AB, FR, SP preferred.

E-7.   AMERICA-MIDEAST EDUCATIONAL AND TRAINING SERVICES, 1100 17th Street NW, Washington, DC 20036.
—Assists several Arabic countries with educational, counseling, job training, and translation services.
—GRD/ counseling, education, international development, Middle Eastern area studies, vocational teaching/ AB, FR preferred.

E-8.   AMERICAN COMMITTEE ON U.S.-RUSSIAN RELATIONS, 109 11th Street SE, Washington, DC 20003.
—Promotes better relations between the United States and the Soviet Union in cultural, artistic, scientific, arms control, and other fields.
—GRD/ foreign policy, international affairs, Russian area studies/ RU.

★E-9.   AMERICAN ENTERPRISE INSTITUTE FOR PUBLIC POLICY RELATIONS, 1150 17th Street NW, Washington, DC 20036.
—Conducts study, research, and publishing programs in the fields of international economic, military, political, and other relations.
—GRD/ economics, international affairs, military studies, political science, publishing, various area studies/ KFL helpful.

E-10.   AMERICAN FEDERATION OF LABOR AND CONGRESS OF INDUSTRIAL ORGANIZATIONS (AFL-CIO), International Affairs Department, AFL-CIO Building, Room 705, 815 16th Street NW, Washington, DC 20006.
—Promotes better living standards, working conditions, freedom, and peace by maintaining contacts with various foreign labor organizations and with foreign embassies.
—UGD/GRD/ area studies, industrial relations, labor

movement history, labor relations, public affairs, public relations/ KFL required.

E-11. AMERICAN FIELD SERVICE INTERNATIONAL/INTERCULTURAL PROGRAMS, 313 East 43rd Street, New York, NY 10017.
—Provides cross-cultural exchange programs for high school students and young adult professionals operating in over 70 countries.
—UGD/ counseling, education, international business, marketing, public administration, plus experience in living abroad/ AB, FR, GE, SP desirable; others optional.

★E-12. AMERICAN FRIENDS SERVICE COMMITTEE, Recruitment Department, 1501 Cherry Street, Philadelphia, PA 19102.
—Quaker organization with programs in over 20 developing countries with emphasis on community services and development, justice, and peace.
—UGD/ any background, but not a must; personal skills, plus at least five years' experience in community work, international relations, agriculture, or peace activities/ AB, AFL, FR, SP useful.

E-13. AMERICAN FUND FOR CZECHOSLOVAK REFUGEES, 1776 Broadway, New York, NY 10019.
—Helps Czechoslovak and Indochinese refugees with adjustment to U.S. life; conducts programs of ESL; and assists with housing, immigration papers, and employment.
—UGD/GRD/ Czech studies, employment market, Indochinese area studies, social work, plus experience with refugees/ CH, CZ, VI.

E-14. AMERICAN INSTITUTE FOR FREE LABOR DEVELOPMENT, 1015 20th Street NW, Washington, DC 20036.
—Provides assistance in strengthening the democratic unions of over 15 Latin American and Caribbean countries through programs in the fields of building, cooperative credit loans, education, etc.
—UGD/GRD/ economic development, industrial relations, Latin American area studies, trade unionism/ PT, SP.

E-15.   AMERICAN JEWISH JOINT DISTRIBUTION COMMITTEE, 711 Third Avenue, 10th Floor, New York, NY 10017.
—Assists Jewish communities in Europe, Africa, Asia, and Latin America with health, education, food, job training, and other programs.
—GRD/ planning, program organization, public administration, social work, plus experience in Jewish social and health services/ FR, GE, HE, RU, SP, YD.

E-16.   AMERICAN LEPROSY MISSION, 1 Alm Way, Greenville, SC 29601.
—Offers medical assistance as well as social and physical rehabilitation programs to people affected by leprosy in Brazil, Ethiopia, India, Nepal, and the United States.
—GRD/ medicine, surgery, physical and occupational therapy/ PT for Brazil.

E-17.   AMERICAN NEAR EAST REFUGEE AID, 1522 K Street NW, Washington, DC 20005.
—Provides assistance to Palestinians in the Middle East with programs in the fields of education, economic well-being, health, etc.
—UGD/GRD/ agronomy, community development, education, engineering, plus at least two years' overseas work experience/AB preferred.

E-18.   AMERICAN ORT FEDERATION, 817 Broadway, New York, NY 10003.
—Conducts vocational and technical training programs for youth in over 30 countries in Africa, East Asia, and Latin America.
—UGD/GRD/ education, engineering, vocational teaching/ AB, FR, SP.

ⓥE-19.   AMERICAN RED CROSS, Office of International Service, 431 18th Street NW, Washington, DC 20006.
—Assists disaster victims and refugees in the United States and abroad, and offers technical advice to foreign Red Cross societies; also provides language banks to help non-English-speaking communities.
—UGD/GRD/ medicine, nursing, social work, plus experience/ AB, CH, FR, GE, HI, NAL, PT, SP, and others.

Ⓥ E-20. AMERICAN REFUGEE COMMITTEE, 2344 Nicollett Avenue, Suite 350, Minneapolis, MN 55404.
—Provides medical care and medical education assistance to Indochinese and Arab refugees.
—UGD/GRD/ laboratory technology, medicine, midwifery, nursing, public health administration, plus two years' medical experience/AB, CA, LO, TH, VI.

★ E-21. AMERICAN SECURITY COUNCIL FOUNDATION, Washington Communications Center, Boston, VA 22713.
—Foundation advocating strong United States defense; cooperates with various educational institutions, and has TV programs and publishing activities.
—UGD/GRD/ communications, government studies, international studies, journalism, mass media, public relations/ SP helpful.

★ E-22. AMERICAS SOCIETY, 680 Park Avenue, New York, NY 10021.
—Promotes understanding of cultural, economical, and political values of Latin American and Caribbean countries, and conducts various programs to meet its objectives.
—GRD/ international affairs, journalism, public relations/ PT or SP fluency.

Ⓥ E-23. AMIGOS DE LAS AMERICAS, 5618 Star Lane, Houston, TX 77057.
—Assists several Latin American countries with young volunteers involved in health projects.
—High school (at least sophomore) and college students, with first aid training/ SP fluency.

★ E-24. AMNESTY INTERNATIONAL USA, 322 Eighth Avenue, New York, NY 10011.
—Concerned with human rights violations, prompt and fair trial of political prisoners, elimination of torture and executions; has affiliated groups in over 50 countries around the world.
—UGD/GRD/ area studies, international relations, political science, social science/ FR, SP useful.

E-25. APPROPRIATE TECHNOLOGY INTERNATIONAL, 1331 H Street NW, Washington, DC 20005.

—Specializes in adapting science and technology to the concrete conditions of various developing countries; conducts programs on small farms, mines, and other places.

—UGD/GRD/ business, economics, engineering, rural industry, plus a minimum of three years' prior relevant experience in similar work/ FR, SP required.

★E-26.   ARMS CONTROL ASSOCIATION, 11 Dupont Circle NW, Washington, DC 20036.

—Concerned with national security issues, including arms control and world peace.

—GRD/ international relations, journalism, national security, political science, plus at least one year's experience in the field of national security/ FR, RU useful.

E-27.   ASIA FOUNDATION, P.O. Box 3223, 465 California Street, San Francisco, CA 94119.

—Encourages and fosters cooperative international relations in several areas (economic, political, social) between the United States and East and South Asian countries.

—GRD/ Asian studies, economics, international relations, law, political science, plus a minimum of two years' experience in government affairs/ CH, JP, KO, and others.

★E-28.   ASIA SOCIETY, Administration Section, 725 Park Avenue, New York, NY 10021.

—Promotes understanding of Asian countries in the field of arts, economics, politics, and other aspects of Asian culture and civilization.

—UGD/GRD/ Asian studies, business administration, education, international relations, plus at least two years of relevant experience/ CH, JP preferred.

E-29.   ASIAN CULTURAL COUNCIL, 280 Madison Avenue, New York, NY 10016.

—Supports cultural exchanges in the field of visual and performing arts between the United States and Asian countries.

—GRD/ Asian area studies, cultural studies, language studies, plus exchange program experience/ CH, FL, JP, KO, TH, and others.

E-30. ASSOCIATION INTERNATIONALE DES ÉTUDIANTS EN SCI-ENCES ÉCONOMIQUES ET COMMERCIALES–US, 135 West 50th Street, 20th Floor, New York, NY 10020.
—Provides international training opportunities for students with leadership potential in the field of business.
—UGD/ accounting, computer science, finance, marketing/ FR, GE, SP useful; exchange students must be members of the organization in their respective countries.

★E-31. BROOKINGS INSTITUTION, 1775 Massachusetts Avenue NW, Washington, DC 20036.
—A research unit specializing in public policy, conveying its findings to scholars, government, and to the public at large.
—GRD/ economics, defense studies, mathematics, statistics/ AB, CH, JP, RU most desirable.

E-32. CARIBBEAN/CENTRAL AMERICAN ACTION, 1211 Connecticut Avenue NW, Suite 510, Washington, DC 20036.
—Provides economic assistance to Caribbean countries, and is supported by major American corporations.
—UGD/GRD/ business, Latin American studies, political science/ SP fluency.

★E-33. CARL DUISBERG SOCIETY INTERNATIONAL, 330 7th Avenue, 9th Floor, New York, NY 10001.
—Sponsors and organizes various work-training and educational-exchange programs between the United States and Germany.
—UGD/GRD/ accounting, agriculture, banking, biomedicine, chemical engineering, computer technology, plus experience in a technical field/ GE required.

★E-34. CARNEGIE ENDOWMENT FOR INTERNATIONAL PEACE, 11 Dupont Circle NW, Washington, DC 20036.
—Sponsors and coordinates programs in the fields of research, education, publishing, and discussion concerning various facets of U.S. foreign policy and international affairs.
—UGD/GRD/ area studies, agriculture, economics, government, international affairs, international politics/ KFL helpful.

E-35.   CATHOLIC RELIEF SERVICES/U.S. CATHOLIC CONFERENCE, Staffing and Manpower Planning, 1011 First Avenue, New York, NY 10022.
—Provides development, relief, and refugee assistance to dozens of countries around the world.
—UGD/GRD/ agriculture, business, economics, health, international affairs, management, sociology/ AB, FR, SP fluency desirable.

E-36.   CENTER FOR DEVELOPMENT AND POPULATION ACTIVITIES, 1717 Massachusetts Avenue NW, No. 202, Washington, DC 20036.
—Assists developing countries with training, technical know-how, and education of professionals specializing in population problems.
—GRD/ family planning, health services, management, teaching/ AB, FR, SP fluency.

E-37.   CENTER FOR INDEPENDENT LIVING, 2539 Telegraph Avenue, Berkeley, CA 94704.
—Provides special programs for persons in wheelchairs to be trained in the computer field, and helps foreign countries to establish similar programs.
—UGD/GRD/ Latin American and Caribbean area studies, occupational therapy, public relations/ SP.

E-38.   CENTER FOR INTER-AMERICAN RELATIONS, 680 Park Avenue, New York, NY 10021.
Absorbed By E-22.

★E-39.   CENTER FOR STRATEGIC AND INTERNATIONAL STUDIES, 1800 K Street NW, Washington, DC 20006.
—Research unit specializing in various aspects of public policy (business, diplomacy, economics, science, military science, etc.); findings are conveyed to legislators, scholars, and the general public.
—GRD/ international economics, international relations, military studies, national security affairs, plus substantial work experience of relevance/ KFL is preferred.

★E-40.   CHICAGO COUNCIL ON FOREIGN RELATIONS, 116 South Michigan Avenue, Chicago, IL 60603.
—Specializes in research and publishing concerning policy topics, economic issues, and general education.

—GRD/ economics, education, international relations, plus relevant experience/ KFL is preferred.

E-41.   CHINA INSTITUTE IN AMERICA, Administration and Development Department, 125 East 65th Street, New York, NY 10021.
—Promotes better understanding of China by Americans through cultural and educational programs, and serves as a meeting place for Chinese visitors from abroad.
—UGD/GRD/ Asian studies, Chinese area studies, fund raising, international relations, public relations/ CH is preferred.

E-42.   CHRISTIAN BLIND MISSION INTERNATIONAL, P.O. Box 175, Wheaton, IL 60187.
—Fights blindness of children in India and East Africa; distributes vitamin capsules to prevent blindness.
—UGD/ African studies, Asian studies, economic development, health care, nutrition, public relations/ AFL, HI desirable.

Ⓥ E-43.   CHRISTIAN CHILDREN'S FUND, P.O.B. 26484, Richmond, VA 23261.
—Provides technical assistance to children without families, and to families with the aim of facilitating child development and educational opportunities.
—UGD/GRD/ education, health, nutrition, vocational training/ FR, GE, SP helpful, depending on assigned country.

E-44.   CHURCH WORLD SERVICE, Overseas Personnel Office, 475 Riverside Drive, New York, NY 10015.
—Operates in 58 countries around the world, and provides international relief, development, and refugee assistance.
—UGD/GRD/ agriculture, business, forestry, international relations, medicine, water resources development, plus at least one year's previous experience in developing countries/ AFL, FR, SP are required.

Ⓥ E-45.   CONCERN, P.O. Box 1790, Santa Ana, CA 92702.
—Provides hunger relief and development assistance to several countries in Latin America, and to Bangladesh and Sierra Leone.

—GRD/ education, engineering, health, water resources development/ SP desirable.

★E-46.   COOPERATIVE FOR AMERICAN RELIEF EVERYWHERE (CARE), Personnel Office, 660 First Avenue, New York, NY 10016.
—Operates health, nutrition, disaster relief, and other programs in over 120 countries around the world.
—UGD/GRD/ agriculture, construction, engineering, fisheries, forestry, international development, medicine, nutrition, public health/ FR, SP required.

E-47.   COUNCIL OF THE AMERICAS, 680 Park Avenue, New York, NY 10021/ 1625 K Street NW, Washington, DC 20006.
—Conducts programs for about 200 U.S. corporations interested in investing in Latin American and Caribbean countries.
—UGD/GRD/ business, economics, finance, Latin American studies/ SP or PT fluency desirable.

★E-48.   COUNCIL ON FOREIGN RELATIONS, Personnel Department, 58 East 68th Street, New York, NY 10021.
—Organizes forums for academic, public, and private institutions to discuss U.S. foreign policy and international relations, human rights, and military assistance.
—UGD/GRD/ economics, history, international affairs, languages, military technology, political science, plus experience in writing, editing, management/ KFL desirable.

E-49.   COUNCIL ON HEMISPHERIC AFFAIRS, 1612 20th Street NW, Washington, DC 20009.
—Brings together leading Americans from the academic, business, professional, and public sectors with the purpose of examining the relations between the United States and Latin American countries in various fields.
—GRD/ economics, industrial relations, international affairs, Latin American area studies/ SP or PT preferred.

★E-50.   COUNCIL ON INTERNATIONAL EDUCATIONAL EXCHANGE, Personnel Department, 205 East 42nd Street, New York, NY 10017.
—Sponsors and organizes various student exchange pro-

grams involving work, study, and travel in other countries.
—UGD/ business, languages, plus experience in travel, study abroad, or sales/ FR, GE, JP, RU, SP preferred.

Ⓥ E-51. DIRECT RELIEF INTERNATIONAL, P.O.B. 30820, Santa Barbara, CA 93130.
—Voluntary organization offering assistance to developing countries in Africa, Asia, the Caribbean area, and Latin America with medical supplies and services.
—GRD/ anthropology, medicine, nursing, public health, plus previous relevant experience/ FR, SP useful.

E-52. EAST COAST MIGRANT HEALTH PROJECT, 1234 Massachusetts Avenue NW, Suite 623, Washington, DC 20005.
—Offers assistance with health and social services to migrant and seasonal farm workers and their families in the U.S.
—UGD/GRD/ health education, medicine, nursing, social work/ FR, H/C, SP.

E-53. EAST-WEST CENTER, 1777 East-West Road, Honolulu, HI 96848.
—Promotes better relations between the United States and Asian countries through cooperative studies, training, and research.
—GRD/ social sciences, plus work experience in the Asian/Pacific area/ CH, FL, JP, KO, and others.

E-54. ERIE DIOCESAN MISSION OFFICE, 246 West Tenth Street, Erie, PA 16501.
INACTIVE(?)
—Provides medical assistance and educational services to local population and physically disabled people in African and Latin American countries.
—UGD/GRD/ health, medicine, nursing, physical therapy, teaching/ SH, SP.

E-55. FAMILY HEALTH INTERNATIONAL, P.O.B. 13950, Durham, NC 27709.
—Conducts contraceptive research programs and assists Asian, African, and Latin American countries with family planning techniques and health care.
—GRD/ demography, epidemiology, public health, statis-

tics, plus previous research experience in developing countries/ FR, PT, SP.

ⓥ★E-56. FORD FOUNDATION, Employment, Training, and Personnel Services, 320 East 43rd Street, New York, NY 10017.
—Provides philanthropic funds to assist dozens of countries around the world in the field of culture, education, government, population, rural and urban poverty, human rights, etc.
—GRD/ area studies, economics, law, political science, rural economics, social science, plus relevant overseas experience/ AB, FR, SP.

E-57. [FOSTER PARENTS] PLAN INTERNATIONAL, P.O.B. 804, 804 Quaker Lane, Warwick, RI 02818.
—Provides assistance to children, their families, and communities in developing countries, with programs in the fields of agriculture, health care, nutrition, job training, and literacy.
—UGD/GRD/ area studies, business, economics, international development, nutrition, social science, plus two years' relevant experience in developing countries/ FR, SP useful.

E-58. FREEDOM HOUSE, 48 East 21st Street, New York, NY 10010.
—Provides free books—as gifts—to schools, libraries, and young readers in over 20 countries around the world.
—UGD/GRD/ education, librarianship, teaching/ KFL helpful.

E-59. HEIFER PROJECT INTERNATIONAL, P.O.B. 808 Little Rock, AR 72203.
—Assists over 20 developing countries with agricultural, farming, and animal-care projects and programs.
—GRD/ agriculture, animal husbandry, veterinary medicine/ AB, FR, SP useful.

ⓥE-60. HELEN KELLER INTERNATIONAL, 15 West 16th Street, New York, NY 10011.
—Conducts blindness prevention programs in various countries through distribution of vitamin A, eye-care projects, and education.

—UGD/ health sciences, international affairs, public health, plus previous work experience in developing countries/ AB, FR, GE, SP preferred.

E-61.   HERITAGE FOUNDATION, 214 Massachusetts Avenue NE, Washington, DC 20002.
—Research organization; advocates limited government, strong national defense, and free enterprise.
—UGD/GRD/ domestic policy, foreign policy, international affairs, plus previous relevant experience in some cases/ KFL desirable.

★E-62.   HUDSON INSTITUTE, Herman Kahn Center, 5395 Emerson Way, P.O.B. 26-919, Indianapolis, IN 46226.
—Research organization specializing in domestic and international affairs, national security, economic development, and international business.
—UGD/GRD/ economics, education, international affairs, national security, political science/ FR, JP, RU, SP most useful.

E-63.   HUMANITAS/INTERNATIONAL, Human Rights Committee, P.O.B. 818, Menlo Park, CA 94026.
—Campaigns against human rights violations, both in the United States and abroad (Soviet Union, Latin America, South Africa, and elsewhere), and advocates humane treatment of political prisoners and a freeze of nuclear weapons.
—UGD/GRD/ area studies, international affairs, law, political science/ KFL helpful.

E-64.   INSTITUTE FOR FOOD AND DEVELOPMENT POLICY (FOOD FIRST), 145 9th Street, San Francisco, CA 94103.
—Researches hunger, agriculture, and farming issues in developing countries.
—UGD/GRD/ agriculture, health, nutrition, U.S. agricultural policies/ SP helpful.

E-65.   INSTITUTE FOR INTERNATIONAL ECONOMICS, 11 Dupont Circle NW, Suite 620, Washington, DC 20036.
—Researches practical approaches to international economic policies.
—UGD/GRD/ computers, economics, international rela-

tions, public policy, statistical analysis/ FR, GE, JP, SP preferred.

★E-66. INSTITUTE FOR POLICY STUDIES, 1901 Q Street NW, Washington, DC 20009.
—Researches U.S. foreign policy, national security, international economics, and human rights matters.
—UGD/GRD/ area studies, conference and seminar organization, economics, international relations/ PT or SP fluency in some cases.

E-67. INSTITUTE OF INTERNATIONAL EDUCATION, 809 United Nations Plaza, New York, NY 10017.
—Facilitates exchange of students, scholars, and teachers, representatives of foreign governments, corporations, and international organizations; conducts programs in over 120 countries.
—UGD/GRD/ consulting, education, research, teaching, technology, plus willingness to work in a developing country/ AB, CH, FR, PT, SH, SP.
—Computer-based referral service for location of qualified applicants; participation is open to employers from dozens of countries.

E-68. INSTITUTE OF PUBLIC ADMINISTRATION, 55 West 44th Street, New York, NY 10036.
—Provides technical assistance to public administration projects; planning, finance, and urban problems in African, Asian, and Latin American countries.
—GRD/ area studies, finance, planning, public administration/ SP.

E-69. INTERNATIONAL AGRICULTURAL DEVELOPMENT SERVICES, 1611 North Kent Street, Suite 6000, Rosslyn Plaza, Arlington, VA 22209.
Absorbed By E-125.

E-70. INTERNATIONAL ASSOCIATION FOR THE EXCHANGE OF STUDENTS FOR TECHNICAL EXPERIENCE, C/O ASSOCIATION FOR INTERNATIONAL PRACTICAL TRAINING, 10 Corporate Center, Suite 250, 10400 Little Patuxent Parkway, Columbia, MD 21044.
—Provides college and graduate students with on-the-job

practical training and experiences outside their country, and operates in over 50 countries.

—UGD/GRD/ agriculture, architecture, forestry, mathematics, technology, and related fields/ FR, GE, JP, PT, SP fluency required by some European, Asian, and Latin American countries.

E-71.   INTERNATIONAL CENTER IN NEW YORK CITY, 119 West 40th Street, 11th Floor, New York, NY 10018.

—Volunteer organization with services aimed at recently arrived foreigners, including students, refugees, and immigrants; conducts cultural programs, counseling, and job-finding assistance.

—UGD/GRD/ area studies, counseling, education, ESL, teaching/ KFL helpful.

E-72.   INTERNATIONAL EYE FOUNDATION, 7801 Norfolk Avenue, Suite 200, Bethesda, MD 20814.

—Assists developing countries with projects to set up eye health-care units, and with prevention of blindness.

—GRD/ epidemiology, ophthalmology, public health administration, plus overseas experience/ AB, FR, SP helpful.

E-73.   INTERNATIONAL EXECUTIVE SERVICE CORPS, 333 Ludlow Street, P.O.B. 10005, Stamford, CT 06904.

—Assists small business owners in developing countries by providing professional management knowledge and referral; operates in over 20 countries in Africa, the Caribbean region, and Latin America.

—UGD/GRD/ accounting, business, finance, management/ KFL useful.

E-74.   INTERNATIONAL HUMAN ASSISTANCE PROGRAMS, 360 Park Avenue South, New York, NY 10010.
INACTIVE(?)

—Assists over a dozen developing countries with programs in vocational training, agricultural techniques, health care, and community development.

—UGD/GRD/ area studies, agriculture, economic development, health science, sociology/ KFL according to assigned country.

E-75.   INTERNATIONAL INSTITUTE FOR ENVIRONMENT AND DE-
VELOPMENT, 1709 Massachusetts Avenue NW, Suite 302,
Washington, DC 20036.
—Provides assistance to over 20 developing countries in
the fields of ecology, draught, famine, flood, and
related subjects.
—UGD/GRD/ economics, international affairs, natural
resource management, science, plus previous relevant
experience/ FR, GE, SP required.

E-76.   INTERNATIONAL INSTITUTE OF RURAL RECONSTRUCTION,
475 Riverside Drive, Room 1270, New York, NY 10115.
—Offers rural reconstruction assistance to several countries in Asia and Latin America.
—GRD/ agriculture, natural resources, science/ SP helpful.

Ⓥ E-77.   INTERNATIONAL RESCUE COMMITTEE, 386 Park Avenue
South, New York, NY 10016.
—Conducts relief and resettlement programs in the U.S.
for refugees from Africa, Asia, and Europe, with
several overseas reception offices.
—UGD/GRD/ medicine, nursing, public health, social
work, plus previous relevant experience in similar pro-
jects/ CH, FR, GE, RU, SP, VI, and other languages
useful.

E-78.   INTERNATIONAL VISITORS INFORMATION SERVICE, 733
15th Street NW, Washington, DC 20005.
—Volunteer organization offering information to foreign
visitors in Washington; 24-hour-a-day service in 52
languages.
—UGD/GRD/ any field, plus language skills and experi-
ence/ KFL fluency.

Ⓥ★E-79.   INTERNATIONAL VOLUNTARY SERVICES, 1424 16th Street
NW, Suite 204, Washington, DC 20036.
—Recruits skilled technicians and volunteers upon the
request of interested governments of developing countries that need assistance in rural projects.
—UGD/GRD/ agriculture, business, irrigation, hydrol-
ogy, nursing, plus a minimum of two years' experience
in developing countries/ FR, SP helpful.

E-80. INTERNS FOR PEACE, 270 West 89th Street, New York, NY 10024.
—Cultivates understanding and respect between Jewish and Arab citizens in Israel.
—UGD/ any field, plus at least six months' living experience in Israel/ HE and/or AB.

E-81. JAPAN PRODUCTIVITY CENTER, 1901 North Forth Meyer Drive, Arlington, VA 22209.
—Provides hospitality services and study tours for Japanese businesspersons and government officials visiting the United States.
—UGD/GRD/ business administration, Japanese studies, plus exchange program experience/ JP fluency.

E-82. LUTHERAN WORLD RELIEF, 360 Park Avenue South, New York, NY 10010.
—Provides relief and development assistance programs in African, Asian, and Latin American countries.
—UGD/GRD/ accounting, agriculture, construction, education, teaching, technology/ FR, SP useful.

ⓥ★E-83. MAP INTERNATIONAL, 2200 Glynco Parkway, P.O. Box 50, Brunswick, GA 31520.
—Provides basic health care services in several developing countries.
—GRD/ education, international public health, medicine, plus at least three years' relevant experience in developing countries/ FR, SP helpful.

★E-84. MEALS FOR MILLIONS FOUNDATION, 815 Second Avenue, New York, NY 10017.
—Provides training assistance to developing countries in the fields of nutrition and health.
—UGD/GRD/ education, nutrition, public health, plus previous experience in developing countries/ FR, SP helpful.

★E-85. MERIDIAN HOUSE INTERNATIONAL, 1630 Crescent Place NW, Washington, DC 20009-9979.
—Advocates world peace through intercultural exchange programs helping foreigners to understand U.S. values, and Americans to understand foreign societies and cultures.

—UGD/GRD/ area studies, international affairs, plus at least two years' relevant experience in similar fields/ KFL desired; SP preferred.

E-86.   METRO-INTERNATIONAL, 55 East 59th Street, New York, NY 10022.
   —Assists foreign students in New York City with adjustment problems, training in the U.S., and job placement services in their native countries.
   —UGD/GRD/ area studies, counseling, education, international affairs, job placement, plus thorough knowledge of New York City and the metropolitan area/ AB, CH, FR, GE, HE, PT, RU, SP, and others.

E-87.   MIDDLE EAST INSTITUTE, 1761 N Street NW, Washington, DC 20036.
   —Promotes better understanding between the United States and countries in the Middle East.
   —GRD/ area studies, business administration, communications, economics, journalism, library science, plus experience in seminars and conference organization/ AB, PE, TU.

★E-88.   NATIONAL COOPERATIVE BUSINESS ASSOCIATION, 1401 New York Avenue NW, Washington, DC 20005.
   —Cooperative services in the fields of agricultural marketing, farm supply, housing, health care; recipients are developing countries that are members of the organization.
   —UGD/GRD/ economics, finance, food processing, international business administration, plus a minimum of three years' experience in developing countries/ FR, PT, SP desirable.

E-89.   NATIONAL COUNCIL FOR COMMUNITY SERVICES TO INTERNATIONAL VISITORS, 1420 K Street NW, Suite 800, Washington, DC 20005.
   —Receives foreign visitors, plans schedules for their trips in the United States, including visits to local communities for exchange of experiences.
   —UGD/GRD/ international relations, plus relevant experience in exchange programs/ KFL desirable according to assignment.

★E-90. NATIONAL COUNCIL FOR INTERNATIONAL HEALTH, 1101 Connecticut Avenue NW, Suite 600, Washington, DC 20006.
—Accords international health assistance to developing countries through job training and placement programs.
—GRD/ business, foreign policy, health care, medicine, public affairs, public health, social work, plus relevant experience/ KFL desirable.

E-91. NATIONAL COUNCIL FOR U.S.-CHINA TRADE, 1050 17th Street NW, Suite 350, Washington, DC 20036.
Absorbed By F-135.

ⓋE-92. NATURE CONSERVANCY, 1815 North Lynn Street, Arlington, VA 22209.
—Advocates preservation of natural biological diversity and of natural resources; conducts educational programs and policy planning in Latin American countries.
—GRD/ business, law, plus at least two years' experience with business or conservation organizations/ SP fluency.

E-93. NEAR EAST FOUNDATION, 342 Madison Avenue, Suite 1030, New York, NY 10173.
—Provides technical and rural development assistance to a dozen countries in Near East and Africa.
—GRD/ agriculture, health, nursing, nutrition, sociology, plus a minimum of two years' experience in developing countries/ AB, AFL, FR.

E-94. NEW YORK ASSOCIATION FOR NEW AMERICANS, 17 Battery Place, New York, NY 10004.
—Provides relief, medical care, housing, counseling, and job placement assistance to thousands of Jewish refugees and immigrants from Eastern Europe, Asia, and Africa.
—UGD/GRD/ counseling, education, public relations, social work, teaching, plus experience with Jewish organizations/ FR, GE, HE, RO, RU, SP, YD, and others.

★E-95. OEF INTERNATIONAL, 1815 H Street NW, 11th Floor Washington, DC 20006.

—Assistance to developing countries in the integration of women, and economic, social, and political progress of women.
—UGD/GRD/ education, health care, international affairs, vocational training/ AB, FR, SP.

E-96.   OPERATION CROSSROADS AFRICA, 475 Riverside Drive, Suite 916, New York, NY 10115.
—Promotes cooperation among youth from North America, Africa, and the Caribbean region, conducts self-help programs and work camps.
—UGD/ African area studies, community development, economic development, sociology, plus leadership training/ AB, FR, SP desirable.

★E-97.   OXFAM AMERICA, 115 Broadway, Boston, MA 02116.
—Assists poor people in over 30 developing countries with self-reliance, agricultural productivity, and community development through food, management, and community development projects.
—GRD/ agriculture, community development, education, various area studies, plus a minimum of three years' experience in developing countries/AB, FR, PT, SP, and others desirable.

Ⓥ E-98.   PAN AMERICAN DEVELOPMENT FOUNDATION, 1889 F Street NW, Washington, DC 20006.
—Assists lower-income people from Latin American and Caribbean countries to improve their standard of living through credit, vocational training, and small-business programs.
—UGD/GRD/ area studies, business, economics, education/ SP desirable.

E-99.   PAN AMERICAN SOCIETY OF THE UNITED STATES, 680 Park Avenue, New York, NY 10021.
—Promotes friendly relations and better understanding between the United States and Latin American countries.
—UGD/GRD/ area studies, cultural affairs, international affairs/ PT or SP.

Ⓥ E-100.   PARTNERS OF THE AMERICAS, 1424 K Street NW, Suite 700, Washington, DC 20005.

—Provides technical assistance and cultural exchange programs between the United States and Latin American and Caribbean countries.

—GRD/ area studies, economic development, health care, teaching, vocational training, plus solid experience in the respective fields/ SP and/or PT.

Ⓥ★E-101. PARTNERSHIP FOR PRODUCTIVITY INTERNATIONAL, 2001 S Street NW, Washington, DC 20009.

—Assists developing countries with income-generating programs in the fields of agriculture, energy, technology, and law.

—UGD/GRD/ accounting, agriculture, anthropology, area studies, economics, political science, sociology, plus substantial experience in the respective field of work/ AB, AFL, FR, SP.

E-102. PATHFINDERS FUND, 9 Galen Street, Suite 217, Watertown, MA 02172.

—Assists developing countries with family planning and population and birthrate projects.

—GRD/ area studies, demography, international affairs, medicine, nursing, sociology/ KFL helpful.

E-103. PEARL BUCK FOUNDATION, P.O. Box 181, Perkasie, PA 18944.

INACTIVE(?)

—Assists Amerasian children—left by U.S. armed forces personnel in various countries—with welfare and education programs.

—GRD/ accounting, administration, international relations, plus work experience in developing countries/ CH, FL, JP, KO, TH required.

Ⓥ E-104. PEOPLE-TO-PEOPLE HEALTH FOUNDATION/PROJECT HOPE, Health Sciences Education Center, Mill Wood, VA 22646.

—Assists developing countries with modern health-care systems and techniques, operates in Africa, Asia, Latin America and some European countries.

—GRD/ health care, health education, medicine, nutrition, public health, sanitation/ AB, CH, FR, PT, SP most useful.

E-105.   PHELPS STOKES FUND, 10 East 87th Street, New York, NY 10028.
—Provides opportunities for U.S. scholars to work in African institutions and for African scholars to work in U.S. universities; also offers grant loans to African students in the U.S.
—GRD/ African area studies, education, teaching, plus exchange program administration experience/ AFL.

E-106.   PLANNED PARENTHOOD FEDERATION OF AMERICA, 810 Seventh Avenue, New York, NY 10019.
—Assists over 30 developing countries with medical care and birth-control programs.
—UGD/GRD/ business administration, demography, economics, public administration, public health, plus a minimum of two years' experience in developing countries/ AB, FR, SP fluency preferred.

E-107.   POPULATION COUNCIL, Personnel Services, 1 Dag Hammarskjöld Plaza, New York, NY 10017.
—Provides research and programs in over 40 developing countries in the fields of human welfare, human reproduction, health, and family planning.
—GRD/ biomedicine, demography, economics, international relations, public health, social science, plus previous experience in developing countries/ FR, SP fluency for some positions.

★E-108.   POPULATION REFERENCE BUREAU, 1875 Connecticut Avenue NW, Suite 520, Washington, DC 20005.
—Researches, collects, interprets, and disseminates information on population growth and change.
—UGD/GRD/ demography, information science, journalism, policy analysis, sociology, plus a minimum of three years' prior experience in population analysis, legislative work, or writing/ FR, SP preferred.

E-109.   PROJECT CONCERN INTERNATIONAL, 3550 Afton Road, P.O.B. 85323, San Diego, CA 92138.
—Provides health care/education, and disease prevention programs to children and mothers in Latin American countries and in Indonesia.

—UGD/GRD/ health education, medicine, nursing, plus a minimum of one year's experience in developing countries/ IN, SP.

E-110. PUBLIC ADMINISTRATION SERVICE, 8301 Greensboro Drive, Suite 420, McLean, VA 22102.
—Provides consulting and research assistance to governments of developing countries, with programs on management system improvements.
—GRD/ area studies, business administration, government affairs, public administration/ AB, FR, SP, PT helpful.

E-111. ROCKEFELLER FOUNDATION, 1133 Avenue of the Americas, New York, NY 10036.
—Promotes well-being of humanity through programs in the fields of agriculture, education, arts, humanities, health care, etc., to over 35 developing countries in Africa, Asia, and Latin America.
—GRD/ African, Asian, Latin American area studies, economics, economic development, education, sociology, teaching/ AB, AFL, ASL, FR, PT, SP.

★E-112. SAVE THE CHILDREN FEDERATION, Personnel Office, 54 Wilton Road, Westport, CT 06880.
—Assists needy children in over 30 developing countries with programs in community development.
—UGD/GRD/ area studies, community development, education, teaching, plus previous experience in developing countries/ FR, PT, SP.

E-113. SELF-RELIANCE FOUNDATION, Box 1, Las Trampas, NM 87576.
INACTIVE(?)
—Assists local population to combine traditional lifestyles with modern technology.
—UGD/ audiovisual production, photography, research, writing/ SP fluency.

E-114. STATE YMCA OF MICHIGAN WORLD AMBASSADORS, 301 West Lenawee Street, Lansing, MI 48914.
Absorbed By E-132.

◨ⓋE-115. SUMMER INSTITUTE OF LINGUISTICS, 19891 Beach Boulevard, Huntington Beach, CA 92647.
—Specializes in language research and applied linguistics among ethnic minority groups from over 40 countries around the world; prepares literacy materials and Bible translations into previously unwritten languages.
—UGD/GRD/ Bible training, language skills, plus previous relevant experience and desire to be a volunteer/ MUL, over 700 languages.

E-116. SURVIVAL INTERNATIONAL, 2122 Decatur Place NW, Washington, D.C. 20008.
—Helps poor people from South American countries to find humane, practical, and constructive solutions for adjustment to modern ways of life.
—UGD/GRD/ anthropology, economic development, Latin American studies, public relations, sociology/ SP fluency.

★E-117. TECHNOSERVE, 148 East Avenue, Norwalk, CT 06851.
—Provides assistance to developing countries in the fields of self-help and business expertise through various programs in Latin America and Africa.
—UGD/GRD/ accounting, agribusiness, agronomy, business administration, engineering, finance, plus a minimum of three years' experience in developing countries/ FR, SH, SP desirable.

E-118. TINKER FOUNDATION, 55 East 59th Street, New York, NY 10022.
—Promotes better understanding among the United States, Spain, Portugal, and Latin American countries through various cultural exchange programs.
—GRD/ administration, area studies, cultural studies, education, plus exchange program experience/ PT, SP.

E-119. TOLSTOY FOUNDATION, 200 Park Avenue South, New York, NY 10003.
—Provides philanthropic assistance to Russian and Eastern European as well as Asian refugees through resettlement and adjustment programs, social and economic aid, teaching ESL, and job placement services.

—UGD/GRD/ humanitarian affairs, immigration law, social work, plus relevant work experience with immigrants/ CA, CZ, GE, HU, LO, PE, PO, RO, RU, VI useful.

E-120.   TRILATERAL COMMISSION, 345 East 46th Street, New York, NY 10017.
—Promotes cooperative relations among the United States, Western European countries, and Japan through programs involving distinguished scholars and other competent persons interested in practical solutions and proposals of mutual interest.
—GRD/ administration, economics, international affairs, Russian and Asian studies, West European studies/ JP, RU.

E-121.   UNITED BOARD FOR CHRISTIAN HIGHER EDUCATION IN ASIA, 475 Riverside Drive, New York, NY 10027.
—Assists over 20 Asian academic institutions with programs encouraging community responsibility and national leadership.
—GRD/ Asian studies, community development, education, public relations/ ASL helpful.

ⓥE-122.   VOLUNTEERS FOR MISSION, Episcopal Church Foundation, 815 Second Avenue, New York, NY 10017.
INACTIVE(?)
—Offers assistance to over 100 developing countries in Africa, Asia, and Latin America in the fields of health, technology, education, social work, etc.
—UGD/GRD/ agriculture, education, health science, social work, teaching/ AFL, FR, GE, JP, SP, UD.

ⓥ★E-123.   VOLUNTEERS IN TECHNICAL ASSISTANCE (VITA), 1815 North Lynn Street, Arlington, VA 22209.
—Provides technical assistance to over 100 developing countries, conducts special programs related to technology, small business, and training.
—GRD/ agriculture, engineering, housing construction, sanitation, water/ FR, SP highly desirable, plus experience in developing countries.

E-124.   WASHINGTON OFFICE ON LATIN AMERICA, 110 Maryland Avenue NE, Suite 404, Washington, DC 20002.
  —Monitors human rights practices and political developments in Central and South American countries, and the implementation of U.S. policies in these countries.
  —UGD/GRD/ foreign affairs, Latin American studies, political science, plus a minimum of experience in legislative or foreign policy/ PT, SP.

Ⓥ E-125.   WINROCK INTERNATIONAL INSTITUTE FOR AGRICULTURAL DEVELOPMENT, Petit Jean Mountain, Route No. 3, Morrilton, AR 72110.
  —Assists about 20 developing countries with programs in agriculture to alleviate hunger, poverty, and reduced productivity.
  —UGD/GRD/ biological science, physical science, program implementation, socioecology, plus a minimum of two years' experience in developing countries/ PT, SP useful.
  —Has absorbed E-69.

E-126.   WORLD CONCERN, P.O. Box 33000, Seattle, WA 98133.
  —Provides assistance to over 40 developing countries with programs in the fields of farming, small business, medical services, and others.
  —GRD/ agriculture, engineering, medicine, public health, plus a minimum of two years' experience in developing countries/ FR, SO, SP.

E-127.   WORLD NEIGHBOR, 4127 NW 122, Oklahoma City, OK 73120.
  —Assists over 20 developing countries in Africa, Asia, and Latin America with community development, family planning, food production, health, and education projects.
  —GRD/ agriculture, education, engineering, health, water/ FR, PT, SP.

E-128.   WORLD REHABILITATION FUND, 332 East 29th Street, New York, NY 10010.
  —Assists disabled people in developing countries with programs providing artificial limbs, braces, and training in self-help routines.

—GRD/ administration, area studies, medicine, public relations/ KFL helpful according to assigned country.

E-129.   WORLD RELIEF CORPORATION, P.O. Box WRC, Wheaton, IL 60189.
—Provides assistance programs to poor people in the Philippines, Indonesia, and Honduras.
—UGD/GRD/ area studies, social work, plus cross-cultural experience and ability to work with the under-privileged/ FL, IN, SP.

E-130.   WORLD VISION RELIEF AND DEVELOPMENT, 919 West Huntington Drive, Monrovia, CA 91016.
—Provides charity assistance to over 80 developing and European countries in the fields of health, agriculture, business, etc.
—GRD/ business, health science, medicine, public health, technology, plus a minimum of five years' experience in developing countries/ FR, SP preferred.

◢E-131.   WYCLIFFE BIBLE TRANSLATORS, P.O.B. 2727, Huntington Beach, CA 92647.
—Evangelical organization services, with emphasis on linguistic analysis of little-known languages and translation of the Bible into these languages; conducts programs in over 40 countries.
—UGD/ Bible studies, language skills/ MUL; dozens of languages.

★E-132.   YMCA-YWCA OF THE UNITED STATES OF AMERICA, 101 North Wacker Drive, Chicago, IL 60606/ 726 Broadway, New York, NY 10003.
—Sponsors partnerships with this organization in over 90 countries around the world; offers assistance to developing countries; and conducts sport, recreational, educational, and vocational training programs.
—UGD/GRD/ Asian studies, international services, teaching ESL, vocational teaching, plus voluntary experience with this or similar organizations/ CH, JP helpful.

★E-133.   YOUTH FOR UNDERSTANDING, 3501 Newark Street NW, Washington, DC 20016.
—Conducts exchange programs for high school students

by sending U.S. students abroad and foreign students
to the U.S., and placing them with host families.
—GRD/ education, international relations, liberal arts,
plus work experience with exchange programs/ FR, JP,
SP preferred.

Addendum Section E

E-134. AFRICARE, 440 R Street NW, Washington, DC 20001.
—Concerned with improvement of life in rural areas of
Africa; promotes development of environmental and
water resources, agricultural training, and health care.
—UGD/GRD/ agricultural development, health care
studies, public health/ KFL desirable, especially AB,
FR, PT.

E-135. AGRICULTURAL DEVELOPMENT COUNCIL, 725 Park Avenue, New York, NY 10021.
—Focuses on research and training to provide manpower
needed in assisting Asian countries and others which are
developing their agricultural resources more affectively.
—GRD/ administration, agricultural economics, Asian
studies, economic development, economics/ KFL
according to area of program.

E-136. AMERICAN COMMITTEE ON U.S.-SOVIET RELATIONS, 109
11th Street SE, Washington, DC 20003.
—Promotes better relations between America and the
former Soviet Union, presently known as CIS (Community of Independent States) by providing accurate information and expert analyses on both countries.
—GRD/ administration, conference organization, Russian area studies/ RU preferred.

E-137. AMERICAN COUNCIL FOR NATIONALITIES SERVICE, 95
Madison Avenue, New York, NY 10019.
—Promotes understanding and cooperation between
various American ethnic, racial, and religious groups;
assists immigrants with adjusting to American society.
—UGD/GRD/ area studies, counseling, international
relations, job placement, social work/ KFL useful.

E-138. AMERICAN COUNCIL FOR VOLUNTARY INTERNATIONAL
ACTION (INTER ACTION), 200 Park Avenue South, New
York, NY 10003.

—Provides a forum for cooperation, planning, and exchange of ideas and information among American voluntary organizations involved in overseas operations.
—UGD/GRD/ agriculture, construction, engineering, forestry, logistics, project management, public health, plus experience in developing countries/ KFL according to area/country of work.

E-139.   AMERICAN COUNCIL ON LEARNED SOCIETIES, 228 East 45th Street, New York, NY 10017.
—Administers programs of fellowships and grants to advance research in the fields of area studies, languages, economics, political studies.
—GRD/ administration, area studies, public relations/ KFL required.

E-140.   AMERICAN EDUCATIONAL TRUST FUND, P.O. Box 53062, Washington, DC 20009.
—Provides the American public with balanced and accurate information concerning United States relations with Middle Eastern States.
—GRD/ area studies, public relations, research, writing/ AB, HE, PE useful.

E-141.   AMERICAN-MIDEAST EDUCATIONAL AND TRAINING SERVICES (AMIDEAST), 1100 17th Street NW, Washington, DC 20036.
—Provides technical training in the areas where economic growth places emphasis on management and technology skills.
—UGD/GRD/ accounting, area studies, business administration, computers, electronics, human resources, vocational training/ AB, HE, PE useful.

E-142.   ATLANTIC COUNCIL OF THE UNITED STATES, 1616 H Street NW, Washington, DC 20006.
—Fosters better relations and ties between Western Europe, North America, Japan, Australia, and New Zealand, by increasing their security and harmonizing their economic, monetary, energy, and other interests.
—GRD/ area studies, foreign policy, international relations, military technology, national security studies/ RU useful.

E-143.   CARE, INC., International Employment, 660 1st Avenue, New York, NY 10016.
—Assists poor people in over 35 countries to become self-supporting by organizing and properly utilizing the existing resources in the areas of nutrition, health, employment, disaster relief, and others.
—UGD/ administration, construction, nutrition, public health, water resources, plus two years of previous experience/FR, SP preferred.

E-144.   CARIBBEAN/CENTRAL AMERICAN ACTION (C/CAA), Suite 510, 1211 Connecticut Avenue NW, Washington, DC 20036.
—Stimulates economic results and long-term constructive public policy by organizing special annual conferences, seminars, and other gatherings on business development and technical assistance issues.
—UGD/GRD/ business, Latin American studies, political science/ SP fluency.

E-145.   CITIZENS EXCHANGE COUNCIL, 18 East 41st Street, New York, NY 10017.
—Organizes intercultural programs between Americans and citizens of nations having different political and/or economic systems.
—UGD/GRD/ cultural studies, exchange programs, area studies on Russia and its neighboring republics/ SLL useful.

E-146.   COALITION FOR NATIONAL SERVICE, 5140 Sherier Place, NW, Washington, DC 20016.
—Brings together American and Russian volunteers to work together in both countries and in other countries in order to meet human and environmental needs.
—UGD/GRD/ area studies, conservation, economic development, education, health care, literacy training/ KFL area or country of program.

E-147.   COMMISSION ON U.S.-CENTRAL AMERICAN RELATIONS, 731 Eighth Street SE, Washington, DC 20003.
—Promotes a new role for the United States in Central America, advocates peace through negotiations and elimination of negative effects of American interference in Central American affairs.

—GRD/ Central American studies, international affairs, political science, public relations/ SP fluency a must.

E-148. COMMITTEE ON MIGRATION AND REFUGEE AFFAIRS c/o American Council of Voluntary Agencies for Foreign Service, 200 Park Avenue South, New York, NY 10003.
—Assists U.S. government officials in processing of refugees for resettlement in America, and represents voluntary agencies in the country of first asylum.
—UGD/GRD/ area studies, social work, work with refugees/ KFL according to area/country of program.

E-149. EXPERIMENT IN INTERNATIONAL LIVING, Brattleboro, VT 05301/1411 K Street NW, Washington, DC 20005.
—Fosters cross-cultural communications and experiments by placing young American students with foreign families abroad, and foreign students with American families in the USA; also maintains a school for international training.
—UGD/GRD/ liberal arts, teaching, plus experience with exchange programs/ KFL helpful.

E-150. FEDERATION FOR AMERICAN IMMIGRATION REFORMS, 1424 16th Street NW, Washington, DC 20036.
—Focuses on stricter border controls and elimination of illegal immigration to America causing damages to unemployed Americans.
—UGD/GRD/ labor relations, Latin American affairs, with emphasis on Mexico, public relations/ SP fluency required.

E-151. FOUNDATION FOR THE MIDDLE EAST, 555 13th Street NW, Washington, DC 20004.
—Promotes peace objectives in the Middle East through public relations and publishing projects.
—GRD/ administration, area studies, public relations, writing/ AB, HE useful.

E-152. FUND FOR PEACE, 823 United Nations Plaza, New York, NY 10017/1755 Massachusetts Avenue NW, Washington, DC 20036.
—Dedicated to the elimination of war as a method of settling international disputes; involved in projects on

international policy, national security, world politics and others.

—GRD/ area studies, economic development, international affairs, national security, public relations, research/ KFL according to program.

E-153. HUMAN RIGHTS WATCH, 36 West 44th Street, New York, NY 10036/712 G Street SE, Washington, DC 20003.
—Monitors human rights practices by various governments, protests against murder, torture, psychiatric, and other abuses violating human rights.
—UGD/GRD/ area studies, administration, foreign policy, international affairs, law, plus strong commitment to human rights/ KFL useful.

E-154. INTERNATIONAL RESEARCH & EXCHANGES BOARD (IREX), 1616 H Street NW, Washington, DC 20006.
—Administers principal academic exchange between the United States and Russia as well as other republics of the former Soviet Union and East European countries based on applications with deadlines.
—GRD/ area studies, history, humanities, languages, literature, and other fields/ KFL fluency (or near fluency) according to country of program.

E-155. INTERNATIONAL STUDENT SERVICE, 356 West 34th Street, New York, NY 10007.
—Offers various services to students and trainees from abroad by meeting students at the airports, facilitating contacts with communities, sponsoring educational travel programs.
—UGD/GRD/ international relations, liberal arts, plus exchange programs experience/ KFL desirable.

E-156. JOINT NATIONAL COMMITTEE FOR LANGUAGES (JNCL), 300 Eye Street NE, Suite 211, Washington, DC 20002.
—Dedicated to the advancement of language studies in America; seeks federal government support for foreign languages and international studies.
—GRD/ foreign languages, international studies, political studies/ KFL preferred.

E-157. NATIONAL ASSOCIATION FOR FOREIGN STUDENTS AFFAIRS, 1860 19th Street NW, Washington, DC 20009.

—Provides training information and other educational services to professionals in the field of international education exchange; keeps contacts with over 50 countries.

—UGD/GRD/ liberal arts, studies of foreign cultures, plus experience in working with foreign students/ KFL desirable.

E-158. NATIONAL COMMITTEE ON U.S.-CHINA RELATIONS, 777 United Nations Plaza, New York, NY 10017.

—Emphasizes necessity of increased knowledge of China as an essential element in American foreign policy; organizes cultural exchanges, sport activities, dances and other programs.

—GRD/ area studies, communications, cultural exchange program experience, public relations/ CH important.

E-159. NATIONAL DEMOCRATIC INSTITUTE FOR INTERNATIONAL AFFAIRS, 1717 Massachusetts Avenue NW, Washington, DC 20036.

—Promotes and supports democratic institutions, movements, and cooperation with political parties in countries with new and emerging democracies in Europe, Asia, and Latin America.

—GRD/ administration, area studies, political science, public relations/ KFL desirable according to country/ area of program.

E-160. SISTERS CITIES INTERNATIONAL, 120 South Paine Street, Alexandria, VA 22314.

—Fosters better understanding and international cooperation through sister city relationships between American and cities from other countries; maintains relationships in over 80 countries.

—GRD/ administration, area studies, international affairs, public relations, plus interest in the concept of sistercities/ KFL fluency according to country of program.

E-161. VOLUNTEERS IN OVERSEAS COOPERATIVE ASSISTANCE, 50 F Street NW, Suite 1075, Washington, DC 20001.

—Recruits and places volunteers on short-term basis to assist agricultural producers in developing countries.

—UGD/GRD/ agricultural economy, agriculture,

engineering, plus experience in similar projects/ KFL desirable, especially FR and SP.

E-162.   WORLD EDUCATION, P.O. Box 745, Old Chelsea Station, New York, NY 10013.
—Uses special techniques developed in India to teach villagers to write and read on the basis of special materials focusing on daily work and expressions.
—UGD/GRD/ area studies, education, teaching/ KFL fluency according to area/country of program.

E-163.   YMCA, INTERNATIONAL STUDENT SERVICE & INTERNA-TIONAL PROGRAMS, 356 West 34th Street, Suite 320, New York, NY 10001.
—Promotes overseas experiences for both the United States and foreign young adults to a better mutual understanding; sponsors youth exchange programs be-tween the United States and dozens of countries.
—UGD/GRD/ counseling, education, teaching/ KFL desirable.

F. PRIVATE SECTOR: BANKING, COMMERCIAL, CONSULTING, RESEARCH, AND OTHER FIRMS

◢F-1.   AD-EX WORLDWIDE, 525 Middlefield Road, Suite 150, Menlo Park, CA 94025.
—Provides translation services from and into English, with emphasis on technical, promotional, and legal literature, as well as other specialized subjects.
—UGD/GRD/ engineering, law, science, technology, and other related subjects, plus professional experience/ MUL.

◢F-2.   ALL-LANGUAGE SERVICES, Personnel Director, 545 Fifth Avenue, New York, NY 10017.
—Provides translation services in over 60 languages in the fields of business, engineering, science, technology, etc.
—UGD/GRD/ business, science disciplines, technology, and other areas, plus considerable professional experi-ence and editing skills/ MUL.

F-3.   AMERICAN EXPRESS BANK, Human Resources Department, American Express Tower, New York, NY 10285-2050.

—Specializes in international financial services with operations in about 40 countries.

—UGD/GRD/ accounting, economics, finance, plus previous banking experience/ CH, FR, GE, SP are valuable.

F-4.　AMERICAN INTERNATIONAL GROUP, International Human Resources, 70 Pine Street, New York, NY 10270.
　　　—Insurance company with operations in 13 countries.
　　　—UGD/GRD/ accounting, business administration, international marketing, plus previous work or overseas experience and desire to travel/ KFL preferred.

F-5.　AMERICAN MOTORS CORPORATION, International Staff [Presently part of Chrysler Corp., P.O.B. 1919 Detroit, MI 48288.]
　　　—Manufactures and assembles passenger cars and jeeps in over 100 countries around the world.
　　　—UGD/GRD/ engineering, marketing, finance, plus a minimum three years' experience/ FR, SP preferred.

F-6.　AMERITRUST COMPANY, Personnel and Organization Department, 900 Euclid Avenue, Cleveland, OH 44101.
　　　—Specializes in financial operations abroad with emphasis on exports and plant expansions overseas.
　　　—UGD/GRD/ accounting, business-related subjects, finance/ SP helpful.

F-7.　ARMCO INTERNATIONAL SALES, 300 Interpace Parkway, Parsippany, NJ 07054.
　　　—Markets steel and metallurgical products overseas, with special interest in Russia and East European countries.
　　　—UGD/GRD/ accounting, business administration, economics, finance/ CZ, HU, PO, RO, RU.

F-8.　ARTHUR D. LITTLE, INC., Personnel Department, Acorn Park, Cambridge, MA 02140.
　　　—Provides consulting services in management, engineering, scientific fields, etc., with operations in 60 countries.
　　　—GRD/ engineering, law, science and related subjects, plus considerable professional and overseas experience/ AB, FR, GE, JP, SP.

F-9.　ARTHUR YOUNG INTERNATIONAL, 277 Park Avenue, New York, NY 10172. [Presently called Ernst & Young International.]

—Provides accounting services with offices in over 65 countries.

—GRD/ accounting, administration, plus area studies/ KFL helpful.

★F-10.   ASSOCIATED PRESS, Human Resources Department, 50 Rockefeller Plaza, New York, NY 10020.

—Agency specializing in news gathering and dissemination of local, national, and international news to over 15,000 newspapers and radio and television stations in over 100 countries.

—UGD/GRD/ broadcasting, journalism, mass media, plus at least two years' experience in daily news as a journalist or broadcaster/ KFL required for overseas assignments according to country of work.

★F-11.   AVON PRODUCTS, Staffing Division, 9 West 57th Street, New York, NY 10019.

—Produces and sells cosmetics, jewelry, and toiletries in over 25 countries.

—GRD/ business administration, international marketing, planning, plus willingness to travel/ CH, FR, GE, SP important.

F-12.   BANKAMERICA, World Banking Division, 555 California Street, San Francisco, CA 94104.

—Provides banking and finance services abroad, and operates in 38 offices outside the United States.

—UGD/GRD/ accounting, administration, finance, law; previous experience is not essential/ CH, GE, JP, RU, SP are important.

F-13.   BANK OF AMERICA NATIONAL TRUST & SAVINGS ASSOCIATION, Personnel Administration, 555 California Street, San Francisco, CA 94104.

—Provides banking and financial services abroad, and operates in 77 countries.

—GRD/ accounting, business subjects, finance/ AB, FR, SP desirable.

F-14.   BANK OF TOKYO TRUST COMPANY, Human Resources Department, 100 Broadway, New York, NY 10005.

—Provides a wide range of banking and financial services and has over 250 offices overseas.

—UGD/GRD/ accounting, finance, marketing; work experience is not essential/ KFL required for some positions.

F-15.   BANKERS TRUST COMPANY, Management Recruiting, 280 Park Avenue, New York, NY 10017.
—Provides multiple banking and financial services, with offices in dozens of countries abroad.
—UGD/GRD/ accounting, finance, marketing, plus analytical, verbal, and interpersonal skills/ KFL and cultural affinity desirable.

★F-16.   BEIJING-WASHINGTON, 4340 East-West Highway, Suite 200, Bethesda, MD 20814.
—Provides export consulting services, and represents the United States, Canada, and European firms in the People's Republic of China.
—GRD/ electronics, engineering, international relations, marketing, technology/ CH(mn) required.

◢★F-17.   BERLITZ TRANSLATION SERVICES, 257 Park Avenue South, New York, NY 10022.
—Provides translation services in several languages and in several fields, and operates language training schools in the United States and abroad.
—UGD/GRD/ engineering, liberal arts, science, social science, technology, etc., translation and interpretation skills on a superior level, plus experience in a specific field of work/ MUL.

F-18.   BOEING COMPANY, Employment Division, 7755 East Marginal Way South, Seattle, WA 98108.
—Produces commercial airplanes, with operations in dozens of countries around the world.
—GRD/ engineering, finance, law, plus previous experience in the aerospace industry, and willingness to travel overseas/ CH, FR, GE, JP, SP are useful.

F-19.   BOYDEN ASSOCIATES, Administration Department, 10 East 53rd Street, New York, NY 10016.
—Recruits executives in the business field for U.S. and foreign firms.
—UGD/GRD/ business administration and other related backgrounds, plus a minimum of ten years' experience in the business field/ KFL needed.

F-20.   BURSON-MARSTELLER INTERNATIONAL, 230 Park Avenue South, New York, NY 10022.
—Provides consulting services in the field of government relations, industrial development, tourism, environmental issues, and consumer affairs.
—UGD/GRD/ banking, business, finance, engineering, law, marketing, medicine, nutrition, science, and other fields/ CH, FR, GE, PT.

F-21.   BUSINESS INTERNATIONAL CORPORATION, 215 Park Avenue South, New York, NY 10022.
—Provides consulting, research, and publishing services; operates offices in Asia, Africa, Europe, and Latin America.
—UGD/GRD/ business, finance, public administration/ KFL helpful.

★F-22. CABLE NEWS NETWORK, 1 CNN Center, Atlanta, GA 30335.
—A local news channel operating 24 hours daily, and covering local, national, and international events.
—UGD/GRD/ broadcasting, journalism, mass media, plus at least ten years' experience as a television reporter/ AB, FR, RU, SP useful.

F-23.   CACI INTERNATIONAL, INC., Personnel Department, 1700 North Moore Street, Arlington, VA 22209.
—Provides management consulting services in demography, computers, transportation, and other fields.
—UGD/GRD/ business administration, computers, economics, political science, psychology, sociology/ KFL very helpful; operates a language center teaching 30 languages.

F-24.   CARL BYOIR AND ASSOCIATES, 380 Madison Avenue, New York, NY 10017.
—Provides public relations services, with dozens of branches operating in Asia, Europe, Latin America, and the Middle East.
—GRD/ communications, journalism, marketing, public relations, research, writing/ AB, FR, GE, JP, SP.

★F-25. CHASE MANHATTAN BANK, College Relations, 1 Chase Manhattan Plaza, 27th Floor, New York, NY 10015.
—Provides a wide range of banking, financial, marketing, and other services in over 100 countries around the world.
—UGD/GRD/ accounting, business administration, economics, finance, international affairs, plus overseas living or working experience, and desire to relocate abroad/ KFL fluency.

F-26. CHECCHI AND COMPANY, Personnel Department, 1730 Rhode Island Avenue NW, Washington, DC 20036.
—Provides consulting services in the fields of agricultural production, business management, education, tourism, and operates in over 20 countries.
—UGD/GRD/ business administration, economics, international relations, plus previous relevant experience/ ASL desirable.

★F-27. CHEMICAL BANKING CORPORATION, Personnel Department, 55 Water Street, 2nd Floor, New York, NY 10041.
—Provides a wide range of banking and financial services, and has offices in over 30 countries.
—GRD/ accounting, business administration, economics, finance, international affairs/ JP, SP required.

F-28. CIGNA, International Employment Division, 1600 Arch Street 11-P, Philadelphia, PA 19103.
—Insurance company with offices operating in dozens of countries.
—UGD/GRD/ accounting, banking, business administration, finance, marketing, plus overseas living experience/ KFL proficiency, at least one foreign language.

F-29. CITICORP AND CITIBANK, Personnel Division, 399 Park Avenue, 26th Floor, New York, NY 10043.
—Provides banking and financial services in over 100 countries in Asia, the Middle East, Europe, and Africa.
—UGD/GRD/ accounting, banking, business administration, finance, international affairs, plus international experience/ AB, FR, SP helpful.

F-30.   CITIZENS AND SOUTHERN NATIONAL BANK, College Relations, 35 Broad Street, Atlanta, GA 30303.
—Provides banking and financial services with offices in Asia, Europe, and Latin America.
—GRD/ area studies, banking, business, foreign economics, international relations, political science/ KFL fluency.

F-31.   CLEARY, GOTTLIEB, STEEN AND HAMILTON, Legal Personnel Section, Liberty Plaza, New York, NY 10004.
—Law firm services with several offices overseas.
—GRD/ law, plus superior academic performance, and ability to work with clients of various nations/ FR, GE, JP, SP important.

★F-32.   COCA-COLA COMPANY, Human Resources Department, 1 Coca-Cola Plaza, Atlanta, GA 30313.
—America's largest producer and distributor of beverages, with overseas operations in over 50 countries.
—UGD/GRD/ business, law, marketing, technical subjects, plus a minimum of two years of overseas experience, and willingness to relocate abroad/ AB, FR, GE, JP, SP preferred.

F-33.   CONTINENTAL ILLINOIS NATIONAL BANK & TRUST COMPANY, College Relations Department, 231 South La Salle Street, Chicago, IL 60693.
—Provides banking and financial services in over 30 countries abroad.
—GRD/ accounting, banking, finance, plus analytical and interpersonal skills, and overseas living experience/ KFL according to assigned country.

◢F-34.   CONWAY ASSOCIATES INTERNATIONAL, 104 East 40th Street, New York, NY 10016.
INACTIVE(?)
—Provides translation and interpretation services for shows, conferences, congresses, and copyrighting in foreign languages.
—UGD/GRD/ liberal arts, linguistics, translation and interpretation training, plus relevant experience/ CH, FR, JP, KO, RU, SP, and others.

F-35.   COUDERT BROTHERS, Hiring Committee, 200 Park Avenue, New York, NY 10166.
        —Law firm operating in the United States and in several countries abroad.
        —GRD/ law, plus superior academic record, maturity, initiative, and innovative approaches/ CH, FR, IN, IT, JP, PT, SP helpful.

F-36.   DATA RESOURCE, Employment Department, 24 Hartwell Avenue, Lexington, MA 02173.
        —Provides consulting services in the fields of software, economic forecasting, financial matters.
        —GRD/ area economics related to Asia, Europe, Latin America, econometrics, international economics, plus a minimum of one year of relevant experience/ CH, FR, GE, JP fluency is preferred.

F-37.   DEVELOPMENT ASSOCIATES, Personnel Department, 2924 Columbia Pike, Arlington, VA 22204.
        —Provides consulting services in the fields of education, social, and economic development in the United States and abroad.
        —UGD/GRD/ computers, engineering, science, technical subjects, plus minimum of three years' experience/ KFL fluency.

F-38.   DRESDNER BANK, Personnel Office, 75 Wall Street, New York, NY 10005.
        —Operates as a branch of a major German bank, and provides banking and financial services.
        —UGD/ accounting, business administration, finance/ GE fluency.

F-39.   EAST-WEST CENTER, 1777 East-West Road, Honolulu, HI 96848.
        —Promotes better relations and understanding between the U.S. and Asian nations through cooperative study, training, and research programs.
        —GRD/ area studies, communications, culture, environment, population resources/ ASL.

★F-40. E. I. DU PONT DE NEMOURS, Professional Staffing/Employment Relations Department, 1007 Market Street, Wilmington, DE 19898.

—Produces chemical and energy products, operating offices in over 50 countries in Africa, Asia, the Middle East, Europe, and Latin America.
—UGD/GRD/ chemical sciences, electrical subjects, life sciences, plus previous relevant experience/ FR, GE, JP preferred.

F-41.   EGON ZEHNDER INTERNATIONAL, 55 East 59th Street, New York, NY 10022.
—Provides consulting services in executive recruiting and management matters, operating in 18 countries.
—GRD/ business administration, plus a second degree in a related major, with extensive business and management experience/ KFL fluency.

F-42.   EMERSON ELECTRIC COMPANY, International Division, 8000 West Florissant Avenue, St. Louis, MO 63136.
—Produces electronic and electric systems for industrial and individual markets, with operations in dozens of countries.
—UGD/GRD/ business administration, engineering, technical subjects, plus at least three years' experience/ CH, FR, GE, JP, RU most useful.

F-43.   ERNST AND WHINNEY, 2000 National City Center, Cleveland, OH 44114.
—Provides accounting services, with offices in over 70 countries around the world.
—GRD/ accounting, administration, area studies/ KFL helpful.

F-44.   EUROPEAN AMERICAN BANK, Employment Division, EAB Plaza, Uniondale, NY 11553.
—Provides banking and financial services in several countries abroad.
—UGD/GRD/ accounting, banking, business management, international studies, plus overseas living experience/ KFL fluency.

F-45.   EXPERIENCE, 1200 Second Avenue South, Minneapolis, MN 55403.
—Provides consulting services in the fields of natural resources, agricultural production, marketing, and technology.

—GRD/ agricultural development, agricultural economics, agronomy, marketing, plus appropriate experience in agricultural development/ AB, CH, FR useful;
SP has priority (fluency in one).

F-46.   FIRST INTERSTATE BANK OF CALIFORNIA, College Relations and Recruitment Department, 707 Wilshire Boulevard, Los Angeles, CA 90017.
—Provides banking and financial services in over 35
countries.
—UGD/GRD/ accounting, banking, finance, plus living
experience abroad/ KFL desirable.

F-47.   FIRST NATIONAL BANK OF BOSTON, College Relations
Department, P.O. Box 1976, Boston, MA 02105.
Absorbed by Bank of Boston Corporation, 100 Federal
Street, Boston, MA 02110.
—Provides banking and financial services with offices
operating in over 40 countries in Africa, Asia, the
Middle East, Europe, the Caribbean, and Latin Amer-
ica.
—UGD/GRD/ accounting, economics, finance, liberal
arts, plus overseas experience/ KFL desirable.

F-48.   FIRST PENNSYLVANIA BANK, Personnel Department, 16th
and Market Streets, Center Square Building, Philadelphia,
PA 19101.
—Provides banking and financial services in several overseas offices.
—UGD/GRD/ accounting, business, economics, finance,
plus previous business experience/ KFL desirable.

F-49.   FIRST WISCONSIN NATIONAL BANK OF MILWAUKEE, Recruitment Department, 777 East Wisconsin Avenue, Milwaukee, WI 53202.
—Provides banking and financial services with connections abroad.
—UGD/GRD/ accounting, banking, finance, liberal arts,
plus demonstrated ability, commitment to banking, and
interest in growing professionally/ KFL desirable, SP
preferred.

F-50.   FMC CORPORATION, 200 East Randolph Drive, Chicago,
IL 60601.

—Produces chemicals and machinery for agriculture, industry, and government; conducts operations in over a dozen countries abroad.

—UGD/GRD/ business management, international analysis, international marketing, plus analytical skills and experience with a manufacturing company and its environment/ KFL helpful.

F-51.   GFE TRANSLATION COMPANY, 6807 Winter Lane, Annandale, VA 22003.
       —Provides translation of technical literature in English into languages of developing countries.
       —UGD/GRD/ computers, engineering, science, technology, plus experience in translating technical literature/ MUL.

F-52.   GIBSON, DUNN AND CRUTCHER, International Department, 333 South Grand Avenue, Los Angeles, CA 90071.
       —Law firm services with operations in three overseas offices in Europe.
       —GRD/ law, superior academic record in top American law schools/ FR, GE, IT.

F-53.   GOODYEAR TIRE AND RUBBER COMPANY, Salaried Personnel Division, 1144 East Market Street, Akron, OH 44316-0001.
       —Produces tires, rubber products, industrial chemicals, and operates in over 40 countries abroad.
       —UGD/GRD/ engineering, international management, management; no previous experience required/ FR, GE, PT, SP preferred.

F-54.   GRAY AND COMPANY PUBLIC COMMUNICATIONS INTERNATIONAL, Recruitment Department, 3255 Grace Street NW, Washington, DC 20007.
       —Consulting firm specializing in information, education, and economic programs abroad.
       —GRD/ accounting, business, policy making on a national scale, and considerable experience in these fields/ MUL proficiency.

F-55.   GRUMMAN CORPORATION, Personnel Department, 1111 Stewart Avenue, Bethpage, NY 11714-3590.

—Manufactures aerospace equipment, data systems, fire apparatus, boats, and other products.
—UGD/GRD/ aerospace engineering, aerospace marketing, international business, military sales, plus a minimum of ten years' experience in the above fields/ FR, GE, SP useful.

F-56. GULF OIL, Gulf Building, P.O. Box 1166, Pittsburgh, PA 15230/ 165 Flanders Road, Westboro, MA 01581.
—Produces petroleum and petroleum products, and operates in dozens of countries in Africa and the Middle East.
—UGD/GRD/ accounting, area studies, business administration, finance, marketing, petroleum engineering/ AB, FR.

F-57. HOECHST-CELANESE CORPORATION, Route 202-206 North Bridgewater, NJ 08876.
—Produces and exports chemicals, fiber, and plastics, and has branches in Asia, Europe, and Central America.
—UGD/GRD/ chemical engineering, mechanical engineering, plus a minimum of three years' experience/ FR, SP desirable.

★F-58. HONEYWELL INTERNATIONAL, Human Resources, Honeywell Plaza, Minneapolis, MN 55408.
—Produces control, navigation, and guidance devices for commercial and military aviation; also manufactures missiles, computers, and other products; branches in 90 countries.
—UGD/GRD/ engineering, finance, international affairs, marketing, science, technology/ KFL is favored.

F-59. IRVING TRUST COMPANY, Professional Recruitment, 48 Wall Street, New York, NY 10015. [Presently part of Bank of New York (same address).]
—Conducts banking and financial operations in over 20 countries around the world.
—UGD/GRD/ accounting, business administration, corporate finance, international marketing/ KFL useful.

F-60. J. WALTER THOMPSON COMPANY, 420 Lexington Avenue, New York, NY 10017.
INACTIVE(?)

—Advertising agency with offices in over 30 countries around the world.
—GRD/ accounting, business administration, design and layout, marketing, media, public relations/ KFL useful.

◢F-61.　KERN CORPORATION, 300 East 45th St. (Met Life Building), New York, NY 10006.
—Provides translation and interpretation services in the fields of engineering, law, insurance, etc.
—UGD/GRD/ chemistry, finance, law, physics, telecommunications, plus previous experience in translation and interpretation/ AB, CH, FR, GE, IT, JP, PT, RO, RU, SP, plus dozens of others.

◢F-62.　LANGUAGE TRANSLATION SERVICES, 319 South Limestone Street, Lexington, KY 40508.
—Provides translation services and production of marketing communications materials, both in printed and audiovisual forms.
—UGD/GRD/ design and layout, marketing, media, public relations, translation and interpretation skills/ FR, GE, SP.

◢F-63.　LINGUISTIC SYSTEMS, 116 Bishop Allen Drive, Cambridge, MA 02139.
—Provides translation, interpretation, and audiovisual services in several languages.
—UGD/GRD/ liberal arts, public relations, translation and interpretation experience/ MUL.

★F-64.　LOS ANGELES TIMES, Times Mirror Square, Los Angeles, CA 90053.
—Daily newspaper covering local, national, and international news, with over 20 offices outside the United States.
—UGD/GRD/ editing, journalism, mass media, reporting, plus previous relevant experience/ AB, CH, JP, RU, SP most helpful.

F-65.　LOUIS BERGER INTERNATIONAL, Personnel Department, P.O.B. 270, 100 Halsted Street, East Orange, NJ 07019.
—Consulting services in the fields of engineering, economics, agriculture, civil engineering, environment,

architecture, urban planning; operating offices in over 70 countries.
—GRD/ agriculture, economics, engineering, environment, business administration, planning/ FR, SP fluency.

★F-66. MANUFACTURERS HANOVER CORPORATION, College Relations Department, 270 Park Avenue, New York, NY 10017.
—Provides banking and financial services in over 40 countries around the world.
—UGD/GRD/ accounting, area studies, business management, corporate finance, international business, political science, plus overseas experience/ KFL fluency according to assigned area.

F-67. McKINSEY AND COMPANY, 55 East 52nd Street, New York, NY 10022.
—Consulting firm specializing in top management matters; 15 offices in Europe and Latin America.
—GRD/ business administration, finance, law, public policy, public relations, plus at least three years' relevant experience/ FR, GE, SP fluency.

★F-68. MEDICAL SERVICES CORP. INTERNATIONAL, Human Resources Department, 1716 Wilson Boulevard, Arlington, VA 22209.
—Provides consultation services in the form of research and advice in the fields of health care, health planning, and medical equipment marketing.
—GRD/ biomedical research, business, education, medicine, nursing, public health, science, plus previous relevant experience/ AB, FR, PT, SP useful.

F-69. MELLON BANK CORPORATION, Management Development Department, Mellon Square, Pittsburgh, PA 15230.
—Provides banking and financial services in dozens of countries in Africa, Asia, Europe, and the Middle East.
—GRD/ accounting, banking, economics, finance, international affairs, political science/ KFL helpful.

F-70. MERRILL LYNCH AND COMPANY, Employment Department Manager, World Finance Center North Tower, New York, NY 10281.

—Provides security, brokerage, and commodity services in several European countries.
—UGD/GRD/ economics, finance, international marketing, plus prior experience as account executive/ KFL useful.

F-71.   MORGAN GUARANTEE TRUST OF NEW YORK, Domestic Recruitment Department, 23 Wall Street, New York, NY 10005.
        —Provides banking and financial services in over 20 countries abroad.
        —GRD/ accounting, business, business administration, economics, finance, marketing, plus previous experience/ KFL fluency according to assigned country.

F-72.   MORGAN STANLEY AND COMPANY, 1251 Avenue of the Americas, New York, NY 10020.
        —Provides investment banking services, and operates several overseas offices.
        —GRD/ business administration, economics, finance; previous experience is not required/ JP useful.

F-73.   MUDGE, ROSE, GUTHRIE, ALEXANDER AND FELDON, 180 Maiden Lane, New York, NY 10038.
        —Law firm with offices in the United States and abroad.
        —GRD/ law, with substantial experience in economic, international, and trade law/ CH, FR, GE, IN, KO, SP preferred.

F-74.   MULTINATIONAL AGRIBUSINESS SYSTEMS, 111 Dupont Circle, Washington, DC 20036.
        —Provides international development and investment services in the field of agribusiness, with operations in developing countries.
        —UGD/GRD/ business management, science, technical subjects, plus experience in international business/ AB, FR, SP proficiency.

F-75.   NATIONAL COMMITTEE ON US-CHINA RELATIONS, 777 United Nations Plaza, New York, NY 10017.
        —Promotes better ties and understanding between the United States and China through cultural, civic, educational, and sports programs.
        —GRD/ Chinese studies, communications, public rela-

tions, plus cultural and educational exchange experience/ CH.

F-76.　NATIONAL WESTMINSTER BANK, USA, Human Resources Department, 175 Water Street, New York, NY 10005.
　　—Provides banking and financial operations in Great Britain, Hong Kong, and Brazil.
　　—UGD/GRD/ accounting, economics, finance; practical and management skills and overseas experience take precedence over educational background/ KFL proficiency.

◢F-77.　NATIONWIDE REPORTING AND CONVENTION COVERAGE, 305 Broadway, New York, NY 10013.
　　—Translation, secretarial, stenotyping, and audiovisual services in various languages.
　　—UGD/GRD/ liberal arts, public relations, translation and interpretation ability/ MUL.

★F-78.　NEW YORK TIMES, Managing Editor/News Department, 229 West 43rd Street, New York, NY 10036.
　　—Leading daily newspaper; covers local, national, and international events, business, sports, literature, arts, and other fields; has dozens of offices overseas.
　　—UGD/GRD/ journalism, liberal arts, plus a minimum of five years' experience with a major U.S. newspaper/ KFL preferred for foreign correspondents in various countries.

★F-79.　NEWSDAY, 235 Pinelawn Road, Melville, NY 11747.
　　—Local newspaper serving New York and Long Island, has four offices abroad.
　　—UGD/GRD/ journalism, plus a minimum of three years' experience with a daily newspaper recording over 200,000 circulation/ KFL useful according to assigned country.

F-80.　NORTHERN TRUST COMPANY, College Recruitment Department, 50 South La Salle Street, Chicago, IL 60675.
　　—Provides banking and financial operations in several countries overseas.
　　—UGD/ accounting, banking, finance, plus relevant experience/ KFL is a strong plus.

F-81.   NORTHWEST BANK OF MINNESOTA, Sixth and Marquette Streets, Minneapolis, MN 55479.
—Provides banking and financial services, and has several offices in various countries.
—UGD/GRD/ accounting, business, economics, finance, international trade, plus prior experience/ FR, GE, SP fluency.

F-82.   ORGANIZATION RESOURCES COUNSELORS, 1211 Avenue of the Americas, New York, NY 10036.
—Provides international comparative cost-of-living and a variety of other data on the United States, foreign corporations, missionary, and government organizations.
—UGD/GRD/ computer science, economics, engineering, international business, journalism, statistics, plus previous experience/ FR, SP.

F-83.   PATTON, BOGGS AND BLOW, Recruitment Committee, 2550 M Street NW, Washington, DC 20037.
—Provides international law services, and has operations in several countries abroad.
—GRD/ law, good academic record from a leading law school, plus willingness to travel abroad/ AB, FR, GE, IT, PE preferred.

F-84.   PENNIE AND EDMONDS, Hiring Partners Committee, 1155 Avenue of the Americas, New York, NY 10036.
—Law firm specializing in domestic and international law, with operations in several countries abroad.
—GRD/ law, plus UGD/GRD in the fields of chemistry, electronics, metallurgy, molecular biology, physics/ AB, CH, FR, GE, JP, RU, SP preferred.

★F-85.   PEPSICO, INC., Personnel Division, 700 Anderson Hill, Building 2/3, Purchase, NY 10057.
—Manufactures soft drinks, snacks, sporting merchandise, etc., and operates in 148 countries around the world.
—GRD/ consumer products, finance, marketing/ AB, CH, FR, GE, JP, PT, RU, SP preferred.

F-86.   PHILADELPHIA NATIONAL BANK, Human Resources Department, 1 North 5th Street, Philadelphia, PA 19101.

[Presently part of CoreStates Bank, same address]
—Provides banking and financial services in several countries abroad.
—UGD/GRD/ business administration, economics, finance, international affairs, plus overseas living experience/ KFL fluency desirable.

F-87. PITTSBURGH NATIONAL BANK, College Relations Department, Fifth Avenue and Wood Street, Pittsburgh, PA 15222.
—Provides banking and financial services in Argentina, Brazil, Mexico, Italy, Hong Kong, and Australia.
—UGD/GRD/ business administration, economic, finance, technical subjects, plus credit analysis skills, and experience overseas/ PT or SP proficiency desirable.

F-88. PLANNING AND DEVELOPMENT COLLABORATIVE INTERNATIONAL, Personnel Department, 1012 N Street NW, Washington, DC 20036.
—Provides training and management services for rural and urban development in Africa, Asia, Latin America, and Near East countries.
—UGD/GRD/ architecture, economics, finance, regional development, urban planning/ AB, FR, PT, SP and others fluently.

F-89. PROMETHEAN CORPORATION, 815 Ritchie Highway, Severna Park, MD 21146.
INACTIVE(?)
—Provides consulting services in the areas of export and trade with African and East European countries.
—GRD/ area studies, business administration, international marketing/ AFL, FR, PO, RU desirable.

F-90. RCA CORPORATION, International Development Division [Presently part of Thompson Consumer Electronics, 600 North Sherman Drive, Indianapolis (South), IN 46201].
—Manufactures radios, television sets, audiovisual materials, electronic communication devices, furnishings for homes, etc.
—UGD/GRD/ engineering, marketing, plus relevant experience/ CH, JP, SP useful.

F-91.   RCA/GLOBAL COMMUNICATIONS, Administrative Employment Division, 201 Centennial Avenue, Piscataway, NJ
08854.
—Coordinates and manages RCA's international communications network, and operates in several countries
abroad.
—GRD/ business, engineering, finance, international affairs, law, marketing/ FR, SP useful.

◢F-92.   RENNERT BILINGUAL TRANSLATIONS, 2 West 45th Street,
5th Floor, New York, NY 10036.
—Provides translation and interpretation services to companies and private persons, and has specialized staff in
several areas.
—UGD/GRD/ finance, law, medicine, science, technology, plus relevant experience in the translation of
same/ AB, CH, FR, GE, IT, JP RO, RU, SP.

F-93.   REPUBLIC BANK CORPORATION, Personnel Recruitment
[Presently Nation's Bank, 100 North Main Street, P.O.B.
613, Dallas, TX 75110].
—Provides banking and financial services outside the
United States, and operates three foreign branches.
—UGD/GRD/ accounting, business, economics, fi-
nance, plus overseas experience/ KFL proficiency is pre-
ferred.

F-94.   REPUBLIC NATIONAL BANK OF NEW YORK, Personnel Department, 452 Fifth Avenue, New York, NY 10018.
—Provides banking and financial services overseas, and
operates several offices abroad.
—GRD/ accounting, business, finance, plus overseas ex-
perience/ KFL proficiency is preferred.

F-95.   REVLON INTERNATIONAL CORPORATION, Human Services
Department, 767 Fifth Avenue, Suite 767, New York, NY
10153.
—Produces and merchandises perfumes, cosmetics, and
toiletries; operates branches in over 130 countries.
—UGD/GRD/ business management, economics, finance, human resources, marketing, plus two years'
relevant experience/ FR, GE, JP, SP fluency.

F-96.   ROBERT R. NATHAN AND ASSOCIATES, International Operations Department, 1301 Pennsylvania Avenue NW, Washington, DC 20004.
INACTIVE(?)
—Provides consulting services in economics, and operates programs in over 20 developing countries.
—GRD/ banking, economics, urban development, plus a minimum of five years' relevant experience/ AB, CH, IN, SP, TH, UR.

★F-97.   RUDER, FINN, INC., 301 East 57th Street, New York, NY 10022.
—Provides public relations services to corporations, foreign governments, nonprofit organizations, and others.
—UGD/GRD/ advertising, business management, languages, law, liberal arts, political science, plus previous experience in public relations/ KFL useful.

F-98.   SEAFIRST CORPORATION, Recruiting Office, 1001 4th Avenue, Seattle, WA 98154.
—Provides banking and financial services overseas, and operates six offices abroad.
—UGD/GRD/ accounting, business, finance, marketing, plus a high degree of self-motivation and passing of accounting exam/ PT or SP useful.

F-99.   SECURITY PACIFIC NATIONAL BANK, College Relations Department, Employment Division, 333 South Hope Street, Los Angeles, CA 90017.
—Provides banking and financial services in several countries in Asia, Europe, and Latin America.
—UGD/GRD/ accounting, business, finance, international relations/ KFL fluency is desirable.

F-100.   SOUTHEAST BANK OF MIAMI, Personnel Recruitment Department, 100 South Biscayne, Miami, FL 33131.
—Provides banking and financial services, with operations in Latin American countries.
—UGD/ accounting, business, economics, finance, international management/ SP fluency.

F-101. SPERRY MARINE, Employment Division/International Division, 1070 Seminole Trail, Charlotsville, PA 22901.
—Produces electronic systems and equipment, computer business machines, and other products.
—UGD/GRD/ engineering, finance, marketing, plus over five years' relevant experience/ DU, FR, GE, JP, SP useful.

F-102. TEXACO, Human Resources, 2000 Westchester Avenue, White Plains, NY 10650/ Texaco Heritage Plaza, 1111 Bagby Street, Houston, TX 77020.
—Petroleum exploration, production, and marketing operations in over 100 countries around the world.
—UGD/GRD/ chemical engineering, geology, geophysics, mechanical engineering, petroleum engineering, plus relevant experience/ FR, GE, IT, PT, SP fluency is often a requirement for any of these.

F-103. TOWERS, PERRIN, Staffing Department, 245 Park Avenue, 17th Floor, New York, NY 10167.
—Consulting firm specializing in the fields of benefits, compensation pay, communications, actuarials, etc.
—UGD/GRD/ communications, computers, economics, energy, engineering, law, science, plus previous relevant experience/ CH, FR, GE, IT, JP, PT, SP preferred.

F-104. TRANSCENTURY CORPORATION, Recruitment Center, 1724 Kalorama Road NW, Washington, DC 20009.
—Provides social science research and international development services in the fields of migration, nutrition, rural and urban public works, and international development.
—UGD/GRD/ business administration, economics, education, engineering, environmental science, international development, public health, plus relevant experience abroad/ KFL fluency according to assignment.

◼★F-105. TRANSLATIONS COMPANY OF AMERICA, 10 West 37th Street, New York, NY 10018.
—Provides translation services in several languages and in several fields.

—UGD/GRD/ advertising, education, law, medicine, transportation, etc./ AB, CH, FR, GE, JP, RU, SP.

F-106. UNION CARBIDE CHEMICAL & PLASTICS, Old Ridgebury Road, Danbury, CT 06810.
—Manufactures antifreeze products, batteries, foamed plastics, electronic materials, etc.
—UGD/GRD/ area studies, accounting, business administration, engineering, finance, marketing, science, technology/ KFL helpful.

F-107. UNITED CALIFORNIA BANK, International Division, 630 Fifth Avenue, New York, NY 10020.
—Provides banking and financial services overseas, and operates in 15 countries.
—UGD/GRD/ accounting, banking, economics, finance, international relations/ AB, FR, SP helpful.

F-108. UNITED PRESS INTERNATIONAL, 1400 Eye Street NW, Washington, DC 20005.
—News gathering organization, operating over 100 offices in the United States, and over 80 offices abroad.
—UGD/GRD/ journalism, mass media, newspaper publications, national and international affairs, plus relevant daily newspaper experience/ KFL fluency required for overseas assignments.

◢F-109. UNIVERSITY LANGUAGE SERVICES, 15 Maiden Lane, Suite 300, New York, NY 10038.
—Provides translation/interpretation services in several languages and in several fields.
—UGD/GRD/ computers, law, medicine, science, technology, plus previous experience in translating/ interpreting work/ AB, CH, FR, GE, IT, JP, PT, RO, RU, SP.

★F-110. U.S. CHAMBER OF COMMERCE, 1615 H Street NW, Washington, DC 20062.
—The world's largest organization of business, trade, and professional associations; has connections with all countries around the world.
—UGD/GRD/ international affairs, international economics, international relations, plus relevant ex-

perience in private or public foreign affairs/ AB, FR, SP preferred.

F-111.   U.S.–RUSSIAN TRADING CORPORATION, 146 West 29th Street, New York, NY 10022.
—Facilitates growth of trade relations between the U.S. and Russia, and provides business support, market, and investment opportunities in both countries for interested individuals or organizations.
—UGD/GRD/ business administration, economics, Russian culture, society, politics, trade/ RU fluency preferred.

★F-112.   WALL STREET JOURNAL, 200 Liberty Street, New York, NY 10007.
—Business and financial newspaper of national and international importance; operates offices in several countries abroad.
—UGD/GRD/ business, journalism, law, liberal arts, plus previous relevant experience/ CH, FR, GE, JP, SP preferred.

★F-113.   WASHINGTON POST, Managing Editor's Department, 1150 15th Street NW, Washington, DC 20005.
—Prominent daily newspaper, covering local, national, and international news; operates offices in about 20 countries.
—UGD/GRD/ journalism, law, liberal arts, mass media, plus a minimum of five years' experience in a subject area or region/ KFL required for overseas assignments.

F-114.   WESTINGHOUSE ELECTRIC CORPORATION, Human Resources International Department, Westinghouse Building–Gateway Center, Pittsburgh, PA 15222.
—Manufactures and markets electric, electronic, and other products, and operates in 40 countries.
—UGD/ accounting, engineering, science; no previous experience is required/ KFL helpful.

F-115.   WEYERHEUSER COMPANY, Corporation Headquarters, 3363 Weyerheuser Way South, Tacoma, WA 98477.
—Produces and markets wood and wood products, with business operations abroad.
—GRD/ finance, marketing, plus relevant experience/ KFL preferred.

F-116. WHITE AND CASE, Legal Employment Office, 1155 Avenue of the Americas, New York, NY 10036.
—Law firm with substantial practice abroad, operates six overseas offices.
—GRD/ law, superior academic record, and interest in the company's practice/ KFL useful for overseas assignments.

Addendum Section F

F-117. AMERICAN MANAGEMENT ASSOCIATION (AMA), 135 West 50th Street, New York, NY 10020.
—Brings together various types of management organizations, provides training, workshops, conferences; operates an international division for Europe, the Middle East, and South America.
—GRD/ business administration, economics, personnel training, public relations, publishing, seminar/ conference organization/ KFL useful.

F-118. AT&T LANGUAGE LINE SERVICES, Recruitment Department, 1 Lower Ragsdale Drive, Building 2, Suite 2-400, Monterey, CA 93940.
—Major telephone/telecommunications company, operates on all continents with services in 134 languages; recruits full-time and freelance translators, interpreters, test evaluators, editors.
—UGD/GRD/ editorial skills, education, interpretation, languages, translation/ KFL fluency in one or more languages.

F-119. BOARD FOR INTERNATIONAL BROADCASTING, 1201 Connecticut Avenue NW, Washington, DC 20036.
—Supervises the operations of Radio Free Europe and Radio Liberty, with broadcasting services to Russia and East European countries.
—GRD/ area studies, liberal arts, research skills, translating ability/ RU, SLL, East European languages.

F-120. BROWN BROTHERS HARRIMAN & COMPANY, 59 Wall Street, New York, NY 10005.
—Provides various financial services (commercial bank-

ing, brokerage, advising, etc.) to major firms in Europe, Asia, Latin America.
—UGD/GRD/ business administration, finance, management/ KFL fluency according to area of assignment.

F-121.   CHRYSLER CORPORATION, College Recruiting, 12000 Chrysler Drive, Highland Park, MI 48288-1919.
—Major American firm, involved in automotive production, financial services, technology and business, with branches in several foreign countries.
—GRD/ business administration, international affairs, plus experience in working/studying overseas/ KFL fluency according to country of assignment.

F-122.   DAVIS, POLK AND WARDWELL, Chase Manhattan Plaza, New York, NY 10005.
—Law firm involved in various foreign financial operations in Europe and Asia.
—GRD/ international studies, law, overseas experience/ FR, JP fluency.

F-123.   DEUTSCHE BANK, AG, NEW YORK BRANCH, 31 West 52nd Street, New York, NY 10019.
—Large German bank, with domestic and foreign branches, provides broad range of financial services on all continents, has special training programs with new recruits.
—GRD/ business administration, international affairs, management, plus experience and willingness to relocate/ GE proficiency required.

F-124.   HILL AND KNOWLTON, 420 Lexington Avenue, New York, NY 10017.
—Leading public relations firm, with dozens of offices in Europe, Latin America, Middle East, Asia, and Australia.
—GRD/ advertising, area studies, economics, international relations, public relations, writing/ KFL useful.

F-125.   INDEX ON CENSORSHIP, 36 West 44th Street, New York, NY 10039.
—Magazine focusing on government repressions against artists, writers, scholars, and other professionals in various countries.

—GRD/ administration, area studies, editorial work, publishing, writing skills/ KFL desirable according to area/country of assignment.

F-126. INTERNATIONAL FOOD POLICY RESEARCH INSTITUTE, 1776 Massachusetts Avenue NW, Washington, DC 20036.
—Focuses on strategies and plans to meet world food needs; constitutes a unit of the Consultative Group of International Agricultural Research.
—GRD/ agricultural planning, agriculture, business management, finance/ KFL fluency of at least two languages according to area of work.

F-127. JONES, DAY, REAVIS AND POGUE, 599 Lexington Avenue, New York, NY 10022.
—Law firm involved in corporate, government, and litigation taxation; operates offices in Europe and Asia.
—GRD/ accounting, area studies, business disciplines, international affairs, law, real estate/ AB, FR helpful.

F-128. KAMSKY ASSOCIATES, 70 Pine Street, New York, NY 10270.
—Trading company, represents over 40 companies involved in joint ventures in China, the Philippines, and Brazil.
—GRD/ business, economics, international studies/ CH(mn), PT fluency.

F-129. THE LANGUAGE CENTER, 144 Tices Lane, East Brunswick, NJ 08816.
—Translation services, editing, printing in various areas such as medicine, law, science and other fields.
—UGD/GRD/ languages, translation and interpretation/ AB, CH, GE, IT, JP, RU, TU and other languages.

F-130. NATHAN ASSOCIATES, 2 Colonial Place, 2101 Wilson Boulevard, Suite 1200, Arlington, VA 22201.
—Consulting firm in economic policy analysis both in America and overseas; provides services in over 70 developing countries and to international organizations.
—GRD/ agricultural economics, business administra-

tion, economics, public policy, urban development/ KFL fluency according to area of assignment.

F-131. PRAGMA CORPORATION, 116 East Broad Street, Falls Church, VA 22046.
—Consulting firm in various fields; provides services to major international organizations covering Asia, Africa, and Latin America.
—GRD/ agriculture, business administration, health disciplines, planning/ KFL fluency according to country/ area of assignment.

F-132. TELENET COMMUNICATIONS CORPORATION, 12490 Sunrise Valley Drive, Reston, VA 22096.
—A subsidiary of U.S. Sprint Corporation, provides packets for data communications networks, products and services; has joint ventures in Asia and Europe.
—UGD/GRD/ business administration, computers, electrical engineering, international business/ KFL required according to area of assignment.

F-133. TOYODA AMERICA, 1 World Trade Center, New York, NY 10048.
—Japanese import/export firm dealing with steel and other metals, textiles, cotton, foodstuffs, and others.
—GRD/ accounting, area studies, business law, finance, marketing, trade/ JP highly desirable.

F-134. UNIVERSE TECHNICAL TRANSLATION, 9330 Memorial Drive, Houston, TX 77024.
—Translation, typesetting, and printing in over 30 languages.
—UGD/GRD/ languages, translation and interpretation skills, writing/ MUL fluency required according to assignment.

F-135. U.S.-CHINA BUSINESS COUNCIL, 1818 N Street NW, Washington, DC 20036.
—Trade and investment operations in China, promotes and facilitates bilateral economic relations; represents over 100 American firms.
—GRD/ business administration, East Asian studies, government studies, international affairs/ CH fluency very helpful.

F-136. U.S. POSTAL SERVICES (USPS), International Postal Affairs, 475 L'Enfant Plaza SW, Washington, DC 20260.
—Coordinates relations and activities with foreign postal administrations, international postal organizations and government agencies related to international postal matters.
—UGD/GRD/ foreign policy studies, international affairs/ KFL fluency required, especially FR and SP.

F-137. WELLS FARGO INTERNATIONAL, 420 Montgomery Street, San Francisco, CA 94163.
—Provides international commercial banking services (deposits, letters of credit, dollar clearance, and others) to clients living both inside and outside the United States.
—UGD/GRD/ accounting, banking, economy, finance, international affairs/ KFL proficiency helpful.

G. ETHNIC AND LANGUAGE CONNECTIONS: FRATERNAL, PROFESSIONAL, TRADE, AND OTHER ORGANIZATIONS

G-1. AFRICAN LITERATURE ASSOCIATION, Cornell University, Africana Studies, 310 Triphammer Road, Ithaca, NY 14850.
—Scholars, teachers, students, writers, and others interested in teaching, research, and promoting African literature; annual directory and annual conventions/ AFL.

G-2. AFRICAN STUDIES ASSOCIATION, Credit Union Building, Emory University, Atlanta, GA 30322.
—Teachers, writers, linguists, historians, librarians, and anthropologists involved in research and writing on Africa; annual conventions/ AFL.

G-3. ALPHA MU GAMA, 855 North Vermont Avenue, Los Angeles, CA 90029.
—Honor society for foreign language specialists, organizes national language weeks, offers scholarships; biennial conventions/ MUL.

G-4.   AMERICAN ARABIC ASSOCIATION, 29 Mackenzie Lane, Wakefield, MA 01880.
—Arabic-American heritage, culture, and language preservation; annual conventions/AB.

G-5.   AMERICAN ASSOCIATION FOR CHINESE STUDIES, 300 Bricker Hall, Ohio State University, Columbus, OH 43210.
—Teachers and scholars involved in teaching Chinese cultural topics in U.S. colleges and universities; annual convention/ CH.

G-6.   AMERICAN ASSOCIATION FOR THE ADVANCEMENT OF SLAVIC STUDIES, 125 Panama Street, Jordan Quad/Acacia Building, Stanford, CA 94305.
—Teachers, librarians, researchers, students, publishers, and others involved in Slavic and East European studies; annual convention; membership directory/ AL, HU, RO, SLL.

G-7.   AMERICAN ASSOCIATION OF HISPANIC CPAS, 1414 Metropolitan Avenue, Bronx, NY 10462.
—Hispanic certified public accountants from public, private, and academic fields; professional seminars; employment services/ SP.

G-8.   AMERICAN ASSOCIATION OF LANGUAGE SPECIALISTS, 1000 Connecticut Avenue NW, Suite 9, Washington, DC 20036.
—Translators, interpreters, and writers; international level; annual convention/ MUL.

G-9.   AMERICAN ASSOCIATION OF MUSEUMS, 1225 I Street NW, Suite 200, Washington, DC 20005.
—Unites various types of museums and professionals serving museums in the field of art, history, science, linguistics, etc.; annual convention; placement service/ MUL.

G-10.   AMERICAN ASSOCIATION OF PROFESSORS OF YIDDISH, NSF Yiddish Studies and Instruction, Queens College, Flushing, NY 11367.
—Scholars, professors, graduate students, and researchers

of Yiddish, as well as individuals interested in this language; various publications/ YD.

G-11.   AMERICAN ASSOCIATION OF TEACHERS OF ARABIC, Brigham Young University, 280 HREB, Provo, UT 84602.
—University and college teachers, scholars, and students in the field of Arabic language, linguistics, and literature; organizes Arabic translation contests; annual conventions/ AB.

G-12.   AMERICAN ASSOCIATION OF TEACHERS OF ESPERANTO, 5140 San Lorenzo Drive, Santa Barbara, CA 93110.
—Teachers of Esperanto who promote this language in American schools; offer scholarships; annual conventions/ EP.

G-13.   AMERICAN ASSOCIATION OF TEACHERS OF FRENCH, 57 East Armory, Champagne, IL 61820.
—Teachers of French in elementary and high schools, colleges, and universities; career information and employment registry/ FR.

G-14.   AMERICAN ASSOCIATION OF TEACHERS OF GERMAN, 112 Haddontowne North 104, Cherry Hill, NJ 08034.
—Teachers of German at high school and college levels; annual convention; placement service/ GE.

G-15.   AMERICAN ASSOCIATION OF TEACHERS OF ITALIAN, c/o Ohio State University, Department of Italian, Columbus, OH 43210.
—Teachers of Italian in high schools and colleges, as well as other persons interested in the Italian language and culture; annual convention; employment registry and placement service/ IT.

G-16.   AMERICAN ASSOCIATION OF TEACHERS OF SLAVIC AND EAST EUROPEAN LANGUAGES, Foreign Language Department, Arizona State University, Tempe, AZ 85287. INACTIVE(?)
—Professors, researchers, students, librarians, and others interested in East European languages, literature, and culture; annual convention/ AL, HU, RO, SLL.

G-17. AMERICAN ASSOCIATION OF TEACHERS OF SPANISH AND PORTUGUESE, P.O. Box 6349, Mississippi State University, State College, MS 39762.
—Teachers of Spanish and Portuguese languages and of Latin American and Hispanic cultures; annual conventions; placement bureau/ PT, SP.

G-18. AMERICAN ASSOCIATION OF TEACHERS OF TURKISH, Princeton University, Near Eastern Studies, 110 Jones Hall, Princeton, NJ 08544.
—Teachers of Turkish language in universities and government institutions; guidelines and standards for teachers; annual conventions/ TU.

G-19. AMERICAN CLASSICAL LEAGUE, Miami University, Oxford, OH 45056.
—Teachers of Latin and Greek in high schools and colleges; annual conventions; placement service/GR, LA.

G-20. AMERICAN COMMITTEE FOR IRISH STUDIES, English Department, Purdue University, Fort Wayne, IN 46805.
—Scholars interested in Irish arts, folklore, language, and literature; information regarding teaching and research opportunities; annual conventions/ IR.

G-21. AMERICAN COUNCIL FOR NATIONALITIES SERVICE, 95 Madison Avenue, New York, NY 10016.
—Unites over 150 American ethnic groups, presents each group without bias, and maintains speaker's bureau.
—Promotes cultural pluralism and assists immigrants with integration into the American society/ MUL.

G-22. AMERICAN COUNCIL OF TEACHERS OF RUSSIAN, 1776 Massachusetts Avenue NW, Washington, DC 20036.
—Teachers and students of Russian in high schools and colleges; exchange programs with the Russian; membership directory; semiannual conventions; placement service via G-6/ RU.

G-23. AMERICAN COUNCIL ON THE TEACHING OF FOREIGN LANGUAGES, 6 Executive Plaza, Yonkers, NY 10701.
—Teachers of classical and modern languages in high schools and colleges; awards for excellent students;

newsletter with job opportunities/ FR, GE, GR, IT, LA, RU.

G-24. AMERICAN HUNGARIAN EDUCATORS ASSOCIATION, 707 Snider Lane, Silver Spring, MD 20904.
—Teachers, librarians, and translators of Hungarian origin involved in teaching or researching Hungarian language, culture, and heritage; annual conventions; directory/ HU.

G-25. AMERICAN INDIAN HERITAGE FOUNDATION, 6051 Arlington Boulevard, Falls Church, VA 22044.
—Preservation of cultural heritage of Native Americans; scholarships for Native American youth; Native American heritage weeks/ NAL.

G-26. AMERICAN INDIAN LIBRARY ASSOCIATION, c/o American Library Association, 50 East Huron Street, Chicago, IL 60611.
—Librarians and other persons or organizations interested in improving library services to Indian reservations and exchange of information among tribes; placement service during American Library Association's conventions/ NAL.

G-27. AMERICAN INDIAN SCIENCE AND ENGINEERING SOCIETY, 1085 14th Street, Suite 1506, Boulder, CO 80302.
—Native American engineers and professionals in science and technology; high school and college students are encouraged to pursue a science or engineering career; placement service/ NAL.

G-28. AMERICAN INSTITUTE OF INDIAN STUDIES, 1130 East 59th Street, Chicago, IL 60637.
—Focuses on studies on India, its culture, and languages; organizes language training programs/ HI and other languages.

G-29. AMERICAN LATVIAN ASSOCIATION IN THE UNITED STATES, P.O. Box 4578, 400 Hurley Avenue, Rockville, MD 20850.
—Preservation of Latvian-American heritage, language, and culture; publication of Latvian textbooks; weekend schools for learning Latvian/ LT.

G-30. AMERICAN LEBANESE LEAGUE, National Press Building, Washington, DC 20005.
INACTIVE(?)
—Preservation of Lebanese-American culture, language, and heritage; various educational and humanitarian programs; annual convention/ AB.

▰G-31. AMERICAN LITERARY TRANSLATORS ASSOCIATION, University of Texas–Dallas, P.O. Box 830688, Richardson, TX 75083-0688.
—Translators of books from various foreign languages into English in the area of literature and the humanities; computerized data base of translators; annual conventions/ MUL.

G-32. AMERICAN LITHUANIAN PRESS AND RADIO ASSOCIATION, P.O. Box 19191, Cleveland, OH 44119.
—Book publishing and broadcasting in Lithuanian; annual awards for translations of short stories/ LI.

G-33. AMERICAN ORIENTAL SOCIETY, University of Michigan, Room 111E, Ann Arbor, MI 48109.
—Research in Asian languages, civilization, and history; annual conventions/ MUL.

G-34. AMERICAN PHILOLOGICAL ASSOCIATION, c/o College of the Holy Cross, Worcester, MA 01610.
—Teachers of Greek and Latin, archaeologists, and comparative linguists; annual conventions; placement service/ GR, LA.

G-35. AMERICAN ROMANIAN ACADEMY OF ARTS AND SCIENCES, 265 Lee Street, Oakland, CA 94610.
—Promotion of Romanian culture, language, and heritage in the United States, Canada, and other countries; publications; annual conventions/ RO.

G-36. AMERICAN-SCANDINAVIAN FOUNDATION, 127 East 73rd Street, New York, NY 10021.
—Cultural relations between the United States and Scandinavian countries through publications, exchange, and other programs; trainee employment program in U.S. and abroad/ DA, FI, NW, SW.

G-37.   AMERICAN SOCIETY OF GEO LINGUISTS, 485 Brooklawn
Avenue, Fairfield, CT 06432.
—Various professionals in the field of languages concerned with the state of existent languages in the world;
bimonthly meetings/ MUL.

G-38.   AMERICAN SOCIETY OF INDEXERS, 1700 18th Street NW,
Washington, DC 20009.
—Indexers, librarians, publishers, and organizations interested and involved in the areas and methods of indexing,
including professionals with language skills; register of
indexers/ MUL.

◪G-39.   AMERICAN SOCIETY OF INTERPRETERS, P.O.B. 9603,
Washington, DC 20016.
—Professional interpreters; information on interpretation
systems; annual conventions; referral services for meeting organizers needing interpreters/ MUL.

◪G-40.   AMERICAN TRANSLATORS ASSOCIATION, 109 Croton Avenue, Ossining, NY 10562.
—Translators and interpreters involved in quality translation; testing and accreditation programs; annual con-
vention/ MUL.

G-41.   AMERICANS BY CHOICE, 225 Broadway, New York, NY
10007.
INACTIVE(?)
—Representatives of about 30 U.S. ethnic groups; awards
for outstanding achievements by U.S. ethnics; annual
conventions/ MUL.

G-42.   ARMENIAN FILM FOUNDATION, 2219 East Thousand Oaks
Boulevard, Thousand Oaks, CA 91362.
—Film producers, editors, writers, and others interested
in film production on Armenians; annual conventions/
AR.

G-43.   ARMENIAN GENERAL BENEVOLENT UNION, 585 Saddle
River Road, Saddle Brook, NJ 07662.
—Promotion of Armenian culture; organizes music, literature, sports, and other programs; operates day schools
in Armenian; annual convention/ AR.

G-44.   ARMENIAN LITERARY SOCIETY, 77 Everett Road, Demarset, NJ 07627.
—Armenian authors; assistance to libraries with Armenian books and promotion of Armenian authors; annual convention/ AR.

G-45.   ARMENIAN RELIEF SOCIETY OF NORTH AMERICA, 80 Bigelow Avenue, Watertown, MA 02172.
—Cultural and educational progress of Armenian-Americans; awards scholarships to deserving students; coordinates 50 Armenian language classes; annual convention/ AR.

G-46.   ASIAN-AMERICAN PSYCHOLOGICAL ASSOCIATION, c/o Queens College/CUNY, School of Education, Flushing, NY 11367.
—Stimulates Asian-Americans to get involved in research and development programs in the field of psychology; annual conventions and placement service/ ASL.

G-47.   ASIAN/PACIFIC-AMERICAN LIBRARIANS ASSOCIATION, c/o American Library Association, 50 East Huron Street, Chicago, IL 60611.
—Librarians and information specialists of Asian or Pacific origin; equal opportunities and career development goals; annual conventions and placement service during American Library Association's conventions (midwinter and summer)/ ASL.

G-48.   ASPIRA OF AMERICA, 1112 16th Street NW, Suite 540, Washington, DC 20036.
—Educational assistance to Latin Americans, student counseling, internships, work/study programs, nutrition and health programs; Latin American doctors encouraged to return to Latin American communities; annual convention; placement services/ SP.

G-49.   ASSOCIATION FOR ARAB-AMERICAN UNIVERSITY GRADUATES, 556 Trapelo Road, Belmont, MA 02178.
—Arab-American professionals; assistance to Arab countries who need professionals in various fields; annual conventions/AB.

G-50.   ASSOCIATION FOR ASIAN STUDIES, c/o University of Michigan, 1 Lane Hall, Ann Arbor, MI 48109.
—Educators, researchers, government officials, students, and others who are involved in studying various Asian countries (Cambodia, Indonesia, Korea, Myanmar, Taiwan, Thailand, Vietnam, and others), their culture and languages; annual conventions/ ASL.

G-51.   ASSOCIATION FOR KOREAN STUDIES, 30104 Avenue Tranquila, Rancho Palos Verdes, Monterey Park, CA 91754.
—Scholars, university professors, students, researchers, and others who are interested in promoting and studying the Korean language; annual conventions/ KO.

G-52.   ASSOCIATION OF AFRICAN PHYSICIANS IN NORTH AMERICA, 2031 Brooks Drive, No. 225, Forestville, MD 20747. INACTIVE(?)
—Physicians, dentists, and other related professionals; facilitates transition of African-trained professionals to U.S. standards and practice; professional counseling, scholarships, annual conventions, and placement service/ AB, AFL, FR, PT, SP.

G-53.   ASSOCIATION OF AMERICAN INDIAN PHYSICIANS, Building D, 10015 South Pennsylvania Street, Oklahoma City, OK 73159.
—Recruitment of Native Americans into the health professions; annual conventions; counseling and placement service/ NAL.

G-54.   ASSOCIATION OF ASIAN INDIANS IN AMERICA, 300 Clover Street, Rochester, NY 14610.
—Preservation of heritage, cultures, and languages of India through college and university Indian studies programs and cultural programs; annual conventions/ HI, MM, MR, PJ, TE, TM, and other languages.

G-55.   ASSOCIATION OF ASIAN/PACIFIC-AMERICAN ARTISTS, 3518 Cahuenga Boulevard, Suite 302, Los Angeles, CA 90068.
—Producers, directors, performers, writers, students, technicians, and others; equal opportunities and career development in the entertainment industry; professional seminars, special directory for members, speaker's bureau, and annual conventions/ MUL.

G-56. ASSOCIATION OF DEPARTMENTS OF FOREIGN LANGUAGES, 10 Astor Place, New York, NY 10003.
—Communication between college and university foreign language departments; seminars for heads of foreign language departments; job information lists; annual conventions/ MUL.

G-57. ASSOCIATION OF FRANCO-AMERICANS, 83 Amherst Street, P.O.B. 2000, Manchester, NH 03105.
—Maintenance of French linguistic heritage in America; annual conferences/ FR.

G-58. ASSOCIATION OF HAITIAN PHYSICIANS ABROAD, 60 Plaza Street, Brooklyn, NY 11238.
—Haitian physicians; eductional programs; assistance for transition to U.S. practice and standards; directory of members and annual conventions/ FR, H/C.

G-59. ASSOCIATION OF HISPANIC ARTS, 173 East 116th Street, New York, NY 10029.
—Hispanic arts promotion through services, and dance, music, theater, and other programs; individual technical assistance and referral services to job hunters/ SP.

G-60. ASSOCIATION OF JEWISH BOOK PUBLISHERS, 192 Lexington Avenue, New York, NY 10016.
—Authors, institutions, and publishing houses involved in producing Jewish textbooks and other publications; annual conventions/ HE, YD.

G-61. ASSOCIATION OF JEWISH LIBRARIES, 330 Seventh Avenue, 21st Floor, New York, NY 10001.
—Promotion of Jewish libraries' interests; consultant services, job clearinghouse, and placement services/ HE, YD.

G-62. ASSOCIATION OF PAKISTANI PHYSICIANS, 4121 South Fairview Avenue, No. 2, Downers Grove, IL 60515.
—Physicians, dentists, and related professionals from Pakistan who practice in North America; assistance with adjustment to newly arrived professionals; seminars on continuing medical education; annual conventions/ BC, B/R, PJ, PS, SD, UR.

G-63. ASSOCIATION OF PHILIPPINE PHYSICIANS IN AMERICA, 2717 West Olive Avenue, Suite 200, Burbank, CA 91505.
—Physicians from the Philippines who are licensed to practice in the United States; continuing education programs for newly arrived colleagues; assistance to medical residents; placement service; annual conventions/ FL, SP.

G-64. ASSOCIATION OF SRI LANKANS IN AMERICA, 2 East Glen Road, Denville, NJ 07834.
—Maintenance of Sri Lankan heritage, culture, and language in the United States; biennial conventions/ SI, TM.

G-65. ASSOCIATION OF STUDENTS AND PROFESSIONAL ITALIAN-AMERICANS, P.O. Box 531, Village Station, New York, NY 10014.
—Professionals and graduate and undergraduate students interested in Italian heritage, culture, and language; special programs; career development; monthly meetings/ IT.

G-66. ASSOCIATION OF TEACHERS OF JAPANESE, c/o Middlebury College, Japanese Program, Hillcrest 1, Middlebury, VT 05753.
—Professors, researchers, and students interested in Japanese language, linguistics, and literature; annual conferences/ JP.

G-67. ASSOCIATION OF TEACHERS OF LATIN AMERICAN STUDIES, 252-58 63rd Avenue, Flushing, NY 11362.
—Teachers, students, researchers, and others who are involved in promoting and encouraging Latin American studies, semiannual conferences/ SP.

G-68. ASSYRIAN BET NAHRAIN, P.O. Box 4116, Modesto, CA 95352.
—Persons involved in studying the Assyrian language and heritage; radio, television, and publishing activities; instruction in Assyrian; monthly meetings/ AS.

G-69. BULGARIAN NATIONAL COMMITTEE, 109 Amherst Street, Highland Park, NJ 08904.
—Assistance to Bulgarian political refugees; educational

programs; semiannual conventions; job placement service/ BL.

G-70. CAMBODIAN BUDDHIST SOCIETY, 13800 New Hampshire Avenue, Silver Spring, MD 20904.
—Preservation of Cambodian culture, religion, heritage, and language; language instruction in Cambodian/ CA.

G-71. CELTIC LEAGUE, P.O. Box 20153, Dag Hammarskjöld Center, New York, NY 10017.
—Dissemination of information about Celtic languages and individual contributions in these languages/ BR, CN, IR, MX, SC, WE.

G-72. CENTER FOR APPLIED LINGUISTICS, 1118 22nd Street NW, Washington, DC 20037.
—Research and resource center in the concrete application of the science of linguistics to cultural, educational, and social issues; conducts adult language education and produces materials in CA, CH, HM, LO, VI; publishes language resource directories.

G-73. CHINESE-AMERICAN FOOD SOCIETY, North Dakota State University, Department of Food and Nutrition, Fargo, ND 58105.
—Engineers, university professors, managers, students, and others involved in food and food-related industries; job listings; annual conferences and placement service/ CH.

G-74. CHINESE-AMERICAN LIBRARIANS ASSOCIATION, Avaria Library, Lawrence Street, Denver, CO 80204.
—Better communication among Chinese-American librarians; equal opportunities for jobs and career development; placement services and convention during American Library Association's conventions (midwinter and summer)/ CH.

G-75. CHINESE-AMERICAN MEDICAL SOCIETY, 218 Edgewood Avenue, Teaneck, NJ 07666.
—Exchange of information and advancement of medical knowledge among physicians of Chinese origin; placement service/ CH.

G-76. CHINESE-ENGLISH TRANSLATION ASSISTANCE GROUP, P.O. Box 400, Kensington, MD 20895.
—Chinese language and computer specialists working for universities, government, and business; data bank for Chinese dictionaries and modalities of translating Chinese/ CH.

G-77. CHINESE INSTITUTE OF ENGINEERS–USA, 2613 Parkview Drive, North, Emmaus, PA 18049.
—Professional engineers, scientists, and others interested in better communication among colleagues; scholarships and professional ties with Taiwan and Singapore; annual conventions/ CH.

G-78. CHINESE LANGUAGE TEACHERS ASSOCIATION, c/o Princeton University, East Asian Studies, 211 Jones Hall, Princeton, NJ 08544.
—Teachers and scholars involved in Chinese language and literature at university and college levels; annual conventions; placement services/ CH.

G-79. COLLEGE LANGUAGE ASSOCIATION, Clark-Atlanta University, Atlanta, GA 30314.
—Teachers of foreign languages and English in black universities and colleges; employment register; annual conventions; placement services/ MUL.

G-80. COMMISSION ON GRADUATES OF FOREIGN NURSING SCHOOLS, 3600 Market Street, Philadelphia, PA 19104.
—Assistance to foreign nurses in becoming registered nurses in the U.S.; conducts English language and nursing proficiency examinations, and is affiliated with the American Nurses Association/ MUL.

G-81. CONGRESS OF RUSSIAN-AMERICANS, P.O. Box 818, Nyack, NY 10960.
—Preservation of Russian heritage, culture, and language in America; contributions of Russian-Americans; triennial conferences/ RU.

G-82. COUNCIL FOR LANGUAGES AND OTHER INTERNATIONAL STUDIES , 300 I Street NE, Washington, DC 20002.
—Concerned with broadening and improving the quality of teaching of foreign languages and ESL; ties with

bilingual and international studies organizations; annual convention/ MUL.

G-83. COURT INTERPRETERS AND TRANSLATORS ASSOCIATION, 12298 Connecticut Drive, Lakewood, CO 80228. (New name: NATIONAL ASSOC. OF JUDICIARY INTER-PRETERS & TRANSLATORS)
—Interpreters serving full time or per diem in federal, state, and municipal courts; works out professional standards; organizes special workshops; produces glossary of legal terms/ MUL.

G-84. CROATIAN WORKERS ASSOCIATION OF AMERICA, P.O. Box 2006, Astoria, New York, NY 11107.
—Assistance to Croatian immigrants in skills, trades, English, and Croatian languages; annual convention/ S/C.

G-85. CUBAN-AMERICAN NATIONAL COUNCIL, 300 West 12th Avenue, 3rd Floor, Miami, FL 33130.
—Assistance to Cuban-Americans in economic and social areas, including vocational training, leadership training, and other programs; biennial conventions; placement service/ SP.

G-86. CZECHOSLOVAK SOCIETY OF ARTS AND SCIENCES, 4064 Woodcliff Road, Sherman Oaks, CA 91403.
—Writers, artists, scientists, university and college professors, and other professionals interested in preserving the Czech and Slovak heritage, culture, and languages in the United States; annual conventions/ CZ, SL.

G-87. DANISH BROTHERHOOD IN AMERICA, P.O. Box 31748, 3717 Harney Street, Omaha, NE 68131.
—Preservation of Danish heritage, culture, and language in America; help to unemployed members, scholarships; quadrennial conventions/ DA.

G-88. DELTA PHI ALPHA, College of Languages, Linguistics, and Literature, Webster 204, 2528 The Mall, University of Hawaii at Manoa, Honolulu, HI 96822.
—Honor society of graduates specializing in German language and German studies; annual conventions/ GE.

G-89. EDUCATIONAL COMMISSION FOR FOREIGN MEDICAL GRADUATES, 3624 Market Street, Philadelphia, PA 19104.
—Evaluation of credentials of foreign medical students, assistance in completion of requirements for practice in the United States; screening agency for hospitals, state licensing boards, and for National Boards of Medical Examiners/ MUL.

G-90. EELAM TAMILS ASSOCIATION OF AMERICA, 21 Lebanon Street, Winchester, MA 01890.
—Promotion of Tamil language and heritage in the United States; semiannual conventions/ TM.

G-91. ESTONIAN LEARNED SOCIETY OF AMERICA, Estonian House, 243 East 34th Street, New York, NY 10016.
—Scholars, teachers, and students interested in Estonian language and culture in the United States; annual conventions/ ES.

G-92. ETHIOPIAN COMMUNITY MUTUAL ASSISTANCE ASSOCIA- TION, 554 West 114 Street, Suite 2R, New York, NY 10025.
—Preservation of Ethiopian culture and language in the U.S.; assistance to Ethiopian refugees with orientation, guidance, and job placement; job data bank/ ET.

G-93. ETHNIC EMPLOYEES OF THE LIBRARY OF CONGRESS, 6100 East View Street, Bethesda, MD 20817.
—Ethnic and racial minority employees of the Library of Congress; equal employment opportunity and carcer development/ MUL.

G-94. ETHNIC MATERIALS INFORMATION EXCHANGE ROUND TA- BLE, c/o American Library Association, 50 East Huron Street, Chicago, IL 60611.
—Exchange of information about various ethnic groups and better library services to ethnocultural communi- ties; placement service during American Library Asso- ciation's conventions (midwinter and summer)/ MUL.

G-95. FEDERATION OF AMERICAN CULTURAL AND LANGUAGE COMMUNITIES, 666 11th Street NW, Suite 800 NIAF, Washington, DC 20001.
—Promotion of the cultural and linguistic rights of various

U.S. ethnic groups; annual convention/ AR, FR, GE, HU, IT, JP, SP, UK, VI.

G-96. FINNISH-AMERICAN HISTORICAL SOCIETY OF THE WEST, P.O. Box 5522, Portland, OR 97208.
—Finnish heritage, culture, and language preservation in the U.S.; research on the Finnish language is encouraged/ FI.

G-97. FOREIGN PHARMACY GRADUATE EXAMINATION COMMISSION, 1300 Higgins Road, Suite 103, Park Ridge, IL 60068.
—Evaluation of qualifications and credentials of foreign pharmacy graduates; assistance in joining the profession in the United States/ MUL.

G-98. FREE ALBANIA ORGANIZATION, 409 West Broadway, South Boston, MA 02127.
—Preservation of Albanian culture, heritage, and language in the United States; annual conventions/ AL.

G-99. FUND FOR THE RELIEF OF RUSSIAN WRITERS AND SCIENTISTS IN EXILE, 519 Eighth Avenue, New York, NY 10018.
—Assistance to needy Russian artists, musicians, actors, writers, and other professionals who have left their homeland; readjustment and placement help; annual conventions/ RU.

G-100. GEORGIAN ASSOCIATION IN THE USA, 136 East 55th Street, Apt. 31, New York, NY 10022.
—Preservation of Georgian culture, heritage, and language in the United States; assistance to Georgian refugees; job placement services/ GG.

G-101. GERMAN-AMERICAN NATIONAL CONGRESS, 4740 North Western Avenue, 2nd Floor, Chicago, IL 60625.
—Preservation of German culture, heritage, and language in the U.S.; support for the study of German in U.S. educational institutions; biennial conventions/ GE.

G-102. GERMAN LANGUAGE CLUB, P.O. Box 5055, Pasadena, CA 91107.
INACTIVE(?)

—Persons interested in learning the German language; produces cassettes for home study/ GE.

G-103. GRADUATES OF ITALIAN MEDICAL SCHOOLS, 360 East 194th Street, Bronx, NY 10458.
—Physicians who graduated from medical schools in Italy; assistance for adjustment in the United States; annual conventions; placement service/ IT.

G-104. HEBREW ACTORS UNION, 31 East Seventh Street, New York, NY 10003.
—Union organization for performing actors and artists; associated with the Actors and Artists of America/ HE, YD.

G-105. HEBREW CULTURE FOUNDATION, 110 East 59th Street, 4th Floor, New York, NY 10022.
—Promotion of studying modern Hebrew in universities and colleges; provides seed grants to qualified institutions/ HE.

G-106. HISPANIC ELECTED LOCAL OFFICIALS, c/o National League of Cities, 1301 Pennsylvania Avenue NW, Washington, DC 20004.
—Sharing of experiences and information among Hispanic elected officials on the local level; semiannual conventions/ SP.

G-107. HISPANIC ORGANIZATION OF LATIN ACTORS, 250 East 65th Street, New York, NY 10023.
—Promotion of work of Hispanic actors; adult theater training, orientation seminars, career development programs, and referral services to casting agencies/ SP.

G-108. INTERLINGUA INSTITUTE, 496-A Hudson Street, Apt. G-34, New York, NY 10014.
—Educators, scientists, students, linguists, translators, and other professionals who are interested in the Interlingua language; annual conventions/ I/L.

G-109. INTERNATIONAL ASSOCIATION FOR LEARNING LABORATORIES, c/o Temple University, Media Learning Center, Philadelphia, PA 19122.
—Promotion of machines and laboratory techniques for

learning languages; language laboratory programs; guidelines for conducting laboratory classes; consultant placement services/ MUL.

G-110. INTERNATIONAL ASSOCIATION OF APPLIED LINGUISTICS, 602 Ballantine Hall, Indiana University, Bloomington, IN 47405.
—Educators, students, researchers, and other professionals interested in such aspects of applied linguistics as language teaching, learning, testing, and related facets; triennial conventions/ MUL.

G-111. INTERNATIONAL SOCIETY OF INDIA CHEMISTS AND CHEMICAL ENGINEERS, Advanced Research Chemicals, 1085 Fort Gibson Road, Catoosa, OK 74015.
—Chemical engineers and chemists from India; courses facilitating transition into U.S. work requirements and standards; semiannual conferences and job referral/ HI and INL.

G-112. ISLAMIC MEDICAL ASSOCIATION, 4121 Fairview Street, Suite 203, Downers Grove, IL 60515.
—Muslim physicians and professionals from related fields in the United States and Canada; assistance to Muslim communities abroad and placement service/ AB.

G-113. ITALIAN ACTORS UNION, 701 West 47th Street, New York, NY 10036.
—Union organization for Italian performing actors; affiliated with the Actors and Artists of America; quarterly meetings/ IT.

G-114. ITALIAN-AMERICAN CULTURAL SOCIETY, 28111 Imperial Street, Warren, MI 48093.
—Preservation of Italian-American heritage, culture, and language in the U.S. and recognition of contributions made by Italian-Americans; Italian language instruction; job placement center/ IT.

G-115. ITALIAN-AMERICAN LIBRARIANS CAUCUS, 6 Peter Cooper Road, Apt. 11-G, New York, NY 10010.
—Italian-American librarians interested in improving

collection of materials on Italian-Americans and better services to Italian-American communities/ IT.

G-116. ITALIAN WELFARE LEAGUE, 8 East 69th Street, New York, NY 10021.
—Assistance to students of Italian origin in completing studies in social work at Columbia University; placement services; annual conventions/ IT.

G-117. JAPAN SOCIETY, 333 East 47th Street, New York, NY 10017.
—Professionals, businesspeople, scholars, organizations, and institutions interested in exchanging ideas and experiences between Japan and the U.S. in various fields of activities; instruction in EN and JP; annual conventions/ JP.

G-118. JEWISH LAWYERS GUILD, 299 Broadway, New York, NY 10007.
—Exchange of information among Jewish judges, attorneys, scholars, and students in the field of legal sciences; monthly meetings/ EN, YD.

G-119. JEWISH TEACHERS ASSOCIATION (MORIM), 45 East 33rd Street, Suite 604, New York, NY 10016.
—Promotion of educational, social, religious, and ethical welfare among Jewish teachers and supervisors who serve in public and private schools; assistance to prospective administrators/ HE, YD.

G-120. JOINT NATIONAL COMMITTEE FOR LANGUAGES, 300 I Street NE, Washington, DC 20002.
—Language organizations interested in improving and expanding the study of foreign languages in U.S. schools of all levels; annual conventions/ MUL.

G-121. KOREAN-AMERICAN COALITION, 610 South Harvard Street, Suite 111, Los Angeles, CA 90005.
—Better communication among Korean-Americans from various parts of the U.S.; assistance in legal matters and in learning English; community networking/ KO.

G-122. KOREAN MEDICAL ASSOCIATION OF AMERICA, 162 Deer Run, Watchung, NJ 07060.

—Korean physicians and medical paraprofessionals interested in exchange of information on Korean medicine; liaison with other health-care organizations; semiannual meetings/ KO.

G-123. KOREAN SCIENTISTS AND ENGINEERS ASSOCIATION OF AMERICA, 6261 Executive Boulevard, Rockville, MD 20852.
—Korean-American scientists and engineers interested in cultural and technological ties with U.S. engineers; biographical archives; annual conventions; placement services/ KO.

G-124. KURDISH HERITAGE FOUNDATION OF AMERICA, 345 Park Place, Brooklyn, NY 11238.
—Preservation of Kurdish heritage, culture, and language; programs in bilingual education; annual conventions/ KD.

G-125. LATIN AMERICAN STUDIES ASSOCIATION, William Pitt Union, 9th Floor, University of Pittsburgh, Pittsburgh, PA 15260.
—Scholars and organizations interested in Latin American studies, training, teaching, and research in this area; international congresses every 18 months/ PT, SP.

G-126. LINGUISTIC ASSOCIATION OF CANADA AND THE UNITED STATES, Box 101, Lake Bluff, IL 60044.
—Linguists and other professionals or organizations with interest in theoretical and applied linguistic studies and research; annual conferences and international membership/ MUL.

G-127. LINGUISTIC SOCIETY OF AMERICA, 1325 18th Street NW, Washington, DC 20036-6501.
—Professors, researchers, scholars, and students interested in researching languages and in applied linguistics; annual conventions/ MUL.

G-128. LITHUANIAN-AMERICAN COMMUNITY, 2713 West 71st Street, Chicago, IL 60629.
—Preservation of Lithuanian heritage, culture, and lan-

guage in the United States; conducts 27 schools teaching Lithuanian; annual conferences/ LI.

G-129. LUSO-AMERICAN EDUCATION FOUNDATION, P.O. Box 1768, Oakland, CA 94604.
—Teachers, students, translators, and other persons interested in studying Portuguese, and promoting this language in high schools and colleges; annual conferences/ PT.

G-130. MEXICAN-AMERICAN ENGINEERING SOCIETY, P.O. Box 3520, Fullerton, CA 92634.
INACTIVE(?) See G-178.
—Mexican-American engineers, scientists, and other professionals in related fields; biographical archives; placement services/ SP.

G-131. MODERN GREEK STUDIES ASSOCIATION, P.O. Box 1826 New Haven, CT 06508.
—Professors, researchers, students, and institutions interested in modern Greek language, literature, and culture; information on professional opportunities, annual conventions/ GR.

G-132. MODERN LANGUAGE ASSOCIATION OF AMERICA, 10 Astor Place, New York, NY 10003.
—University and college professors and students interested in foreign languages and English, researchers in this field, and others who aspire to teach at college level; data base for languages and linguistic fields; awards; annual conventions and job information service/ MUL.

G-133. MONGOLIA SOCIETY, 321-322 Goodbody Hall, Indiana University, Bloomington, IN 47405.
—Academics, students, librarians, and other professionals who are interested in Mongolian language and culture; publishes textbooks and dictionaries in Mongolian; annual conventions/ MO.

G-134. NATIONAL AMERICAN INDIAN COURT CLERKS ASSOCIATION, 1000 Connecticut Avenue NW, Washington, DC 20036.

—Training and continuing education; support for Native American court officers at a professional level; improvement of Native American court system/ NAL.

G-135.   NATIONAL AMERICAN INDIAN COURT JUDGES ASSOCIATION, 1000 Connecticut Avenue NW, Washington, DC 20036.

—Improvement of the Native American court system; continuing education programs and periodic training sessions/ NAL.

G-136.   NATIONAL ASSOCIATION/FEDERATION OF HISPANIC PUBLICATIONS, P.O.B. 23605, Orlando, FL 32802.

—Publishers and editors representing over 100 Spanish magazines, newspapers, and other periodicals interested in supporting and promoting Hispanic media; annual conventions/ SP.

G-137.   NATIONAL ASSOCIATION FOR ASIAN AND PACIFIC AMERICAN EDUCATION, 310 Eight Street, Suite 301, Oakland, CA 94607.

—Asian-American educators, librarians, and related professionals interested in improvement of school curricula on Asian and Pacific subjects; operates special workshops, bilingual multicultural programs; annual conventions/ ASL.

G-138.   NATIONAL ASSOCIATION FOR BILINGUAL EDUCATION, Union Center Plaza, 810 1st Street NE, Washington, DC 20002.

—Educators, administrators, and paraprofessionals interested in promoting bilingual education for ethnic minorities; annual conventions/ SP.

G-139.   [NATIONAL ASSOCIATION OF] ASIAN-AMERICAN CERTIFIED PUBLIC ACCOUNTANTS, 580 California Street, 16th Floor, San Francisco, CA 94104.

—Asian-American certified public accountants or persons aspiring to become CPAs; continuing education programs, employment opportunities, and referral services/ ASL.

G-140.   NATIONAL ASSOCIATION OF CUBAN ARCHITECTS IN EXILE, 940 North East 79th Street, Causeway Suite, Miami, FL 33138.

INACTIVE(?) See G-178.
—Professional Cuban-American architects and students involved in various projects of social welfare and urban planning; annual conventions/ SP.

G-141.   NATIONAL ASSOCIATION OF HISPANIC JOURNALISTS, National Press Building, No. 1193, Washington, DC 20045.
—Journalists and communications professionals of Hispanic descent who are supporting educational and career opportunities for their colleagues and students in the field of journalism; training workshops; scholarships; annual conventions/ SP.

G-142.   NATIONAL ASSOCIATION OF HISPANIC NURSES, 6905 Alamo Downs Parkway, San Antonio, TX 78238.
—Hispanic registered nurses and nursing students supporting equal educational, career, and economic opportunities with other groups in the field; biennial conventions/ SP.

G-143.   NATIONAL ASSOCIATION OF PROFESSORS OF HEBREW, 1346 Van Hise Hall, University of Wisconsin, 1220 Linden Drive, Madison, WI 53706.
—Professors, students, scholars, and others interested in studying Hebrew language, literature, and related subjects; annual conventions/ HE.

G-144.   NATIONAL ASSOCIATION OF SELF-INSTRUCTIONAL LANGUAGE PROGAMS, c/o Critical Language Center, Box 38, Temple University, Philadelphia, PA 19122.
—University, college, and high school students of foreign languages involved in independent-study programs; audiovisual and textual materials are provided; annual conventions/ MUL.

G-145.   NATIONAL COALITION OF HISPANIC HEALTH AND HUMAN SERVICES ORGANIZATIONS, 1501 16th Street NW, Washington, DC 20005.
—Organizations and individuals encouraging Hispanic youth to pursue health professions; various educational programs; biennial conventions/ SP.

G-146. NATIONAL COUNCIL OF STATE SUPERVISORS OF FOREIGN
LANGUAGES, State Education Building, 4 Capitol Mall,
Little Rock, AR 72201.
—State supervisors of foreign languages interested in
upgrading the standards of teaching modern foreign
languages; annual conventions/ MUL.

G-147. NATIONAL COUNCIL ON THE EVALUATION OF FOREIGN
EDUCATIONAL CREDENTIALS, c/o AACRAO, 1 Dupont
Circle NW, Suite 330, Washington, DC 20036.
—Verification and recommendation of United States
grade equivalencies for students with credentials from
foreign countries/ MUL.

G-148. NATIONAL FEDERATION OF MODERN LANGUAGE TEACH-
ERS ASSOCIATIONS, 659 North 57th Avenue, Omaha, NE
68132.
—Network of state, regional, and national organizations
of teachers of modern languages interested in exchange
of information and experiences; annual conventions
and placement services/ MUL.

G-149. NATIONAL HEBREW CULTURE COUNCIL, 14 East 14th
Street, New York, NY 10012.
—Support for teaching Hebrew in universities, colleges,
and high schools; student awards; workshops for teach-
ers/ HE.

G-150. NATIONAL INDIAN COUNSELORS ASSOCIATION, P.O. Box
20007, Institute of American Indian Arts, Santa Fe, NM
87504.
—Native American counselors serving Native American
communities and interested in improved educational
services to these communities; data base; annual con-
ventions/ NAL.

G-151. NATIONAL INDIAN EDUCATION ASSOCIATION, 1819 H
Street, NW, Washington, DC 20006.
—Improvement of the educational level of Native Americans and establishment of libraries for Native American communities/ NAL.

G-152. NATIONAL INDIAN SOCIAL WORKERS ASSOCIATION,
P.O.B. 27463 Albuquerque, NM 87125.

—Counseling, development, planning, and administration programs for Native American organizations; encourages Native American youth to pursue the field of social work; annual conferences/ NAL.

G-153. NATIONAL ORGANIZATION OF ITALIAN-AMERICAN WOMEN, 445 West 59th Street, Room 1248, New York, NY 10019.
—Support for Italian-American women's professional and social advancement; annual conferences/ IT.

G-154. NATIONAL ORGANIZATION OF MINORITY ARCHITECTS, 120 Ralph McGill Boulevard, Atlanta, GA 30308.
—Black, Chinese, and Hispanic architects interested in professional opportunities for minority architects; roster of minority architecture firms; regional meetings and annual conventions/ CH, SP.

G-155. NORTH AMERICAN SINGERS ASSOCIATION, 6236 North Kildare Avenue, Chicago, IL 60646.
—German-American singers and members of men's, women's, or mixed choruses interested in promotion of German-language songs and customs/ GE.

G-156. NORTH AMERICAN TAIWANESE PROFESSORS ASSOCIATION, 5632 South Woodlawn Street, Chicago, IL 60637. INACTIVE(?)
—Professors, researchers, and scientists of Taiwanese descent interested in the upgrading and promotion of scientific knowledge; biographical archives; scholarships; annual conventions/ CH.

G-156/a. NORTHEAST CONFERENCE ON THE TEACHING OF FOREIGN LANGUAGES, P.O. Box 623, Middlebury, VT 05753.
—Educational organizations interested in promoting the teaching of foreign languages in the U.S.; awards for students and teachers; annual conventions/ MUL.

G-157. NORWEGIAN SINGERS ASSOCIATION OF AMERICA, Route 2, Box 137 Kenyon, MN 55946.
—Male chorus music featuring Scandinavian songs; biennial conventions/ NW.

G-158. PHI SIGMA IOTA, 5211 Essen Street, Suite 2, Baton Rouge, LA 70809.
—Honor society of foreign language specialists; scholarships; biennial conferences/ MUL.

G-159. PI DELTA PHI, Sam Houston State University, Box 2147, Huntsville, TX 77341.
—Honor society of French language and literature students; scholarships; triennial conventions/ FR.

G-160. PLA/MULTILINGUAL LIBRARY MATERIALS AND SERVICES COMMITTEE, c/o American Library Association, 50 East Huron Street, Chicago, IL 60611.
—Librarians and language specialists interested in multilingual library collections in the United States and Canada; guidelines for building such collections and offering better services to patrons; placement service during American Library Association's conventions (midwinter and summer)/ MUL.

G-161. REFORMA: NATIONAL ASSOCIATION TO PROMOTE LIBRARY SERVICES TO THE SPANISH SPEAKING, c/o American Library Association, 50 East Huron Street, Chicago, IL 60611.
—Librarians and institutions interested in improving library services to Spanish-speaking communities and patrons in the United States; placement service during American Library Association's conventions (midwinter and summer)/ SP.

G-162. SERBIAN-AMERICAN BAR ASSOCIATION, c/o Deyon-Branko-Brashich, 1040 6th Avenue, New York, NY 10018.
—Judges, attorneys, and other related professionals of Serbian descent interested in promoting educational services consistent with Serbian heritage; annual conventions/ S/C.

G-163. SERBIAN NATIONAL FEDERATION, 3 Gateway Center Pittsburgh, PA 15222.
—Preservation of Serbian heritage, culture, and language in the United States; quadrennial conventions/ S/C.

G-164.   SIGMA DELTA PI, P.O. Box 55125, Riverside, CA 92517.
—Honor society for Spanish language and literature specialists; scholarships; triennial meetings/ MUL.

G-165.   SLOVAK WRITERS AND ARTISTS ASSOCIATION, c/o Slovak Institute, 10510 Buckeye Boulevard, Cleveland, OH 44104.
—Writers, journalists, editors, painters, composers, and other professionals of Slovak descent interested in promoting Slovak literature, language, and culture; irregular conventions/ SL.

G-166.   SLOVENE NATIONAL BENEFIT SOCIETY, 166 Shore Drive, Burr Ridge, IL 60521.
—Preservation of Slovenian heritage, culture, and language; quadrennial conventions/ SV.

G-167.   SLOVENIAN RESEARCH CENTER OF AMERICA, 29227 Eddy Road, Willoughby Hills, OH 44092.
—Promotion and study of Slovenian language, culture, and heritage; Slovenian publications and courses in Slovenian/ SV.

G-168.   SOCIEDAD DE BIBLIOTECARIOS DE PUERTO RICO, Digan Escalare, Rio Piedras, PR 00931-2898.
See G-161.
—Professional librarians affiliated with the American Library Association and specializing in Spanish; placement service during American Library Association's conventions (midwinter and summer)/ SP.

G-169.   SOCIÉTÉ DE PROFESSEURS FRANÇAIS ET FRANCOPHONES EN AMERIQUE, 22 East 60th Street, New York, NY 10022.
—American and French teachers of French in the United States; organizes competitions and offers scholarships; quarterly meetings/ FR.

G-170.   SOCIETY FOR INTER-CELTIC ARTS AND CULTURE, 98 Marguerite Avenue, Waltham, MA 02154.
—Preservation of Celtic culture, heritage, and languages through various educational and artistic programs;

serves also as booking agency for Celtic artists/ BR, CL, CN, IR, MX, SC.

G-171.   SOCIETY FOR IRANIAN STUDIES, c/o Middle East Institute, SIA Building, Room 113, 420 West 118th Street, Columbia University, New York, NY 10027.
—Scholars, professors, and students involved in the study of Iranian language, culture, history, and related subjects; annual conferences/ PE.

G-172.   SOCIETY FOR LINGUISTIC ANTHROPOLOGY, c/o American Anthropological Association, 1703 New Hampshire Avenue NW, Washington, DC 20009.
—Scholars and studies involved in anthropological study of languages; annual conventions/ MUL.

G-173.   SOCIETY FOR ROMANIAN STUDIES, c/o Department of History, Huntington College, Huntington, IN 46750.
—Professors, students, researchers, and others interested in the study of Romanian language, culture, politics, and other aspects of contemporary Romania; annual conventions/ RO.

G-174.   SOCIETY FOR THE ADVANCEMENT OF SCANDINAVIAN STUDY, c/o Department of Germanic Languages, University of Oregon, Eugene, OR 97403.
—Teachers, scholars, researchers, and students involved in the study and fostering of Scandinavian languages, including teaching; annual conventions/ DA, FI, NW, SW.

G-175.   SOCIETY OF BASQUE STUDIES IN AMERICA, 600 Central Avenue, Riverside, CA 92507.
—Preservation and promotion of Basque heritage, culture, and language in the U.S.; speaker's bureau/ BS.

G-176.   SOCIETY OF FEDERAL LINGUISTS, P.O. Box 7765, Washington, DC 20044.
—Teachers, librarians, catalogers, and other related professionals using foreign languages on the job and working for the U.S. government; annual conventions/ MUL.

G-177. SOCIETY OF HISPANIC PROFESSIONAL ENGINEERS, 5400 East Olympic Boulevard, Suite 120, Los Angeles, CA 90022.
—Hispanic engineers and students interested in attracting and motivating other Hispanics to the field of engineering; annual conventions and placement services/ SP.

G-178. SOCIETY OF SPANISH ENGINEERS, PLANNERS AND ARCHITECTS, 384 East 149th Street, Suite 300, Bronx, NY 10455.
—Hispanic professionals in the field of engineering, urban planning, and architecture who are interested in better cooperation among industry, the academic community, and government; counseling for students, annual conventions, and placement services/ SP.

G-179. SPECIAL LIBRARIES ASSOCIATION, 1700 18th Street NW, Washington, DC 20009.
—Librarians, information specialists, and related professions from public, private, and academic libraries, specializing in various areas, including languages and literature; annual conventions; placement services/ MUL.

G-180. TAIWANESE ASSOCIATION OF AMERICA, P.O.B. 3302, Iowa City, IA 52244.
—Friendship between Taiwanese Americans and better understanding of other ethnic groups; annual conventions; placement services/ CH.

G-181. TEACHERS OF ENGLISH TO SPEAKERS OF OTHER LANGUAGES, 1600 Cameron Street, Suite 300, Alexandria, VA 22314.
—Teachers of ESL from colleges, high schools, and adult education programs; annual conventions; placement services/ ESL.

G-182. TIBET SOCIETY, P.O. Box 1968, Bloomington, IN 47402.
—Teachers, students, scholars, researchers, institutions, and organizations interested in research and study of the history, religion, languages, and other aspects of Tibet/ TI.

G-183.   TRANSLATION RESEARCH INSTITUTE, 5914 Pulaski Avenue, Philadelphia, PA 19144.
—Translators of various languages in various areas of specialization; membership directory with language qualifications; referral services/ MUL.

◼G-184.   TRANSLATOR'S AND INTERPRETER'S EDUCATIONAL SOCIETY, 1259 El Camino Road, Suite 160, Menlo Park, CA 94025.
—Teachers, students, researchers, and other professionals interested in translation and interpretation activities and specialization in Western Hemisphere languages; data base directory; courses in translation and interpretation; seminars for teachers/ MUL.

G-185.   TURKISH-AMERICAN PHYSICIAN ASSOCIATION, 222 Middle County Road, Smithtown, NY 11787.
—Turkish-American physicians interested in better professional ties between colleagues from the United States and Turkey; annual meetings/ TU.

G-186.   TURKISH STUDIES ASSOCIATION, c/o History Department, Colorado State University, Fort Collins, CO 80524.
—Teachers, students, researchers, and organizations interested in the study of Turkish culture, language, history, etc., in cooperation with Turkish scholars; annual conventions/ TU.

G-187.   UKRAINIAN ARTISTS ASSOCIATION IN THE U.S.A., 1022 North Lawrence Street, Philadelphia, PA 19123.
—Ukrainian painters, sculptors, graphic artists, and related professionals interested in sponsoring shows, exhibits, and other programs; assistance to needy artists; annual conventions/ UK.

G-188.   UKRAINIAN ENGINEERS SOCIETY OF AMERICA, 300 Winston Drive North 116, Cliffside Park, NJ 07010.
—Professional engineers, architects, economists, and other related professionals interested in Ukrainian scientific terminology, professional development programs, and attracting youth to the field of engineering; annual conventions/ UK.

G-189. UKRAINIAN LIBRARY ASSOCIATION OF AMERICA, P.O. Box 4555, New York, NY 10956.
—Professional and paraprofessional librarians and others who are interested in Ukrainian language, literature, and other topics for scholarly research; annual conventions and placement services during American Library Association's conventions (midwinter and summer)/ UK.

G-190. UKRAINIAN MEDICAL ASSOCIATION OF NORTH AMERICA, 2247 West Chicago Avenue, Chicago, IL 60622.
—Physicians, surgeons, dentists, and other related professionals interested in better professional ties and career development; biographical archives; placement services/ UK.

G-191. UNION AND LEAGUE OF ROMANIAN SOCIETIES OF AMERICA, 23203 Lorain Road, North Olmstead, OH 44070.
—Preservation of Romanian heritage, culture, language, and fraternal ties; scholarships to deserving students of Romanian descent; biennial congress/ RO.

G-192. U.S. BRANCH OF THE INTERNATIONAL COMMITTEE FOR THE DEFENSE AND PRESERVATION OF THE BRETON LANGUAGE, 169 Greenwood Avenue, B-4 Jenkintown, PA 19046.
—Preservation of the Breton language and culture/ BR.

G-193. VIETNAM FOUNDATION, 6713 Lumsden Street, McLean, VA 22101.
—Preservation of Vietnamese heritage, culture, and languages, and integration of Vietnamese refugees in American society; classes in Vietnamese and English; counseling services/ VI.

G-194. WELSH SOCIETY, 450 Broadway, Camden, NJ 08103.
—Preservation of Welsh heritage, culture, and language in America; awards to outstanding Welsh-Americans and scholarships to deserving students; annual conventions/ WE.

G-195. WOMEN'S CAUCUS FOR MODERN LANGUAGES, Department of English, Louisiana State University, Women's Studies, Baton Rouge, LA 70803.

—Professional women from universities and colleges who are interested in the study and teaching of foreign languages; annual conventions/ MUL.

G-196. YIDDISH WRITERS UNION, 45 East 33rd Street, New York, NY 10016. INACTIVE(?) See G-212.
—Union organization of Yiddish journalists; professional lectures; annual conventions/ YD.

Addendum Section G

G-197. AFGHANISTAN STUDIES ASSOCIATION c/o Center for Afghanistan Studies, University of Nebraska/Omaha, Ash 238, Omaha, NE 68182-0006.
—Students and scholars involved in Afghan studies, have teaching, research, and cultural programs focusing on Afghan culture, language, and heritage/ PE(dr), PS.

G-198. AMERICAN COUNCIL ON GERMANY, 14 East 60th Street, Suite 606, New York, NY 10022.
—Promotes better understanding between the United States and Germany, sponsors joint working projects, fellowship exchanges and group discussions/ GE.

G-199. AMERICAN LITHUANIAN MUSICIANS ALLIANCE, 7310 South California Avenue, Chicago, IL 60061.
—Promotes Lithuanian music, organizes various musical programs such as operas, concerts, folklore festivals, and maintains a musicology library/ LI.

G-200. AMERICAN HUNGARIAN FOUNDATION, 300 Somerset Street, P.O. Box 1084, New Brunswick, NJ 08903.
—Conducts academic, cultural, and educational programs related to Hungarian cultural and historical heritage in America; maintains library and museum/ HU.

G-201. ASSEMBLY OF TURKISH AMERICAN ASSOCIATIONS, 1522 Connecticut Avenue NW, Washington, DC 20036.
—Reunites various Turkish-American organizations, offers assistance to Turkish-American schools, sponsors

annual heritage weeks; maintains job placement service/ TU.

G-202. BUDDHIST COUNCIL FOR REFUGEE RESCUE AND RESETTLEMENT, 1777 Murchison Drive, Burlingame, CA 94010.
—Helps Indo-Chinese refugees with resettlement in America, provides ESL courses, job training, and placement services/ CA, LO, VI.

G-203. BYELORUSSIAN INSTITUTE OF ARTS AND SCIENCE, 230 Springfield Avenue, Rutherford, NJ 07070.
—Scholars, writers, artists, and students interested in Byelorussian heritage in America, achievements of Byelorussian Americans/ BY.

G-204. CENTER FOR FOREIGN JOURNALISTS, A Sunrise Valley Drive, Reston, VA 22091.
—Promotes exchanges of professional experiences between journalists from various countries; maintains an educational center, consulting and referral services/ MUL.

G-205. CROATIAN ACADEMY OF AMERICA, P.O. Box 1767, Grand Central Station, New York, NY 10163-1763.
—Preservation of Croatian history, literature, religion, and other aspects of Croatian-American heritage/ S/C.

G-206. CUBAN AMERICAN NATIONAL FOUNDATION, 1000 Thomas Jefferson Street NW, Suite 601, Washington, DC 20007.
—Concerned with political, economic, social, and other aspects related to Cubans inside and outside their land of origin/ SP.

G-207. ERIC CLEARINGHOUSE ON LANGUAGES & LINGUISTICS CENTER FOR APPLIED LINGUISTICS, 1118 22nd Street NW, Washington, DC 20037.
—Deals with theoretical and practical aspects of teaching foreign languages and applied linguistics; holds over 300,000 specialized microfiches/ MUL.

G-208. ESPERANTO LEAGUE FOR NORTH AMERICA, P.O. Box 1129, El Cerrito, CA 94530.

—Promotes Esperanto language in schools via correspondence courses, and maintains library and information center, as well as book services (dictionaries, manuals, etc.)/ EP.

G-209. ETHIOPIAN COMMUNITY DEVELOPMENT COUNCIL, 1036 South Highland Street, Arlington, VA 22204.
—Provides assistance to Ethiopian refugees in the process of integrating into the American society; assists small businesses, operates training, counseling and outreach services/ ET.

G-210. GERMAN AMERICAN WORLD SOCIETY, 529 A Central Avenue, Jersey City, NJ 07307.
—Provides information on German-American history, culture, arts; maintains library, referral, and placement services/ GE.

G-211. LAOTIAN CULTURAL AND RESEARCH CENTER, 1413 Meriday Lane, Santa Ana, CA 92706.
—Preserves Laotian culture and heritage in America, maintains special library and archives/ LO.

G-212. LEAGUE FOR YIDDISH, 200 West 72nd Street, Suite 40, New York, NY 10023.
—Promotes the use of the Yiddish as a living language, organizes seminars, maintains library, and provides book sale services/ YD.

G-213. MEXICAN-AMERICAN OPPORTUNITY FOUNDATION, 6252 Telegraph Road, Commerce, CA 90040.
—Conducts several programs for Mexican-Americans, including vocational training, apprenticeships, ESL courses, employment services/ SP.

G-214. NATIONAL ASSOCIATION FOR THE EDUCATION AND ADVANCEMENT OF CAMBODIAN, LAOTIAN, AND VIETNAMESE AMERICANS, Illinois Research Center, 1855 Mount Prospect Road, Des Plaines, IL 60018.
—Seeks to provide equal educational, job, and developmental opportunities for Indo-Chinese Americans; organizes workshops, contests, and referral services for professionals and networking; provides scholarships/ CA, LO, VI.

G-215. NATIONAL ASSOCIATION OF ASIAN AMERICAN PROFESSIONALS, P.O. Box 772, New York, NY 10002.
—Assists Asian-American professionals through networking programs and encourages high school students to pursue college studies/ ASL.

G-216. NATIONAL FEDERATION OF HISPANICS IN COMMUNICATION, P.O. Box 2106, Fairfax, VA 22031.
—Reunites writers, editors, audiovisual specialists, moviemakers, photographers, and others; encourages exchanges of experiences and networking, and organizes training and professional development programs/ SP.

G-217. NATIONAL SLAVIC CONVENTION, 16 South Patterson Park Avenue, Baltimore, MD 21231.
—Organizes individuals and associations of Slavic descent; offers social, legal, educational and health assistance; maintains library and placement service/ SLL.

G-218. SOCIETY OF TURKISH ARCHITECTS, ENGINEERS AND SCIENTISTS IN AMERICA, 821 United Nations Plaza, 2nd Floor, New York, NY 10017.
—Reunites Turkish professionals, and helps members to obtain professional licenses in America; sponsors social programs/ TU.

G-219. UNITED STATES-JAPAN FOUNDATION, 145 East 32nd Street, New York, NY 10016.
—Supports educational and scientific exchanges between the United States and Japan/ JP.

G-220. YIVO INSTITUTE FOR JEWISH RESEARCH, 1048 Fifth Avenue, New York, NY 10028.
—Conducts research and training programs in Yiddish language, Jewish literature, folklore, history and other related fields; maintains library and archives with over 20 million items/ YD.

3. FOREIGN EMPLOYMENT AND BUSINESS RESOURCES

This chapter has two sections—H) United Nations: Administrative, Specialized, Regional, and Other Related Units, with 43 entries, and I) Worldwide Contacts: Country-by-Country Review, with 191 entries.

Section H lists for job-hunting purposes all United Nations units in alphabetical order rather than by rank, administrative subordination, or importance. Each entry shows the name of the unit, address, activities in brief, job requirements (graduate or undergraduate studies, educational background or occupation), and desirable languages. One has to keep in mind that, even though the United Nations has over 600 offices all around the world, staffed by about 65,000 employees, only about 7,000 employees (representing about 11 percent) are U.S. citizens. The competition is very tough, and standards of hiring are very high (requirements include advanced graduate studies combined with solid experience and fluency in languages). In recent years, the United Nations has experienced serious financial difficulties, which is also a factor to be considered by job hunters. United Nations official languages are AB, CH, EN, FR, RU, and SP. Many employees are fluent in two or more languages. Applicants for United Nations positions should also refer to items D-24 and D-64.

Section I entries differ from those in the previous section. Each entry shows the name of country, capital, population, official language(s) and other widely used languages (separated by a dash from the official), the country's embassy and commercial or trade office addresses in the United States, and number of firms (if any) in this country; U.S. embassy and commercial or trade office addresses in the respective country, number of U.S. firms there, plus United Nations Information and Development Program offices in each country. Such an arrangement permits job hunters willing to work abroad—for U.S. or for foreign employers—as well as businesspeople to have important contacts for each country at their fingertips.

It is useful to remember that international work requires adaptability to various climates, cultures, and customs; and patience, flexibility, and sensitivity to other people; and a good command of foreign languages.

Population statistics for each country were extracted from *World Statistics in Brief* (United Nations, 1986).

H. UNITED NATIONS: ADMINISTRATIVE, SPECIALIZED, REGIONAL, AND OTHER RELATED UNITS

H-1. FOOD AND AGRICULTURE ORGANIZATION (FAO), Liaison Office for North America: 1001 Second Street NW, Washington, DC 20437/ Main Office: Via delle Terme di Caracalla, 00100 Rome, Italy.
—Undertakes and coordinates agricultural and rural development, food and nutrition research, and is a specialized agency.
—GRD/ agricultural economics, economic development, economics, nutrition subjects, rural planning, world resources/ AB, CH, FR, SP are important.

H-2. GENERAL AGREEMENT ON TARIFFS AND TRADE (GATT), Centre William Rappard, 154, Rue de Lausanne, 1211 Geneva 21, Switzerland.
—An autonomous organization, its objective is to remove trade barriers between nations and expand international trade and economic development.
—GRD/ economic development, economics, tariffs and trade studies/ AB, FR, SP.

H-3. INTER-AMERICAN DEVELOPMENT BANK, Employment Section, 1300 New York Avenue NW, Washington, DC 20577.

—Regional organization, promotes economic development of member countries in Latin America.

—GRD/ banking, economic development, economics, environment, finance, Latin American studies/ FR, PT, SP, fluency in two languages preferred.

H-4. INTER-AMERICAN INSTITUTE FOR COOPERATION ON AGRI-CULTURE (IICA), 1889 F Street NW, Suite 840, Washington, DC 20006.

—Autonomous agency within the Organization of American States (OAS), specializing in agriculture and supporting agricultural and rural development of member states.

—GRD/ agricultural science, development economics, plus several years of relevant experience/ FR, PT, SP, fluency in two.

H-5. INTERGOVERNMENTAL COMMITTEE FOR MIGRATION (ICM), 440 National Press Building, 529 14th Street NW, Washington, DC 20045.

—Specialized agency, deals with processing, resettlement, and assistance to refugees from Africa, Central America, and Eastern Europe.

—GRD/ economics, international relations, law, management, public relations, sociology, plus research experience/ FR or SP.

H-6. INTERNATIONAL ATOMIC ENERGY AGENCY (IAEA), Vienna International Center, P.O. Box 100, A-1400 Vienna, Austria.

—Specialized agency, its objective is to encourage and accelerate the uses of atomic energy for peaceful purposes.

—GRD/ administration, economics, international relations, public relations/ CH, FR, RU, SP.

H-7. INTERNATIONAL CIVIL AVIATION ORGANIZATION (ICAO), P.O. Box 400, 1000 Sherbrooke Street West, Montreal, Quebec, Canada H3A 2R2.

—Specialized agency, its function is to administer technical cooperation programs in civil aviation.

—GRD/ aeronautics, business adminstration, economics, meteorology, plus solid professional experience and training/ FR, SP.

H-8.   INTERNATIONAL COMMISSION FOR THE CONSERVATION OF ATLANTIC TUNA, Príncipe de Vergara 17, Madrid 28001, Spain.
—Specialized agency, cooperates closely with H-1 and is concerned with rational exploitation of tuna and related species in the Atlantic Ocean; reviews statistical and research programs.
—GRD/ economics, marine studies, statistics, world economics/ FR, SP.

H-9.   INTERNATIONAL FUND FOR AGRICULTURAL DEVELOPMENT, United Nations, New York, NY 10017/ 107 Via Del Serafico 00142 Rome, Italy.
—Specialized agency, helps increase agricultural production in developing countries, has over 140 member states.
—GRD/ agricultural economics, economic development, finance, food resources, sociology, studies in area countries/ AB, FR, PT, SP.

★H-10. INTERNATIONAL LABOR ORGANIZATION (ILO), USA Branch Office: 1750 New York Avenue NW, Washington, DC 20006/ Headquarters: 4, Route de Morillons, CH-1211, Geneva 22, Switzerland.
—Specialized organization, its function is to implement international programs for improving global labor conditions.
—GRD/ area studies, economics, industrial relations, international relations, labor economics, labor law, public administration, social sciences, statistics, plus minimum five years' experience/ FR, SP.

H-11. INTERNATIONAL MARITIME ORGANIZATION (IMO), 4 Albert Embankment, London, SE1 7SR, United Kingdom.
—Specialized organization dealing with safety of international shipping and prevention of maritime pollution from ships; also concerned with respecting standards for shipbuilding.
—GRD/ international studies, international trade, maritime law, plus extensive experience and expertise in the field of international trade/ FR, SP. Recruitment is done through United Nations central office.

★H-12. INTERNATIONAL MONETARY FUND (IMF), Recruiting and Training Division, 700 19th Street NW, Washington, DC 20431.
—Specialized agency, performs several global monetary management functions.
—GRD/ area studies, business administration, economics, finance, statistics, plus extensive experience in the respective fields/ AB, FR, SP important.

H-13. INTERNATIONAL TELECOMMUNICATION UNION (ITU), Palais des Nations, 1211 Geneva 10, Switzerland.
—Undertakes and coordinates technical cooperative projects with the aim of improving and accelerating global telecommunications systems.
—GRD/electronics, engineering, mathematics, physical science, statistics, telecommunications, plus extensive experience in the respective fields/ FR, SP, RU.

H-14. NORTH ATLANTIC TREATY ORGANIZATION (NATO), 1110 Brussels, Belgium.
—A regional, intergovernmental defense organization, aimed at protecting Western Europe, its members—15 North and Western European countries and the United States—cooperate in cultural, economic, military, political, and social fields.
—GRD/ international studies, law, liberal arts, military subjects, political sciences, and other related fields/ FR, RU.
—American NATO staff is usually recommended by U.S. Department of State.

H-15. ORGANIZATION FOR ECONOMIC COOPERATION AND DEVELOPMENT (OECD), 2 Rue André-Pascal, 75018 Paris Cedex 16, France.
—Regional organization concerned with the cooperation of its members—advanced industrial nations, including the United States—in economic, industrial, cultural, and other fields.
—GRD/ administration, business, economic development, economics, European studies, industrial relations, manpower studies, statistics/ FR, SP and other languages helpful.

H-16.   ORGANIZATION OF AMERICAN STATES (OAS), Constitution Avenue and 17th Street NW, Washington, DC 20006.
  —Regional organization, promotes cooperation among the nations of North and South America in cultural, economic, educational, and other fields, and also serves as an arena for inter-American negotiations.
  —GRD/ American studies, area studies, economic development, economics, international studies, Latin American studies, public relations/ FR, SP fluency.

★H-17.   PAN AMERICAN HEALTH ORGANIZATION (PAHO), 525 23rd Street NW, Washington, DC 20037.
  —Regional organization responsible for the administration of health-care services in the countries that are members of H-16.
  —GRD/ medicine, health administration, public health, sanitary engineering, plus a minimum of five years' experience in the respective fields/ FR or PT, SP.

H-18.   SOUTH PACIFIC COMMISSION (SPC), P.O. Box D-5, Nouméa Cedex, New Caledonia/ or South Pacific Commission, c/o U.S. Department of State, Washington, DC 20520.
  —Technical organization, provides training and assistance in cultural, economic, and social fields to over 20 countries in the region, as well as in Australia and New Zealand.
  —GRD/ education, management, marine resources, technology/ MUL.
  —American personnel is recommended by the U.S. Department of State.

H-19.   UNITED NATIONS CHILDREN'S FUND (UNICEF), Recruitment and Staff Development, 866 United Nations Plaza, Room A-3K, New York, NY 10017.
  —Provides basic services to needy children in developing countries.
  —GRD/ area studies, civil engineering, economics, education, health, nutrition, social work, teaching, plus experience in developing countries/AB, FR, PT, or SP required.

H-20.   UNITED NATIONS CONFERENCE ON TRADE AND DEVELOPMENT (UNCTAD), Palais des Nations, 1121 Geneva 10, Switzerland.

—Provides a forum for developing countries to debate economic issues, and researches the impact upon participating countries.
—GRD/ economic development, economics, legal background, studies of area countries, trade/ AB, FR, SP.

★H-21.   UNITED NATIONS DEVELOPMENT PROGRAM (UNDP), 1 United Nations Plaza, New York, NY 10017.
—Helps developing countries in Africa, Asia, parts of Europe, Latin America, and the Middle East to better use their natural resources and available manpower.
—GRD/ economic development, economics, public administration, sociology, plus solid experience in developing countries/ AB, CH, FR, SP, fluency in at least two.
—Countries with UNDP offices are listed in Section I.

H-22.   UNITED NATIONS EDUCATIONAL, SCIENTIFIC AND CULTURAL ORGANIZATION (UNESCO), Liaison Office: United Nations Plaza, Room DC2-0934, New York, NY 10017/ Headquarters: 7, Place de Fontenoy, 75700 Paris, France.
—Specialized agency, has an extensive network of research and dissemination programs in the areas of culture, education, mass communications, and science.
—GRD/ archaeology, arts, broadcasting, communications, cultural affairs, engineering, journalism, mass media, teaching, plus relevant experience/ AB, CH, FR, RU, SP.

H-23.   UNITED NATIONS ENVIRONMENT PROGRAMME, Liaison Office: Room DC2-8, United Nations, New York, NY 10017/ Headquarters: P.O. Box 30552, Nairobi, Kenya.
—Coordinating unit for solving environmental problems on an international level.
—GRD/ economic development, economics, energy studies, environmental studies, population, world resources/ AB, FR, PT, SP, fluency in at least two.

H-24.   UNITED NATIONS HIGH COMMISSIONER FOR REFUGEES (UNHCR), Palais des Nations, 1211 Geneva 10, Switzerland/ Liaison Office: 1785 Massachusetts Avenue NW, Washington, DC 20036.
—Helps refugees with political asylum and protection of their rights to employment, education, and freedom of movement, and cooperates with governments and or-

ganizations offering the asylum and assisting refugees to become self-supporting.

—GRD/ economic development, economics, international relations, social work, plus experience with displaced persons or refugees/ AB, FR, RU, SP, and other languages.

★H-25. UNITED NATIONS INDUSTRIAL DEVELOPMENT ORGANIZATION (UNIDO), Vienna International Center, Room EO-554, P.O. Box 300, A-1011, Vienna, Austria.

—Promotes and coordinates the acceleration of industrialization in the developing countries.

—GRD/ area studies, business administration, economic development, economics, industrial relations, plus a minimum of three years' experience in a relevant field/ FR essential, other languages helpful (according to area of work).

★H-26. UNITED NATIONS INSTITUTE FOR TRAINING AND RESEARCH (UNITAR), 801 United Nations Plaza, New York, NY 10017.

—Administers various training programs aimed at educating national and foreign service officers in the functioning of the United Nations apparatus and other aspects related to multifaceted cooperation.

—GRD/ area studies, economic development, economics, foreign policy, international relations, political science, world resources, plus relevant experience, research, and training ability/ FR important, other languages helpful.

H-27. UNITED NATIONS INTERNATIONAL SCHOOL, 24-50 East River Drive, New York, NY 10010.

—A school for students whose parents are associated with the United Nations and come from outside the United States; accepts students from the age of five through preparation for college.

—UGD/GRD/ elementary and high school subjects, language studies, plus relevant teaching experience/ AB, CH, FR, RU, SP.

H-28. UNITED NATIONS RELIEF AND WORKS AGENCY (UNRWA), Vienna International Center, P.O. Box 700, A-1400, Vienna, Austria/ P.O. Box 484, Amman, Jordan.

—Provides services to Palestinian refugees who live in camps in Israel (West Bank and Gaza), Jordan, Lebanon, and Syria; operates hundreds of schools, health programs, and food distribution.

—GRD/ accounting, administration, education, engineering, health, law, nutrition, personnel administration, technology, various language studies, plus five years' of experience with relief organizations/ AB, FR, GE in demand.

H-29.   UNITED NATIONS SECRETARIAT/GENERAL RECRUITMENT OFFICE, Room 200, United Nations Plaza, New York, NY 10017.
—Posts vacancies for international positions.

★H-30.   UNITED NATIONS SECRETARIAT/PROFESSIONAL RECRUITMENT, Room 2465, United Nations Plaza, New York, NY 10017.
—Accepts applications from professionals who apply for a specific posted position or vacancy announcement, and dispatches the applications to the hiring departments, except H-3, H-12, H-14, H-16, and H-37; applications for these agencies must be sent directly.

H-31.   UNITED NATIONS SECRETARIAT/PUBLIC INFORMATION DEPARTMENT, Room S-037-G, United Nations Plaza, New York, NY 10017.
—Promotes the work of the United Nations and maintains information offices all around the world. Countries with such offices are listed in Section I.
—GRD/ broadcasting, exhibitions, films, graphic arts, journalism, press, publication, radio, television, visual media/ AB, CH, FR, RU, SP.

H-32.   UNITED NATIONS SECRETARIAT/PUBLIC INFORMATION DEPARTMENT, NON-GOVERNMENT ORGANIZATIONS (NGO), Room S-1037-J, United Nations Plaza, New York, NY 10017.
—Consultative agency of the United Nations, with multiple links to nongovernment agencies around the world.
—Has lists of volunteer opportunities.

H-33.   UNITED NATIONS SECRETARIAT/RECRUITMENT PROGRAMME SECTION, Room 2475, United Nations Plaza, New York, NY 10017.

—Accepts applications for professional positions in the Secretariat.

—GRD/ agriculture, demography, developmental agriculture, economics, engineering, finance, health services, international affairs, language studies, political studies, public administration, statistics, translating and interpreting services/ AB, CH, FR, RU, SP.

H-34. UNITED NATIONS UNIVERSITY, Toho Seimei Building, 29th Floor, 15-1 Shibuya 2-chome, Shibuya-ku, Tokyo, Japan.

—Involved in research programs in the fields of human and social development, natural resource management, and world hunger.

—GRD/ agriculture, area studies, demography, developing countries studies, language studies, world resources, and related subjects, plus teaching credentials and experience/ JP especially helpful.

H-35. UNITED NATIONS VOLUNTEERS, Palais des Nations, 1211 Geneva 10, Switzerland/ Coordinating Committee for International Volunteer Service, 1 Rue de Miollis, Paris 15, France/ or 1889 F Street, Ground Floor, Washington, DC 20006.

—Recruits youth from many countries to help developing countries in the fields of community development, education, health services, road reconstruction, etc.

—UGD/GRD/ administration, business, economics, engineering, nursing, teaching, urban planning, veterinary science/ FR, SP.

H-36. UNIVERSAL POSTAL UNION (UPU), Welt Post Strasse H, Case Postal 3000, Berne 15, Switzerland.

—Promotes freedom of transit, technical cooperation among organization's members, and improvement of the international postal system.

—GRD/ communications, electronics, engineering, mass media/ FR, GE, SP.

H-37. WORLD BANK, Personnel Department, 1818 H Street NW, Washington, DC 20433.

—An umbrella organization of three related agencies: INTERNATIONAL BANK FOR RECONSTRUCTION AND DEVELOPMENT (IBRD), THE INTERNATIONAL DEVELOPMENT ASSOCIATION (IDA), AND THE INTERNATIONAL FI-

NANCE CORPORATION (IFC); provides loans, policy advice, and technical assistance to developing countries.
—GRD/ banking, business administration, economic development, economics, finance, technical subjects/ AB, CH, FR, PT or SP.

H-38.   WORLD FEDERATION OF UNITED NATIONS ASSOCIATIONS (WFUNA), Room DC1-1177, United Nations, New York, NY 10017.
—Promotes appreciation of objectives and principles of the United Nations worldwide.
—GRD/ broadcasting, graphic arts, journalism, publications, radio, television, and related areas/ AB, CH, FR, RU, SP.

H-39.   WORLD HEALTH ORGANIZATION (WHO), 20, Avenue Appia, 1211 Geneva 27, Switzerland or c/o Pan American Sanitary Bureau, 525 23rd Street NW, Washington, DC 20037.
—Provides multiple programs assisting member nations to upgrade their health services and train health workers.
—GRD/ economics, engineering, entomology, health education, medical studies, nursing, sanitary engineering, statistics, plus experience in developing countries/ MUL, languages of areas preferred.

H-40.   WORLD INTELLECTUAL PROPERTY ORGANIZATION (WIPO), 34, Chemin des Colombettes, 1211 Geneva 20, Switzerland.
—Concerned with the protection of intellectual property—copyrights, patents, trademarks, etc.—throughout the world.
—GRD/ administration, business, cultural subjects, law, science, technology/ FR, SP.

H-41.   WORLD METEOROLOGICAL ORGANIZATION (WMO), 41, Avenue Giuseppe-Motta, 1211 Geneva 20, Switzerland.
—Coordinates, standardizes, and improves world meteorological activities and encourages exchange of information among member nations.
—GRD/ meteorological studies, plus considerable experience in the field/ FR, SP.

H-42. WORLD TOURISM ORGANIZATION (WTO), Calle Capitán Haya 42, E-Madrid 20, Spain.
—Promotes tourism with the aim of advancing participating countries in the areas of culture, economy, and social welfare.
—GRD/ administration, area studies, cultural studies, language studies, tourism, plus experience in tourism/ MUL, area languages preferred.

Addendum Section H

H-43. UNITED NATIONS FUND FOR POPULATION ACTIVITIES (UN-FPA), 220 East 42nd Street, New York, NY 10017.
—Largest international agency promoting awareness of population problems and assistance to developing countries.
—GRD/ demography, economics, public health, sociology, plus several years of relevant experience/ AB, CH, FR, RU, SP, fluency in two required.

I. WORLDWIDE CONTACTS: COUNTRY-BY-COUNTRY REVIEW

I-1. AFGHANISTAN/Kabul/16.5 mil./ PE(dr), PS
—EMB in USA: 2341 Wyoming Avenue NW, Washington, DC 20008.
—USA EMB: Wazir Akbar Khan Mina, Kabul.
—UND: Sardar Shah Mahmoud Ghazi Wat, P.O. Box 5, Kabul.
—UNI: *Same as above.*

I-2. ALBANIA/Tirana/3.2 mil./ AL-GR, IT
—EMB in USA: 1150 18th Street NW, Washington, DC 20036.
—USA EMB: RRUGA Labinoti 103, Room 2921, Tirana.
—UND: *See* Yugoslavia
—UNI: Same as UNI.

I-3. ALGERIA/Algiers/25.3 mil./ AB-BB, FR
—EMB in USA: 2118 Kalorama Road NW, Washington, DC 20008.

—USA EMB: 4 Chemin Cheich Bachir Brahimi, P.O. 549 (Alger-Gare), Algiers/U.S. firms: 25.
—UND: P.O.B. 823, Algiers 1600.
—UNI: *Same as above.*

I-4. ANDORRA/Andorra/34,000/ CT-FR, SP
—Interests represented by Spain.

I-5. ANGOLA/Luanda/8.5 mil./ PT, UM-BN
—EMB in USA: Not established yet.
—USA EMB: Predio Bia, 11 Andal Street, Luanda, C.P. 6484 (Liaison Office)
—UND: Avenida dos Restauradores, 128-1, Caixa Postal 910, Luanda.

I-6. ANTIGUA AND BARBUDA/St. Johns/85,000/ EN-EN(pt)
—EMB in USA: 3400 International Drive NW, Suite 4M, Washington, DC 20008.
—USA EMB: FPO Miami 34054.
—UNI: *See* Trinidad and Tobago.

I-7. ARGENTINA/Buenos Aires/32.6 mil./ SP-FR, GE, IT
—EMB in USA: 1600 New Hampshire Avenue NW, Washington, DC 20009.
—CTR in USA: 50 West 34th Street, 6th Floor, Suite C2, New York, NY 10001/ Argentinian firms in the U.S.: 6.
—USA EMB: 4300 Colombia, Palermo, 1425 Buenos Aires.
—USA CTR: Avenida Pte. Roque Sáenz Peña 567, 6° Piso, 1352 Buenos Aires/ U.S. firms: 256.
—UND: Casilla de Correo 2257, 1000 Capital Federal, Buenos Aires.
—UNI: Junín 1940 1er Piso, 1113 Buenos Aires.

I-8. AUSTRALIA/Canberra/17.2 mil./ EN
—EMB in USA: 1601 Massachusetts Avenue NW, Washington, DC 20036.
—CTR in USA: 636 Fifth Avenue, New York, NY 10111/Australian firms in the U.S.: 29.
—USA EMB: Moonah Place, Canberra, A.C.T. 2600.
—USA CTR: 39-41 Lower Fort Street, Sydney, N.S.W. 2000/ U.S. firms: 704.
—UNI: 44 Market Street, 16th Floor, P.O. Box 4045, Sydney, N.S.W. 2001.

I-9. AUSTRIA/Vienna/7.8 mil./ GE-HU, S/C, SV
—EMB in USA: 2343 Massachusetts Avenue NW, Washington, DC 20008.
—CTR in USA: 165 West 46th Street, New York, NY 10036/ Austrian firms in the U.S.: 12.
—USA EMB: Boltzmanngasse 16, A-1091, Vienna.
—USA CTR: Porzellangasse 35, A-1090, Vienna/ U.S. firms: 145.
—UNI: International Center, Wagramer Strasse 5, P.O.B. 500, A-1400, Vienna.

I-10. BAHAMAS/Nassau/250,000/ EN
—EMB in USA: 2220 Massachusetts Avenue NW, Washington, DC 20008.
—CTR: 767 Third Avenue, New York, NY 10017.
—USA EMB: Queen Street, P.O. Box N-8197, Nassau/ U.S. firms: 50.
—UNI: *See* Trinidad and Tobago.

I-11. BAHRAIN/Manama/486,000/ AB-EN
—EMB in USA: 3502 International Drive NW, Washington, DC 20008.
—CTR in USA: 2 United Nations Plaza, 25th Floor, New York, NY 10017.
—USA EMB: Building 979, Road 3119, P.O. Box 26431, Manama/ U.S. firms: 52.
—UND: Jufair, P.O. Box 26814, Manama.
—UNI: King Faisal Road, Gufool, P.O.B. 26004, Manama.

I-12. BANGLADESH/Dhaka/108 mil./ BG-EN
—EMB in USA: 2201 Wisconsin Avenue NW, Washington, DC 20007.
—CTR in USA: 821 United Nations Plaza, 8th Floor, New York, NY 10017.
—USA EMB: Diplomatic Enclave, Madani Avenue, G.P.O. Box 323, Dhaka 1212/ U.S. firms: 23.
—UND: New House No. 60, New Road No. 11/A, P.O. Box 224, Ramna, Dhaka 1000.
—UNI: House 12, Road 6, Dhamandi, GPO Box 3658, Dhaka 1205.

I-13. BARBADOS/Bridgetown/257,000/ EN
—EMB in USA: 2144 Wyoming Avenue NW, Washington, DC 20008.

—CTR in USA: 800 Second Avenue, New York, NY 10017.
—USA EMB: P.O. Box 302, Bridgetown/ U.S. firms: 29.
—UND: Jemmot's Lane, P.O. Box 625 C, Bridgetown.
—UNI: *See* Trinidad and Tobago.
—CARIBBEAN DEVELOPMENT BANK: P.O. Box 408 Wildey, St. Michael.

I-14.   BELGIUM/Brussels/9.9 mil./ FR, DU-GE
—EMB in USA: 3330 Garfield Street NW, Washington, DC 20008.
—CTR: 50 Rockefeller Plaza, New York, NY 10020/ 437 Madison Avenue, New York, NY 10022/ Belgian firms in the U.S.: 39.
—USA EMB: 27 Boulevard du Régent, B-1000 Brussels.
—USA CTR: Avenue des Arts, B-1040, Brussels/ U.S. firms: 466.
—UNI: Avenue De Broqeville 40, 1200 Brussels.

I-15.   BELIZE/Belmopan/193,000/ EN-SP
—EMB in USA: 3400 International Drive NW, Suite 25, Washington, DC 20008.
—USA EMB: Gabourel Lane, P.O.B. 286, Belize City.
—UNI: *See* Trinidad and Tobago.

I-15/a.   BENIN/Porto-Novo/4.7 mil./ FR-DE, F/O, M/I, YO
—EMB in USA: 2737 Cathedral Avenue NW, Washington, DC 20008.
—USA EMB: Rue Caporal Anani Bernard, P.O. Box 2012, Cotonou/ U.S. firms: 7.
—UND: Lot III, Zone Résidentielle, B.P. 506, Cotonou.
—UNI: *See* Togo.

I-16.   BERMUDA/Hamilton/54,670 (1980)/ EN
—USA CTR: P.O. Box 325, Hamilton 5/ U.S. firms: 39.

I-17.   BHUTAN/Thimphu/0.6 mil./ TI-NE
—No diplomatic relations with U.S.
—UND: Hydel Building, G.P.O. Box 162, Thimphu.
—UNI: *See* India.

I-18.   BOLIVIA/La Paz/6.4 mil./ SP-AY, QC
—EMB in USA: 3014 Massachusetts Avenue NW, Washington, DC 20008.

—CTR in USA: 211 East 43rd Street, Room 802, New York, NY 10017.
—USA EMB: Banco Popular Building, P.O. Box 425, La Paz.
—USA CTR: Avenida 6 de Agosto No. 2570, P.O. Box 8268, La Paz/ U.S. firms: 39.
—UND: Avenida Ara No. 2529, Casilla 686, La Paz.
—UNI: Plaza Isabel La Católica, Apartado Postal 686, La Paz.

I-19. BOTSWANA/Gaborone/1.3 mil./ EN-AF, SE
—EMB in USA: 3400 International Drive NW, Suite 7M, Washington, DC 20008.
—USA EMB: P.O. Box 90, Gaborone.
—UND: Barclays Bank Building, P.O. Box 54, Gaborone.
—UNI: *See* Zambia.

I-20. BRAZIL/Rio de Janeiro/155.6 mil./ PT(br)-GE, IT, JP
—EMB in USA: 3006 Massachusetts Avenue NW, Washington, DC 20008.
—CTR in USA: 630 Fifth Avenue, New York, NY 10111/ 22 West 48th Street, New York, NY 10036/ Brazilian firms in the U.S.: 12.
—USA EMB: Avenida das Nações, Lote 3, Brasilia.
—USA CTR: Caixa Postal 916, Praça Pio X-15, 5° Andar, 20040 Rio de Janeiro/ U.S. firms: 516.
—UND: Edificio Venancio II, 3° Andar, Caixa Postal 07-0285, 7000 Brasilia.
—UNI: Avenida Marechal Floriano 196, 20060 Rio de Janeiro.

I-21. BRUNEI/Bandar Seri Begawan/256,000/ ML-CH
—EMB in USA: The Watergate, 2600 Virginia Avenue NW, Suite 300, Washington, DC 20037.
—USA EMB: P.O. Box 2991, Bandar Seri Begawan.

I-22. BULGARIA/Sofia/8.9 mil./ BL-AR, GR, TU
—EMB in USA: 1621 22nd Street NW, Washington, DC 20008.
—USA EMB: 1 A Stamboliski Boulevard, Sofia.
—UNI: *See* Switzerland.

I-23. BURKINA FASO (UPPER VOLTA)/Ouagadougou/8.7 mil./FR-GS, LB, M/S, S/M
—EMB in USA: 2340 Massachusetts Avenue NW, Washington, DC 20008.
—USA EMB: P.O. Box 1, Ouagadougou.
—UND: P.O. Box 575, Ouagadougou.
—UNI: 218, Rue de la Gare, Secteur No. 3, P.O.B. 135, Ouagadougou.

I-24. No Entry.

I-25. Burma. *See* Myanmar.

I-26. BURUNDI/Bujumbura/5.5 mil./ FR, KU-SH
—EMB in USA: 2233 Wisconsin Avenue NW, Suite 212, Washington, DC 20007.
—USA EMB: Avenue des etats unis, P.O. Box 1720, Bujumbura.
—UND: 3 Rue de Marche, P.O. Box 1490, Bujumbura.
—UNI: Place de l'Indépendence and Avenue de la Poste, P.O.B. 2160, Bujumbura.

I-27. CAMEROON/Yaoundé/9.4 mil./ FR, EN-AFL various
—EMB in USA: 2349 Massachusetts Avenue NW, Washington, DC 20008.
—USA EMB: Rue Nachtigal, P.O. Box 817, Yaoundé/ U.S. firms: 23.
—UND: P.O. Box 836, Yaoundé.
—UNI: Immeuble Kamden, Rue Joseph Clère, P.O.B. 836, Yaoundé.

I-28. CANADA/Ottawa/27 mil./ EN, FR-GE, IT, UK
—EMB in USA: 501 Pennsylvania Avenue NW, Washington, DC 20001.
—CTR: 1251 Avenue of the Americas, New York, NY 10020/ Canadian firms in the U.S.: 267.
—USA EMB: 100 Wellington Street, Ottawa, K1P 5T1, P.O.B. 5000.
—USA CTR: *Same as above*/ U.S. firms: 1,145.

I-29. CAPE VERDE/Praia/369,000/ P/C, PT
EMB in USA: 3415 Massachusetts Avenue NW, Washington, DC 20007.
—USA EMB: Rua Hojl Ya Yenna 81, C.P. 201, Praia.

—UND: Casa Moeda, Caixa Postal 62, Praia.
—UNI: *See* Senegal.

I-30. CENTRAL AFRICAN REPUBLIC/Bangui/3.1 mil./ FR, S/H
—EMB in USA: 1618 22nd Street NW, Washington, DC 20008.
—USA EMB: Avenue President Dacko, P.O. Box 924, Bangui/ U.S. firms: 4.
—UND: Avenue d'Indépendence, P.O. Box 872, Bangui.
—UNI: *See* Cameroon.

I-31. CHAD/N'Djamena/5.5 mil./ FR-AB, M/A, MU, S/A
—EMB in USA: 2002 R Street NW, Washington, DC 20009.
—USA EMB: Avenue Félix Éboué, P.O. Box 413, N'Djamena/ U.S. firms: 4.
—UND: Route de Farcha, P.O. Box 906, N'Djamena.
—UNI: *See* Upper Volta.

I-32. CHILE/Santiago/13.7 mil./ SP-GE, IT
—EMB in USA: 1732 Massachusetts Avenue NW, Washington, DC 20036.
—CTR in USA: 866 United Nations Plaza, New York, NY 10017/ 220 East 81st Street, New York, NY 10028.
—USA EMB: Codina Building, 1343 Agustinas, Santiago.
—USA CTR: Avenida Americo Vespucio, Sur 80, 9 Piso, 4131 Correo Central, Santiago.
—UND: Bandera 341, Casilla 197-D, Santiago.
—UNI: Comisión Económica para América Latina, Casilla 179-D, Santiago.

I-33. CHINA (PEOPLE'S REPUBLIC)/Beijing/1,114 mil./ CH various dialects-TI, UI
—EMB in USA: 2300 Connecticut Avenue NW, Washington, DC 20008.
—CTR in USA: 520 12th Avenue, New York, NY 10036/ 1 Pennsylvania Plaza, New York, NY 10001/ Chinese firms in the U.S.: 7.
—USA EMB: Xiu Shui Bei Jie, Beijing.
—USA CTR: Babcock & Wilcox, P.O.B. 4354, Beijing 100043/ U.S. firms: 60.
—UND: 2 Dong Quije Sanlitun, Beijing.

I-34. COLOMBIA/Bogotá/33 mil./ SP
—EMB in USA: 2118 Leroy Place NW, Washington, DC 20008.
—CTR in USA: 10 East 46th Street, New York, NY 10017/ 111 Broadway, Room 1408, New York, NY 10006.
—USA EMB: Calle 38, No. 8-61, Bogotá. (P.O.B. AA 3831).
—USA CTR: Apartado Aéreo 8008, Bogotá/ U.S. firms: 185.
—UND: Transversal 15 Norte 119-81, Bogotá.
—UNI: Calle 72, No. 12-65, Apartado Aéreo 058964, Bogotá 2.

I-35. COMOROS/Moroni/503,000/ AB, FR-SH (local dialect)
—EMB in USA: 336 East 45 Street, New York, NY 10017.
—USA EMB: P.O. Box 1318, Moroni.
—UND: Route du Bord de Mer, P.O. Box 648, Moroni.
—UNI: *Same as above.*

I-36. CONGO/Brazaville/2.2 mil./ FR-KK, LG
—EMB in USA: 4891 Colorado Avenue NW, Washington, DC 20011.
—USA EMB: Avenue Amilcar Cabral, P.O. Box 1015, Brazaville.
—UND: Avenue Pointe-Hollandaise, Quartier M'Pila, P.O.B. 465, Brazaville.
—UNI: P.O.B. 13210, Brazaville.

I-37. COSTA RICA/San José/2.9 mil./ SP-EN
—EMB in USA: 1825 Connecticut Avenue NW, Suite 211, Washington, DC 20009.
—CTR in USA: 80 Wall Street, Suite 1117, New York, NY 10005.
—USA EMB: Avenida 3 and Calle I, San José.
—USA CTR: Avenida 2 Calle 30-32, No. 3034, P.O. Box 4946, San José/ U.S. firms: 76.
—UND: 100 Metros al Sur, Apartado Postal 4540, San José.
—UNI: *See* El Salvador.

I-38. COTE D'IVOIRE (IVORY COAST)/Abidjan/12.1 mil./ FR-DY
—EMB in USA: 2424 Massachusetts Avenue NW, Washington, DC 20008.

—USA EMB: 5 Rue Jesse Owens, 01, P.O. Box 1712, Abidjan.
—USA CTR: 01, P.O. Box 1083, Abidjan/ U.S. firms: 36.
—UND: Angle de la Rue Courgaset et l'Avenue Marchand, 01, P.O. Box 1747, Abidjan.
—UNI: *See* Senegal.

I-39. CUBA/Havana/10.6 mil./ SP
—No diplomatic relations with the U.S.: Cuban interests in U.S.: 2630 16th Street NW Washington, DC 20009. U.S. interests in Cuba are represented by Switzerland.
—UND: Calle 18 No. 110, Apartado Postal 4138, Havana.
—UNI: *See* Mexico.

I-40. CYPRUS/Nicosia/702,000/ GR, TU
—EMB in USA: 2211 R Street NW, Washington, DC 20008.
—CTR: 13 East 40th Street, New York, NY 10016.
—USA EMB: Therissos and Dositheos Streets, Nicosia/ U.S. firms: 23.
—UND: P.O. Box 3521, Nicosia.
—UNI: *See* Greece.

I-41. CZECH REPUBLIC/Prague/10.5 mil./ CZ, SL-GE, HU
—EMB in USA: 3900 Linnean Avenue NW, Washington, DC 20008.
—USA EMB: Trziste 15-12548, Prague/ U.S. firms: 5.
—UNI: Panska 5, 11100, Prague 1.
(See also Slovakia, I-185.)

I-42. DENMARK/Copenhagen/5.1 mil./ DA-EN, NW, SW
—EMB in USA: 3200 Whitehaven Street NW, Washington, DC 20008.
—CTR: 825 Third Avenue, New York, NY 10022/ Danish firms in the U.S.: 31.
—USA EMB: Dag Hammarsjölds Alie 24, 2100 Copenhagen/ U.S. firms: 191.
—UNI: 37 H. C. Andersens Boulevard, DK-1553, Copenhagen V.

I-43. DJIBOUTI/Djibouti/510,000/ FR-AB, SO
—EMB in USA: 1156 15th Street NW, Washington, DC 20005.

—USA EMB: Plateau du Serpent, Boulevard Maréchal Joffre, P.O. Box 185, Djibouti.
—UND: Boulevard de la République, P.O. Box 2001, Djibouti.

I-44.   DOMINICA/Roseau/108,812/ EN-F/C
—CTR in USA: 89-19 191st Street, Hollis Park, NY 11423.
—UNI: *See* Trinidad and Tobago.

I-45.   DOMINICAN REPUBLIC/Santo Domingo/7.2 mil./ SP
—EMB in USA: 1715 22nd Street, Washington, DC 20008.
—CTR in USA: 17 West 60th Street, New York, NY 10023/ 1 World Trade Center, Room 86065, New York, NY 10048.
—USA EMB: Calle César Nicolás Pensón y Calle Leopoldo Navarro, Santo Domingo.
—USA CTR: Torre B.H.D., Avenida W. Churchill, P.O. Box 95-2, Santo Domingo/ U.S. firms: 50.
—UND: Avenida Anacoana No. 9, Apartado 1424, Santo Domingo.
—UNI: *See* Mexico.

I-46.   ECUADOR/Quito/9.6 mil./ SP-QC
—EMB in USA: 2535 15th Street NW, Washington, DC 20009.
—CTR in USA: 18 East 41st Street, New York, NY 10017/ 115 Broadway, Room 1408, New York, NY 10006.
—USA EMB: 120 Avenida Patria, P.O. Box 538, Quito.
—USA CTR: Edificio Multicentro, La Niña y 6 de Diciembre, P.O. Box 2432, Quito/ U.S. firms: 101.
—UND: 10 de Agosto 5470, P.O. Box 4731, Quito.
—UNI: *See* Colombia.

I-47.   EGYPT/Cairo/56 mil./ AB-EN, FR
—EMB in USA: 2310 Decatur Place NW, Washington, DC 20008.
—CTR in USA: 1110 Second Avenue, New York, NY 10022/ 1 World Trade Center, Suite 8741, New York, NY 10048.
—USA EMB: Lazougi Street, Garden City, Cairo.
—USA CTR: Cairo Marriott Hotel, Suite 1541, P.O. Box 233 Zamalek, Cairo/ U.S. firms: 112.

—UND: 29 Sharia Taha Hussein, P.O. Box 982, Cairo.
—UNI: 1 Osiris Street, Tagher Building, P.O.B. 262, Cairo.

I-48. EL SALVADOR/San Salvador/5.4 mil./ SP-NA
—EMB in USA: 2308 California Street NW, Washington, DC 20008.
—CTR in USA: 46 Park Avenue, New York, NY 10016.
—USA EMB: 25 Avenida Norte No. 1230, San Salvador.
—USA CTR: 65 Avenida Sur No. 159, P.O. Box (05) 9, San Salvador/ U.S. firms: 49.
—UND: Paseo General Escalón, P.O. Box 399, San Salvador.
—UNI: Paseo General Escalón, y 87 Avenida Norte, P.O.B. 2157, San Salvador.

ENGLAND *See* UNITED KINGDOM, I-154.

I-49. EQUATORIAL GUINEA/Malabo/417,000/ SP-BI, FN
—EMB in USA: 801 Second Avenue, Suite 1403, New York, NY 10017.
—USA EMB: P.O. Box 597, Malabo.
—UND: Calle de Kenia, P.O. Box 399, Malabo.
—UNI: *Same as above.*

I-50. ETHIOPIA/Addis Ababa/45 mil./ AM-AB, EN, IT
—EMB in USA: 2134 Kalorama Road NW, Washington, DC 20008.
—USA EMB: Entoto Street, P.O. Box 1014, Addis Ababa/ U.S. firms: 8.
—UND: Menelik II Avenue, P.O. Box 5580, Addis Ababa.
—UNI: Economic Commission for Africa, P.O. Box 3001, Addis Ababa.

I-51. FIJI/Suva/747,000/ EN-FJ, HI
—EMB in USA: 2233 Wisconsin Avenue NW, Washington, DC 20007.
—CTR in USA: 1 United Nations Plaza, New York, NY 10017.
—USA EMB: 31 Loftus Street, P.O. Box 218, Suva.

—UND: National Bank of Fiji Building, Private Mail Bag, Suva.
—UNI: *See* Australia.

I-52.   FINLAND/Helsinki/4.9 mil./ FI, SW-LP
—EMB in USA: 3216 New Mexico Avenue NW, Washington, DC 20016.
—CTR in USA: 540 Madison Avenue, New York, NY 10022/ 35 East Wacker Drive, No. 1900, Chicago, IL 60601/ Finnish firms: 172.
—USA EMB: Itainen Puistotie 14/A, Helsinki/ U.S. firms: 81.
—UNI: *See* Denmark.

I-53.   FRANCE/Paris/56.6 mil./ FR-BR, BS, CT, GE, IT, SP
—EMB in USA: 4101 Reservoir Road NW, Washington, DC 20007.
—CTR in USA: 934 Fifth Avenue, New York, NY 10021/ 509 Madison Avenue, Suite 1900, New York, NY 10022/ French firms in the U.S.: 121.
—USA EMB: 2, Avenue Gabriel, 75382 Paris, Cedex 8.
—USA CTR: 21, Avenue Georges V, 75008 Paris/ U.S. firms: 687.
—UNI: 1 Rue Miollis, 75732 Paris, Cedex 15.

I-54.   GABON/Libreville/1.2 mil./ FR-BN, FN
—EMB in USA: 2034 20th Street NW, Washington, DC 20009.
—USA EMB: Boulevard de la Mer, P.O. Box 4000, Libreville.
—UND: Immeuble "Les Tropiques," P.O. Box 553, Libreville.
—UNI: *See* Cameroon.

I-55.   GAMBIA/Banjul/875,000/ EN-ML, WO
—EMB in USA: 1030 15th Street NW, Washington, DC 20008.
—CTR in USA: Devell Road, Stanfordville, NY 12581.
—USA EMB: Fajara (East) Kairaba Avenue, P.O. Box 19, Banjul.
—UND: Bungalow Road, P.O. Box 553, Banjul.
—UNI: *See* Senegal.

I-56. GERMANY, EAST (Presently part of I-57 after unification with West Germany in 1900).

I-57. GERMANY (FEDERAL REPUBLIC)/Bonn/80/ mil./ GE-EN, FR
—EMB in USA: 4645 Reservoir Road NW, Washington, DC 20007.
—CTR in USA: 460 Park Avenue, New York, NY 10022/ 666 Fifth Avenue, New York, NY 10103/ German firms in the U.S.: 366.
—USA EMB: Deichmanns Avenue, 5300 Bonn.
—USA CTR: Rossmarkt 12, Postfach 100-162, D-6000, Frankfurt am Main 1/ U.S. firms: 821.
—UNI: *See* Austria.

I-58. GHANA/Accra/14.9 mil./ EN-FA, GA, HS, and other tribal languages
—EMB in USA: 3512 International Drive NW, Washington, DC 20008.
—CTR in USA: 19 East 47th Street, New York, NY 10017.
—USA EMB: Ring Road, East, P.O. Box 194, Accra/ U.S. firms: 23.
—UND: Ring Road, Dual Carriage, P.O. Box 1423, Accra.
—UNI: Gamel Abdul Nasser and Liberia Roads, P.O.B. 2339, Accra.

I-59. GREECE/Athens/10.2 mil./ GR-EN, TU
—EMB in USA: 2221 Massachusetts Avenue NW, Washington, DC 20008.
—CTR in USA: 69 East 79th Street, New York, NY 10021/ 29 Broadway, Room 1508, New York, NY 10006/ Greek firms in the U.S.: 6.
—USA EMB: 91 Vasilissis Sophias Boulevard, 10160 Athens.
—USA CTR: 16 Kanari Street, 3rd Floor, Athens/ U.S. firms: 164.
—UND: 36 Amalia Avenue, 58 Athens, GR-105.
—UNI: *Same as above.*

I-60. GRENADA/St. George's/91,000/ EN- F/C.
—EMB in USA: 1701 New Hampshire Avenue NW, Washington, DC 20009.

—CTR in USA: 820 Second Avenue, Suite 1100, New York, NY 10017.
—USA EMB: P.O. Box 54, St. George's.
—UNI: *See* Trinidad and Tobago.

I-61.   GUAM/Agana/106,000/ GM-EN
—USA CTR: P.O. Box 283, Agana/ U.S. firms: 13.

I-62.   GUATEMALA/Guatemala City/9 mil./ SP-MY various dialects
—EMB in USA: 2220 R Street NW, Washington, DC 20008.
—CTR in USA: 57 Park Avenue, New York, NY 10016.
—USA EMB: 7-01 Avenida de la Reforma, Zona 10, Guatemala City.
—USA CTR: Apartado Postal 832, 7a Avenida, 14-44, Zona 9, Oficina 19, 2do. Nivel, Apartado Postal 832, Guatemala City/ U.S. firms: 89.
—UND: 64, Avenida 20-20, Zona 110, Apartado Postal 23-A, Guatemala City.
—UNI: *See* El Salvador.

I-63.   GUINEA/Conakry/6.7 mil./ FR-FU, MD and other languages
—EMB in USA: 2112 Leroy Place NW, Washington, DC 20008.
—USA EMB: 2nd Boulevard and 9th Avenue, P.O. Box 603, Conakry.
—UND: Immeuble ex Urbaine e Seine, P.O. Box 222, Conakry.
—UNI: *See* Senegal.

I-64.   GUINEA-BISSAU/Bissau/966,000/ P/C, PT
—EMB in USA: 211 East 43rd Street, Suite 604, New York, NY 10017.
—USA EMB: Avenida Domingos Ramos, 1067, Bissau.
—UND: Avenida Domingos Ramos, 34-E, P.O. Box 179, Bissau.
—UNI: *See* Senegal.

I-65.   GUYANA/Georgetown/990,000/ EN-HI, NAL, UR
—EMB in USA: 2490 Tracy Place NW, Washington, DC 20008.
—CTR in USA: 622 Third Avenue, New York, NY 10017.

—USA EMB: 31 Main Street, Georgetown/ U.S. firms: 11.
—UND: 42 Brickdam, P.O. Box 10960, Georgetown.
—UNI: *See* Trinidad and Tobago.

I-66.   HAITI/Port-au-Prince/5.7 mil./ H/C-FR
—EMB in USA: 2311 Massachusetts Avenue, Washington, DC 20008.
—CTR in USA: 60 East 42nd Street, New York, NY 10017.
—USA EMB: Harry Truman Boulevard, P.O. Box 1761, Port-au-Prince.
—USA CTR: Complexe 384, Delmas (59), P.O. Box 13486, Port-au-Prince/ U.S. firms: 31.
—UND: 18, Avenue Ducoste, P.O. Box 557, Port-au-Prince.
—UNI: *Same as above.*

HOLY SEE *See* VATICAN, I-157.

I-67.   HONDURAS/Tegucigalpa/4.4 mil./ SP-EN
—EMB in USA: 3007 Tilden Street NW, Washington, DC 20008.
—CTR in USA: 18 East 41st Street, New York, NY 10017.
—USA EMB: Avenida La Paz, Tegucigalpa.
—USA CTR: Hotel Honduras Maya, Apartado Postal 1838, Tegucigalpa/ U.S. firms: 36.
—UND: Edificio Comercial Maya, Apartado Postal 976, Tegucigalpa.
—UNI: *See* El Salvador.

I-68.   HONG KONG/Hong Kong/5.95 mil./ CH-EN
—Hong Kong firms in the U.S.: 55.
—USA EMB: 26 Garden Road, P.O. Box 30, Hong Kong.
—USA CTR: 1030 Swire House, Central, Hong Kong/ U.S. firms: 392.
—UNI: *See* Thailand.

I-69.   HUNGARY/Budapest/10.7 mil./ HU-CZ, RO, S/C, SL
—EMB in USA: 3910 Shoemaker Street NW, Washington, DC 20008.
—CTR in USA: 8 East 75th Street, New York, NY 10021.
—USA EMB: V. Szabadsag Ter 12, Budapest/ U.S. firms: 7.
—UNI: *See* Switzerland.

I-70.   ICELAND/Reykjavík/255,708/ IC
—EMB in USA: 2022 Connecticut Avenue NW, Washington, DC 20008.
—CTR in USA: 3701 Lexington Avenue, New York, NY 10017.
—USA EMB: Laufasvegur 21, Reykjavík.
—UNI: *See* Denmark.

I-71.   INDIA/New Delhi/845 mil./ HI, EN-BG, MM, MR, PJ, TE, TM, and other national languages
—EMB in USA: 2107 Massachusetts Avenue NW, Washington, DC 20008.
—CTR in USA: 3 East 64th Street, New York, NY 10021/ 445 Park Avenue, 18th Floor, New York, NY 10022/ Indian firms in the U.S.: 13.
—USA EMB: Shanti Path, Chanakyapuri 110021, New Delhi/ U.S. firms: 227.
—UND: 55 Lodi Estate, P.O. Box 3059, New Delhi 110-003.
—UNI: *Same as above.*

I-72.   INDONESIA/Jakarta/80 mil./ IN, EN
—EMB in USA: 2020 Massachusetts Avenue NW, Washington, DC 20036.
—CTR in USA: 5 East 68th Street, New York, NY 10021/ 12 East 41st Street, Suite 701, New York, NY 10017/ Indonesian firms in the U.S.: 4.
—USA EMB: Medan Merdeka Selatan 5, Jakarta.
—USA CTR: Landmark Centre, 22nd Floor, Suite 2204, 55, Jakarta/ U.S. firms: 129.
—UND: 14 Jalan M.H. Thamrin, P.O. Box 2338, Jakarta.
—UNI: Gedung Dewan Pers, 5th Floor, 32-34 Jalan Kebon Sirih, Jakarta.

I-73.   IRAN/Teheran/54 mil./ PE-AB, KD, TU
—No diplomatic relations with the U.S.: Iranian interests in US: 2209 Wisconsin Avenue NW, Washington, DC 20007, and U.S. interests in Iran are represented by Switzerland/ U.S. firms: 86.
—UND: P.O. Box 15875-4557, Teheran.
—UNI: P.O. Box 1555, Teheran.

I-74.   IRAQ/Baghdad/17.8 mil./ AB-EN, KD
—Diplomatic relations with the U.S. broken during the Gulf War.

—EMB in USA: 1801 P Street NW, Washington, DC 20036. (Presently closed.)
—USA EMB: P.O. Box 2447 Alwiyah, Baghdad/U.S. firms: 15. (Presently closed.)
—UND: Abi Nuwas Street (102), P.O. Box 2048, Alwiyah, Baghdad.
—UNI: Economic Commission for Western Asia, P.O. Box 27, Baghdad.

I-75. IRELAND/Dublin/3.5 mil./ IR, EN
—EMB in USA: 2234 Massachusetts Avenue NW, Washington, DC 20008.
—CTR in USA: 515 Madison Avenue, 18th Floor, New York, NY 10022/ 460 Park Avenue, New York, NY 10022/ Irish firms in the U.S.: 6.
—USA EMB: 42 Elgin Road, Ballsbridge, Dublin.
—USA CTR: 20 College Green, Dublin 20/ U.S. firms: 213.
—UNI: *See* United Kingdom.

I-76. ISRAEL/Jerusalem/4.9 mil./ HE, AB-EN
—EMB in USA: 3514 International Drive NW, Washington, DC 20008.
—CTR in USA: 800 Second Avenue, New York, NY 10017/ 500 Fifth Avenue, Room 5416, New York, NY 10036/ Israeli firms in the U.S.: 24.
—USA EMB: 71 Hayakron Street, Tel Aviv.
—USA CTR: Shaul Hamelach Boulevard, P.O. Box 33174, Tel Aviv/ U.S. firms: 135.
—UNI: *See* Greece.

I-77. ITALY/Rome/57.7 mil./ IT-AL, FR, GE, GR, SV
—EMB in USA: 1601 Fuller Street NW, Washington, DC 20009.
—CTR in USA: 690 Park Avenue, New York, NY 10021/ Empire State Building, 350 Fifth Avenue, Suite 3015, New York, NY 10001/ Italian firms in the U.S.: 32.
—USA EMB: Via Veneto 119/A, 00187-Rome.
—USA CTR: Via Cantu I, 20213 Milan/ U.S. firms: 440.
—UNI: Palazzeto Venezia, Piazza San Marco 50, Rome.

I-78. JAMAICA/Kingston/2.4 mil./ EN-C/R (local dialect)
—EMB in USA: 1850 K Street NW, Suite 355, Washington, DC 20006.

—CTR in USA: 866 Second Avenue, New York, NY 10017.
—USA EMB: Jamaica Mutual Life Center, 2 Oxford Road, 3rd Floor, Kingston.
—USA CTR: Wyndham Hotel, 77 Knutsford Boulevard, Kingston/ U.S. firms: 55.
—UND: 1 and 3 Lady Musgrave Road, P.O. Box 280, Kingston.
—UNI: *See* Trinidad and Tobago.

I-79. JAPAN/Tokyo/124 mil./ JP-CH, EN
—EMB in USA: 2520 Massachusetts Avenue NW, Washington, DC 20008.
—CTR in USA: 299 Park Avenue, New York, NY 10017/ 145 West 57th Street, New York, NY 10019/ 244 San Pedro Street, Los Angeles, CA 90012/ Japanese firms in the U.S.: 375.
—USA EMB: 10-11, Akasaka, 1-chome, Minato-ku (107), Tokyo.
—USA CTR: Fukide Building, No. 2, 4-1-21 Toronamon, Minato-ku, Tokyo 105/ U.S. firms: 690.
—UND: Shin Aoyama Building, Nishikan (Room 2255), 1-1 Minami Aoyama, 1-chome, Minato-ku, Tokyo 107.
—UNI: *Same as above.*

I-80. JORDAN/Amman/3.3 mil./ AB-EN
—EMB in USA: 3504 International Drive NW, Washington, DC 20008.
—USA EMB: Jebel Amman, P.O. Box 354, Amman/U.S. firms: 26.
—UND: P.O. Box 35286, Amman.
—UNI: *See* Lebanon.

I-81. KAMPUCHEA (CAMBODIA)/Pnom Penh/8.3 mil/ CA-FR
—No diplomatic relations with the U.S./ U.S. firms: 3.
—UNI: *See* Thailand.

I-82. KENYA/Nairobi/24 mil./ EN, SH-KK, several other languages
—EMB in USA: 2249 R Street NW, Washington, DC 20008.
—CTR in USA: 424 Madison Avenue, New York, NY 10017.

—USA EMB: Moi/Haile Selassie Avenue, P.O. Box 30137, Nairobi/ U.S. firms: 79.
—UND: Kenya Railways Headquarters, P.O. Box 30218, Nairobi.
—UNI: UN Office, Gigiri, P.O.B. 34135, Nairobi.

I-83.   KOREA, NORTH (DEMOCRATIC REPUBLIC)/Pyongyang/22.5 mil./ KO
—No diplomatic relations with the U.S.
—UND: Building 21, Munsondong, P.O. Box 27, Pyongyang.

I-84.   KOREA, SOUTH/Seoul/42.8 mil./ KO-EN, JP
—EMB in USA: 2370 Massachusetts Avenue NW, Washington, DC 20008.
—CTR in USA: 460 Park Avenue, New York, NY 10022/ 725 Park Avenue, New York, NY 10021/ 981 South Western Avenue, Room 201, Los Angeles, CA 90006/ Korean firms in the U.S.: 27.
—USA EMB: 82 Sejong-Ro, Chongro-ku, Seoul.
—USA CTR: Chosun Hotel, Room 307, Seoul/ U.S. firms: 154.
—UND: Central P.O. Box 143, Seoul 100.

I-85.   KUWAIT/Kuwait/2 mil./ AB-EN
—EMB in USA: 2940 Tilden Street NW, Washington, DC 20008.
—USA EMB: P.O. Box 77 SAFAT, 13001 Safat/ U.S. firms: 67.
—UND: Dasman Square, P.O. Box 2993, Safat 13030.
—UNI: *See* Lebanon.

I-86.   LAOS/Vientiane/4 mil./ LO-FR
—EMB in USA: 2222 S Street NW, Washington, DC 20008.
—USA EMB: Rue Bartholonie, P.O. Box V, Vientiane.
—UND: Rue Phone Keng, P.O. Box 345, Vientiane.
—UNI: *See* Thailand.

I-87.   LEBANON/Beirut/2.6 mil./ AB-EN, FR
—EMB in USA: 2560 28th Street NW, Washington, DC 20008.
—CTR in USA: 9 East 76th Street, New York, NY 10021/

1 World Trade Center, Suite 1345, New York, NY 10048.
—USA EMB: Avenue de Paris, P.O. Box 70-840 Antelias, Beirut/ U.S. firms: 81.
—UND: Kamal Jabra Building, P.O. Box 11-3216, Beirut.
—UNI: Apartment 1, Fakhouri Building, Ardati Street, P.O.B. 4656, Beirut.

I-88. LESOTHO/Maseru/1.72 mil./ S/T-EN
—EMB in USA: 2511 Massachusetts Avenue NW, Washington, DC 20008.
—USA EMB: P.O. Box 333, Maseru 100.
—UND: BWP Center, Kingsway and Hilton Roads, P.O.B. 301, Maseru 100.
—UNI: *Same as above.*

I-89. LIBERIA/Monrovia/2.44 mil./ EN-AFL various
—EMB in USA: 5201 16th Street NW, Washington, DC 20011.
—CTR in USA: 820 Second Avenue, New York, NY 10017.
—USA EMB: 111 United Nations Drive, P.O. Box 98, Monrovia/ U.S. firms: 26.
—UND: Liberian Bank for Development and Investment Building, Tubman Boulevard, P.O. Box 274, Monrovia.
—UNI: *Same as above.*

I-90. LIBYA/Tripoli/4 mil./ AB-EN, IT
—No diplomatic relations with the U.S.
—USA CTR: Shari Mohammad Thabit, P.O. Box 289, Tripoli.
—UND: 67-71 Turkiya Street, P.O. Box 358, Tripoli.
—UNI: Muzafar al Aftas Street, Hay El-Andolous, P.O.B. 286, Tripoli.

I-91. LUXEMBOURG/Luxembourg/374,500/ FR-GE, local dialect
—EMB in USA: 2220 Massachusetts Avenue NW, Washington, DC 20008.
—CTR in USA: 801 Second Avenue, New York, NY 10017/ Luxembourgian firms in the U.S.: 5.
—USA EMB: 22, Boulevard Emmanuel-Servais, 2535, Luxembourg/ U.S. firms: 35.
—UNI: *See* Belgium.

I-92. MADAGASCAR/Antananarivo/11.4 mil./ MG, FR-HV and others
  —EMB in USA: 2374 Massachusetts Avenue NW, Washington, DC 20008.
  —CTR in USA: 801 Second Avenue, New York, NY 10017.
  —USA EMB: 14 and 16 Rue Rainitivo, Antsahavola, P.O. Box 620, Antananarivo.
  —UND: 26 Laulana Razafimahandry, P.O. Box 1348, Antananarivo.
  —UNI: 22 Rue Rainitivo, Antsahavola, P.O.B. 1348, Antananarivo.

I-93. MALAWI/Lilongwe/8 mil./ CC, EN-BN various dialects
  —EMB in USA: 2408 Massachusetts Avenue NW, Washington, DC 20008.
  —USA EMB: P.O. Box 30016, Lilongwe/ U.S. firms: 11.
  —UND: Plot No. 7, Area 40, P.O. Box 30135, Lilongwe.
  —UNI: *See* Zambia.

I-94. MALAYSIA/Kuala Lumpur/17.8 mil./ ML-CH, EN, TM and others
  —EMB in USA: 2401 Massachusetts Avenue NW, Washington, DC 20008.
  —CTR in USA: 140 East 45th Street, New York, NY 10017.
  —USA EMB: 376 Jalan Tun Razak, P.O. Box 10035, 50700 Kuala Lumpur.
  —USA CTR: 1501 15th Floor, Amoda, Jalan Imbi, Kuala Lumpur/ U.S. firms: 147.
  —UND: K 9 and 10, Jalan Duta, P.O. Box 2544, Kuala Lumpur.
  —UNI: *See* Thailand.

I-95. MALDIVES ISLANDS/Malé/213,215/ SI(Divehi dialect)-AB, EN
  —No diplomatic relations with the U.S.
  —UND: P.O. Box 2058, Malé.
  —UNI: *See* Sri Lanka.

I-96. MALI/Bamako/ FR-BM, DY, M/N
  —EMB in USA: 2130 R Street NW, Washington, DC 20008.

—USA EMB: Rue Testard and Rue Mohamed V, P.O. Box 34, Bamako.
—UND: P.O. Box 120, Bamako.
—UNI: *See* Burkina Faso.

I-97. MALTA/La Valletta/360,000/ EN, MT-IT
—EMB in USA: 2017 Connecticut Avenue NW, Washington, DC 20008.
—CTR: 249 East 35th Street, New York, NY 10016.
—USA EMB: Development House, St. Anne Street, Floriana, P.O. Box 535, La Valletta.
—UNI: *See* Italy.

I-98. MAURITANIA/Nouakchott/1.9 mil./ AB, FR-TK, WO
—EMB in USA: 2129 Leroy Place NW, Washington, DC 20008.
—USA EMB: P.O. Box 222, Nouakchott.
—UND: Avenue Gamal Abdel Nasser, Plot K, Lot 208, P.O. Box 620, Nouakchott.
—UNI: *See* Senegal.

I-99. MAURITIUS/Port Louis/1.1 mil./ EN-CH, C/R, FR, HI, UR
—EMB in USA: 4301 Connecticut Avenue NW, Suite 134, Washington, DC 20008.
—USA EMB: Rogers Building, 4th Floor, John Kennedy Street, Port Louis.
—UND: P.O. Box 253, Port Louis.
—UNI: *Same as above.*

I-100. MEXICO/Mexico City/81 mil./ SP-NAL various dialects
—EMB in USA: 1911 Pennsylvania Avenue NW, Washington, DC 20006.
—CTR in USA: 8 East 41st Street, New York, NY 10017/ 233 Broadway, New York, NY 10017/ Mexican firms in the U.S.: 6.
—USA EMB: Paseo de la Reforma 305, Mexico 5, D.F. 06500.
—USA CTR: Lucerna 78, 20° Piso, P.O. Box 82-B15, Mexico, D.F./ U.S. firms: 637.
—UND: Apartado Postal 6719, 06600 Mexico, D.F.
—UNI: Presidente Masaryk 29, 11570 Mexico, D.F.

I-101.   MONACO/Monaco/30,000/ FR-EN, IT
—CTR in USA: 845 Third Avenue, 2nd Floor, New York, NY 10022.
—U.S. firms in Monaco: 5.

I-102.   MONGOLIA/Ulan Bator/2.1 mil./ MO-TR, KZ and various dialects
—EMB in USA: 1021 Iron Gate Road, Potomac, MD 20854.
—USA EMB: *See* China.
—UND: Microregion 12, House 19, Apt. 49, P.O. Box 49/207 Ulan Bator.
—UNI: *Same as above.*

I-103.   MOROCCO/Rabat/25 mil./ AB-BB, FR
—EMB in USA: 1601 21st Street NW, Washington, DC 20009.
—CTR in USA: 437 Fifth Avenue, New York, NY 10016.
—USA EMB: 2 Avenue de Marrakech, Rabat.
—USA CTR: Immeuble "Xerox," 30, Avenue des Forces Armées Royales, Casablanca/ U.S. firms: 43.
—UND: Angle del' Avenue Moulay Hassan et Rue Assafi, "Casier ONU," Rabat-Chellah.
—UNI: P.O. Box 601, Rabat.

I-104.   MOZAMBIQUE/Maputo/16.1 mil./ PT-BN various dialects
—EMB in USA: 1990 M Street NW, Washington, DC 20036.
—USA EMB: Avenida Kaunda 193, P.O. Box 783, Maputo/ U.S. firms: 6.
—UND: Avenue Kenneth Kaunda 931, P.O. Box 4595, Maputo.
—UNI: *Same as above.*

I-104/a. MYANMAR/Yangon/40.7 mil./ BU-CH, EN, HI, TM
—EMB in USA: 2300 S Street NW, Washington, DC 20008.
—CTR in USA: 10 East 77th Street, New York, NY 10021.
—USA EMB: 581 Merchant Street, GPO Box 521, Yangon.
—UND: No. 24, Mawa-Itari Road, P.O. Box 650, Yangon.
—UNI: 28/A Manawhari Road, P.O.B. 230, Yangon.

I-105.   NEPAL/Kathmandu/18.9 mil./ NE-BU, EN, TI
—EMB in USA: 2131 Leroy Place NW, Washington, DC
20008.
—CTR: 820 Second Avenue, Suite 1200, New York, NY
10017.
—USA EMB: Pani Pokhari, Kathmandu.
—UND: P.O. Box 107, Lainchaur, Lazimpat, Kath-
mandu.
—UNI: Pulchowk, Patan P.O.B. 107, Kathmandu.

I-106.   THE NETHERLANDS/The Hague/15 mil./ DU-EN, FS, GE
—EMB in USA: 4200 Linean Avenue NW, Washington,
DC 20008.
—CTR in USA: 1 Rockefeller Plaza, 11th Floor, New
York, NY 10020/ Dutch firms in the U.S.: 82.
—USA EMB: Lange Voorhout 102, The Hague.
—USA CTR: Carnegieplein 5, 2517 KJ, The Hague/ U.S.
firms: 53.
—UNI: *See* Belgium.

I-107.   NETHERLANDS ANTILLES/Willemstad/267,000/ DU, P/P-
EN
—USA EMB: St. Anna Boulevard 19, P.O.B. 158,
Willemstad.
—USA CTR: P.O. Box 158, Willemstad, Curaçao.
—UNI: *See* Trinidad and Tobago.

I-108.   NEW ZEALAND/Wellington/3.4 mil./ EN-M/O
—EMB in USA: 37 Observatory Circle NW, Wash-
ington, DC 20008.
—CTR in USA: 630 Fifth Avenue, New York, NY 10111/
10960 Wilshire Boulevard, Suite 1530, Los Angeles,
CA 90024/ New Zealand firms in the U.S.: 9.
—USA EMB: 29 Fitzherbert Terrace, Thorndon, P.O.B.
1190, Wellington.
—USA CTR: Corner Featherston and Johnston Streets,
P.O. Box 3408, Wellington/ U.S. firms: 209.
—UNI: *See* Australia.

I-109.   NICARAGUA/Managua/3.8 mil./ SP-EN
—EMB in USA: 1627 New Hampshire Avenue NW,
Washington, DC 20009.
—USA EMB: Km. 4½ Carretera Sur., Managua.
—USA CTR: Apartado 202, Managua/ U.S. firms: 27.

—UND: Plaza España, 2 cuadras abajo, Apartado Postal 3260, Managua.
—UNI: *Same as above.*

I-110. NIGER/Niamey/8 mil./ FR-DJ, FU, HS, T/K
—EMB in USA: 2204 R Street NW, Washington, DC 20008.
—USA EMB: P.O. Box 11201, Niamey.
—UND: Maison de l'Afrique, P.O. Box 11207, Niamey.
—UNI: *See* Burkina Faso.

I-111. NIGERIA/Lagos/88.5 mil./ EN-ED, HS, IG, YO, and many others
—EMB in USA: 2201 M Street NW, Washington, DC 20037.
—CTR in USA: 575 Lexington Avenue, New York, NY 10022.
—USA EMB: 2 Eleke Crescent, P.O. Box 554, Lagos/ U.S. firms: 106.
—UND: 11 Queen's Drive, Ikoyi, P.O. Box 2075, Lagos.
—UNI: 17 Kingsway Road, Ikoyi, P.O.B. 1068, Lagos.

I-112. NORWAY/Oslo/4.2 mil./ NW-FI, LP
—EMB in USA: 2720 34th Street NW, Washington, DC 20008.
—CTR in USA: 825 Third Avenue, New York, NY 10022/ World Trade Center, 350 South Figueroa Street No. 360, Los Angeles, CA 90017/ Norwegian firms in the U.S.: 23.
—USA EMB: Drammensvein 18, Oslo 2/ U.S. firms: 136.
—UNI: *See* Denmark.

I-113. OMAN/Muscat/1.5 mil./ AB-BC, EN, HI, PE, UR
—EMB in USA: 2342 Massachusetts Avenue NW, Washington, DC 20008.
—USA EMB: P.O.B. 50202 Madinat Qaboos, Muscat/ U.S. firms: 20.
—UND: House No. 20, Road 10, P.O. Box 5287, Ruwi, Muscat.
—UNI: *Same as above.*

I-114.   PAKISTAN/Islamabad/114 mil./ EN, UR-BC, B/R, PJ, PS, SD
—EMB in USA: 2315 Massachusetts Avenue NW, Washington, DC 20008.
—CTR in USA: 12 East 65th Street, New York, NY 10021/ 17 Battery Place, New York, NY 10004.
—USA EMB: Diplomatic Enclave, Ramna, P.O. Box 1048, Islamabad.
—USA CTR: Abbasi Shaheed Road of Smaria Faisal, GPO Box 1322, Karachi/ U.S. firms: 61.
—UND: Block No. 2, Diplomatic Enclave No. 1, P.O. Box 1051, Islamabad.
—UNI: House No. 26, 88th Street, Ramna 16/3, P.O.B. 1107, Islamabad.

I-115.   PANAMA/Panama City/2.3 mil./ SP-EN
—EMB in USA: 2862 McGill Terrace NW, Washington, DC 20008.
—CTR in USA: 1270 Avenue of the Americas, New York, NY 10020/ Panamanian firms in the U.S.: 4.
—USA EMB: Apartado 6959, Panama 5.
—USA CTR: P.O. Box 168, Balboa-Ancon, Panama/ U.S. firms: 115.
—UND: Calle 47-E No. 1, Esquina Avenida 5 Sur A, Apartado 6314, Panama 5.
—UNI: Calle 54 y Avenida 3 Sur, Edificio 17, Apartado 6-9083, Panama.

I-116.   PAPUA NEW GUINEA/Port Moresby/3.7 mil./ EN-PI (Melanesian), HR
—EMB in USA: 1330 Connecticut Avenue NW, Suite 350, Washington, DC 20036.
—USA EMB: P.O. Box 1492, Port Moresby.
—UND: P.O. Box 1041, Port Moresby.
—UNI: *See* Philippines.

I-117.   PARAGUAY/Asunción/4.1 mil./ SP-GU
—EMB in USA: 2400 Massachusetts Avenue NW, Washington, DC 20008.
—CTR in USA: 1 World Trade Center, New York, NY 10048.
—USA EMB: 1776 Avenida Mariscal López, Casilla Postal 402, Asunción.

—USA CTR: Edificio Finansud, Avenida Mariscal López y Saravi, Asunción/ U.S. firms: 21.
—UND: Edificio City, Calle Estrella 345, Casilla de Correo 1107, Asunción.
—UNI: *Same as above.*

I-118.   PERU/Lima/19.2 mil./ SP, QC-AY
—EMB in USA: 1700 Massachusetts Avenue NW, Washington, DC 20036.
—CTR in USA: 805 Third Avenue, New York, NY 10022/ 50 West 34th Street, 6th Floor, New York, NY 10001.
—USA EMB: P.O. Box 1995, Lima-100.
—USA CTR: Avenida Ricardo Palma 836, Lima 18/ U.S. firms: 156.
—UND: Apartado 4480, Naciones Unidas, Lima.
—UNI: Mariscal Blas Cardeña 450, San Isidro, Apartado Postal 14-0199, Lima.

I-119.   PHILIPPINES/Manila/60.9 mil./ FL-EN, SP
—EMB in USA: 1617 Massachusetts Avenue NW, Washington, DC 20036.
—CTR in USA: 565 Fifth Avenue, New York, NY 10036/ 711 Third Avenue, 17th Floor, New York, NY 10017/ 447 Sutter Street, San Francisco, CA 94108.
—USA EMB: 1201 Roxas Boulevard, Manila.
—USA CTR: P.O. Box 1578, MCC, Manila/ U.S. firms: 205.
—UND: Mia Road, Pasay City, P.O. Box 7285 (ADC), Metro Manila 3120.
—UNI: *Same as above.*

I-120.   POLAND/Warsaw/38 mil./ PO-RU, UK
—EMB in USA: 2640 16th Street NW, Washington, DC 20009.
—CTR in USA: 233 Madison Avenue, New York, NY 10016.
—USA EMB: Aleje Ujazdowskle 29/31, Warsaw/ U.S. firms: 15.
—UNI: *See* Switzerland.

I-121.   PORTUGAL/Lisbon/10.3 mil./ PT-SP
—EMB in USA: 2125 Kalorama Road NW, Washington, DC 20008.

—CTR in USA: 630 Fifth Avenue, New York, NY 10011/ 5 West 45th Street, 4th Floor, New York, NY 10036.
—USA EMB: Avenida das Forças Armadas, 1600 Lisbon.
—USA CTR: Rua de D. Estefania 155, 5-Q, Esq., Lisbon 1200/ U.S. firms: 93.
—UNI: Rua Latino Coelho No. 1, Edificio Aviz Bloco 1 A-1-10, 1000 Lisbon.

I-122. QATAR/Doha/371,863/ AB-EN
—EMB in USA: 600 New Hampshire Avenue NW, Suite 1180, Washington, DC 20037.
—USA EMB: Fariq Bin Omran, P.O. Box 2399, Doha.
—UND: Al-Hitmi New Villas, Box 3233, Doha.
—UNI: *See* Bahrain.

I-123. ROMANIA/Bucharest/23 mil./ RO-FR, GE, HU, UK
—EMB in USA: 1607 23rd Street NW, Washington, DC 20008.
—CTR in USA: c/o Chamber of Commerce, 1615 H Street, Washington, DC 20062.
—USA EMB: Strada Tudor Arghezi 7-9, Bucharest/ U.S. firms: 7.
—UND: 79362 Strada Aurel Vlaicu No. 16, Bucharest.
—UNI: Strada Aurel Vlaicu 16, P.O.B. 1-701, Bucharest.

I-124. RWANDA/Kigali/6.7 mil./ FR, K/R, K/S
—EMB in USA: 1714 New Hampshire Avenue NW, Washington, DC 20009.
—USA EMB: Boulevard de la Révolution, P.O. Box 28, Kigali.
—UND: Avenue de l'Armée, P.O. Box 445, Kigali.
—UNI: *Same as above.*

I-125. SAINT KITTS AND NEVIS/Basseterre/45,000/ EN
—EMB in USA: 2100 M Street NW, Washington, DC 20037.
—UNI: *See* Trinidad and Tobago.

I-126. SAINT LUCIA/Castries/146,000/ EN-F/C
—EMB in USA: 2100 M Street NW, Washington, DC 20037.

—CTR in USA: 801 Second Avenue, 21st Floor, New York, NY 10017.
—UNI: *See* Trinidad and Tobago.

I-127.   SAN MARINO/San Marino/23,000/ IT
—CTR in USA: 350 Fifth Avenue, S-3107, Empire State Building, New York, NY 10001.

I-128.   SÃO TOMÉ and PRÍNCIPE/São Tomé/124,000/ PT-P/C
—EMB in USA: 801 Second Avenue, Suite 1504, New York, NY 10017.
—UND: Avenida das Nações Unidas, Caixa Postal 109, São Tomé.
—UNI: *Same as above.*

I-129.   SAUDI ARABIA/Riyadh/12 mil./ AB
—EMB in USA: 601 New Hampshire Avenue NW, Washington, DC 20037.
—CTR in USA: 866 United Nations Plaza, New York, NY 10017/ Saudi Arabian firms in the U.S.: 5.
—USA EMB: Collector Road M, Riyadh Diplomatic Quarter, Riyadh.
—USA CTR: c/o Aramc P.O.B. 1329, Dhahran 31311/ U.S. firms: 224.
82—UND: Al-Washam Street Marubba, P.O. Box 558, Riyadh.
—UNI: *See* Egypt.

I-130.   SENEGAL/Dakar/7.3 mil./ FR-DY, FU, ME, M/G, WO
—EMB in USA: 2112 Wyoming Avenue NW, Washington, DC 20008.
—USA EMB: P.O. Box 49, Avenue Jean XXIII, Dakar/ U.S. firms: 8.
—UND: 2, Avenue Roume, P.O. Box 154, Dakar.
—UNI: Allée Robert Delmas, P.O.B. 154, Dakar.

I-131.   SEYCHELLES/Victoria/67,378/ EN, F/C
—EMB in USA: 820 Second Avenue, Suite 900F, New York, NY 10017.
—USA EMB: Victoria House, Box 251, Victoria.
—UNI: *See* Kenya.

I-132. SIERRA LEONE/Freetown/4.1 mil./ EN-ME, PI, T/N
—EMB in USA: 1701 19th Street NW, Washington, DC 20009.
—USA EMB: Corner of Walpole and Siaka Stevens Streets, Freetown/ U.S. firms: 8.
—UND: Bank of Sierra Leone Building, Siaka Stevens Street, P.O. Box 1011, Freetown.
—UNI: *See* Ghana.

I-133. SINGAPORE/Singapore/2.7 mil./ CH, EN, ML, TM
—EMB in USA: 1824 R Street NW, Washington, DC 20009.
—USA EMB: 30 Hill Street, Singapore 0617.
—USA CTR: c/o GM Singapore, 501 Ang Mo Kio Industrial Park I, Singapore/ U.S. firms: 415.
—UNI: *See* Thailand.

I-134. SOMALIA/Mogadishu/7.6 mil./ SO-AB, EN, IT
—EMB in USA: 600 New Hampshire Avenue NW, Suite 710, Washington, DC 20037. (Ceased operations in May 1991.)
—USA EMB: Corso Primo Luglio, P.O. Box 574, Mogadishu/ U.S. firms: 5.
—UND: United Nations Compound, P.O. Box 24, Mogadishu.
—UNI: *See* Sudan.

I-135. SOUTH AFRICA/Cape Town/33.1 mil./ AF, EN-AFL, GJ, HI, TE
—EMB in USA: 3051 Massachusetts Avenue NW, Washington, DC 20008.
—CTR in USA: 326 East 48th Street, New York, NY 10022/ 1080 Park Avenue, New York, NY 10128.
—USA EMB: Thibault House, 225 Pretorius Street, Pretoria.
—USA CTR: P.O. Box 62280, Johannesburg/ U.S. firms: 286.

I-136. SOVIET UNION/Moscow/274 mil./ RU-AR, AZ, BY, ES, GG, KZ, K/Z, LI, LT, RO(mo), TJ, T/M, UK, UZ, and dozens of other languages
—The Soviet Union was replaced by the Commonwealth of Independent States, (a loose alliance) after the collapse of communism in 1991.

—All 15 former Soviet republics became independent states (*see* entries in the appendix to this section).
—UNI: Ulitsa Lunacharskogo 4/16, Moscow 121002.

I-137. SPAIN/Madrid/38.7 mil./ SP-BS, CT, GC, VL
—EMB in USA: 2700 15th Street NW, Washington, DC 20009.
—CTR in USA: 150 East 58th Street, New York, NY 10022/ 500 Fifth Avenue, New York, NY 10036/ Spanish firms in the U.S.: 20.
—USA EMB: Serrano 75, Madrid 28006.
—USA CTR: Hotel EuroBuilding, Padre Damian 23, Madrid 16/ U.S. firms: 376.
—UNI: Avenida General Perón 32-1, P.O.B. 3-400, 28080 Madrid.

I-138. SRI LANKA/Colombo/17 mil./ SI, TM-EN
—EMB in USA: 2148 Wyoming Avenue NW, Washington, DC 20008.
—CTR in USA: 630 Third Avenue, New York, NY 10017.
—USA EMB: 210 Galle Road, Colombo 3/ U.S. firms: 29.
—UND: 204 Bauddhaloka Mawatha, P.O. Box 1505, Colombo 7.
—UNI: *Same as above.*

I-139. SUDAN/Khartoum/25.6 mil./ AB-AFL, EN
—EMB in USA: 2210 Massachusetts Avenue NW, Washington, DC 20008.
—CTR in USA: 210 East 49th Street, New York, NY 10017.
—USA EMB: Sharia Ali Abdul Latif, P.O. Box 699, Khartoum/ U.S. firms: 20.
—UND: House No. 7, Block 5, Gama's Avenue, P.O. Box 913, Khartoum.
—UNI: P.O. Box 1992, Khartoum.

I-140. SURINAME/Paramaribo/416,839/ DU-EN, D/C, T/T
—EMB in USA: 4301 Connecticut Avenue NW, Washington, DC 20008.
—USA EMB: Dr. Sophie Redmondstraat 129, P.O. Box 1821, Paramaribo/ U.S. firms: 13.
—UND: *See* Trinidad and Tobago.
—UNI: *Same as above.*

I-141.   SWAZILAND/Mbabane/581,000/ EN, S/W
—EMB in USA: 3400 International Drive NW, Washington, DC 20008.
—USA EMB: P.O. Box 199, Mbabane.
—UND: Embassy House, Morris Street, Private Mail Bag, Mbabane.
—UNI: *See* Zambia.

I-142.   SWEDEN/Stockholm/8.6 mil./ SW-FI, LP
—EMB in USA: 600 New Hampshire Avenue NW, Suite 1200, Washington, DC 20037.
—CTR in USA: 825 Third Avenue, New York, NY 10022/ World Trade Center, San Francisco, CA 94111/ Swedish firms in the U.S.: 303.
—USA EMB: Strandvagen 101, S-115, 27 Stockholm/ U.S. firms: 302.
—UNI: *See* Denmark.

I-143.   SWITZERLAND/Bern/6.75 mil./ FR, GE, IT, RM
—EMB in USA: 2900 Cathedral Avenue NW, Washington, DC 20008.
—CTR in USA: 444 Madison Avenue, New York, NY 10022/ 645 Fifth Avenue, New York, NY 10001/ Swiss firms in the U.S.: 59.
—USA EMB: Jubilaeumstrasse 93, 3005 Bern.
—USA CTR: Talacker 41, 8001 Zurich/ U.S. firms: 387.
—UND: United Nations Office in Geneva, Palais des Nations, 1211 Geneva 10.
—UNI: *Same as above.*

I-144.   SYRIA/Damascus/11.3 mil./ AB-AR, EN, FR, KD
—EMB in USA: 2215 Wyoming Avenue NW, Washington, DC 20008.
—USA EMB: Abu Rumaneh, Al Mansur Street North 2, P.O. Box 29, Damascus/ U.S. firms: 15.
—UND: Abu Rumaneh, 28, Al Jala's Street, P.O. Box 2317, Damascus.
—UNI: *See* Lebanon.

I-145.   TAIWAN (REPUBLIC OF CHINA)/Taipei/18.7 mil./CH(mn), CH(ta), EN, JP
—USA CTR: Room 1012, Chia Hsin Building Annex, Taipei/ U.S. firms: 170; Taiwanese firms in the U.S.: 7.

I-146.   TANZANIA/Dar es Salaam/ 25 mil./ EN, SH-BN various dialects
—EMB in USA: 2139 R Street NW, Washington, DC 20008.
—USA EMB: 36 Laibon Road, P.O. Box 9123, Dar es Salaam/ U.S. firms: 11.
—UND: P.O. Box 9182, Dar es Salaam.
—UNI: Matasalamat Building, 1st Floor, P.O.B. 9224, Dar es Salaam.

I-147.   THAILAND/Bangkok/56 mil./ TH-CA, CH, LO, ML
—EMB in USA: 2300 Kalorama Road NW, Washington, DC 20008.
—CTR in USA: 53 Park Place, Room 505, New York, NY 10007.
—USA EMB: 95 Wireless Road, Bangkok.
—USA CTR: P.O. Box 11-1095, 145 Wireless Road, Kian Gwan Building, Bangkok/ U.S. firms: 146.
—UND: Radjamnern Avenue, G.P.O. 618, Bangkok.
—UNI: United Nations Building, United Nations Economic and Social Commission, Radjamnern Avenue, Bangkok 10200.

I-148.   TOGO/Lomé/3.4 mil./ FR-EW, HS, TW, and dozens of other languages
—EMB in USA: 2208 Massachusetts Avenue NW, Washington, DC 20008.
—USA EMB: Rue Pelletier Caventou and Rue Vouban, P.O. Box 852, Lomé.
—UND: 40, Avenue des Nations Unies, P.O. Box 911, Lomé.
—UNI: 107 Boulevard du 13 Janvier, P.O.B. 911, Lomé.

I-149.   TRINIDAD AND TOBAGO/Port-au-Spain/1.24 mil./ EN-HI and others
—EMB in USA: 1708 Massachusetts Avenue NW, Washington, DC 20036.
—CTR in USA: 420 Lexington Avenue, New York, NY 10170/ 400 Madison Avenue, Room 803, New York, NY 10017.
—USA EMB: 15 Queen's Park West, P.O. Box 752, Port-au-Spain/ U.S. firms: 59.
—UND: 19 Keate Street, P.O. Box 812, Port-au-Spain.
—UNI: 15 Keate Street, P.O.B. 130, Port-au-Spain.

I-150.   TUNISIA/Tunis/8.1 mil./ AB-FR
—EMB in USA: 1515 Massachusetts Avenue NW, Washington, DC 20005.
—CTR: 870 United Nations Plaza, New York, NY 10017.
—USA EMB: 144 Avenue de la Liberté, Tunis 1002/ U.S. firms: 46.
—UND: 61 Boulevard Bab Benat, P.O. Box 863, Tunis 1035.
—UNI: *Same as above.*

I-151.   TURKEY/Ankara/56.5 mil./ TU-AB, KD
—EMB in USA: 1714 Massachusetts Avenue NW, Washington, DC 20036.
—CTR in USA: 821 United Nations Plaza, New York, NY 10017.
—USA EMB: 110 Ataturk Boulevard 06043 Ulus, Ankara/ U.S. firms: 65.
—USA CTR: Balumcu 80700 Istanbul.
—UND: 197 Ataturk Boulevard, P.O. Box 407, Ankara.
—UNI: *Same as above.*

I-152.   UGANDA/Kampala/15.1 mil./ EN-LN, SH
—EMB in USA: 5909 16th Street NW, Washington, DC 20011.
—USA EMB: Parlament Avenue, P.O. Box 7007, Kampala/ U.S. firms: 14.
—UND: IPS Building, Obote Avenue, P.O. Box 7184, Kampala.
—UNI: *See* Kenya.

I-153.   UNITED ARAB EMIRATES/Abu Dhabi/1.8 mil./ AB-EN
—EMB in USA: 600 New Hampshire Avenue NW, Washington, DC 20037.
—USA EMB: P.O. Box 4009 Al Sudan Street, Abu Dhabi.
—USA CTR: International Trade Center, Suite 1609, P.O.B. 9281, Dubai/ U.S. firms: 134.
—UND: Corner Istiqual Street and Airport Road, P.O. Box 3490, Abu Dhabi.
—UNI: *See* Bahrain.

I-154.   UNITED KINGDOM/London/57.4 mil./ EN-SC, WE
—EMB in USA: 3100 Massachusetts Avenue NW, Washington, DC 20008.

—CTR in USA: 845 Third Avenue, New York, NY 10022/ 275 Madison Avenue, New York, NY 10016/ 3150 California Street, San Francisco, CA 94115/ British firms in the U.S.: 305.
—USA EMB: 24/31 Grosvenor Square, London W1A 1AE.
—USA CTR: 75 Brook Street, London W1Y 2EB/ U.S. firms: 1,186 in England, 98 in Scotland, 16 in Wales, 12 in Northern Ireland.
—UNI: Ship House 20, 20 Buckingham Gate, London SW1 6LB.

I-155.   UNITED STATES/Washington, DC/254 mil./ EN-CH, GE, FR, IT, PO, SP, and dozens of other languages.
—US EMB abroad are listed for countries with diplomatic relations.
—US Mission to the United Nations: 799 United Nations Plaza, New York, NY 10017.
—US Chamber of Commerce: 1615 H Street NW, Washington, DC 20062.
—UND: 2102 L Street NW, Washington, DC 20037.
—UNI: 1889 F Street NW, Washington, DC 20006.

I-156.   URUGUAY/Montevideo/3.1 mil./ SP
—EMB in USA: 1918 F Street NW, Washington, DC 20006.
—CTR in USA: 747 Third Avenue, 37th Floor, New York, NY 10017.
—USA EMB: Lauro Muller 1776, Montevideo.
—USA CTR: Calle Bartolomé Mitre 1337, Casilla de Correo 809, Montevideo/ U.S. firms: 66.
—UND: Edificio Artigas, Rincón 487, 10° piso, Casilla de Correo 1207, Montevideo.
—UNI: *See* Argentina.

I-157.   VATICAN (HOLY SEE)/Vatican City/1,000/ IT
—EMB in USA: 3339 Massachusetts Avenue NW, Washington, DC 20008.
—USA EMB: Via Aurelia 294, 00165 Rome.
—UNI: *See* Italy.

I-158.   VENEZUELA/Caracas/9.2 mil./ SP
—EMB in USA: 1099 30th Street NW, Washington, DC 20007.

—CTR in USA: 7 East 51st Street, New York, NY 10022/ 115 Broadway, Room 1110, New York, NY 10006/ Venezuelan firms in the U.S.: 13.

—USA EMB: Avenida Francisco de Miranda y Avenida Principal de la Floresta, P.O. Box 62291, Caracas.

—USA CTR: Torre Credival, piso 10, 2 da, Avenida Campo Alegre, Apartado 5181, P.O. Box 5181, Caracas/ U.S. firms: 297.

—UND: Edificio Torre Central, 4° piso, Avenida Luis Roche y Transy de Palos Grandes Altamira, Apartado 69005, 1062-A Caracas.

—UNI: *See* Colombia.

I-159.   VIETNAM/Hanoi/65 mil./ VI-CA, CH, FR, and other languages
—No diplomatic relations with U.S.A.
—UND: *See* Thailand.
—UNI: *Same as above.*

I-160.   WESTERN SAMOA/Apia/200,000/ EN, SM
—EMB in USA: 1155 15th Street NW, Washington, DC 20037.
—USA EMB: P.O. Box 3430, Apia.
—UND: Lauofo Meti's Building, Private Mail Bag, Apia.
—UNI: *See* Australia.

I-161.   YEMEN/Sana'a/12 mil./ AB-EN
—EMB in USA: 600 New Hampshire Avenue NW, Washington, DC 20037.
—USA EMB: P.O. Box 1088, Sana'a.
—UND: Al-Haj Hassan Kassin Al-Wusta Building, 202 Zubeiry Street, P.O. Box 551, Sana'a.
—UNI: *See* Egypt.

I-162.   YEMEN, SOUTH/Aden/2.1 mil./ AB-EN, M/H (Presently part of I-161, after unification)

I-163.   YUGOSLAVIA/Belgrade/10 mil./ MA, S/C, SV-HU, RO
—EMB in USA: 2410 California Street NW, Washington, DC 20008.
—CTR in USA: 767 Third Avenue, New York, NY 10017.
—USA EMB: Kneza Milosa 50, Belgrade/ U.S. firms: 18.

—UND: Svetozara Markovica 58, P.O. Box 157, 11001 Belgrade.
—*See also* separate entries for former republics of Yugoslavia [Appendix to this section].
—*Note:* Yugoslavia presently consists only of Serbia and Montenegro.

I-164. ZAIRE/Kinshasa/38.5 mil./ FR-KK, KW, LG, T/S
—EMB in USA: 1800 New Hampshire Avenue NW, Washington, DC 20009.
—CTR in USA: 529 Fifth Avenue, New York, NY 10017.
—USA EMB: 310 Avenue des Aviateurs, Kinshasa/ U.S. firms: 25.
—UND: Bâtiment II République, Boulevard du 30 Juin, P.O.B. 7248, Kinshasa.
—UNI: *Same as above.*

I-165. ZAMBIA/Lusaka/8.5 mil./ EN-BE, BN, LU, LZ, TG, and others
—EMB in USA: 2419 Massachusetts Avenue NW, Washington, DC 20008.
—USA EMB: P.O. Box 31617, United Nations Avenue, Lusaka/ U.S. firms: 35.
—UND: P.O. Box 31966, Lusaka.
—UNI: P.O. Box 32905, Lusaka.

I-166. ZIMBABWE/Harare/9.6 mil./ EN-ND, SN
—EMB in USA: 1608 New Hampshire Avenue NW, Washington, DC 20009.
—USA EMB: P.O. Box 3340, 1724 Herbert Chitapo Avenue, Harare/ U.S. firms: 44.
—UND: U.D.C. Centre, 1st Street and Union Avenue, P.O. Box 4775, Harare.
—UNI: Dolphin House, 123 Moffat Street and Union Avenue, P.O.B. 4408, Harare.

Addendum Section I

I-167. ARMENIA/Yerevan/3.3 mil./ AR-AZ, RU
—EMB in USA: 122 C Street NW, Suite 360, Washington, DC 20001.
—USA EMB: 18 General Bagramiani, Yerevan.

I-168.   AZERBAIJAN/Baku/7.1 mil./ AZ-AR, RU
—EMB in USA: 747 3rd Avenue, 17th Floor, New York, NY 10017 (Serves also as Mission to the United Nations).
—USA EMB: Hotel Intourist, 77 Prospekt Neftyanikov, Baku.

I-169.   BOSNIA and HERZEGOVINA/Sarajevo/4.3 mil./ S/C-AL, TU
—EMB in USA: 1345 Avenue of the Americas, 43rd Floor, New York, NY 10105 (Serves also as Mission to the United Nations).
—USA EMB: Not established yet because of the war in various regions of Bosnia and Herzegovina.

I-170.   BYELARUS (BELORUSSIA)/Minsk/10.2 mil./ BY-PO, RU, UK
—EMB in USA: 1511 K Street NW, Suite 619, Washington, DC 20005.
—USA EMB: Storovilenskaya No. 6, Minsk.

I-171.   CROATIA/Zagreb/4.7 mil./ S/C, SV
—EMB in USA: 236 Massachusetts Avenue NE, Washington, DC 20002.
—USA EMB: Andrije Hebranga 2, Zagreb.

I-172.   ESTONIA/Tallinn/1.58 mil./ ES-RU, UK
—EMB in USA: 630 Fifth Avenue, Suite 2415, New York, NY 10111 (Serves also as Mission to the United Nations).
—USA EMB: Kentmanni 20, Tallinn, EE 0001

I-173.   GEORGIA/Tbilisi/5.5 mil./ GG-AR, AZ, RU
—EMB in USA: *See* I-183.
—USA EMB: 25 Antonely Street, Tbilisi.

I-174.   KAZAKHSTAN/Alma-Ata/16.7 mil./ KZ, RU-GE, UK
—EMB in USA: Temporary representation by I-183 (Russia).
—USA EMB: 551 Seyfalline Street, Alma-Ata.

I-175.   KYRGYZSTAN/Bishkek/4.4 mil./ K/Z, RU-UZ
—EMB in USA: Temporary representation by I-183 (Russia).
—USA EMB: Erkindik Prospekt No. 66, Bishkek.

I-176. LATVIA/Riga/2.7 mil./ LT-RU
—EMB in USA: 4325 17th Street NW, Washington, DC 20011.
—USA EMB: Raina Boulevard 7, Riga 22650.

I-177. LITHUANIA/Vilnius/3.7 mil./ LI, RU-PO
—EMB in USA: 2622 16th Street NW, Washington, DC 20009.
—USA EMB: Akmenu 6, Vilnius 232600.

I-178. MACEDONIA/Skopje/1.9 mil./ MA, S/C-AL, GR, TU
—EMB in USA: Not established yet.
—USA EMB: *See* I-163 (Yugoslavia).

I-179. MARSHALL ISLANDS/Majuro/45,563/ EN, Marshallese
—EMB in USA: 2433 Massachusetts Avenue NW, Washington, DC 20008.
—USA EMB: P.O. Box 1379, Majuro.

I-180. MICRONESIA/Kolonia/107,900/ EN, local (indigenous) languages
—EMB in USA: 1725 N Street NW, Washington, DC 20036.
—USA EMB: P.O. Box 1286 Phonpei 96941, Kolonia.

I-181. MOLDOVA/Chisinau/4.4 mil./ RO, RU-UK
—EMB in USA: Temporary representation by I-183 (Russia).
—USA EMB: Str. Alexei Mateevich No. 103, Chisinau.

I-182. NAMIBIA/Windhoek/1.3 mil./ EN-AF, GE, and various others
—EMB in USA: P.O. Box 34728, Washington, DC 20043.
—USA EMB: 14 Lossen Street, Windhoek.

I-183. RUSSIA/Moscow/150 mil./ RU-BY, UK, and dozens of other languages
—EMB in USA: 1125 16th Street NW, Washington, DC 20036
—USA EMB: Ulitsa Chikovskogo 19/21/23, Moscow/ U.S. firms: over 200.
—UNI: Ulitsa Lunacharskogo 4/16, Moscow 121002.

I-184.   ST. VINCENT AND THE GRENADINES/Kingstown/114,000/
EN
—EMB in USA: 1717 Massachusetts Avenue NW,
Washington, DC 20036.
—USA EMB: No embassy.

I-185.   SLOVAKIA/Bratislava/5.3 mil./ SL-CZ, HU, RU, UK
—EMB in USA: 3900 Spring and Freedom Streets NW,
Washington, DC 20008.
—USA EMB: Hviezdoslavovo Namestie 4, Bratislava.

I-186.   SLOVENIA/Ljubljana/2 mil./ SV-S/C, GE
—EMB in USA: 1300 19th Street, Suite 410, Washington, DC 20036.
—USA EMB: P.O. Box 254, Cankarevo, Ljubljana
6100.

I-187.   SOLOMON ISLANDS/Honiara/325,000/ EN and Melanisian
languages
—EMB in USA: 820 Second Avenue, Suite 800, New
York, NY 10017 (Serves also as Mission to the United
Nations).
—USA EMB: Mud Alley, P.O. Box 561, Honiara.
—UNI: *See* Philippines.

I-188.   TAJIKISTAN/Dushanbe/5.2 mil./ TJ-RU, UZ
—EMB in USA: Temporary representation by I-183
(Russia).
—USA EMB: Aini Street No. 39, Dushanbe (Closed
on October 24, 1992 because of Civil War in the
country.)

I-189.   TURKMENISTAN/Ashkhabat/3.6 mil./ T/M-RU, UZ
—EMB in USA: Temporary representation by I-183
(Russia).
—USA EMB: Hotel Yubileinaya, Ashkhabat (tempo-
rary headquarters).

I-190.   UKRAINE/Kiev/52 mil./ UK, RU
—EMB in USA: 20001 L Street NW, Suite 200, Wash-
ington, DC 20036.
—USA EMB: Ulitsa Yurija Kotsyubinskoho No. 10,
Kiev.

I-191.   UZBEKISTAN/Tashkent/20.3 mil./ UZ-KZ, RU, TJ
      —EMB in USA: Temporary representation by I-183 (Russia).
      —USA EMB: 55 Chelanzanskaya, Tashkent.

APPENDIX: REMINDERS AND RECOMMENDATIONS FOR SUCCESSFUL JOB HUNTING

1. JOB SEARCH SUGGESTIONS

—Treat your job search as a full-time job—work at it for seven to eight hours daily and involve your family in the process of job hunting.

—Never be discouraged by setbacks: disappointments are part of the process before finding the right job.

—Be patient and persevere, the job hunt can take several months, with ups and downs on the road.

—Always be honest with yourself and with others, but build up your assets and tone down your shortcomings during interviews.

—Have a positive attitude, display your positive characteristics.

—Associate yourself with successful people who share similar goals.

—Have a clear idea of your goals and achievement objectives.

—Plan your actions, steps of implementation, and strategies.

—Organize thoroughly your research materials (file, appointment calendar, and other data).

—Be a clear communicator both orally and in writing.

—Be enthusiastic and energetic, and strive to ask intelligent and interesting questions.

—Be a good listener and let the interviewer know you are listening.

—Be polite, tactful, and courteous under all circumstances.

—Keep a professional stance both in your attire and your speaking.

—Demonstrate your competence, intelligence, and other skills and this will generate confidence and credibility in you.

—Balance your job search time with recreational activities.

—Be open-minded, periodically evaluate your progress, and be flexible by reorganizing activities and priorities.

2. EMPLOYERS' EXPECTATIONS IN POTENTIAL EMPLOYEES

—Ability of the potential employee to organize thoughts and communicate them clearly both in writing and speech.

—Ability to intelligently understand assignments.

—Sense of maturity that enables the employee to deal effectively with difficult situations and people.

—The potential employee's acceptance of responsibility and willingness to do the job.

—Initiative of the employee to improve his or her performance and to bring creative ideas to his or her work.

—Ability to lead others and give a positive example.

—Energy and flexibility in performing duties.

—Ability to compete with others, and to cope successfully in stressful situations.

—The potential employee knows his or her own capabilities, strengths, and weaknesses, and has a clear picture of his or her direction and goals for the future.

3. COVER LETTER SUGGESTIONS

—A cover letter acts as "an introduction card" for your résumé.

—The main purpose of writing is to interest the employer in hiring you.

—Address the letter to a specific person by name (personnel interviewer, chief of unit, etc.) and spell the name correctly.

—The first twenty words should attract the reader's interest and tell your viewpoint in terms of contributions you can make to the employer.

—Always refer to the résumé for a more specific listing of your skills.

—Use simple, direct language, correct grammar, and type neatly on standard size paper (8½ × 11).

—Keep your letter short—limit it to one page.

—Avoid being aggressive, familiar, overbearing, or "humorous" in your letter, but try to reflect some individuality.

—End your letter by stating what the reader can expect next

from you. (For example, that you will call to follow up in a week, or wait for a call from the reader.)

4. RÉSUMÉ SUGGESTIONS

—One page only (in virtually all cases) and only in exceptional cases (for example many years of experience, variety of noted achievements) two pages, including publications.

—Size should be 8½ × 11, oversized or small-sized résumés are not acceptable.

—Typesetting is the best résumé preparation process even though it is more costly. This process allows the résumé to be kept on disk, makes clear copies, and allows for flexibility in design.

—When using a computer, try to have your résumé printed out using a laser printer.

—Proofreading your résumé *is a must.*

—Use action verbs rather than passive ones (e.g. "supervised," not "watched over").

—Try to be clear and direct, without being long-winded in describing your skills.

—Be neat, well organized, and professional in the résumé's presentation.

—Use ample spacing and highlighting (e.g. caps, underlining) for different emphases.

—Maintain an aesthetic balance by centering your contact information on the top, keeping information categories on the left in all caps (for example, employers and dates of employment), while the description of the categories should be to the right of the information category.

—Check very carefully for correct spelling, grammar, and punctuation. Ask a friend to help check objectively.

—Always bring to the employer's attention *your strongest points first.*

—In compiling the résumé, one should avoid using abbreviations (except the middle initial of your name), and cramped or crowded typing.

5. INTERVIEW SUGGESTIONS

—Sit up straight and look interested in what the interviewer has to say.

—Project your voice clearly to the interviewer.

—Have clean and trimmed nails, comb your hair, and wear

it in a conservative style, use a moderate amount of perfume or cologne, and be appropriately dressed.
—Get a good night's sleep before the interview, and use the restroom before being called by the interviewer.
—Smile during the interview, maintain eye contact with the interviewer, appear enthusiastic, and let the interviewer set the pace of the interview.
—Take notes during the interview, have your questions prepared in advance, and allow the interviewer to close the interview.
—Leave plenty of time to reach the interview on time.
—Do not mention the salary in the initial interview.
—Do not glance at your watch during the interview.

Negative impressions left by job hunters:
Tardiness, sloppiness, evasiveness, arrogance, abrasiveness, indecisiveness, lack of preparation, negative attitudes, begging for a job, apologizing for lack of experience, using unsuitable jokes, trying very hard to please, lack of self-control, touching irrelevant topics, uncertainty about the future, overstaying the welcome, a weak or half-hearted handshake, lack of self-confidence, looking uninterested or intimidated, boastfulness, egotism, super-aggressiveness, treating the secretary or receptionist in a cavalier or condescending manner.
REMEMBER: What you do and say during the first ten seconds of an interview may determine whether you are hired according to Robert Half, president of Robert Half International, a well-known employment agency.

6. INTERVIEWING THE INTERVIEWER SUGGESTIONS
—Before deciding to join a company or to decline an offer, the interviewee should ask questions during the interview and clarify several aspects: duties and responsibilities of the future job, the relationship between that position and other positions, who is the future boss and what is his/her background, who were the previous people who occupied the vacant position, what are the opportunities for further development and promotions, does the employer use periodic performance reviews, what is the work schedule and how flexible is it, and any other aspects of the position in which you are interested.
—The job-seeker should also clarify after being offered the

position the salary range, 401K plan, and other investment matching programs, cafeteria, insurance plan (i.e. health, dental, optical, life, and others), car allowance and/or gasoline allowance if applicable, compensation days for unpaid overtime/business travel, health club membership, accidental death insurance, employment contract and/or termination of the contract, expense account (if any), paid sick leave, personal days, number of paid holidays, short- or long-term disability compensation plans, stock options, vacation time, forms of compensation (if any) upon retirement.

FOR DETAILS REGARDING THE JOB HUNTING PROCESS, RÉSUMÉS AND INTERVIEWS, THE FOLLOWING BOOKS ARE RECOMMENDED:
a) **Job Search.** Ronald Krannich and Caryl Rae Krannich, *Discover the Best Jobs for You* (Manassas Park, VA: Impact Publications, 1993); Michelle Le Compte, ed., *Job Hunter's Sourcebook: Where to Find Employment Leads and Other Job Search Resources* (Detroit: Gale Research Company, 1993); Harry Levinson, *Career Mastery: Keys to Taking Charge of Your Career* (San Francisco: Berret-Koehler, 1992).
b) **Résumés.** Richard Beatty, *The Résumé Kit* (New York: Wiley and Sons, 1984); Burdette Bostwick, *Résumé Writing* (New York: Wiley and Sons, 1985); Thomas Jackson, *The Perfect Résumé* (New York: Anchor Books, 1981). *See also* "Selective Bibliography" section.
c) **Interviews.** Anthony Medley, *Sweaty Palms: The Neglected Art of Being Interviewed* (New York: Time-Life Learning Publications, 1984); Stephen Merman and John McLaughlin, *Outinterviewing the Interviewer* (New York: Prentice Hall, 1983); Martin J. Yate, *Knock'em Dead with Great Answers to Tough Interview Questions* (Boston: Bob Adams, 1987).

7. SELECTIVE POSITIONS OF AMERICAN COLLEGE GRADUATES WITH FOREIGN LANGUAGE SKILLS (OR MAJORS) WORKING IN THE USA

A
Abstractor, Accountant (Auditor, Account Executive), Actor, Advertising Agent, Agricultural Specialist, Airline Flight Attendant, Airline Pilot, Airline Flight Reservation Specialist, Announcer (Radio, Television), Anthropologist, Architect, Archi-

vist, Area Studies Specialist (Latin America, Middle East, Far East, Russian, and East European), Astronaut, Astronomer

B

Bank Officer (Loans, International Transactions), Biologist, Bookkeeper, Broadcaster (Radio, Television), Budget Analyst, Business Executive

C

Cartographer, Child Care Worker (Nanny, Nursery), Clergy (all denominations, including missionaries), Communications Specialist, Community Development Specialist, Compensations Specialist, Computer Systems Specialist, Consultant (various fields), Controller, Copywriter, Counselor (School, College, Private), Credit Analyst, Customs Officer

D

Dentist, Doctor-Medical (various fields)

E

Economist, Editor, Education Administrator (or Specialist), Electronics Engineer, Environmental Specialist, Etymologist, Executive Secretary, Export/Import Manager

F

Fashion Model, Financial Analyst, Financial Manager (or officer), Foreign Service Officer (consular, diplomatic, agricultural, military, commercial), Free Lance Writer

G

Geographer, Geologist, Government Worker (federal, state, municipal), Guide (tourist, conventions)

H

Health Administrator, Health Educator, Historian, Home Economist, Hotel Manager

I

Immigration Officer, Indexer, Information Officer, Insurance Agent, Intelligence Specialist, Interpreter

J

Journalist (radio and TV networks, newspaper, journal)

L
Law Enforcement Officer (police, F.B.I., Secret Service, Security), Lawyer (various fields), Librarian (acquisitions, bibliographer, cataloging, reference, foreign collections, special collections), Linguist, Literary Agent

M
Marketing Specialist (manager, buyer), Media Executive (or performer), Medical Assistant, Medical Researcher, Meteorologist, Museum Curator, Musician

N
National Park Officer, Navy (officer, passenger agent), Nurse (registered), Nutritionist

O
Office Manager, Optician

P
Peace Corp Volunteer, Personnel Officer (manager, interviewer, labor relations specialist), Philologist, Physician (all fields), Physicist, Police Officer, Production Manager, Public Health Specialist, Public Information Officer, Public Relations Specialist, Publisher, Purchasing Agent

Q
Quality Control Supervisor

R
Realtor, Receptionist, Recording Industry Specialist, Reporter, Research Analyst, Restaurant Manager (Captain, Maitre D')

S
Sales Specialist (manager, representative, customer service), Scientific Information Specialist, Scientist (various fields), Secretary (bilingual, multilingual, executive, administrative), Singer, Social Worker, Sociologist, Space Specialist, Statistician, Stenographer, Switchboard Operator, Systems Analyst

T
Teacher (kindergarten, elementary and high school, college/ university, tutor), Technical Writer, Telex/Telegraph Engineer, Therapist (various fields), Translator, Transportation Specialist, Travel Agent

8. SELECTIVE POSITIONS OF AMERICAN COLLEGE GRADUATES WITH FOREIGN LANGUAGE SKILLS (OR MAJORS) WORKING OVERSEAS OR FOR MULTINATIONAL COMPANIES

A

Accountant, Advertising Manager, Aeronautical Engineer, Agricultural Engineer, Agronomist, Air-Conditioning Specialist, Aircraft Pilot, Anesthetist, Animal Husbandry Specialist, Architectural Engineer, Atomic/Nuclear Specialist, Auditor.

B

Bacteriologist, Bilingual Secretary, Biochemist, Biologist, Botanist, Budget Analyst, Business Machines/Materials Salesperson.

C

Chemical Engineer, Chemist, City Planner, Civil Engineer, Community Organizer, Computer Specialist (Programmer, Systems Analyst), Construction Engineer, Controller.

D

Data Processor Supervisor, Dentist, Design Engineer, Detective, Dietetic Specialist.

E

Economist, Electrical Engineer, Electronics Engineer, Engineer (other fields), Environmental Protectionist, ESL Teacher, Executive (various fields), Export/Import Manager.

F

Farm Business Specialist (Manager, Equipment), Finance Executive, Fiber Optics Specialist, Food Chemist, Foreign Operations Specialist (Executive, Controller), Forestry Specialist.

G

Geological Engineer, Geologist, Geophysicist, Gerontologist, Guidance Counselor.

H

Heating/Refrigeration Equipment Engineer, Horticulture Specialist, Hospital Administrator, Hotel Manager.

I

Industrial Designer, Industrial Engineer, Instrumentation Engineer, International Market Analyst, International Personnel Manager, International Sales Executive.

L

Landscape Architect, Laser Specialist, Lawyer (Taxes, Banking), Librarian, Livestock Production Specialist.

M

Manufacturing Engineer, Marketing Research Manager, Mechanical Engineer, Medical Engineer, Metallurgical Engineer, Meteorologist, Microbiologist, Multinational Operations Executive.

N

Nurse (Professional Registered), Nursery Operations Specialist.

O

Occupational Therapist, Oceanographer, Ophthalmologist, Optician, Optometrist, Overseas Regional Manager.

P

Paramedic, Personnel Manager, Petroleum Engineer, Pharmacist, Physician, Physicist, Physiotherapist, Production Manager, Programmer (Computer, Business, Engineer), Psychiatrist, Public Relations Manager, Publisher's Sales Manager.

R

Realtor, Rehabilitation Counselor, Robotics Specialist.

S

Sales Executive, Sanitation Engineer, Science Teacher, Secondary School Teacher, Soil Scientist, Speech Pathologist and Audiologist, Surgeon, Surveyor, Systems Analyst Manager.

T

Tax Accountant, Teacher (Kindergarten, Elementary School), Technical Writer, Textile Design Specialist, Traffic Manager, Tree Expert Specialist.

U

Urban Planner Engineer.

V
Veterinarian, Vocational Counselor, Vocational Teacher.

W
Water and Waste Water Specialist, Wildlife and Conservation Specialist, Woodwork Sales Manager.

Z
Zoologist.

*　　*　　*

Note:
In order to work overseas or for international organizations, five important elements are expected by recruiters:
(1) Language skills
(2) Willingness to relocate
(3) Ability to operate in a team made up of various nationalities
(4) Experience in working and living overseas
(5) General professional and educational requirements

SELECTIVE BIBLIOGRAPHY

The information herein was verified through 1993. Annual publications were marked accordingly to enable consultation of later editions.

BOOKS AND PAMPHLETS FOR CHAPTER 1

Ash, Lee. *Subject Collections,* 7th ed. New York: R. R. Bowker, 1993. 2 vols.
Hundreds of academic, public, and private libraries with language collections in the U.S. and Canada, with description of size and other characteristics.

The College Blue Book. New York: Macmillan, 1991. 5 vols.
Profiles of over 3,000 U.S. and Canadian universities and colleges by state or province, including language courses and majors. Also listings of grants, scholarships, fellowships, and loans.

The College Handbook, 1993. New York: College Entrance Examination Board, 1988. [Annual publication.]
Over 3,000 colleges and universities in the U.S. listed by state; index of majors includes languages and area studies; addresses do not have zip codes.

Directory of Foreign Language Service Organizations (Sophia Behrens, compiler). Washington, DC: ERIC Clearinghouse on Languages and Linguistics, 1987.
Lists over 150 organizations for foreign-language teachers and researchers, dozens of publications, and distributors of foreign-language materials.

Directory of Language Collections in North American Public Libraries (Sylva Manoogian and Natalia Bezugloff, compilers). Chicago: American Library Association, 1986.
Over 200 U.S. and Canadian public libraries with language collections, arranged by language and by geographical location; size of collections and services provided by libraries are described.

Directory of Programs in Linguistics in the USA and Canada. Washington, DC: Linguistic Society of America, 1987.
Over 180 colleges, universities, and other institutions teaching foreign languages for degrees or specialization; includes uncommonly taught languages.

Global Guide to International Education (David Hoopes and Kathleen Hoopes, editors). New York: Facts on File, 1984.
Comprehensive reference work, lists hundreds of U.S. universities, colleges, government, and private organizations, foundations, and other nonprofit units with foreign language and/or area studies programs. Very good annotations and bibliographic resources. Needs updating.

Guide to Non-English-Language Schools. Rosslyn, VA: National Clearing House for Bilingual Education/Inter-American Research Associates, 1988.
Lists private schools sponsored by various ethnic groups and languages used in classes; good for teachers of various languages.

Index to Majors, 1992–93. New York: College Entrance Examinations Board, 1987. [Annual publication.]
Dozens of language majors and area studies in U.S. colleges and universities.

Lovejoy's College Guide (Charles Straughn II and Barbarasue Lovejoy Straughn, compilers). New York: Monarch Press, 1993.
Over 2,700 U.S. colleges and universities listed by state; has index to several language studies, career curricula, and special programs.

Multilanguage Vendors List. Toronto: Metropolitan Toronto Library Board and Multilingual Biblioservice of the National Library of Canada, 1988.

Lists dozens of vendors from the United States, Canada, and other countries by language; good annotations regarding vendor services (language, payment, mail order, etc.), supplemented by alphabetical list of vendors.

Peterson's Annual Guides: Undergraduate Study Guide to Four-Year Colleges, 1992 (Andrea Lehman, editor). Princeton, NJ: Peterson's Guides, 1988. [Annual publication.]

Standard reference work, lists thousands of college and university profiles in alphabetical order, including foreign language majors; has a major directory.

Peterson's Annual Guides: Undergraduate Study Guide to Two-Year Colleges, 1989 (Andrea Lehman, editor). Princeton, NJ: Peterson's Guides, 1988. [Annual publication.]

Same structure as the previous item, for two-year colleges only.

A Selected List of Foreign-Language Book Dealers in New York City (Donnell Foreign Language Library and New Americans Project of Queens Borough Public Library, compilers). New York: American Library Association Convention, 1986.

Dozens of book dealers, with addresses and telephone numbers, listed by language; especially prepared for ALA convention.

A Selected List of Language Materials Vendors in the Metropolitan Los Angeles and San Francisco Areas (Staff of the Bay Area Library Information System and Metropolitan Cooperative Library System, compilers). San Francisco: American Library Association Convention, 1987.

Dozens of vendors arranged by language, with annotations regarding services provided; especially prepared for ALA convention.

A Selected List of Vendors of Audio-Visual Materials (Staff of Foreign Language Department of the Chicago Public Library, compilers). New Orleans: American Library Association Convention, 1988.

Dozens of vendors arranged in alphabetical order; especially prepared for ALA convention.

Where to Buy Multilingual Books in Ontario. Toronto: Ministry of Citizenship and Culture, 1986.

Several dozen vendors arranged by language of specialization, and also listed in alphabetical order, with addresses and telephone numbers.

Wynar, Lubomyr, and Buttlar, Lois. *Guide to Ethnic Museums, Libraries, and Archives in the United States.* Kent, Ohio: Program for the Study of Ethnic Publication/School of Library Science, Kent State University, 1978.

Covers over 1,400 organizations belonging to over 70 U.S. ethnic groups, with detailed descriptions of language collections and services, including teaching of languages, internships, and courses for credit.

BOOKS AND PAMPHLETS FOR CHAPTERS 2 AND 3

Angel, Juvenal, compiler. *Multinational Marketing and Employment Directory.* New York: Uni World Business Publications, 1982.

Description of thousands of U.S. firms offering opportunities for international jobs overseas; special section on interviewing and résumés. Needs updating, but basically still valid information.

Angus, Susan. *Invest Yourself: The Catalogue of Volunteer Opportunities.* New York: Commission on Voluntary Service, 1991.

Lists over 200 private volunteer organizations with dozens of overseas job opportunities.

Aulick, June. *Résumés for Employment in the U.S. and Overseas,* 3rd ed. New York: World Trade Academy Press, 1988.

Methods of preparing résumés accompanied by samples of

résumés and cover letters, plus some foreign countries in profile.

Beard, Marna, and McGahey, Michael. *Alternative Careers for Teachers*. New York: Arco, 1985.
Job changing for educators, with a special section on opportunities for foreign-language majors.

Beckmann, David; Mitchell, Timothy; and Powers, Linda. *The Overseas List: Opportunities for Living and Working in Developing Countries*. Minneapolis, MN: Augsburg Publishing House, 1985.
Lists hundreds of private development assistance, religious, teaching, United States government, United Nations, and business organizations. Detailed descriptions of activities in various countries.

Broadcasting & Cable Market Place. New York: Bowker, 1992. [Annual publication.]
Lists all U.S. and Canadian stations with programs in 26 languages ranging from AB, CH, CZ, to SP, UK, VI. Good for translators, majors in journalism and broadcasting, editors, and others with language skills.

Burgoin, Edward. *Foreign Languages and Your Career*. Washington, DC: Columbia Languages Services, 1984.
Describes dozens of fields of work in which foreign-language skills are needed; has index to hundreds of occupations.

Cantrell, Will, and Marshall, Terry. *101 Ways to Find an Overseas Job*. Merrifield, VA: Cantrell Corporation, 1987.
Good information on how to find jobs overseas, U.S. and foreign organizations with jobs overseas, volunteer agencies, bibliographic recommendations (books, periodicals, pamphlets), plus tax information.

Career Associates. *Career Choices Encyclopedia: Guide to Entry-Level Jobs*. New York: Walker and Company, 1986. [New edition in preparation.]

Describes several careers requiring fluency in foreign languages.

Career Employment Opportunities Directory (Alvin Renetzky, editor). Santa Monica, CA: Ready Reference Press, 1985. 4 vols.
Volume 1, *Liberal Arts and Social Sciences,* lists several opportunities for graduates with foreign-language skills under the subject heading "Foreign Language Capability."

A Career Guide for Ph.D.s and Ph.D. Candidates in English and Foreign Languages. New York: Modern Language Association, 1988.
Assists job hunters with advice on seeking college and university employment; has samples of résumés, vitae, and cover letters. It is a revised version of *A Guide for Job Candidates and Department Chairmen in English and Foreign Languages,* published in 1978.

Career Information Center, 3rd ed. Mission Hills, CA: Glencoe Publishing Company, 1992. 13 vols. [New edition in preparation.]
Volumes 10, *Marketing and Distribution,* and 11, *Public and Community Service,* discuss positions for which foreign languages are an asset.

Casewit, Curtis. *Foreign Jobs: The Most Popular Countries.* New York: Monarch Press, 1984.
Work opportunities in European and Asian countries; includes immigration, visa, and work permit information.

———. *How to Get a Job Overseas.* New York: Arco, 1984.
Several work areas, volunteer opportunities, and self-employment, plus résumé advice.

Congrat-Butlar, Stefan, compiler. *Translations and Translators: An International Directory and Guide.* New York: R. R. Bowker, 1979.
Lists associations, training, guidelines, access to the profession, marketplaces, plus names of translators by language

and specialty in the United States and other countries. Needs updating but is still in print.

CPC Annual: A Directory of Employment Opportunities for College Graduates, 1992/93. Bethlehem, PA: College Placement Council, 1988. [Annual publication.]
   Lists foreign-language opportunities with U.S. and foreign companies; gives detailed descriptions of employer's requirements; has samples of résumés, cover letters, and advice on interviewing.

Directory of American Firms Operating in Foreign Countries. New York: World Trade Academy Press, 1991. 3 vols.
   Thousands of firms arranged by country, with addresses and industrial specializations; gives access to over 120 countries around the world.

Directory of Community Services 1992: The Bronx, Manhattan and Staten Island. New York: New York Public Library, 1988. [Annual publication.]
   Lists hundreds of ethnic, cultural, social, health, and other organizations in New York City serving various ethnic communities, and able to utilize qualified employees with language skills.

Directory of Foreign Firms Operating in the United States. New York: World Trade Academy Press, 1991.
   Hundreds of foreign firms arranged by country, with addresses and industrial specializations.

Directory of International Internships: A Guide to International Internships Sponsored by Educational Institutions, Government Agencies, and Various Organizations (Jeffrey E. Roberts et al., editors). Lansing, MI: Michigan State University, Office of Overseas Study/Office of International Students and Scholars Placement Services, 1987.
   Lists several sponsors with their objectives, number of internships, location, duration, and eligibility requirements for applicants, including foreign-language competence; indexes of topics and geographical areas.

Edwards, E. W. *Exploring Careers Using Foreign Languages.* New York: Rosen Publishing Group, 1986.
Describes various opportunities for persons with language skills; lists organizational, government, and private employers.

Encyclopedia of Associations, 1993. Detroit: Gale Research Company, 1988. 3 vols. [Annual publication.]
Standard reference work, with thousands of ethnic, professional, trade, voluntary, philanthropic, and other organizations related to persons with language skills; each entry has name, address, and detailed description of purpose and activities.

The Fourth of July Resource Guide for the Promotion of Careers in Public, Community, and International Service (Devon Smith, editor). Allentown, PA: Middle Atlantic Placement Association, 1987.
Annotated entries on publications covering several areas, including international careers, internships, and voluntary work requiring knowledge of foreign languages.

Griffith, Susan. *Work Your Way Around the World.* Cincinnati, OH: Writer's Digest Books, 1986.
Short-term jobs and volunteer opportunities overseas.

Guide to Careers in World Affairs (Foreign Policy Association, editor). New York: Foreign Policy Association, 1986.
Lists over 250 U.S. and foreign employment opportunities, with detailed descriptions of organizations, their activities, and needs.

Honig, Lucille, and Brod, Richard. *Foreign Languages and Careers.* New York: Modern Language Association, 1979.
Pamphlet; discusses foreign-language utilization in business, commerce, civil service, education, library science, medical science, and other fields. Bibliography is outdated, but the rest is valid.

Howard, Marguerite, and Weeg, Carol. *Teaching Abroad.* New York: Institute of International Education, 1988.
Describes hundreds of exchange programs, with employment and information resources for elementary, junior high, and high school teachers, college and university faculty, and education administrators.

Hueber, Theodore, and Arnold, Edwin. *Opportunities in Foreign Language Careers.* Lincolnwood, IL: VGM Career Books, 1986.
Overview of foreign-language careers, employment outlook, educational requirements, salaries, lists of careers, selected agencies, and organizations with interest in bilinguals and multilinguals.

Immigrant Services in New York City: An Agency Directory. New York: New York City Department of City Planning, Office of Immigrant Affairs, 1988.
Comprehensive reference work listing hundreds of organizations that provide vocational training, teach ESL, and offer other forms of assistance, including services in dozens of languages.

International Directory for Youth Internships with the United Nations, its Specialized Agencies and Non-Governmental Organizations: A Directory of Intern/Volunteer Opportunities, 1984–1985. New York: Council on International and Public Affairs, 1984.
Lists names and addresses of organizations and agencies; gives addresses of United Nations information centers and development programs by country around the world. Pamphlet edited by Cynthia Morehouse.

Johnson, Willis, editor. *Directory of Special Programs for Minority Group Members: Career Information Services, Employment Skill Banks, Financial Sources.* Garrett Park, MD: Garrett Park Press, 1990.
Lists hundreds of organizations of interest to African-Americans, Native Americans, Chinese-Americans, Hispanic-Americans and Japanese-Americans, with opportunities for those who speak relevant languages.

Kocher, Eric. *International Jobs: What They Are and How to Get Them.* Reading, MA: Wesley Publishing, 1990.
Over 500 career opportunities around the world, including U.S. and foreign employers, with very good descriptions and job requirements. Some addresses need updating.

Kregar, Shirley; Gentile, Linda; and Adelman, Alan. *After Latin American Studies: A Guide to Employment for Latin Americanists.* Pittsburgh, PA: Center for Latin American Studies/University of Pittsburgh, 1987.
Lists opportunities in advertising, insurance, hotel, marketing, publishing, and specialized translating fields, teaching ESL, and government job opportunities. Pamphlet.

Looking for Employment in Foreign Countries, 8th ed. New York: World Trade Academy Press, 1990.
Gives several country profiles, with opportunities for foreign nationals; has résumé and cover letter samples. Data on country profiles need updating since new edition is only a reprint of older edition.

Malnig, Lawrence. *What Can I Do with a Major in . . . How to Choose and Use Your College Major.* Ridgefield, NJ: Abbott Press, 1984.
Discusses careers and opportunities for foreign-language majors; lists current occupations of those with language skills.

Marquez, Alex, and Marquez, Ana. *The New Interpreter's Handbook: A Step-by-Step Guide to Becoming a Professional Interpreter.* Anaheim, CA: Iberia Language Services, 1987.
Overview of the profession, translation, and interpretation varieties, freelancing, techniques, schools for training and self-study programs, examinations, certification, and sources of work.

Minority Organizations: A National Directory, 3rd ed. Garrett Park, MD: Garrett Park Press, 1987.
Thousands of organizations for Chinese, Filipino, Japanese, Korean, Afro-American, and Southeast Asian ethnics

in the U.S.; a special index covers academic and professional fields for ethnics.

Muckie, Jim. *How to Find Jobs Teaching Overseas.* New York: By the author, 1988.
Pamphlet, lists over 150 foreign agencies and schools; has samples of résumés and cover letters.

Occupational Outlook Handbook, 1992–93. Washington, DC: U.S. Department of Labor, 1988. [Annual publication.]
Standard reference work; thousands of occupations and training requirements, job outlook, salaries, etc. Includes many occupations using language skills.

Overseas Employment Opportunities for Educators, 1988–1989. Alexandria, VA: U.S. Department of Defense, Dependents Schools, 1988. [Annual publication.]
Describes teaching and other positions in elementary, junior high, and high schools for U.S. military dependents abroad. Need for teachers of FR, GE, LA, SP. Pamphlet issued yearly.

Peterson's Annual Guides/Business and Management Jobs, 1988. Princeton, NJ: Peterson's Guides, 1987. [Annual publication.]
Lists hundreds of organizations, including those hiring graduates who know FR, GE, IT, JP, PE, RU, SP, and other languages.

Powers, Linda. *Careers in International Affairs.* Washington, DC: Georgetown University, 1992.
Describes the international affairs job market, hundreds of U.S. and international employers, including U.S. government and United Nations agencies; business, consulting, and banking firms; and research and teaching organizations. Needs for foreign languages mentioned.

Reilly, George. *Guide to Cruise Ship Jobs.* Babylon, NY: Pilot Books, 1991.
Pamphlet; lists several employment opportunities for professionals, but mostly for nonprofessionals, for which lan-

guage skills are an asset. Has a list of recruitment agencies and techniques of interviewing.

Schuman, Howard. *Making It Abroad: The International Job Hunting Guide.* New York: Wiley and Sons, 1988.
Presents various aspects in preparing for and considering a job abroad, including knowledge of languages; lists consultants and useful newsletters and books; examines job market options; and has résumé samples.

Sheriff, June. *Careers in Foreign Languages: A Handbook.* New York: Regents Publishing Company, 1975.
Good introduction to the field of foreign languages, courses, degrees, proficiency, and job opportunities with government and international organizations; has useful appendixes and a directory of foreign-language newsletters. Some parts of the book need updating.

The Source Book: 1989–90: Social and Health Services in the Greater New York Area. Lanham, MD: UNIPUB, 1988.
Thousands of organizations and their services, including knowledge of various languages for various ethnic communities or patients. Listed are CH, FR, GR(mo), HE, IN, IT, JP, KO, RU, SP, YD, and others.

Specialized Study Options U.S.A.: A Guide to Short-Term Educational Programs in the United States for Foreign Nationals. New York: Institute of International Education Overseas, 1987. 2 vols.
Lists over 1,500 academic, vocational, and professional programs for foreign nationals, leading to various fields of work.

Translation Services Directory. Ossining, NY: American Translators Association, 1988.
Lists hundreds of translation organizations and individual members specializing in translations; covers several dozen languages.

U.S. Government Manual 1992/93. Washington, DC: U.S. Government Printing Office, 1992. [Annual publication.]

Detailed description of U.S. government departments, agencies, and other units, with functions, names, and addresses; good documentation for job hunters with language skills interested in working for the federal government.

U.S. Non-Profit Organizations in Development Assistance Abroad: TAICH Directory, 1983. New York: Technical Assistance Information Clearing House, 1983.
Describes thousands of U.S. nonprofit organizations on all continents, their aims, functions, number of employees inside and outside the U.S., volunteers, and other related subjects. Many addresses need updating.

Volunteer! The Comprehensive Guide to Voluntary Service in the U.S. and Abroad, 1992. Yarmouth, ME: Intercultural Press, 1992. [New edition in preparation.]
Lists hundreds of organizations, their activities, and aims. Some addresses need updating.

Wharton, John. *Jobs in Japan: Complete Guide to Living and Working in the Land of Rising Opportunity.* Denver, CO: Global Press, 1991.
Describes working conditions, schools, and hundreds of contact organizations. Useful tips.

Williams, John W. *Career Preparation and Opportunities in International Law.* Washington, DC: American Bar Association and International Law Institute, 1984.
Presents international legal career opportunities in the public, private, and nonprofit sectors, and respective requirements, including proficiency in foreign languages.

Win, David. *International Careers: An Insider's Guide.* Charlotte, VT: Williamson Publishing, 1987.
A how-to manual discussing international careers in foreign countries, strategies and tactics, creative opportunities, and various U.S. and foreign employers. Special attention accorded foreign languages.

Work, Study and Travel Abroad 1992–93: The Whole World Handbook (Marjorie Adoff Cohen, compiler). New York: Council on International Educational Exchange/St. Martin's Press, 1992.

Presents various opportunities to work abroad short term—a few months to two years—and to combine a job with travel and study.

Worldwide Chamber of Commerce Directory, 1992. Washington, DC: Worldwide Chamber of Commerce, 1992. [Annual publication.]

Thousands of chamber of commerce organizations in the United States, Mexico, and many foreign countries, with addresses, telephone numbers, and a list of foreign embassies and U.S. representatives abroad.

Woodworth, David. *1992 Directory of Overseas Summer Jobs: Where the Jobs Are and How to Get Them.* Princeton, NJ: Peterson's Guides, 1988.

Various summer job opportunities in several European countries, plus visa and work permit regulations for each country.

PERIODICALS FOR CHAPTERS 2 AND 3

Career Opportunities News, P.O. Box 190, Garrett Park, MD 20896.

Bimonthly; features articles on foreign-language careers in various fields of work.

Employment Opportunities Digest, International Publications, P.O. Box 19749, Indianapolis, IN 46210.

Listings of mostly professional jobs in various countries. Quarterly.

Equal Opportunity, Equal Opportunity Publications, 44 Broadway, Greenlawn, NY 11740.

Quarterly; recruitment for black, Native American, Asian, and Hispanic college graduates.

Executive Search Newsletter, I.C.A., 575 Madison Avenue, New York, NY 10022.
Monthly; management positions in various developing countries.

Federal Career Opportunities, Federal Research Service, P.O. Box 1059, Vienna, VA 22180-1059.
Biweekly; professional and nonprofessional jobs with U.S. government agencies; involves work in Asia, Europe, and Latin America.

Foreign and Domestic Teacher's Bureau, Foreign and Domestic Teacher's Bureau, Box 1063, Vancouver, WA 98666.
Listings of positions for teachers—including of foreign languages—in the United States and abroad. Monthly.

International Employment Hotline, P.O. Box 6170, McLean, VA 22106.
Monthly listing of professional jobs in dozens of countries in Africa, Asia, and Latin America.

International Jobs Bulletin, University Placement Center, South Illinois University, Carbondale, IL 62901.
Lists mainly professional jobs in several countries; also describes volunteer and internship programs. Biweekly.

Job Opportunities Bulletin, Transcentury Recruitment Center, 1724 Kalorama Road NW, Washington, DC 20009.
Bimonthly with positions in Asia, Africa, Latin America, and the Middle East; also has classified ads by job hunters.

Jobs Worldwide, A. Boggio, P.O. Box 357, South Pasadena, CA 91030.
Monthly; lists mostly professional positions culled from other sources such as the *New York Times, National Employment Business Weekly,* and others.

Language Paper, Le Grande Eliason International, 1341-F Main Street, Walnut Creek, CA 94596.
Encourages language study related to employment; presents résumé abstracts by professionals with language skills. Bimonthly.

Match Net, Match, 1100 17th Street NW, Suite 300, Washington, DC 20036.
Lists professional jobs mostly in the Middle East and requiring knowledge of Arabic. Bimonthly.

Modern Language Association of America—Job Information List, Modern Language Association of America, 10 Astor Place, New York, NY 10003.
Quarterly; lists teaching positions for English and foreign languages in colleges and universities. February issue has positions for two-year colleges.

National Business Employment Weekly, Institutional Investor, 488 Madison Avenue, New York, NY 10022.
Professional positions both in the United States and abroad, plus brief articles on job hunting, interviews, salaries, etc.

The New York Times, The New York Times Company, 229 West 43rd Street, New York, NY 10036.
Leading newspaper; has daily and weekly supplements of classified ads for professional and nonprofessional bilinguals and multilinguals.

Overseas Employment Newsletter, Overseas Employment Service, P.O. Box 460, Mount Royal, PQ, H3P 3C7, Canada.
Lists professional jobs in Africa, Asia, Australia, and Europe. Biweekly.

Work Abroad, Mr. Information, 1775 Robson Street, Suite 205, Vancouver, BC V6G 1C9, Canada.
Professional and nonprofessional positions in Europe, Asia, Africa, and Latin America.

PERIODICALS REFERENCE WORKS FOR ALL CHAPTERS

The Standard Periodicals Directory, 1988. New York: Oxbridge Communications, 1988. [Annual publication.]
    Standard reference tool; includes thousands of ethnic and language periodicals; useful for both job hunting and language learning purposes.

Wynar, Lubomyr. *Encyclopedic Directory of Ethnic Newspapers and Periodicals in the United States.* Littleton, CO: Libraries Unlimited, 1972.
    Annotates over 900 periodicals and newspapers published by over 40 U.S. ethnic groups in their respective languages or in bilingual publications. Some publications have classified ads for job opportunities. Book needs updating, but is basically still valid.

Addendum Selective Bibliography

Books for Chapter 1

Chronicle Four-Year College Data Book: A College Guide for 1991–1993 School Year. Moravia, New York: CGP, 1993.
    Lists thousands of colleges, including those offering majors in foreign languages. Appended by language indexes.

Chronicle Two-Year College Data Book: A College Guide for 1991–1992 School Year. Moravia, New York: CGP, 1992.
    Lists thousands of junior colleges, including those with foreign language courses. Appended by language indexes.

Books for Chapters 2 and 3

Carland, Maria Pinto and Spate, Daniel, editors. *Careers in International Affairs.* Washington, DC: Georgetown University, 1991.
    Emphasizes the necessity of knowing foreign languages to

understand and reach foreign societies by American job hunters willing to work abroad. Examines various options and their requirements.

Directory of Opportunities in International Law. Charlottesville, VA: University of Virginia Law School, 1992.
Offers various opportunities for law school graduates, and describes position requirements, including knowledge of foreign languages.

Krannich, Ronald and Krannich, Sheryl. *Almanac of International Jobs and Careers.* Woodbridge, VA: Impact Publications, 1991.
Lists names, addresses, and telephone numbers of over 1,000 key employers for job hunters with language skills.

Seelye, H. Ned and Day, J. Laurence. *Careers for Foreign Language Aficionados and Other Multinational Types.* Lincolnwood, IL: VGM Career Horizons, 1992.
Descriptions of dozens of jobs that involve knowledge of foreign languages; includes a listing of contact organizations.

Periodicals for Chapters 2 and 3

Community Jobs. ACCESS, 50 Beacon Street, Boston, MA 02108.
Monthly; listings of jobs and internships in the nonprofit sector, including those in foreign countries. Shows requirements and salaries.

Federal Jobs Digest. Federal Jobs Digest, Box 594, Millwood, NY 10549.
Monthly; has a section with overseas job vacancies with the U.S. Army, Navy, Department of State, and other units.

Federal Times. Army Times Publishing, 6883 Commercial Drive, Springfield, VA 22159.
Weekly; lists hundreds of federal civil-service jobs, including U.S. Army and Navy positions in several foreign countries.

International Employment Gazette. 1525 Wade Hampton Boulevard, Greenville, SC 29609.

Biweekly; lists hundreds of vacancies in construction and business fields. Also describes a placement network for job hunters.

Monday Development. Interaction, 200 Park Avenue South, New York, NY 10003.

Biweekly; lists vacancies with nonprofit organizations assisting various countries in Africa, Asia, and Latin America.

INDEXES

In order to facilitate the research process, this directory provides three indexes:

1. Index to Languages
2. Index to Educational and Occupational Backgrounds
3. Index to Geographic Names.

The first index identifies both language resources for educational purposes (sections A, B, C) and language resources for employment or business aims (sections D, E, F, G, H, I).

The second index refers to educational and occupational backgrounds desired by employers (sections D, E, F, G, H), in addition to knowledge of languages.

The third index leads to states and territories as well as to Canadian provinces, since they can be found in various sections of the book. The 191 countries mentioned in section I were not included in the index since these countries are already arranged alphabetically (I/1 through I/191).

All three indexes are alphabetized word by word, and geared to entry code numbers rather than page numbers, thus making the identification of desired items quick and easy.

INDEX TO LANGUAGES

Afghan. *See* Pushto
African languages (AFL), **A**/103, 198, 293, 465, 894; **B**/70, 76, 158, 247; **D**/43; **E**/3, 4, 12, 42, 44, 93, 101, 105, 111, 122; **F**/89; **G**/1, 2, 52; **I**/27, 89, 135, 139

138, 139, 142, 144–47, 152, 169, 177, 185, 187, 189, 191, 193, 194, 197, 207, 212, 221, 223, 249, 265, 278, 293–95, 305–7, 311, 317, 320, 330, 337, 344, 356, 367, 404, 411, 418, 429, 438, 451–53, 463–66, 482, 497, 507, 516, 517, 522, 523, 532, 535, 544, 558, 564, 575, 580, 583, 633, 634, 647, 661–63, 666, 667, 673, 675, 681, 684, 686, 691, 694, 704, 721–23, 736, 738, 739, 748, 781, 802, 809, 825, 830, 853, 863, 869, 871, 872, 880, 903, 914, 927, 938–40, 942, 955, 961, 975, 1007, 1068, 1069, 1077, 1081, 1092, 1115, 1137, 1156, 1168, 1169, 1190, 1192, 1193, 1195, 1198, 1208, 1210, 1219, 1220, 1223; **B**/12, 24, 35, 36, 71, 73, 96, 132, 137, 144, 159, 171, 187, 199, 212, 227, 237, 243, 245, 248, 254, 255, 258, 264, 265, 269, 276, 289, 295, 297, 316, 349, 356, 361, 371, 374, 375, 378, 379; **C**/102, 113, 114, 174, 184, 216; **E**/15, 80, 86, 94; **G**/60, 61, 104, 105, 119, 143, 149; **I**/76; Addendum (p. 332)

Hindi (HI), **A**/71, 136, 138, 139, 144, 255, 305, 307, 328, 465, 507, 544, 591, 673, 675, 681, 723, 738, 757, 942, 943, 955, 1069, 1077, 1090, 1115, 1137, 1168, 1193, 1195, 1220; **B**/96, 111, 137, 159, 212, 243, 245, 254, 255, 258, 268, 363, 364, 366–68, 370–76, 378–80, 382, 384; **C**/25, 90, 143, 157, 169, 206, 279; **D**/67; **E**/19, 42; **G**/28, 54, 111; **I**/51, 65, 71, 99, 104a, 113, 135, 149

Hindi-Urdu (H/U), **A**/30, 71, 305, 307, 452, 673, 675, 757, 942, 1193, 1210

Hiri Moto (HR), **I**/116

Hittite (HT), **A**/139, 189, 305, 307, 453, 465, 704, 942, 1081, 1169, 1210

Hmong (HM), **A**/139, 825; **C**/73; **G**/72

Hopi (HO), **A**/21, 28

Hova (HV), **I**/92

Hualapi (HL), **A**/391

Huichol (HC), **A**/675

Hungarian (HU), **A**/138, 139, 142, 144, 320, 404, 673, 725, 825, 940, 943, 1077, 1195, 1210, 1219; **B**/12, 24, 27, 50, 54, 56, 60, 64, 65, 71, 73, 82, 87, 96, 108, 132, 159, 178, 187, 193, 196, 198–200, 212, 213, 227, 232, 243, 245, 254, 255, 258, 265, 267, 269, 272, 273, 276, 277, 289, 297, 350, 356, 361, 363, 367–76, 378–80, 382, 384; **C**/109, 140, 188; **D**/39, 56, 67; **E**/119; **F**/7; **G**/6, 16, 24, 95, 200; **I**/9, 41, 69, 123, 163, 185

Ibo. *See* Igbo

Icelandic (IC), **A**/21, 71, 139, 142, 169, 185, 249, 320, 404, 482, 516, 544, 673, 675, 722, 781, 830, 942, 1041, 1077, 1115, 1137, 1139, 1168, 1193, 1195, 1213; **B**/42, 71, 137, 263, 350, 361, 364, 373, 382, 384; **I**/70

781, 825, 830, 836, 853, 863, 869, 900, 927, 940, 942, 943, 955, 975, 1007, 1069, 1086, 1087, 1090, 1092, 1100, 1115, 1123, 1137, 1139, 1142, 1150, 1168, 1169, 1190, 1193, 1198, 1210, 1213, 1214, 1219, 1220; **B**/12, 18, 22, 27, 29, 30, 33, 36, 40, 42, 43, 47, 49, 50, 52, 54, 56, 60, 71, 73, 88, 94, 96, 115, 132, 137, 144, 159, 178, 187, 226, 227, 234, 243, 245, 254, 258, 265, 269, 297, 350, 356, 363, 367, 371, 374–76, 378, 379, 384; **C**/7, 24, 26, 30, 32, 67, 71, 83, 123, 129, 131, 135, 164, 186, 187, 196, 197; **D**/3, 8, 21, 34, 44; **E**/27–29, 31, 53, 62, 65, 70, 81, 103, 120, 122, 132, 133; **F**/8, 12, 18, 24, 27, 31, 32, 34, 35, 37, 42, 61, 64, 72, 84, 85, 90, 92, 95, 101, 103, 105, 109, 112; **G**/66, 95, 117; **H**/34; **I**/20, 79, 84, 145; Addendum (p. 332)
Javanese (JV), **A**/189, 255, 675
Judeo-Arabic (J/A), **A**/632
Judeo-Persian (J/P), **B**/71

Kamayura (KM), **A**/1069
Kanada (KA), **A**/144, 1069
Kansa (KN), **A**/391
Kashmiri (KS), **A**/307
Kazakh (KZ), **A**/728; **D**/56; **I**/174, 191
Khakhas (KH), **B**/245
Khalkha. *See* Mongolian
Khmer. *See* Cambodian
Kihunde (KI), **A**/320
Kikungo (KK), **I**/36, 82, 164
Kikuyo (KY), **B**/247
Kimeru (K/U), **A**/307
Kinairuanda (K/R), **I**/124
Kingwan (KW), **I**/164
Kirghiz (K/Z), **D**/56; **I**/136, 175
Kirundi/Rundi (KU), **A**/320; **B**/247; **I**/26
Kiswahili (K/S), **I**/124
Kituba (KT), **A**/189
Knowledge of a foreign language (KFL), **D**/1, 2, 4, 5, 7, 9, 12, 14–17, 19, 20, 22, 25, 26, 28, 30, 31, 34, 36, 38, 39a, 41, 47, 49, 50–52, 60–62, 65, 66; **E**/9, 10, 33, 39, 40, 48, 58, 61, 63, 73, 74, 78, 85, 89, 90, 102, 114, 128; **F**/4, 9, 10, 14, 15, 19, 23, 25, 28, 30, 33, 37, 41, 43, 44, 46–50, 58–60, 66, 69–71, 76, 78–80, 86, 93, 94, 97, 99, 102, 106, 108, 113–16; Addendum (p. 332)
Kongo (KG), **B**/247
Korean (KO), **A**/47, 71, 138, 139, 142, 144, 153, 189, 255, 307, 309, 320, 391, 443, 465, 507, 532, 633, 664, 673, 681, 723, 736, 825, 940, 943, 955, 1077, 1124, 1137, 1139, 1210; **B**/22, 27, 29, 30, 36,

Luba/Lubi (LB), **B**/247; **I**/23
Lubi. *See* Luba
Luganda (LN), **I**/152

Macedonian (MA), **A**/465, 675, 781, 825; **B**/71, 165, 245, 250, 366, 371, 379; **C**/147; **I**/163, 178
Mahri (M/H), **I**/162
Mainke/Malinke (M/N), **I**/96
Makua (MK), **A**/307
Malagasy (MG), **B**/247; **I**/92
Malay (ML), **A**/71, 139, 144; **B**/71; **I**/21, 55, 94, 133, 147
Malaylam (MM), **A**/1069, 1169; **B**/71; **G**/54; **I**/71
Malaysian (MS), **A**/295
Malecite (MC), **A**/1197
Malinke. *See* Mainke
Maltese (MT), **B**/71, 167, 364, 370, 378; **C**/179; **I**/97
Manchu (MN), **A**/139, 434, 465, 632, 673
Mande/Mende (ME), **A**/295; **B**/247; **I**/130, 132
Mandingo (M/G), **B**/247; **I**/130
Mandinka (MD), **A**/295, 307, 452; **I**/63
Manx (MX), **B**/71, 103, 283; **G**/71, 170
Maori (M/O), **A**/1077; **I**/108
Marathi (MR), **A**/255, 507, 516, 544, 742, 942; **B**/71, 243, 245, 265, 370–72, 376; **C**/25, 143, 157, 169; **G**/54; **I**/71
Mari. *See* Cheremyssian
Masa (M/A), **I**/31
Mayan (MY), **A**/344, 803, 942, 1077; **I**/62
Maya-Quiche (M/Q), **A**/721
Maya-Yukatan (M/Y), **A**/305, 418, 591, 721, 1069
Mende. *See* Mande
Micmac (MI), **A**/1198
Mina (M/I), **I**/15a
Miwok-Lake (MW), **A**/825
Modern languages (MOL), **A**/39, 46, 93, 167, 376, 378, 384a, 548, 553, 632, 777, 867, 1008, 1010, 1022, 1064, 1116
Mohawk (MH), **A**/1219
Mongolian/Khalkha (MO), **A**/139, 142, 320, 434, 465, 632, 673, 728, 1169, 1210; **B**/245; **G**/133; **I**/101
Montagnaise (M/T), **A**/1198, 1219
Mossi (M/S), **I**/23
Moudang (MU), **I**/31
Multiple/various languages (MUL), **A**/17, 64, 120, 155, 160, 166, 174, 209a, 229, 245, 253, 258, 273, 285, 343, 374, 382, 460, 556, 616, 627, 677, 679, 693, 701, 737, 752, 759, 775, 805, 815, 816,

Peul. *See* Fulani

Pidgin (PI), **A**/189, 255, 507; **I**/116, 132

Polish (PO), **A**/138, 139, 142, 144, 153, 177, 185, 189, 197, 221, 223, 293, 295, 305–7, 320, 391, 451, 465, 473, 498, 516, 517, 544, 673, 675, 721, 725, 738, 757, 781, 813, 877, 878, 906, 926, 940, 955, 1041, 1069, 1077, 1092, 1115, 1137, 1150, 1168, 1190, 1193, 1195, 1210, 1214, 1219, 1220; **B**/12, 36, 45, 46, 50, 56, 60, 64, 65, 71, 73, 74, 82, 96, 104, 105, 132, 137, 141, 142, 144, 151, 159, 161, 166, 174, 175, 178, 179, 187, 194, 196, 199, 200, 212, 213, 215, 227, 235, 243, 245, 251, 252, 254, 255, 258, 265, 269, 276, 277, 280, 283, 289, 297, 315, 316, 350, 356, 361, 363, 364, 366–80, 382, 384, 385; **C**/43, 59, 96, 108, 142, 150, 162, 191–93, 217, 232, 279; **D**/39, 56, 67; **E**/119; **F**/7, 89; **I**/120, 155

Portuguese (PT), **A**/11, 20, 21, 30, 56, 67, 105, 114, 128, 139, 142–46, 153, 169, 185, 189, 207, 221, 223, 248, 255, 294, 295, 303–7, 311, 319, 320, 344, 365, 391, 410, 418, 452, 464, 465, 476, 477, 507, 516, 517, 544, 591, 615, 632, 637, 638, 640, 642, 650, 654, 666, 667, 673, 675, 681, 704, 721, 723, 728, 736, 741, 781, 825, 830, 942, 955, 975, 1007, 1041, 1060, 1069, 1077, 1115, 1137, 1150, 1168, 1169, 1190, 1193, 1198, 1207, 1210, 1214, 1219, 1220, 1228, 1244; **B**/12, 43, 50, 58, 60, 64, 69, 71, 73, 96, 103, 132, 137, 142, 144, 148, 149, 182, 183, 187, 197, 199, 200, 209, 212, 227, 239, 243, 245, 254, 258, 265, 269, 276, 297, 310–12, 315–17, 350, 356, 361, 363, 364, 366–80, 382, 384; **C**/24, 35, 63, 66, 104, 129, 146, 149, 163, 183, 189, 194, 217, 239, 261, 276; **D**/42, 67; **E**/14, 16, 19, 22, 38, 47, 49, 55, 66, 67, 70, 86, 88, 97, 99, 100, 104, 110–12, 118, 124, 125, 127, 134; **F**/20, 35, 53, 61, 68, 85, 87, 88, 98, 102, 103, 109, 128; **G**/17, 52, 125, 129;**H**/3, 4, 9, 16, 19, 37; **I**/5, 20, 29, 64, 104, 121, 128

Portuguese/Creole (P/C), **I**/29, 64, 128

Prakrit (PK), **A**/139, 189, 255, 942, 1168

Provençal (PV), **A**/139, 169, 249, 404, 451, 465, 544, 654, 675, 682, 704, 781, 869, 942, 1137, 1169, 1210, 1220; **B**/71, 245

Prussian (PR), **A**/942; **B**/245

Punjabi (PJ), **B**/254, 265, 361, 363, 364, 366–68, 370–74, 376, 378, 379, 382, 384; **C**/37, 90, 143, 157, 169, 279; **G**/54, 62; **I**/71, 114

Pushto/Afghani (PS), **A**/465; **B**/71; **D**/67; **G**/62, 197; **I**/1, 114

Quechua (QC), **A**/142, 307, 320, 654, 675, 723, 943, 1069, 1077, 1169; **B**/71; **I**/18, 46, 118

Rhaeto-Romance/Rumansh (RM), **A**/465; **B**/71; **I**/143

Romanian/Rumanian (RO), **A**/139, 142, 249, 305, 307, 320, 451, 465, 675, 742, 781, 825, 869, 1137, 1169, 1190; **B**/71, 96, 114,

137, 159, 172, 212, 243, 245, 254, 256, 267, 269, 270, 371, 375, 379, 384; **C**/226, 236, 266; **D**/39, 56, 67; **E**/94, 119; **F**/7, 61, 89, 92, 109; **G**/6, 16, 35, 173, 191; **I**/69, 123, 136, 163
Rumanian. *See* Romanian
Rumansh. *See* Rhaeto-Romance
Rundi. *See* Kirundi
Russian (RU), **A**/3, 11, 13, 16, 19, 21, 30, 51, 57, 58, 62, 84, 86, 107, 118, 123–25, 138–43, 145, 146, 153, 169, 172, 173, 178, 184, 185, 187, 189, 191, 193, 195–98, 204, 209, 213, 219, 222, 223, 255, 283, 291, 293, 305–7, 313, 319, 320, 329, 337, 341, 347, 352, 353, 361, 365, 391, 398, 404, 405, 410, 413, 418, 431, 432, 441, 442, 447, 451–53, 464, 465, 468–70, 476, 480, 482–84, 486, 487, 498, 499, 507, 509, 516, 517, 520, 523, 525, 527, 529, 530, 532, 533, 541, 544, 575, 580, 583, 591, 604, 609, 615, 621, 633, 635, 637, 639, 640, 642, 645, 653, 654, 662, 663, 665–67, 673, 675, 682, 686, 695–97, 703, 704, 718, 721, 722, 725, 732, 736, 738, 742, 747, 757, 792, 798, 801, 804, 813, 823, 825, 826, 829–31, 836, 853, 865, 866, 869, 875, 880, 881, 884, 891–93, 897, 900, 907, 909, 911–13, 917, 923, 925, 938, 940, 942, 943, 947, 949, 955, 959, 1003, 1007, 1014, 1041, 1046, 1063, 1068, 1069, 1077, 1081, 1086–88, 1092, 1100, 1103, 1107, 1114, 1115, 1124, 1126, 1131, 1137, 1139, 1141, 1150, 1152, 1159, 1168, 1169, 1174, 1178, 1191, 1193, 1195, 1197, 1200, 1204, 1206, 1207, 1209, 1211, 1214, 1217, 1219, 1220, 1222, 1223; **B**/1, 2, 12, 27, 36, 38, 43, 49, 50, 52, 54, 56, 60, 64, 66, 71, 73, 77, 79, 82, 86, 96, 103, 115, 132, 137, 138, 144, 151, 159, 161, 169, 175, 178, 179, 182, 183, 187, 196, 198–200, 212, 215, 227, 228, 243, 245, 254, 255, 258, 260, 265, 267, 269, 271, 272, 276, 277, 280, 289, 290, 293, 295, 297, 316, 324, 332, 343, 347, 350, 351, 355, 356, 361, 363, 364, 366, 368–76, 378–80, 382, 384; **C**/43, 65, 69, 70, 75, 112, 120, 137, 207, 209; **D**/3, 21, 23, 34, 39, 46, 48, 56, 59, 67; **E**/8, 15, 26, 31, 62, 77, 86, 94, 119, 120; **F**/7, 12, 22, 34, 42, 61, 64, 84, 85, 89, 92, 105, 109, 111; **G**/21, 23, 81, 89; **H**/6, 13, 14, 22, 24, 27, 33, 38; **I**/120, 136; Addendum (p. 332)
Rwanda (RW), **B**/245

Salishan-Coast (SA), **A**/1193, 1213
Salish-Puget (S/P), **A**/1137
Samo (S/M), **I**/23
Samoan (SM), **A**/255, 1077
Sangho (S/H), **I**/30
Sanskrit (SS), **A**/57, 58, 60, 71, 136, 139, 145, 146, 189, 197, 249, 255, 305, 307, 365, 391, 418, 434, 451, 452, 465, 507, 516, 523, 532, 544, 580, 591, 664, 675, 704, 722, 723, 736, 742, 927, 942,

955, 1081, 1092, 1115, 1137, 1191, 1193, 1195, 1198, 1210, 1213, 1219; **B**/245
Sara (S/A), **I**/31
Saxon, Old (SX), **A**/465, 544, 633, 675, 721, 728, 942, 1041, 1169
Scandinavian Languages (SCL), **A**/464, 516, 528, 533, 1297
Scottish/Gaelic-Scottish (SC), **A**/136, 191, 465, 527, 675, 830, 1210, 1213; **B**/71, 307, 309, 361, 364, 382; **G**/71, 170; **I**/154
Serbo-Croatian (S/C), **A**/138, 139, 142, 143, 153, 185, 189, 295, 305–7, 320, 451, 452, 465, 516, 532, 673, 675, 720, 723, 781, 813, 825, 869, 1069, 1115, 1137, 1168, 1169, 1193, 1210, 1213; **B**/36, 50, 60, 71, 96, 97, 132, 137, 159, 243, 245, 254, 269, 277, 295, 296, 322, 356, 358, 367–69, 371, 372, 374–80; **C**/43, 125, 147, 170, 177, 182, 215, 282; **D**/67; **G**/84, 162, 163, 205; **I**/9, 69, 163
Sesotho (S/T), **I**/88
Setswana (SE), **A**/452; **I**/19
Shona (SN), **A**/221, 307, 320, 507; **B**/71, 247; **I**/166
Shuar (SR), **A**/1069
Sindhi (SD), **A**/30, 465; **B**/71, 245; **G**/62; **I**/114
Sinhalese (SI), **A**/673; **B**/245; **G**/64; **I**/95, 138
Si-Swati (S/W), **I**/141
Skokleng (SK), **A**/1069
Slavic languages (SLL), Addendum (p. 332)
Slavic/Slavonic, Old Church (S/S), **A**/139, 169, 197, 209, 295, 305–7, 320, 391, 451, 453, 465, 482, 544, 615, 675, 723, 781, 825, 880, 890, 927, 955, 1081, 1115, 1137, 1168, 1190, 1193, 1195, 1210, 1219; **B**/245
Slovak (SL), **A**/142, 465, 813, 1210, 1219; **B**/64, 71, 98, 116, 132, 137, 164, 173, 196, 243, 245, 254, 258, 267, 269, 277, 279, 293, 299, 300, 303, 340, 356, 361, 363, 364, 370–73, 378–80, 382; **C**/43, 202; **D**/56, 67; **G**/86, 165; **I**/41, 69, 185
Slovenian (SV), **A**/307, 320, 391, 465, 813, 825, 943, 955; **B**/60, 71, 96, 137, 159, 177, 269, 322, 356, 371; **C**/147, 177; **D**/67; **G**/166, 167; **I**/9, 77, 163, 171, 186
Sogdian (SG), **A**/465, 942; **I**/30
Somali (SO), **A**307, 320; **B**/247; **E**/126; **I**/43, 134
Songhai (S/G), **B**/247
Sorbian. *See* Wendic
Sotho (ST), **A**/1168; **B**/247
Soyot. *See* Tuva
Spanish (SP), **A**/2–12, 14–16, 19–28, 30–33, 35–38, 40, 43–45, 47–49, 51–59, 61–65, 67–92, 94–96, 98–102, 104–8, 110–14, 116–18, 121–46, 149–66, 168–73, 175–77, 179, 180, 182–86, 188–96, 198, 200–206, 208–10, 213–17, 219, 220, 222, 224–28, 230–36, 238, 239, 241–52, 254–57, 259–64, 266–72, 274–77,

1041, 1069, 1077, 1137, 1139, 1169, 1193, 1213; **B**/12, 36, 50, 54, 56, 60, 71, 73, 96, 107, 132, 137, 159, 176, 178, 179, 184, 187, 199, 212, 213, 233, 243, 254, 258, 263, 269, 276, 287, 289, 292, 297, 316, 343, 350, 351, 355, 356, 361, 363, 364, 370, 371, 373, 375, 379, 382, 384; **C**/171, 195; **G**/36, 174; **I**/42, 52, 142
Syriac (SY), **A**/54, 65, 139, 189, 249, 465, 633, 1007, 1195, 1223; **B**/71, 278
Syryenian (S/Y), **B**/245

Tagalog. *See* Filipino
Tahitian (TA), **A**/255, 1077
Tajik (TJ), **B**/245; **D**/56; **I**/136, 188, 191
Taki Taki (T/T), **I**/140
Tamashek (T/K), **I**/110
Tamil (TM), **A**/305, 452, 675, 942, 1069, 1168; **B**/71, 243, 259, 371, 372; **C**/25, 157, 169; **G**/54, 64, 90; **I**/71, 94, 104a, 133, 138, 189
Tangale (TN), **A**/307
Tartar (TT), **A**/320; **B**/71; **D**/56
Tegrinya (TY), **A**/307
Telugu (TE), **A**/675, 942, 1069, 1168; **B**/243; **G**/54; **I**/71, 135
Tenne (T/N), **A**/132
Thai (TH), **A**/21, 138, 139, 141, 144, 189, 255, 293, 307, 516, 675, 723, 869, 943, 1092, 1137, 1168; **B**/40, 56, 71, 187, 243, 245, 265, 356; **C**/4, 227; **D**/31, 67; **E**/20, 29, 103; **F**/96; **I**/147
Tibetan (TI), **A**/138, 139, 144, 189, 255, 320, 465, 516, 633, 673, 723, 736, 869, 1092, 1168, 1191, 1210; **B**/71, 100, 235, 245, 269; **G**/182; **I**/17, 33, 105
Tiv (TV), **A**/320
Tlingit (TL), **A**/19
Tocharian (TO), **A**/71, 675
Tonga (TG), **A**/1077; **B**/247; **I**/165
Tshiluba (T/S), **I**/164
Tsimshian (TS), **A**/19, 1211
Tsonga (T/G), **B**/247
Tswana (T/W), **B**/247
Tukolor (TK), **I**/98
Turkic (TR), **A**/465, 942, 1081, 1137; **B**/71; **I**/102
Turkish (TU), **A**/30, 138, 141, 144, 146, 185, 189, 293, 305, 320, 465, 516, 633, 673, 675, 704, 622, 722, 723, 728, 781, 825, 942, 955, 1069, 1081, 1137, 1169, 1210, 1219; **B**/71, 137, 243, 245, 258, 261, 269, 371; **D**/31, 67; **E**/87; **F**/129; **G**/18, 185, 186, 201, 218; **I**/22, 40, 59, 73, 151, 169, 178
Turkoman (T/M), **B**/245; **I**/136
Turko-Tataric (T/U), **B**/245; **D**/56

INDEX TO EDUCATIONAL AND OCCUPATIONAL BACKGROUNDS

Writing, editing, and publishing, **E**/9, 48, 108, 113, 140, 151; **F**/2, 24, 64, 108, 117–18, 124–25, 134; **G**/1, 2, 8, 31, 38, 42, 55, 60, 86, 99, 142, 165, 196; **H**/31, 38

INDEX TO GEOGRAPHIC NAMES (AMERICAN AND CANADIAN)

Vermont, **A**/1084–92; **B**/345; **C**/131; **D**/113
Virgin Islands, **A**/1189; **D**/121
Virginia, **A**/1093–1121, 1360–63; **B**/347, 348; **C**/132, 133, 265; **D**/114, 150

Washington, **A**/1122–41, 1364–67; **B**/349–51; **C**/134; **D**/115, 151
West Virginia, **A**/1144–51, 1368; **B**/353; **D**/116
Wisconsin, **A**/1152–74, 1369–70; **B**/354–59; **D**/117
Wyoming, **A**/1175–79, 1371–72; **B**/360; **D**/118

NOTE: All foreign countries are arranged alphabetically in section I (I/1 through I/191)

ADDENDUM-INDEX TO LANGUAGES

Biblical Languages (BIL), **A**/50, 147, 273, 278, 394, 497, 558, 809, 871, 987, 1009, 1032, 1131, 1138, 1225, 1272, 1285, 1292, 1301, 1308, 1312, 1335/a, 1339, 1341–42, 1349–50, 1355, 1360, 1369–70

Chinese (CH), **A**/133, 141, 153, 253, 261, 495, 520, 541, 657, 669, 682, 685, 814, 829, 831, 866, 1084, 1124, 1134, 1159, 1128, 1281, 1306, 1334, 1364, 1366; **C**/262–63, 275, 279; **D**/10; **E**/158; **F**/129, 135; **H**/43

French (FR), **A**/24, 30, 76/a, 79, 150, 253, 306, 364, 419, 475, 481, 549, 566, 579, 646, 698, 723, 730, 735, 739, 752, 790, 853, 876, 962, 976, 996, 1026, 1050, 1111, 1164, 1185, 1198, 1224, 1226, 1230–32, 1244–46, 1248–50, 1252–57, 1260–62, 1267, 1271–73, 1282–84, 1287–89, 1291, 1293, 1295, 1298–1300, 1302, 1306, 1309, 1314, 1318, 1323–25, 1329, 1332, 1334–36, 1344, 1347, 1352, 1354, 1357–58, 1360–63, 1375–76; **B**/251, 389; **C**/228–29, 238, 241, 244, 248, 275–76, 279, 283; **D**/49; **E**/79, 134; **F**/102, 122, 127, 136; **H**/43

German (GE), **A**/9, 76/a, 79, 99, 221, 294, 300, 318, 329, 336, 338, 361, 408, 456, 475, 504, 549, 584, 586, 596, 741, 752, 879, 951, 962, 976, 996, 1164, 1182, 1198, 1218, 1224, 1226, 1230, 1244, 1245, 1254, 1257, 1261–62, 1267, 1271, 1275, 1281–82, 1289, 1298, 1300, 1306, 1318, 1329, 1332–37, 1347, 1354, 1358, 1363, 1375–76; **B**/387–88; **C**/228–29, 241, 244, 269, 273, 277, 279; **D**/49; **F**/102, 123, 129; **G**/198, 210; **I**/174, 182, 186

1224, 1226–31, 1235, 1244–45, 1248, 1250, 1252–55, 1257–59,
1261–62, 1264–65, 1267–68, 1271, 1277, 1282–83, 1286, 1288–89,
1293, 1299, 1300, 1302, 1305–06, 1309, 1313–21, 1340, 1344,
1347, 1352, 1354, 1357–58, 1362–63, 1367–68, 1373–74; **C**/228–
31, 233, 238, 241, 244, 258, 260, 266–67, 273, 279; **E**/143–44,
147, 150, 161; **F**/102, 136; **G**/206, 213, 216; **H**/43

ADDENDUM-INDEX TO EDUCATIONAL
BACKGROUNDS

Area studies, **E**/135–37, 139, 140–42, 144–48, 150–54, 157–160,
162; **F**/66, 119, 124, 125, 127, 133, 135; **G**/197, 200, 203, 205,
210–11

ABOUT THE AUTHOR

VLADIMIR F. WERTSMAN graduated from University "A.I. Cuza" Law School (Romania) and earned his Master's degree in Library Science from Columbia University (1967). He served as Adult Services Librarian and Branch Librarian in various branches of the Brooklyn Public Library, was Russian and Romanian languages specialist at Donnell Foreign Language Library, New York, and worked as Senior Librarian at the Job Information Center, Mid-Manhattan Library, New York. He is a member of the American Romanian Academy of Arts and Sciences, International Social Science Honor Society, American Association for the Advancement of Slavic Studies, and the American Library Association. He chaired the PLA/Multilingual Library Service Committee and presently is Chair of Publishers & Multicultural Materials Committee of Ethnic Materials Round Table, American Library Association. He is the author of *The Romanians in America, 1748–1974* (Oceana, 1975), *The Ukrainians in America, 1608–1975* (Oceana, 1976), *The Russians in America, 1727–1976* (Oceana, 1977), *The Armenians in America, 1616–1976* (Oceana, 1978), *The Romanians in America and Canada* (Gale Research, 1980), *The Librarian's Companion* (Greenwood Press, 1987) as well as *Career Opportunities for Bilinguals and Multilinguals, (first edition)* (Scarecrow Press, 1991) and co-author of the *Ukrainians in Canada and the United States* (Gale Research, 1981) and *Free Voices in Russian Literature, 1950s–1980s* (Russica, 1987). His biography is included in *Who's Who in America* (47th ed.) and *Contemporary Authors* (New Revision Series).